Storage Network Performance Analysis

Dr. Huseyin Simitci

WILEY

Wiley Publishing, Inc.

Storage Network Performance Analysis

Published by
Wiley Publishing, Inc.
10475 Crosspoint Boulevard
Indianapolis, IN 46256
www.wiley.com

Copyright © 2003 by Wiley Publishing, Inc., Indianapolis, Indiana
Published simultaneously in Canada

Library of Congress Control Number: 2002114877

ISBN: 0-7645-1685-X

Manufactured in the United States of America

10 9 8 7 6 5 4 3 2 1

1Q/SS/QU/QT/IN

Credits

ACQUISITIONS EDITOR
Katie Feltman

PROJECT EDITORS
Marcia Ellett
Kevin Kent

TECHNICAL EDITOR
Kenneth Smallwood

COPY EDITOR
Gabrielle Chosney

EDITORIAL MANAGER
Mary Beth Wakefield

VICE PRESIDENT & EXECUTIVE GROUP PUBLISHER
Richard Swadley

VICE PRESIDENT AND EXECUTIVE PUBLISHER
Bob Ipsen

EXECUTIVE EDITORIAL DIRECTOR
Mary Bednarek

PROJECT COORDINATOR
Nancee Reeves

GRAPHICS AND PRODUCTION SPECIALISTS
Beth Brooks
Heather Pope

QUALITY CONTROL TECHNICIANS
Carl William Pierce
Charles Spencer

PROOFREADING AND INDEXING
TECHBOOKS Production Services

About the Author

Dr. Huseyin Simitci is currently an engineering staff member of XIOtech Corporation, where he applies performance analysis techniques to evaluate and design current and future technologies. Before working with XIOtech, he was a researcher in the Advanced Technologies Group of Seagate Technology, where he helped model network attached storage technologies.

He holds a Ph.D. in Computer Science from the University of Illinois at Urbana-Champaign (2000), and an M.S. in Computer Engineering from Bilkent University, Ankara (1994).

He has authored several research papers in the areas of high performance input/output systems, applications of adaptive techniques in parallel file systems, and storage network interfaces. His work contributed to the national Scalable I/O Initiative (SIO) and NSF-funded Grand Challenge programs, as well as to commercial storage products.

His research interests include the areas of performance evaluation and modeling of advanced storage systems, file systems, storage network protocols, data distribution, and adaptive tuning.

To my parents, Kezban and Mustafa

Preface

Networking increased the value (or usefulness) of data by enabling information sharing among several hundreds, even millions, of computers and human beings. Similarly, networked storage increased the value of stored data by enabling shared, ubiquitous, secure access to this data.

Storage networks brought together the best aspects of networking and storage technologies to provide cost-effective, high-performance data storage. However, this synergy also brought together all the problems associated with networks and storage devices. One of the biggest problems arose in data access performance, which can be hampered because of the contention for networks and storage devices.

Storage Network Performance Analysis provides the reader with the essential information and tools to tackle performance issues in storage networks. It includes performance analysis methodologies for storage, networks, and storage networks.

Performance analysis is an all-encompassing term that can include the understanding or design of system architectures, benchmarking, analytical modeling, simulation modeling, capacity planning, management, monitoring, prediction, tuning, upgrading, downgrading, visualization, and many other similar tasks.

This book provides a connection between the theory of performance analysis and the practice of storage system performance engineering. It is a unique collection of ideas, practices, guidelines, and frameworks to help you approach the performance-related issues arising in many data storage systems. Storage systems researchers will find information on modeling and simulating their storage system designs and forecasting prospective performance improvements. Storage field engineers will find information on evaluating implementation alternatives. System administrators will find hints on tuning the performance of their storage subsystems and networks.

A final word about what this book is not: The book is not a reference that you can use find performance information on specific products. It aims to provide you with the information you need to design, implement, or purchase storage systems. In addition, the main focus of the book is performance. Thus, many aspects of storage networks that do not directly affect performance — that might otherwise be very important — are not treated explicitly. In other words, it is up to you to weigh the significance of performance in your projects.

What's in this Book

The book contains six parts that lead you from the theoretical foundations of performance analysis to the practical aspects of storage performance design and tuning.

Part I: Performance Analysis Techniques

Part I provides the theoretical foundations for performance modeling and analysis in general. After defining the performance metrics for storage systems, it introduces analytical modeling techniques. Then, it discusses the use of simulation for performance analysis. Later, the design of experimental performance studies is presented.

Part II: Performance Analysis and Modeling of Storage System Components

Part II introduces several layers of storage systems and provides guidelines for modeling the performance of each system component. It starts with the storage device layer, moves on to storage interconnects and networks, and then discusses modeling and forecasting techniques for storage workloads.

Part III: Storage Performance Engineering

Part III introduces Quality of Service and Service Level Agreement notions for data storage networks. Then, capacity planning techniques for storage systems and networks are presented. The discussion includes system-level performance analysis and price/performance considerations.

Part IV: Storage Performance Tools

Part IV provides an overview of software tools available to performance engineering practitioners. After discussing component and system-level benchmarks, software for performance data collection and storage performance management is reviewed.

Part V: Storage Performance Tuning

Part V contains an optimization and tuning discussion for several layers of the storage network, presenting host system tuning issues, and optimizations at the application, storage subsystem, and storage network layers.

Part VI: Case Studies

Part VI concludes the book with case studies of storage performance analysis. These chapters contain in-depth analysis and discussion of performance modeling, benchmarking, tuning, and design of network attached storage, remote storage replication, and e-commerce data centers.

How to Use this Book

This book can be read at many levels; for example, you can read it for its theoretical perspective, or it can be read with a view to the practical application of its concepts.

You should read each chapter in sequence, because later chapters build on the information that is provided in earlier chapters. However, certain chapters can be skipped, depending on your interests.

A researcher or engineer who wants to understand, design, and model storage network architectures is encouraged to read the entire book in sequence.

Part I is the basis for almost all the discussions in the rest of the book. So, review Part I if you need to fill in any gaps in your knowledge base, or if you simply want to reacquaint yourself with the material.

The chapters in Part II can be read almost independently based on need or interest. Those who want to design, install, and manage storage networks should read Parts III and IV for their discussion of performance engineering tools.

Part V provides practical performance tuning techniques and tips for individuals who want to know detailed information on various storage network components.

The case studies in Part VI assume that the reader is familiar with the performance analysis information provided in Parts I and II.

Although all new storage network and performance analysis concepts are defined and explained before they are first used in the book, the scope of the book prevents in-depth coverage of any one topic. Extensive reference lists at the end of each chapter enable you to explore certain areas in more detail.

Conventions Used in this Book

Every chapter starts with a section describing the topics found in that chapter. Then, the first few sections provide background information about the topics. The chapter continues with a performance analysis discussion and example studies, where applicable. Most chapters end with a review of available software tools for that subject. All chapters end with a summary of chapter highlights and a list of references.

Display equations are shown in monospace type, and inline math uses the font type of the paragraph it is in.

All new terms are shown in italics and explained before their first usage.

Three supplementary information formats are used throughout the book:

Provides additional information about the subject that does not fit into the flow of the normal text.

Provides information, mostly based on my personal experience, that helps simplify the reader's work.

Provides information, again based on my own experience, that draws the reader's attention to possible pitfalls or errors so they do not repeat the same mistakes I made.

How to Reach the Author

You can contact me if you have comments about the contents of the book, or any errors found therein. E-mail me at `huseyin@simitci.net`. Errata and additional information about the book will be kept and updated at `http://simitci.net`.

Acknowledgments

This book project is the outgrowth of collective work and exchange of ideas that I have had over the years with many talented and helpful friends and colleagues. Although all of their names may not appear here, I am grateful to all of them.

First, I want to thank Daniel A. Reed for steering my career into the performance analysis field, which I enjoy greatly.

Thanks to Kenneth Smallwood, who referred me to Wiley and initiated the entire book process. Katie Feltman, Acquisitions Editor, helped me to conceptualize the book and took me through the entire process. Project Editors, Marcia Ellett and Kevin Kent, took care of the manuscript, and Gabrielle Chosney helped as the Copy Editor. I'm grateful to all of them for helping to make this book the best that it could be.

Storage industry veteran, Kenneth Smallwood, of XIOtech, served as the Technical Editor, and helped verify the technical content and improved the book's readability.

Several past and current engineering colleagues, including Dave Aune, Lyle Bergman, Steve Brueggeman, Ayman M. Ghanem, Paul Greenblatt, Vamsi Gunturu, Bill Hunt, Chris Malakapalli, Kenton Maguire, Steve Nowakowski, Robert Peglar, Brad Rapp, Satish L. Rege, Gary Ronneberg, Osman N. Sen, Eric Wendel, Zhigao Yao, and Fumin Zhang, provided their help and insight in developing many ideas expressed in this book.

Randy Fardal, Francesca Harbert, Timothy Radlick, and Joshua Tseng, all of Nishan Systems, helped formulate, have provided help in the formation of some of the examples provided in the book.

I am especially grateful to XIOtech Corporation, and its managerial staff, for supporting this book project.

Special thanks to all the members of my extended family for the support and encouragement they have provided throughout my educational and professional career. I am grateful to my beloved wife, Aysun, for bearing with me for the duration of the writing and the late-night tea services. Finally, I hope my children, Yusuf and Yeliz, will some day understand why "the book" required so much time that could have been otherwise devoted to them.

Contents at a Glance

Part V   Storage Performance Tuning

Part VI   Case Studies

Contents

Part I

Performance Analysis Techniques

Chapter 1
Introduction to Storage Networking Performance

Chapter 2
Data Analysis Review

Chapter 3
Analytical Modeling

Chapter 4
Simulation Modeling

Chapter 5
Experimental Analysis

Chapter 1

Introduction to Storage Networking Performance

In This Chapter

How did storage and networking, two traditionally separate fields of study in computer science, become joined in the same term—*storage networking*? How do we define and measure the performance of storage networks? These questions are answered in this chapter, as it introduces the following storage networking performance analysis areas:

- ✓ Defining a storage networking model that provides a framework for storage architecture discussions

- ✓ Considering examples of popular storage architectures represented in the storage networking model

- ✓ Reviewing definitions of metrics for measuring the performance of storage networks

- ✓ Identifying systematic performance evaluation techniques for storage networks

Storage Networking

Computer technology incorporates various fields of study. Advances in one field are passed on to other fields, resulting in innovations there. The effect of networking on data storage technology is an example of this. At one time, two mostly uncorrelated computer technology areas, networking and storage, now seem to be inseparable.

Data storage was previously thought to belong to the inside of server cases or right next to a mainframe computer. However, as networking technology started to affect storage device connections, the placement and distance of storage systems gradually changed. First, they moved to their own storage subsystems; then, they were located at almost any distance from the computers they serve. Formerly known as *peripheral devices*, storage systems became the center of many Information Technology (IT) operations. Today, data storage systems constitute major portions of many IT budgets. In data centers, computing nodes (servers) became peripheral to the storage systems; servers are upgraded and connected to storage systems to satisfy the data processing requirements.

One of the main thrusts behind this change is the Internet and its concomitant requirements. Exponential data growth, fueled by the exchange of information without any distance limitations in many data-rich formats—audio, video, picture, and text—and by the proliferation of *electronic business (e-business)* processes, requires data storage systems that are massive in terms of storage capacity and access performance.

As the importance of data storage increased, so did the interest of computer professionals and the computer industry in the new storage architectures and devices. A number of new approaches to storage problems were thus developed, and several new architectures defined and marketed. Even though these approaches all depend on similar architectural foundations, the marketing that surrounds them is confusing because it makes them sound very distinct.

This book presents the fundamental similarities between the varied approaches to the data storage problem. You will see that even the approaches that seem most unique share many common components and processes. A unified look at storage enables the study of the advantages and disadvantages of many architectural choices. Throughout the book, I use the term *storage networking* to encompass the study of all the storage-related components, processes, and architectures.

In the next section, I define the *storage networking model* that encapsulates most of the storage architectures in use today. The development, implementation, improvement, tuning, and management of a system are greatly assisted by a conceptual model, which provides a framework for expressing the relationships between the model components.

Defining the Storage Networking Model

Storage access is an integral part of the *Input/Output (I/O) path*. To be useful, computers must accept input data and present the results in the form of output data. The storage networking model shows the I/O path from the user application down to the physical storage platters. At the end, this path determines the data storage performance.

Initially, it is more important to focus on the similarities of various architectural options and determine the overlapping components. Then, the performance analyst can start looking at the components and processes that make the architectures different. This way of thinking forces one to make baseline comparisons. When a difference occurs, it is easier to understand the root cause.

The storage networking model parallels and is inspired by the Storage Networking Industry Association's (SNIA) *Shared Storage Model* (SNIA, 2001). Both models can be used to express many storage networking architectures in existence today. However, the two models are laid out differently. The storage networking model used in this book is specifically developed to enable the study of storage networking performance. It can be used as a base for the design of performance models, which requires explicit treatment of component and process entities and the data flows between them. I had to refrain from using the Shared Storage Model because the copyright terms surrounding it prohibit any expansions and alterations.

Figure 1-1 depicts the layered structure of the storage networking model. On the left, the logical layers of storage access are presented. The physical layers of storage access are on the right. In the next section, I show that most of the storage networking architectures can be expressed (modeled) by assigning the logical layers on the left to the physical layers on the right. The logical layers include:

✓ **Application:** The application layer generates all the I/O transfers, including the storage accesses. In Chapter 9, I show that the workload characteristics of the applications have a profound effect on storage performance. Therefore, application requirements determine the type and size of the storage network that needs to be implemented. Applications access storage through file system calls or database queries.

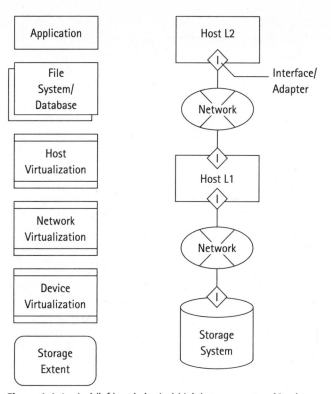

Figure 1-1: Logical (left) and physical (right) storage networking layers

✓ **File System/Database:** This layer maps the logical placement of data in a file or a database table onto the underlying physical storage. As I discuss in the virtualization layer, what looks like physical storage at the file system layer might be a *virtualized* set of storage extents that span multiple physical devices. File systems map a continuous space (a file) onto the underlying storage block units. In this respect, database systems are no different than the file systems and they should be treated as file systems until you definitely need to make a distinction. Instead of mapping files, database systems map database tables onto storage blocks. They must perform all the customary file system operations such as opens, closes, reads, writes, backups, and so on.

✓ **Virtualization:** This layer and the layers below it deal only with blocks of storage. Access to storage is made in units of storage blocks without regard to their placement in a file or database table. Virtualization is one of the most popular and overused terms in the storage networking field. I define *virtualization* as the process of collecting several underlying storage extents and presenting them to the upper layers as a different set of storage logical units (as seen in Figure 1-2), possibly after applying some complex transformation functions. These functions include *aggregation*, for collecting various extents into a large storage pool; *partitioning*, for dicing this large storage pool into pieces that are presented to the higher levels; and *redundancy*, for redundantly storing the data while distributing it onto the underlying storage extents. Note that virtualization is not bound to storage capacity management — you can virtualize performance, cost, management, and reliability characteristics of storage, too. Historically, virtualization has been present in one form or another at various levels in computing systems. I model virtualization at three levels:

- **Host Virtualization:** Virtualization on the host system can be implemented using Logical Volume Manager (LVM) software. Some operating systems provide this functionality as part of the operating system. Alternatively, it can be purchased as a commercial LVM package.

- **Network Virtualization:** Increasingly, the network devices — switches, directors, or specialized appliances — include storage management functionalities like virtualization. These devices can access all the underlying storage units, and they can be set to present virtualized storage to the hosts.

- **Device Virtualization:** Device virtualization has been, and still is, the most prevalent form of storage virtualization. Host Bus Adapters (HBAs) that connect storage devices to the host computers have long been providing RAID (Redundant Array of Inexpensive Disks) functionality, which is the most widely used virtualization technique. Similarly, specialized RAID subsystems provide many forms of virtualization inside the array boxes.

In a given storage network, all, some, or none of the virtualization layers might be present.

Each layer has its own merits and is discussed in detail in Chapters 16 and 17.

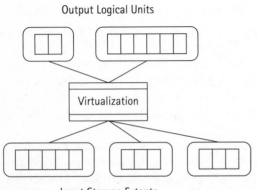

Figure 1-2: Virtualization distributes logical units onto storage extents.

✓ **Storage Extent:** The bottom of the logical storage layers is the storage extents. Each storage extent is a continuous piece of storage space on some storage device. The virtualization layer gathers and partitions these extents into a set of logical units.

Obviously, these are not the only logical layers that operate on the storage data. Nevertheless, they represent the most important and general set of modeling entities that can be used as a foundation for more detailed study. In this book, wherever possible, I try to use this storage networking model and expand each piece to study the alternatives therein.

The physical layers of the storage networking model are:

✓ **Host (Level 2):** These host computers constitute the "client" computers in a traditional local area network (LAN) environment. Level 2 hosts are connected to Level 1 hosts, which are generally "servers." Level 2 hosts might be desktop computers running office applications or compute nodes running enterprise applications.

✓ **Network:** In terms of high-level modeling, I make no distinction between communication networks and storage networks. All connection mediums will be represented as *network* links. Whether it is a LAN connection or a SCSI (Small Computer System Interface) connection, the job of a "network" medium is to carry data between two or more computing entities (computers, disk drives, and so on).

✓ **Interface/Adapter:** These interface cards connect physical components to a network. I use interfaces to denote Network Interface Cards (NICs) and Host Bus Adapters (HBAs).

✓ **Host (Level 1):** Level 1 hosts are servers in the storage network. They could be file servers, database servers, or any other form of specialized storage server that provides data storage services to the Level 2 Hosts (clients).

✓ **Storage Device:** Any storage end device that stores data physically on a storage medium is in this level. Examples are physical memory, disk drives, array controllers, tape libraries, and so on.

Exploring Storage Networking Model Examples

In this section, I use the storage networking model to represent several widely used storage architectures. These usage examples are constructed by assigning the logical layers to the physical layers in various combinations. The overall intention is to show that these architectures have many common building blocks, and that the storage networking model can be used to discuss the similarities and differences explicitly.

DIRECT-ATTACHED STORAGE

Figure 1-3 illustrates how a monolithic host with direct-attached storage inside the host chassis can be represented using the logical and physical layers of the storage networking model. In this example, the host contains the application, the file system, the disk drives, and the storage network (the disk connections) inside the host box. The host also has host virtualization (LVM) to manage the internal, direct-attached storage devices.

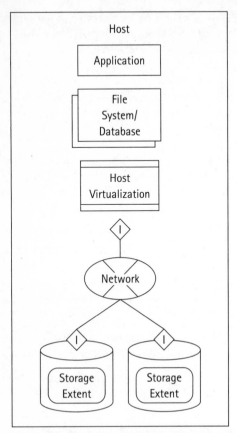

Figure 1-3: Host with direct-attached storage and LVM

Just from looking at the layout of the model, some very simple but important observations can be made:

✓ Direct-attached storage restricts storage to a single host and hinders sharing between multiple hosts.

✓ Addition and removal of storage devices affects the host directly and probably requires host shutdown.

✓ As long as the storage device is connected to a single host, it doesn't really matter whether the devices are inside the host box. In Figure 1-3, you can equally draw the host line above the network and still get the same configuration.

SAN ATTACHED STORAGE WITH DEVICE VIRTUALIZATION

Storage area networks (SANs) are specialized networks for storage data that can connect multiple hosts to multiple storage devices. The example in Figure 1-4 shows that multiple hosts can share a storage device over a network. In this case, I chose to model the virtualization layer inside the storage device, which might be a RAID array. The array controller presents the storage extents to the hosts as logical units (LUs). The hosts can share access to a particular LU or they can use separate, unshared LUs. Note that even if the LUs are not shared, the storage device is shared.

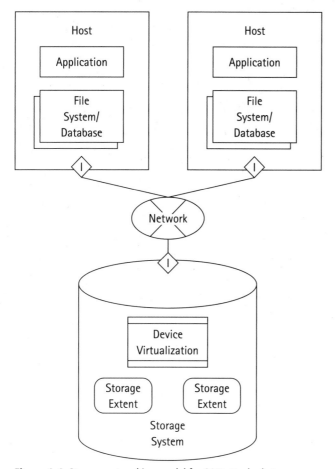

Figure 1-4: Storage networking model for SAN attached storage

SAN attached storage exhibits the following characteristics:

✓ SANs permit device sharing. If necessary, individual LUs can also be shared. This configuration enables the consolidation of storage resources.

✓ Addition or removal of storage devices does not necessarily require host shutdowns. The storage can be updated independent of the host computers.

SAN ATTACHED STORAGE WITH NETWORK VIRTUALIZATION

In a networked storage environment, the virtualization can be performed inside the network elements. Such an architecture is shown in Figure 1-5 using the storage networking model.

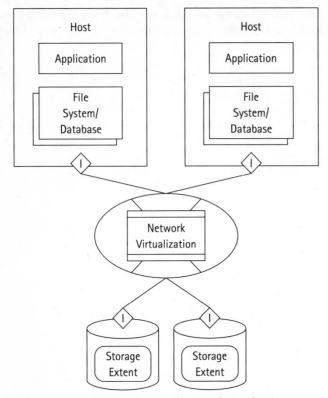

Figure 1-5: SAN attached storage with network virtualization

Virtualization at the network means that:

✓ Even if the underlying storage devices do not have virtualization, the network can be used to virtualize them.

✓ A uniform management of virtualization over diverse sets of storage devices is maintained.

Virtualization at the network layer requires support from all the switches on the network. A switch that does not participate in this virtualization might expose the underlying storage devices directly to the hosts. Therefore, the layout of the network becomes very critical when network virtualization is used.

NAS SERVER

Specialized file servers that serve file system data over a network are generally referred to as network attached storage (NAS) servers. I use the term *NAS server* when the storage devices are an integral part of the NAS device, as opposed to using SAN attached storage as backend storage. Figure 1-6 depicts a NAS server using the storage networking model. The first thing to note is the placement of the file system layer. The file system is divided into two halves. The first half is on the client hosts and performs access operations over a network to the second half of the file system, which is on the NAS server. This is how *network file systems* will be modeled.

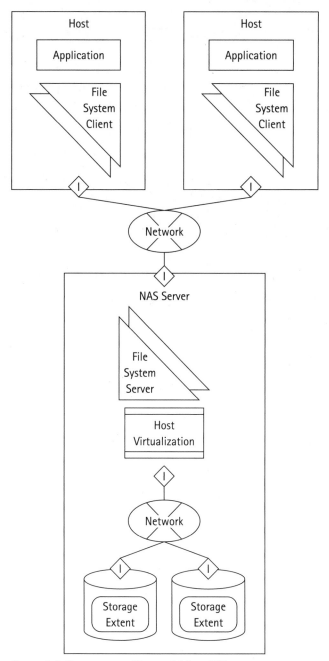

Figure 1-6: Storage networking model for a NAS server

A NAS server exhibits the following characteristics:

✓ Storage is separate from the application hosts, which allows independent upgrades and management.

✓ Storage is consolidated in a server, which allows consolidation of storage management tasks.

✓ NAS servers can be optimized for file serving, since this is the only function they are supposed to perform. Specialized storage devices and virtualization software can be contained inside the NAS servers.

NAS HEAD

When a NAS server uses SAN attached storage as backend storage instead of integrated storage devices, it is referred to as a *NAS head*. Figure 1-7 illustrates how a NAS head can be shown using the storage networking model. Compared to the NAS server in Figure 1-6, the storage devices are now external and accessed using an external storage network.

NAS heads exhibit the following characteristics:

✓ NAS device and storage devices are independent and can be purchased, upgraded, and managed separately.

✓ NAS heads can be used to add NAS functionality to existing SAN storage installations.

✓ Similar to NAS servers, NAS heads can be optimized just for file serving.

Storage Networking Performance

Data (information, that is) is probably an institution's most valuable asset. It must be handled swiftly and with care. In fact, the speed with which data is handled determines the success of many projects and commercial endeavors. In computer systems, data travels on the I/O path. Unfortunately, the elements on the I/O path have historically been the most performance-limiting factors. As important as I/O performance is for overall system performance, it is extremely difficult to define and measure.

In general, *performance* refers to the functioning of a particular entity, especially with regard to effectiveness. Operational speed is not the only factor here; how well a given architecture or product scales to bigger installations, or how well it realizes the reliability specifications, for example, can also contribute to effective performance. Although I try to use *performance* in its most general sense in this book, it is sometimes necessary to use it in the sense of operational speed, in order to align more fully with industry usage.

In order to talk more concretely about various performance issues, it is necessary to define the metrics, the quantitative measures of performance. The next section discusses the metrics of performance that are used in the rest of the book.

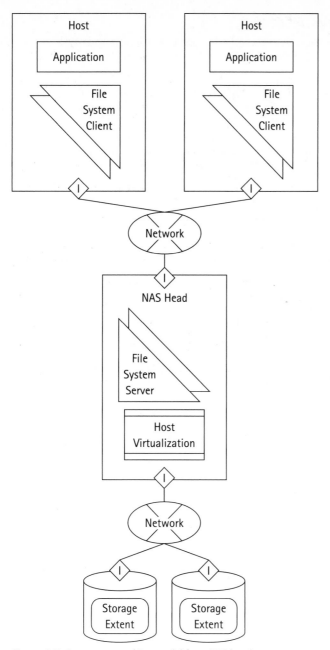

Figure 1-7: Storage networking model for a NAS head

Storage Performance Metrics

Performance is the result of complex interactions that take place among numerous system components. Therefore, it is difficult to quantify it with a few simple numbers.

The next sections define and explain several metrics commonly used in the performance analysis of storage systems. The overall performance of a system or a component is a combination of many of these metrics. In this chapter, I define the metrics in broad terms. Formal mathematical definitions can be found in Chapter 3.

Table 1-1 shows the units of magnitude commonly used in many of the metrics. One confusing point often found in the computing literature is whether the units represent powers of 10 or powers of 2. For example, in many contexts, K (kilo) denotes a thousand (1×10^3) and in others it denotes 1,024 (1×2^{10}). Unfortunately, the terminology still hasn't been consistently defined.

TABLE 1-1 Units of Magnitude

Symbol	Name	Magnitude
K	Kilo, thousand	1,000 or 1,024
M	Mega, million	1,000,000 or 1,024K
G	Giga, billion	1,000,000,000 or 1,024M
T	Tera, trillion	1,000,000,000,000 or 1,024G
P	Peta, quadrillion	1,000,000,000,000,000 or 1,024T
E	Exa, quintillion	1,000,000,000,000,000,000 or 1,024P
Z	Zetta, sextillion	1,000,000,000,000,000,000,000 or 1,024E
Y	Yotta, septillion	1,000,000,000,000,000,000,000,000 or 1,024Z

The symbols K, M, G, T, P, and so on, denote powers of 1,000 when they are applied to measurements of bandwidth and powers of 1,024 when they are applied to measurements of storage capacity. For example, a transmission line can have a bandwidth of 1.5 Mbps (1,500,000 bps), and a read buffer can have a capacity of 4KB (4,096 bytes).

Table 1-2 presents the common symbols of time used in the performance metrics.

TABLE 1-2 Units of Time

Abbreviation	Time Unit
ns	Nanosecond, 1/1,000,000,000 of a second
μs, us	Microsecond, 1/1,000,000 of a second
ms	Millisecond, 1/1,000 of a second
sec, s	Second
min, m	Minute

BANDWIDTH

Bandwidth is the total amount of data transferred through a medium or system per unit of time. It is a synonym for *data transmission rate*. Units generally used for bandwidth are shown in Table 1-3. Bandwidth is usually expressed at two different levels:

✓ **Raw bandwidth** or **line-speed** is the specified, theoretical transmission rate of a component. A transmission line or bus will have a physical signal rate that determines the maximum possible data rate. The user is guaranteed not to observe anything faster than this specified rate.

✓ **Sustained bandwidth** is the data rate after accounting for all the overheads that might be needed for the transmission operations. The sustained bandwidth will always be less than the raw bandwidth if the transmission medium has contention or if parts of the transmission are not considered usable data. Sustained bandwidth is a better representation of the performance a user observes when using the component.

TABLE 1-3 Units of Bandwidth

Acronym	Bandwidth Unit
KB/s, KBs, KBps	Kilobytes per second
MB/s, MBs	Megabytes per second
GB/s, GBs	Gigabytes per second

Continued

TABLE 1-3 Units of Bandwidth (Continued)

Acronym	Bandwidth Unit
TB/s, TBs	Terabytes per second
Kb/s, Kbs, kbs, kbps	Kilobits per second
Mb/s, Mbs, mbs	Megabits per second
Gb/s, Gbs	Gigabits per second
Tb/s, Tbs	Terabits per second

In the computing literature, it is common to use both *B* and *b* as an abbreviation for both *byte* and *bit*, interchangeably. This is quite confusing. In this book, I use B for byte and b for bit in every context, consistently.

Some bandwidth quotes that you might encounter in the storage networking context are shown in Table 1-4. For example, Fibre Channel (FC) has a physical signal bandwidth of 1 Gbs (1000 Mbs), while it has a data bandwidth of 100 MBs (800 Mbs). I discuss the reason for the difference and all the component bandwidths at appropriate times in the book.

TABLE 1-4 Storage Bandwidth Examples

Disk drive media transfer	440 Mbs
ULTRA160, SCSI bus	160 MBs
Fibre Channel physical bandwidth	1 Gbs
Fibre Channel data bandwidth	100 MBs
PCI bus, 32-bit, 33 MHz	133 MBs
T1 WAN link	1.5 Mbs
OC-12 WAN link	622 Mbs
NAS device, network file access	300 Mbs

THROUGHPUT

Throughput is the amount of work performed by a component or system over unit time. As shown in Table 1-5, throughput is generally expressed in operations per second or transactions per second. Although throughput and bandwidth are sometimes used interchangeably, there is a fundamental difference between the two terms. The difference stems from the fact that operations reported in the throughput can have different data sizes. This affects the bandwidth directly. For example, suppose that a transmission line can support 100 IOPS when each operation is 4KB long. Then, the bandwidth of the line is 400 KBps (4×100). The same line might be able to perform 20 IOPS when the operation sizes are 100KB long. This amounts to a bandwidth of 2,000 KBps (20×100).

TABLE 1-5 Units of Throughput

Abbreviation	Throughput Unit
IOPS, IOps	I/O operations per second
TPS, tps	Transactions per second
TPM, tpm	Transactions per minute

Table 1-6 shows some throughput examples. Throughputs of a disk drive and a RAID array are reported in IOPS. These throughput numbers depend on the operation types and parameters. Consequently, it is necessary to state the access parameters (the workload) while claiming certain throughput numbers. When using a standard benchmark like TPC-C (Transaction Processing Council Benchmark C), which has a standard workload definition, you may not need workload specifications explicitly while reporting throughput measurements.

TABLE 1-6 Storage Throughput Examples

Disk drive, 4KB, random reads	100 IOps
RAID array, 4KB, random writes	10,000 IOps
TPC-C benchmark on a single server	105,000 tpm
TPC-C benchmark on a clustered server	709,220 tpm

DELAY

Delay and *latency* are terms that are often used interchangeably. In this book, however, I use *delay* to indicate the wait time induced by contention within a system component. This corresponds to the *queuing time* (wait time in a queue), which will be defined formally in Chapter 3. In contrast, I use the word *latency* to indicate the amount of time between the initiation of an action and the actual start of the action. In general, delay is specified on individual component basis, and latency is defined end-to-end. Some delay examples encountered in storage networking are provided in Table 1-7.

TABLE 1-7 Storage Delay Examples

Delay in a network router with a light load	3 ms
Delay in an overloaded network router	40 ms
Delay in a layer-2 switch	200 ns

LATENCY

As I mentioned in the previous section, *latency* is used to specify the amount of time between the initiation of a request and the first reaction to it. One example is a communication line where latency defines the time between the start of a data packet transmission at the source and the start of receipt at the destination.

> *Latency* is generally inherent to the physical structure of a device or process. An example is the latency on a fiber-optic cable due to its length. *Delay*, on the other hand, is a result of the usage pattern, which causes resource contention. An example is the delay of packets at an overloaded network router.

Table 1-8 provides example latency values..

TABLE 1-8 Storage Latency Examples

Disk drive rotational latency	4 ms
Packet latency on a LAN segment	3 ms
Latency on a satellite link	300 ms

RESPONSE TIME

Response time, one of the most important storage performance metrics, denotes the time it takes to finish a given storage operation. The operation could be defined as any of these storage operations: read, write, open, close, search (or a combination thereof). The response time is measured from the initiation of the operation (request) to the completion of the operation (reply). It is an end-to-end measurement and includes wait times (delays and latencies) and service times (actual work time).

In addition to the operation type, many factors affect response time. The storage device determines the actual work time. The intensity of the demand on the device creates contention on the storage device. Contention for a service causes delays while waiting, which adds to the response time. The intensity of contention on a device is inversely proportional to its throughput. Therefore, it is common practice in storage literature to present response time data as a response time versus throughput graph. An example response time graph is shown in Figure 1-8. At high throughput rates, the response time increases exponentially because of long waiting times in the storage component under study.

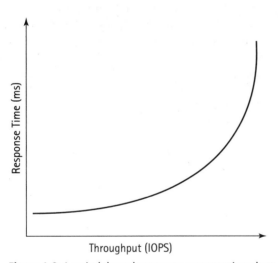

Figure 1-8: A typical throughput versus response time chart

Table 1-9 shows some response time examples. When response time is given without a system load (or throughput) qualifier, it is assumed that the given response time is under very light load. As shown in Figure 1-8, the response time is almost stable for some range of throughput values under light load.

TABLE 1-9 Storage Response Time Examples

Disk drive response time, 4KB, random reads	6.5 ms
RAID array, 4KB, random writes	15 ms
NAS file server, file creation	30 ms
HTTP, 15KB file get operation	2.5 sec

ACCESS DENSITY

For the last several decades, the data density of disk drives increased steadily by doubling the stored bits in a square inch of platter surface every two years. For the last couple of years, this doubling of data density occurred in less than a year. This technological advancement produced tremendous increases in disk capacity, which unfortunately was not matched by increases in access speed. Because the disk rotation and seek times improve at a much lower pace than the disk capacity, an imbalance of disk performance occurs. Every year, the access speed (throughput) per gigabyte of storage is decreasing.

To identify this imbalance, I define *access density* as a performance metric. Access density is computed as throughput (in IOPS) divided by the capacity (in gigabytes). Assume that a disk drive has a throughput of 100 IOPS and a capacity of 36GB. The drive has an access density of $100 \div 36 = 2.78$ IOPS/GB. If, the next year, this disk drive family has a throughput of 120 IOPS and a capacity of 73GB, its access density is $120 \div 73 = 1.64$ IOPS/GB. Even though both the throughput and the capacity of the disk drive increased, its access density decreased from 2.78 to 1.64 IOPS per GB.

Access density should be considered for storage systems as well as individual storage components. For example, the access density of a RAID array is its throughput divided by its usable capacity. As discussed in Chapter 6, the throughput of a RAID array is proportional to the number of disk drives (spindles) it has. You might conclude that to keep access density high, it's necessary to use a greater number of lesser capacity disk drives, rather than a fewer number of higher capacity drives. A disk array of 20 disks with 36GB each has almost the same capacity as an array of 10 disks with 73GB each. However, the former array has twice the number of spindles (more workers) to distribute the jobs. Table 1-10 presents the access density values discussed in the examples used in this section. I discuss how to model the performance of disk arrays and many other storage components in Part II of this book.

TABLE 1-10 Storage Access Density Examples

Disk drive, 36GB, 100 IOps	2.78 IOps/GB
Disk drive 73GB, 120 IOps	1.64 IOps/GB
RAID array, 20 disks, 36GB each	2.5 IOps/GB
RAID array, 10 disks, 73GB each	1.4 IOps/GB

SCALABILITY

The ability of a system to grow without adversely affecting its service performance is called *scalability*. Growth is inevitable. When growth occurs, the computing systems are stressed. If the system is able to function within acceptable performance limits, it is called a *scalable* system.

I consider scalability at two levels:

✓ First, when the demand on a system increases, the system is limited in the amount of extra load it can accept. For example, consider the response time versus throughput chart in Figure 1-9. There is a defined acceptable response time limit. When the workload increases from the current load, the response time starts to increase. At a later throughput level, the response time will cross over the acceptable level. Therefore, the system is scalable up to this point, without any system changes.

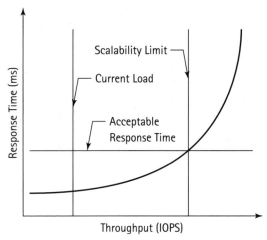

Figure 1-9: Throughput versus response time chart, showing the scalability limit

✓ Secondly, if growth beyond the capabilities of the current system is expected, you can add additional hardware to the same system. If the performance increases in proportion to the increase in hardware capabilities, the system is able to *scale up*. Consider the performance chart in Figure 1-10 for a system that is upgraded by additional hardware. You can see that the new throughput limit is higher after the hardware upgrade. An additional hardware upgrade does not necessarily improve the performance, or the improvement might be very small considering the expense of the upgrade. Moreover, additional hardware might sometimes even degrade system performance. Such a system is clearly not scalable.

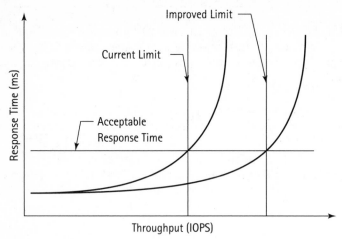

Figure 1-10: Throughput scalability after a hardware update

A scalable system architecture allows the user to start small and grow as necessary. This provides flexibility in planning and management. Although it is not as popular as scaling up, *scaling down* might be a usable feature in some situations. If a system has a modular architecture, it might be possible to shrink the system hardware and expect a proportional, gradual decrease in performance. A system that is able to scale down allows the user to manage downsizing instead of growth.

RELIABILITY

Reliability is the degree to which a given computing component produces consistent results repeatedly without any incapacitating failures. Although it is very difficult to quantify a system's overall reliability claim, it is easier to quantify its failure characteristics.

Quantitative measures of reliability are provided in Table 1-11. Mean Time Between Failures (MTBF) is the amount of time a component is expected to work without a serious failure. MTBF can be computed by dividing the number of observed failures by the length of the observation time. Note that this type of direct computation is impossible for components that have MTBF of millions of hours. In such cases, an extrapolation technique is used by observing multiple (hundreds of) components at the same time. The underlying premise is that the probability of a failure is proportional to the number of items observed. For example, for a component with an MTBF of f, the MTBF of m of these components is f ÷ m. Consequently, multiple items can be used to reduce the observation (testing) time.

MTBF can be used to denote the amount of time a user can expect a component to work without a failure. In other words, it is an *estimate* of the equipment's reliability.

A related notion is Mean Time to Recovery (MTTR). MTTR is the average repair time to fix or replace a failed component and start using the system again. MTTR can be used to define service level agreements with a service provider. In this case, MTTR is the maximum amount of time the provider would take to fix the problem. Lower MTTR times would cost higher amounts of money. Both MTBF and MTTR are generally expressed in terms of hours.

TABLE 1-11 Reliability Measurement Units

Acronym	Reliability Measure
MTBF	Mean time between failures (or faults)
MTTR	Mean time to repair (or recovery)

Table 1-12 presents some example MTBF and MTTR values.

TABLE 1-12 Reliability Examples

MTBF for an enterprise disk drive	1,000,000 hours
MTBF for a NAS server	1,000 hours
MTTR for a NAS server	1 hour

AVAILABILITY

A system's *availability* is the degree to which it stays up (running) within acceptable limits of performance and without any unrecoverable failures. It is usually measured as the percentage of uptime with respect to the overall elapsed time. If the MTBF and MTTR of a component are known, its availability can be computed using the following equation:

```
Availability = MTBF ÷ (MTBF + MTTR)
```

Since MTTR is the time required for repairs, it represents the downtime. Assuming the component is expected to have a failure every MTBF, the above equation represents the percentage of uptime, which is the availability. In the computing literature, it is common to refer to availability by the number of 9s in the availability percentage. For example, if a system has 99.999 percent uptime, it is said to have five 9s availability. Some examples of system availability values are presented in Table 1-13.

TABLE 1-13 Availability Examples

Availability of a NAS server	99.9%
Availability of clustered NAS servers	99.99%
Availability of remote mirrored enterprise data centers	99.999%

It is a common practice to sum up the robustness of computing systems with the acronym *RAS* (Reliability, Availability, Serviceability).

Serviceability is the ease of maintenance on a system. It correlates to the MTTR measurements I discussed in the last two sections.

Evaluating Storage Performance Requirements

Storage performance means different things to different people. A user, using application software on his/her desktop, wants that software to run faster to save time and does not care much about underlying data storage performance issues. A system administrator in a midsize business cares about finishing the system backups sooner. A storage administrator in an enterprise data center cares about the speed of data replication between remote sites and whether or not the current storage network will scale when new servers are added. End-users and system administrators are users of the storage networks, and they only want to do their job better, faster, and probably cheaper.

Table 1-14 shows the relative importance of the storage performance metrics defined earlier in four different environments—a personal PC, a small office (workgroup) server, a midsize data center, and an enterprise data center. A typical PC user generally cares only about the response time of the data operations; the other metrics are invisible to him/her. In a small office server and midsize data center, the other performance metrics are important as well. These environments, for example, are careful about the throughput of their storage systems. In enterprise data centers, all of the performance metrics become important. Such systems need to perform at their best, with the highest possible bandwidth, extreme scalability, and five 9s availability.

**TABLE 1-14 Relative Importance of Storage Performance Metrics
in Different Environments**

Metric	Personal PC	Small Office Server	Midsize Data Center	Enterprise Data Center
Bandwidth	Low	Low	Medium	High
Throughput	Low	Medium	Medium	High
Response Time	Medium	Medium	High	High
Access Density	Low	Low	Medium	High
Scalability	Low	Low	Medium	High
Reliability	Medium	Medium	High	High
Availability	Low	Medium	High	High

On the other side of the coin are the storage system designers who want to provide these services to the users. The network designer checks the number of switching ports and connections to see if the network has enough aggregate bandwidth. A data center implementer worries about balancing the load across multiple storage arrays. An array implementer tries to provide enough outward connection ports to enable maximum throughput out of the array.

The overall I/O system, including the storage I/O, is immensely complex. Managing the complexity of the I/O system requires tradeoffs between cost and performance. Many performance problems can be solved by throwing in more money and new (and newer) equipment. However, this is not an economical solution, if possible at all. Therefore, at each level compromises must be made to optimize performance versus cost.

From CPU down to the disk, intelligence is distributed according to cost performance analysis. The storage networking model discussed earlier in this chapter provides a tool for understanding this point. An example of the placement of intelligence is storage virtualization. If you look back at Figures 1-1 through 1-6, you can see that virtualization can be performed at several layers of the storage network—the host, the network, the device. Each of these choices has advantages and disadvantages depending on circumstance. A host-based, software-only solution is cheaper, but consumes host CPU cycles. A device-based solution might be more costly, but it is more efficient.

Even inside the host, these cost-performance choices must be made. For example, some I/O protocols might be implemented more cheaply if the CPU is responsible for moving data around. For example, programmed I/O and many network protocols with software stacks use the host CPU for data transfers. On the other hand, if, instead of the CPU, specialized hardware devices are used to move I/O data around, the implementation will be much faster but more costly because of the additional hardware. Examples of this kind of I/O include the Direct Memory Access (DMA) and network protocol implementations with hardware-assisted stacks.

It is the purpose of this book to provide the reader with the tools to understand, evaluate, and manage these storage performance requirements and tradeoffs in the most efficient way.

Conducting a Systematic Performance Evaluation

There are many ways to handle a performance analysis project. I place them in three main categories—intuition, experimental, and modeling.

- ✓ **Intuition:** Every user, system administrator, or system designer has some prior experiences with the systems they are dealing with. Over time, they develop intuitive rules of thumb for performance management. In most cases, these rules should not be taken lightly when they are based on historical data. Intuition is the fastest way to arrive at a decision and does not consume any resources. However, the consequences might be costly. In performance analysis, intuition is best used for developing hypotheses and verifying the results of other formal techniques.

- ✓ **Experimental:** If the system under study is available for experimental testing, very reliable, direct performance data can be obtained. Compared to intuition and modeling, experimental performance analysis provides the most accurate results. However, even if the systems exist, it may not always be possible to experiment with them. Generally, it is not wise to disrupt a critical system used in production. Still, it might be possible to collect data without disturbing the service of the system. The most advanced computing and storage systems and networks have performance data collection capabilities built into them. However, you should note that any system that is probed for data collection will be disturbed from its normal behavior pattern and the collected data will not be an exact representation of normal behavior. Collecting data has additional overhead, which might further overload an already overloaded system. Care must therefore be taken when collecting performance data to balance overhead with accuracy. You should not overdo it.

I discuss the techniques for systematic experimental analysis in Chapter 5. The tools for collecting experimental performance data are discussed in Chapter 13.

✓ **Modeling:** Models are abstract descriptions of systems under study. Oftentimes, they concentrate on the most important aspects of the system and leave out details. Decades of modeling research have shown that a relatively small number of high-level parameters can provide surprisingly accurate estimates. As a result, complex I/O systems do not require complex modeling. A modeling study can start with the most basic features and can be expanded with increasing levels of detail. Developing models takes time. It requires more resources than an analysis based on intuition alone. On the other hand, modeling is simpler, and sometimes more cost-effective, than experimental studies performed on physical systems. Sometimes, it may not even be possible to acquire or build a physical system. Once a good, accurate model is developed, it can be used for many purposes, including cost-performance analysis, capacity planning, and similar what-if analysis. Modeling techniques can be grouped into two categories:

■ **Analytical Modeling:** If the abstract description of the system is constructed using mathematical expressions, it is an *analytical* model. The analytical model focuses on the relationships of modeled system features. The modeler, using some assumptions, chooses system parameters that he/she believes have the most effect on the behavior of the system. The relationships between these parameters are represented by mathematical equations. An analytical model can be very accurate if the assumptions and the relationships closely reflect the real system. Analytical modeling techniques are discussed in Chapter 3 in detail.

■ **Simulation Modeling:** A *simulation* models system behavior by executing specialized computer programs. Simulation models represent the interactions between system components. The assumption is that the analytical relationships are an outcome of these interactions. Several specialized programming languages are used for constructing simulations (for example, SIMULA, SimScript, and MODSIM). In addition, certain software packages, most of which have graphical user interfaces, make it easier to build models by providing building blocks for the models (for example, SIMULINK, Hyperformix/Workbench, and OPNET Modeler). Simulation models generally take more time to build compared to analytical models, and they certainly take more time to compute results. However, simulation models provide more accurate results compared to the analytical models. Simulation techniques are discussed in Chapter 4 in more detail.

It is possible to combine analytical and simulation models. Individual blocks in a simulation model can include analytical sub-models. Such an approach provides the advantages of both approaches.

A model is useful only under the circumstances that are foreseen by its assumptions. Out of its scope, a model is invariably useless.

Whether you depend on your intuition or use experimental or modeling analysis, a systematic performance study consists of the following three basic steps (just like any other scientific study):

1. Build a hypothesis.

2. Test your hypothesis.

3. Evaluate the results. If necessary, modify your hypothesis and return to step 2.

Suppose, for example, that you realize that a certain file server is experiencing degraded performance. First, you hypothesize that the increased client load is causing the problem. Then, you check the system logs and the historical performance data to verify your hypothesis. In addition, you run experiments with different load levels if possible. If you are not satisfied that the load level is the problem, you will check another potential cause. If you are satisfied that the load level is the problem, you will make a similar performance study for the solution of the problem. First, you hypothesize that the memory in the server is not enough for the increased load. To test this, you can simply add more memory and check the resulting performance. While you are changing the memory, you might also think about upgrading the network card of the server. Be forewarned: if you do this, you will ruin your performance analysis because you won't be able to tell whether it was the memory expansion or the network card upgrade that solved the problem. Therefore, controlled, step-by-step testing is very important.

Indeed, this seemingly simple procedure is the basis for all scientific research. If followed with consistency, it eases the planning, implementation, and evaluation phases of your performance analysis projects.

Summary

This chapter introduced some key concepts about both storage networking and storage networking performance.

Storage Networking

✓ Advances in networking technology affected the traditional data storage architectures and helped the formation of storage networks.

✓ Storage systems are no longer peripheral devices; they are the central components in data centers.

✓ The growth of data size, partially fueled by the Internet and e-business requirements, enables opportunities for new, highly available, scalable, faster storage architectures.

✓ The storage networking model provides a unified modeling framework to represent the I/O path from the CPU down to the disks for various types of storage architectures.

✓ The storage networking model has logical functional layers and physical layers.

✓ Many existing storage architectures can be represented in the storage networking model by mapping the logical layers to physical entities. The models for various popular storage system architectures are shown as examples.

✓ The storage networking model provides the framework for the storage performance analysis in this book.

Storage Networking Performance

✓ Even though data is an organization's most valuable asset, the components that handle the data (the I/O path) have historically been the slowest link in computing performance.

✓ Performance refers to the functioning of a particular entity, especially with regard to effectiveness.

✓ Besides referring to operational speed, performance also encompasses a system's availability, scalability, reliability, and so on.

✓ Performance metrics are the quantitative measures of system performance.

✓ Bandwidth, throughput, delay, latency, response time, access density, scalability, reliability, and availability are defined as the performance metrics for storage networks.

✓ Performance requirements have different meanings for different types of users and for different types of institutions. Depending on requirements, some performance metrics become more important than others.

✓ Performance evaluation projects can be based on intuition, experimental tests, or modeling. Each approach has its advantages and disadvantages, but all are useful as available tools for the performance analyst.

✓ Performance analysis studies must be based on a scientific approach that entails creating a hypothesis, testing it, and then revising it.

References and Additional Resources

Barker, Richard and Paul Massiglia. November 2001. *Storage Area Network Essentials: A Complete Guide to Understanding and Implementing SANs*. John Wiley & Sons.

Provides the essentials for SAN designs. Discusses strategies for moving from a server-centric storage system to a SAN-based system, where the data is the center of computing.

Clark, Tom. September 1999. *Designing Storage Area Networks: A Practical Reference for Implementing Fibre Channel SANs*. Addison-Wesley.

A concise guide for Fibre Channel–based SAN implementations.

Clark, Tom. December 2001. *IP SANS: A Guide to iSCSI, iFCP, and FCIP Protocols for Storage Area Networks*. Addison-Wesley.

Introductory chapters provide information on the SNIA shared storage model and the synergy between the storage and networking worlds. It provides examples for the layered approach in both storage and networking protocols.

Farley, Marc. May 2001. *Building Storage Networks*, Second Edition. McGraw-Hill.

A comprehensive guide to everything related to storage networks.

Marcus, Evan and Hal Stern. January 2000. *Blueprints for High Availability: Designing Resilient Distributed Systems*. John Wiley & Sons.

Treatment of availability from storage systems up to the application layer.

Musumeci, Gian-Paolo D. and Mike Loukides. February 2002. *System Performance Tuning*, Second Edition. O'Reilly & Associates.

Performance tuning must be handled at all layers of the system. This is a guide for tuning the performance of UNIX computing systems from top to bottom.

Storage Networking Industry Association. October 2001. *A Dictionary of Storage Networking Terminology*, available at http://www.snia.org/English/Resources/Dictionary.html.

SNIA provides a dictionary of common storage networking–related terms to standardize their usage among storage professionals. The dictionary provides the technical context of each definition to clarify their usage.

Chapter 2

Data Analysis Review

In This Chapter

While analyzing the performance of storage networks, you will obtain experimental performance data and derive similar numbers from analytical or simulation models. However, these numbers, in and of themselves, are not significant or interesting to many people. You need mathematical methods to summarize and characterize your data. This short review of statistical techniques teaches the following:

✓ Measures of central tendency in data — mean, median, and mode

✓ Measures of dispersion in data — histograms, distributions, standard deviation, and variance

✓ Confidence interval and statistical significance

✓ Probability distribution functions that are commonly used in modeling studies

Summarizing Data

Like other experimental scientific studies, performance analysis requires many data points. The data might be used to define a particular workload or the resulting product performance. In any case, presenting hundreds of numbers in a table is not an effective way to communicate information. You must summarize the input parameters and the output performance data using established statistical techniques. This chapter presents a short overview of the mathematical terms and techniques that are used in extracting information from numbers — *statistics*.

This chapter provides only the basic statistical techniques that enable you to understand the rest of the book. You are encouraged to consult the resources listed at the end the chapter for further details. You can be easily misled by statistical analysis, knowingly or unknowingly. Therefore, every performance analyst and performance reviewer must be on the lookout for the statistical validity of any statement of performance.

When you are faced with hundreds of data points, you must first identify what the *average* data looks like. If this set consists of related data, there must be measures to show the *central tendency* of the data points. This is the subject of the next section.

The same data set probably exhibits some dispersion — not all the data points are the same. To describe how the data is scattered, in an orderly manner, the measures of *spread* are used. These measures tell you if there is a particular pattern of data distribution. This is the subject of the latter half of the chapter.

Measures of central tendency and spread provide useful information about the data. This information is used to generate models of performance and analyze performance, as you'll see in the rest of the book.

Measures of Central Tendency

In statistics, a *random variable* denotes a term that can take on a value according to a given probability. The set of all the possible values for that variable is called a *population*. Because analyzing the whole population may not be possible, a *sample* is taken and tested. The sample is a random subset of the population. The assumption is that the sample, if taken correctly, will exhibit the characteristics of the whole population. Therefore, studying the sample and making generalizations about the population becomes possible.

The first generalization technique is used to find the characteristics of an average data point. You can find the average by summing all the numbers and dividing by the number of measurements (*observations*). The resulting number is called the *mean* or the *expected value* and can be formulated for a random variable x, as shown in the following equation.

Equation 2-1

$$\mu = \Sigma_i x_i \div n$$

The mean, μ, is obtained by summing all the possible values, x_i, and dividing by the number of elements, n.

The value that occurs the greatest number of times in a sample is the *mode*. By definition, mode corresponds to one of the sample values. The value in the middle of the sample is the *median*. The median can be found by sorting the set and then identifying the value that falls in the middle of the set. For a set with an odd number of elements, the median is the middle value. For a set with an even number of elements, the median is the average of the two middle values. The computation of mean, median, and mode is illustrated in Example 2-1.

Figure 2-1 illustrates Example 2-1's data set in a graphical format. The x-axis shows the sample values. You can see a square on the y-axis for each occurrence of the corresponding sample value. Note that the mean value does not necessarily correspond to any existing sample values.

Example 2-1 Averaging Data

Suppose that the following numbers result from 10 response time measurements:

5   6   6   8   9   9   9   10   10   12

In this data set, the mean value computed using Equation 2-1 is 8.4. Because 9 occurs three times, it is the mode. The two middle values are 9s; therefore the median is 9, the average of the two.

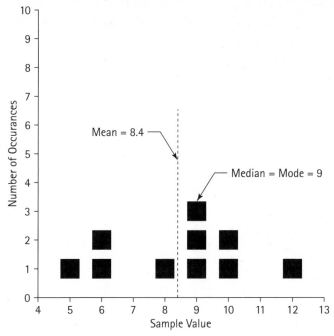

Figure 2-1: Measures of central tendency for a sample

Although the mean is useful for describing the entire sample set, the median is a better measure for describing the average element. In a skewed sample like the one shown in Example 2-2, the mean, median, and mode can have very different values.

The data in Example 2-2 is plotted in Figure 2-2. You can see that the set is skewed to the left.

Example 2-2 Averaging Skewed Data

The following is a skewed sample relative to the sample in Example 2-1.

5   6   8   8   10   10   11   11   11   12

In this data set, the mean is 9.2, the median is 10, and the mode is 11.

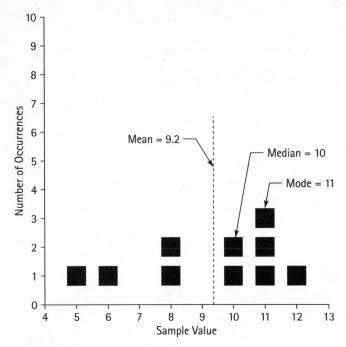

Figure 2-2: Measures of central tendency for a skewed sample

For such a skewed set, the mode indicates where most of the data points are; the median indicates where the data points are divided in half. The mean is closer to the skewed tail relative to the median and mode and represents the whole set, not the average element. Because of this property, the mean is more susceptible to outliers in the set.

Measures of Data Spread

In addition to finding the central tendencies, or the average data, you can also describe how the data is scattered around the mean value. If you look back at Figure 2-1, the graph that shows the sample data points can be used to visualize the shape of the distribution. Such graphs are known as *histograms*. On the y-axis, they show the frequency of each data point's occurrence. You can also group data into *bins* (non-overlapping subsets of the data) and plot the frequency of the elements corresponding to the bins. A histogram is shown in Figure 2-3 for the sample data set given in Example 2-1. In this histogram, the bins are two units wide. For example, you can see that four elements exist between the values 7 and 9.

This kind of histogram is easily obtained using Microsoft Excel spreadsheets. Go to the Tools menu, and within that menu go to the Data Analysis menu; choose Histogram, and then choose your input data range and output chart options.

The histogram chart in Figure 2-3 also includes the cumulative percentage function. It is formally called the *cumulative distribution function (CDF)*, and shows the percentage of all elements up to a point on the x-axis. For example, in Figure 2-3, CDF(11) is 90 percent, meaning that 90 percent of the elements are equal to or less than 11.

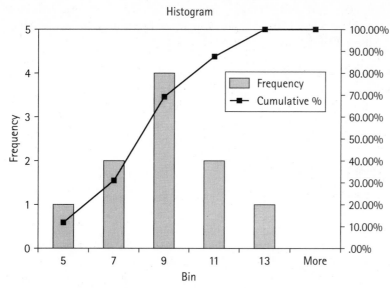

Figure 2-3: Histogram of a sample data set

Also note that the shape of the histogram is a bell-shaped curve if it is plotted continuously. This bell-shaped curve is actually a special distribution called *normal distribution*. A generic normal distribution is plotted in Figure 2-4.

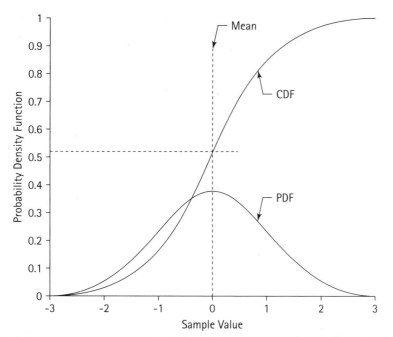

Figure 2-4: A generic normal distribution curve

In Figure 2-4, the y-axis shows the frequency of occurrence for each sample value. By dividing each frequency value by the total number of observations, you obtain probability distribution. For a continuous distribution, this is called *probability density function (PDF)*. The area under the PDF curve has a special meaning. The area between two values, *a* and *b*, denotes the probability that the random variable will fall between *a* and *b*. More formally, PDF is the first derivative of CDF. The exact mathematical definitions are beyond the scope of this book, and I encourage you to consult the resources given at the end of the chapter. If you plot the CDF and PDF of a variable with a normal distribution, you obtain a graph like that shown in Figure 2-4. Some other important distribution functions are discussed later in this chapter.

Variance and Standard Deviation

To quantify the difference between all the observations and the mean value, you can use Equation 2-2:

Equation 2-2

$$\sigma^2 = \Sigma_i \ (x_i - \mu)^2 \div (n-1)$$

The symbol σ^2 is used to indicate the *sample variance*. It is the sum of all squared distances from the mean, divided by (n-1). The other widely used statistical value, *standard deviation* (σ), is simply the square root of the variance. It can be computed as shown in Equation 2-3.

Equation 2-3

$$\sigma = \sqrt{\sigma^2}$$

Although showing variance on a graph isn't practical, statisticians prefer to use it as a theoretical tool. To my mind, standard deviation is more useful for practical researchers. Standard deviation is expressed in the same unit as the sample data, and you can show the standard deviation on a distribution graph for visual clues of data spread. For example, for normal distribution, 68 percent of the elements lie within one standard deviation distance from the mean, as shown in Figure 2-5. Similarly, 95 percent of the area is within two standard deviation distances from the mean.

In normal distribution, about two-thirds of the data lies within one standard deviation distance from each side of the mean value. Consequently, the higher the value of standard deviation relative to the mean value, the more widely dispersed the data.

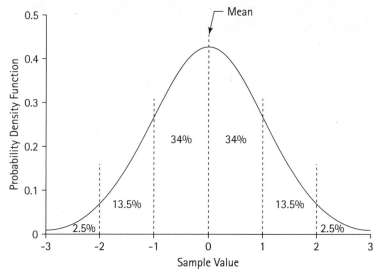

Figure 2-5: The area under the normal distribution curve

Standard Error of the Mean

Every time you draw a sample from a population, the sample has a slightly different mean from the previous samples. The *central limit theorem* states that these mean values approximate a normal distribution regardless of the original population's distribution. However, the spread of the normal distribution depends on the spread of the original population. The more diverse the original population, the more different the observed means will be. As you have seen, the measure of diversity in a population is the standard deviation. Because it may not be practical to obtain the standard deviation of the whole population, the standard deviation of the sample set in hand can be used as an approximation. *Standard error of the mean (SEM)*, or simply *standard error*, is obtained by dividing the standard deviation by the square root of the number of experiments in the sample, as shown in Equation 2-4.

Equation 2–4

$$SEM = \sigma \div \sqrt{n}$$

SEM is an approximate measure of the variation in the mean value if you were to repeat the set of experiments several times. Even if your experiments are perfectly controlled, you will see this variation by pure chance, depending on which sample set you chose in that population. It's common sense that the more experiments you have, the more accurate your estimates will be.

Standard deviation describes the data — it measures how representative the mean value is in that population (see Example 2-3). On the other hand, SEM describes an experiment — the reliability of estimates in that experiment against random variations.

Example 2-3 Computing the Standard Error

Compute the standard error of the mean for the data set shown in Example 2-1.

In Example 2-1, the mean was computed as 8.4. There are 10 observations (n = 10).

Using Equation 2-2, the variance can be computed as 4.71. The standard deviation is 2.17, which is the square root of the variance. Using Equation 2-4, SEM is 2.17 ÷ $\sqrt{10}$ ~= 0.686. This means that if you were to perform similar sets of experiments (with 10 data points in each), you should expect to have a standard deviation of 0.686 ms between the mean values of each set.

Confidence Interval and Confidence Level

In the previous section, you saw an expected deviation between the sample mean and the "true" population mean. You can show this expected range by μ±r, which is a range around the sample mean. The width of this range is called the *confidence interval*. In addition, the probability that the population mean lies within this interval is called the *confidence level*. Traditionally, this probability is shown in percentages (for example, 95 percent confidence level).

As previously stated, sample means have a normal distribution, and their standard deviation is σ ÷ $\sqrt{n}$, which is the standard error. The confidence interval for the population mean can be calculated by using Equation 2-5.

Equation 2-5

```
confidence interval = μ ± t × (σ÷√n)
```

This range is a multiple (t) of the standard error around the sample mean. You have previously seen that for normal distribution, 95 percent of the area is within two standard deviations of the mean. So, the confidence interval with a 95 percent confidence level can be computed by substituting t = 2. Unfortunately, this statement is accurate only if the number of observations (n) is greater than 30. For n less than 30, t should be calculated using the t-distribution function. In Microsoft Excel, it can be computed using the function TINV(p, n-1). Here, p denotes the significance level where 100(1-p) gives the confidence level. For example, for 95 percent confidence level, the significance level, p, is 0.05. The confidence interval for Example 2-1 is computed in Example 2-4.

All the statistical analysis metrics described above for a single random variable can easily be computed using Microsoft Excel's data analysis tools. Go to the Tools menu and then, within that menu, go to the Data Analysis menu; choose the Descriptive Statistics item to obtain all the statistical values shown in Table 2-1, for the sample values given in Example 2-1.

Example 2-4 Computing the Confidence Interval

Compute the confidence interval of the population mean for the sample data set given in Example 2-1, with 95 percent confidence level.

Because there are 10 (<30) observations in the sample, you must find the t-distribution for significance level 0.05. Using Microsoft Excel, you can compute TINV (0.05, 10 - 1) as 2.26. Then, the range is $2.26 \times 2.17 \div \sqrt{10} = 1.55$.

The confidence interval of the population mean with 95 percent confidence level is 8.4 ± 1.55.

TABLE 2-1 Data Analysis Output from Microsoft Excel

Descriptive Statistics

Mean	8.4
Standard Error	0.686375
Median	9
Mode	9
Standard Deviation	2.170509
Sample Variance	4.711111
Kurtosis	-0.58802
Skewness	-0.15647
Range	7
Minimum	5
Maximum	12
Sum	84
Count	10
Largest(1)	12
Smallest(1)	5
Confidence Level (95.0%)	1.55269

So far, you have seen the statistical analysis techniques for a single variable (univariate). Other statistical techniques are useful for studying the relationship between two or more random variables (correlation, regression, and so on).

Statistical techniques dealing with multiple random variables are discussed in Chapter 5.

Random Numbers and Probability Distributions

Systems are complex. Modeling a complex system deterministically is very difficult. You must often use random variables to reduce the complexity of modeling.

In addition, modeling system parameters using just the mean value does not provide enough information. You must describe how the parameters take on different values by defining distribution functions. As discussed in the next several chapters, many analytical modeling techniques require assumptions about certain distributions of variables for simplicity and tractability.

This section reviews the most commonly used distribution functions, along with their usage in modeling. To reiterate, the area under the curve of a continuous probability density function between the points *a* and *b* is equal to the probability of the random variable being between *a* and *b*. For a discrete *probability mass function* (equivalent of PDF, for integer-valued random variables), the function shows the probability that the variable equals x.

Normal Distribution

Normal distribution has essential importance in statistics because of the central limit theorem. Normal distribution is used to model randomness when the variable is the sum of a large number of independent factors.

Parameters of normal distribution include the following:

✓ Mean

✓ Standard deviation

You can generate normal distribution values using the NORMDIST function in Microsoft Excel. Some example usages for normal distribution follow:

✓ Sample means of a large number of observations

✓ A parameter, which is the result of the combination of several other random variables

✓ Modeling error, which is the result of several, unaccounted-for factors

A variable with normal distribution was previously shown in Figure 2-5. A normal distribution with mean = 0 and standard deviation = 1 is called the *unit normal distribution*, or the *standard normal distribution*.

Exponential Distribution

Exponential distribution is a continuous distribution with the *memoryless property*, meaning that previous values of the random variable do not have any effect on successive values. This seemingly simplistic property is very important in modeling and is the required assumption for the solution of many models. It is generally used to model the time between independent events.

The single parameter of the exponential distribution is: Scale parameter = Mean = a

You can generate exponential distribution values using the EXPONDIST function in Microsoft Excel. The mean is a, and the variance is a^2.

Some usages for the exponential distribution include the following:

✓ Time between successive events, where the events are the result of a number of independent factors

✓ Inter-arrival time between successive arrivals to a service center (device)

✓ Service time at a device

✓ Time between device failures, or length of repairs

Two exponential distribution functions with means 0.5 and 1 are plotted in Figure 2-6.

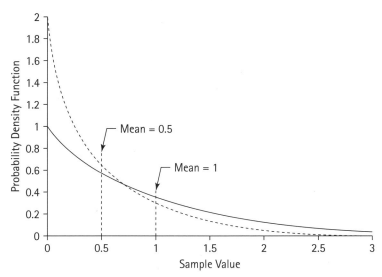

Figure 2-6: PDF for two example exponential distributions

Poisson Distribution

Poisson distribution is a discrete distribution used widely in modeling. It is utilized to model the number of events in unit time if the events are caused by independent factors. It is a memoryless distribution similar to exponential distribution. The number of future events does not depend on the events that have already happened.

The single parameter of the Poisson distribution is: Mean = γ

You can generate Poisson distribution values using the POISSON function in Microsoft Excel. The mean and the variance are both equal to γ.

Some example usages for the Poisson distribution include the following:

✓ The number of arrivals to a device per unit time

✓ The number of requests to a file server in a given time interval

✓ The number of equipment failures in a given time interval

Figure 2-7 shows an example probability mass function for a Poisson distribution with a mean of two. Because Poisson distribution is a discrete distribution, only the integer values of the variable are shown. A process where the number of arrivals conforms to the Poisson distribution is called a *Poisson process*.

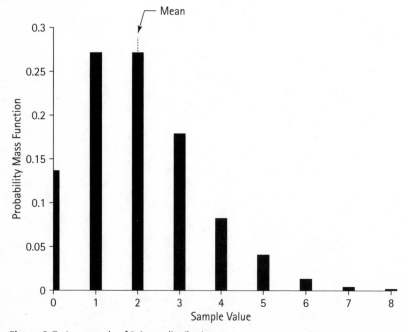

Figure 2-7: An example of Poisson distribution

Uniform Distribution

If a random variable has known minimum and maximum boundaries and can take on values in this range with equal probability, it is modeled with the uniform distribution.

Uniform distribution has the following parameters:

✓ Minimum value, a

✓ Maximum value, b

You can generate normal distribution values easily by using the PDF formula, $f(x) = 1 \div (b - a)$. Similarly, the mean can be computed as $(a + b) \div 2$, and the variance as $(b - a)^2 \div 12$.

Usages for the uniform distribution include the following:

✓ A random variable with known minimum and maximum values, where no other information is known about the variable

✓ Rotational latency on a disk

✓ Propagation delay in a network

Figure 2-8 illustrates the PDF and CDF for a uniform distribution. The straight, horizontal PDF line points to the fact that the probability is uniformly distributed in the range between a and b.

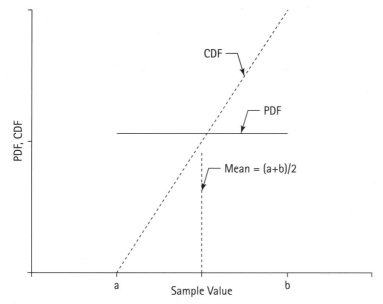

Figure 2-8: PDF and CDF for a uniform distribution between a and b

Statistical Games

"Lies, damn lies, and statistics." — Anonymous

Deliberately or unknowingly, statistics can be used to erroneously reinforce any statement without much substance. Someone who uses statistics in this way is said to be playing *statistical games*.

For example, assume that two alternative systems are being compared using a metric with a mean value of 8.5 on system A and 9.2 on system B. If the metric is a lower-value-better metric, you might conclude that system A is better on this metric. However, if you know that the 95 percent confidence intervals are 8.5±2.1 and 9.2±1.8, you see that a lot of overlap exists between the two intervals and that the difference of the means is not statistically significant.

Do not compare two sample means without checking their confidence intervals. To be able to say that the means are statistically different, the confidence intervals should not overlap.

Also, watch out for the assumptions being made. Many statistical calculations depend on the assumption of *independence of observations*. In other words, they have no effect on the value of other data points. In experimental analysis, this means that successive tests should not disturb one another's results. For example, if you are measuring file system performance, do not forget to clear the file system cache between successive tests. Otherwise, the data collected in the file system cache in the previous experiment will cause a bias when the later experiment is performed.

Charts without a robust statistical basis represent another frequently encountered statistical game. It is very easy to be misled visually by charts that are drawn with confusing axis scales, crowded data, incompatible units, and so on.

When good statistical comparisons don't exist, people sometimes resort to other deceptive games. Bailey summarized this in his paper (Bailey, 1991) on parallel computing performance pitfalls, which are applicable to other areas of performance analysis as well.

"If all else fails, show pretty pictures and animated videos, and don't talk about performance."

— D. Bailey.

Summary

This chapter explained the mathematical methods (statistics) you need to characterize your experimental data, and included the following information:

Summarizing Data

✓ Presenting hundreds of performance data numbers is not useful. The data must be summarized.

✓ The characteristics of average data points are defined by the measures of central tendency.

✓ The measures of spread define the distribution of data.

Measures of Central Tendency

✓ Mean is the arithmetic average of all the data points.

✓ Median is the number in the middle of a data set, and it is a better measure of central tendency than the mean when the sample is skewed.

✓ Mode is the value that occurs most frequently in the sample.

Measures of Data Spread

✓ Frequency distributions can be plotted using histograms.

✓ Probability density function shows the distribution of data in graphical form.

✓ Standard deviation measures the average distance from the mean.

✓ The standard error is the standard deviation of the population mean when the experiments are repeated several times.

✓ The confidence interval for the mean can be calculated using the standard error.

Random Numbers and Probability Distributions

✓ Random numbers and probability distributions are required tools for simplifying models.

✓ Normal distribution is used for modeling the sum of many distribution means.

✓ Exponential and Poisson distributions are memoryless and are used to model arrival times and arrival rates, respectively.

✓ Uniform distribution is used to model bounded variables with no other information.

Statistical Games

✓ Statistics, if not used appropriately, can easily become deceptive.

✓ Check the statistical significance of your statements by looking at the confidence intervals.

✓ Comparison charts should be reviewed carefully for statistical accuracy.

References and Additional Resources

Arsham, Hossein. 2000. *Excel for Introductory Statistical Analysis*. Available at http://ubmail.ubalt.edu/~harsham/excel/excel.htm.

An online guide for using Microsoft Excel 2000 for statistical analysis.

Bailey, David H. August 1991. *Twelve Ways to Fool the Masses When Giving Performance Results on Parallel Computers,* Supercomputing Review, pp. 54–55. Also available at www.supercomp.org/sc2000/bell/twelve-ways.txt.

Required reading for all performance analysts who want to prevent performance analysis mistakes.

Dretzke, Beverly J. and Kenneth A. Heilman. June 2001. *Statistics with Excel,* 2nd Edition. Prentice Hall.

A manual for using Microsoft Excel for data analysis.

Gottfried, Byron S. August 1999. *Spreadsheet Tools for Engineers*. McGraw-Hill.

A guide for utilizing Microsoft Excel 2000 for practical engineering analysis. Provides step-by-step instructions for statistical analysis and presentation.

Tufte, Edward R. May 2001. *The Visual Display of Quantitative Information,* 2nd Edition. Graphics Press.

A classic guide for presenting quantitative information without confusing the reader.

Chapter 3

Analytic Modeling

In This Chapter
Sometimes, simple formulations provide valuable insight about relationships between system parameters. Abstracting these relationships using mathematical equations is the realm of analytic modeling. This chapter discusses the foundations of analytic modeling, including the following:

- ✓ The concept of queues and queuing networks
- ✓ Performance laws stemming from simple observations
- ✓ Formulas for response time and throughput modeling
- ✓ Practical ways to determine performance low and high bounds

Introduction to Analytic Modeling

If you've ever tried to explain a physical phenomenon using mathematical equations, you are familiar with *analytic modeling*. For the scope of this book, analytic modeling is restricted to the study of computer system performance. Although this performance is a function of all the computer system's components and their interactions, the rest of the book focuses on modeling the performance of data storage systems and networks.

The mathematical relations between computer system parameters can be expressed in many ways. You can implement these models using a spreadsheet program, which allows fast evaluation of a wide parameter space. A more formal approach is to use *queuing network models* and the associated mathematical formulas.

Queuing networks have been used to study computer system performance for several decades with great success (Jain, 1991). Queuing networks represent the systems as a network of service centers and their associated queues. The behavior of each individual queue is the focus of *queuing theory* (Gross, 1997). Some of the basic results and techniques of queuing theory have been very useful, even in the study of complex systems.

The main advantage of analytic and queuing network modeling is the ease of model construction. Compared with the alternatives, simulation modeling and experimental analysis, analytic models require much less development time. In addition, once the models are constructed, they are fast to evaluate and can produce results quickly. Because of their simplicity, analytic models are easier to refine and modify.

The disadvantages of analytic models include their relative inaccuracy compared to the simulation models and experimental studies. Analytic models use simplifying assumptions to maintain tractability. If the system under study differs significantly from these assumptions, the results may not be reliable. Because of such concerns, the results produced using analytic models are easy targets for skeptics.

Nonetheless, the fundamental understanding enabled by analytic models, especially queuing models, is essential to the analysis of computer system performance.

Analytic queuing models are useful for double-checking and understanding the results of simulation models or experimental benchmarks. In addition, you can use them in pre-planning such experiments.

Fundamental Performance Laws

Several performance metrics can be calculated simply by observing the transactions arriving at or departing from a system. These operational analyses were introduced in a paper by Denning (Denning, 1977), and are considered the basis for many other performance studies. Figure 3-1 depicts a black-box look of a system where transactions (*customers or jobs*, in queuing theory terminology) arrive on one side and depart on the other. Assume that the system is observed for a period of T seconds. The number of customer arrivals during the observation period is denoted by A, and the number of customer departures (completions) is denoted by C. The average number of customers in the system waiting for service and being serviced is N. The average time it takes for a customer to pass through the system is R — the *response time* or the *residence time*.

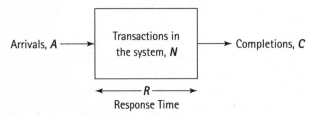

Figure 3-1: A black-box, transaction processing system

In addition, the following rates are defined. The customer arrival rate, γ, can be computed by dividing the total number of arrivals by the observation period, T.

Equation 3-1

```
Arrival rate = γ = A ÷ T
```

The rate of completions is the throughput of the system and is denoted by X. It can be computed by dividing the number of completions by the length of the observation period.

Equation 3–2

```
Throughput = X = C ÷ T
```

For a steady system, the rate of customer arrivals is equal to the rate of customer departures. In this case, γ equals X.

Equation 3–3

```
Steady State Throughput = X = γ
```

Defining a Queuing Center

Customers arriving at a system like the one shown in Figure 3-1 receive some service. If the resources are limited, the customers must wait in a queue until the resource is free. This queuing behavior is formalized with *queuing centers*, in the field of *queuing theory* (Gross, 1997).

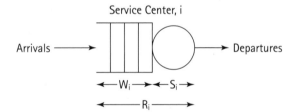

Figure 3-2: A service center with a queue

Figure 3-2 shows the symbol for a queuing center, which is sometimes called a *service center* or a *service station*. A system like the one seen in Figure 3-1 might consist of a single service center or a network of service centers. The latter is called a *queuing network*. The metrics of the service center i, in a queuing network, are subscripted by i to differentiate them from the overall system metrics.

For example, the arrival rate to the service center i is denoted by γ_i, the throughput by X_i, and the response time by R_i. W_i denotes the average time spent by a customer waiting in the queue (*queuing time*), and S_i denotes the average time it takes to receive service (*service time*). The number of customers in the service center, waiting for or receiving service, is called the *queue length* (Q_i). These and additional queuing network notations are summarized in Table 3-1 for easy reference.

TABLE 3-1 Queuing Network Analysis Symbols

Symbol	Description
S	Service time
T	Observation time
A	Number of arrivals
C	Number of completions
R	Response time
W	Waiting time
Z	Think time, or delay
N	Number of active customers/transactions
γ	Arrival rate
Q	Queue length, including the one in service
X	Throughput
U	Utilization

Little's Law

The most important operational performance law is called Little's Law, after its author J.D.C. Little (Little, 1961). This law states that the average number of customers (N) in a system is equal to the product of average throughput (X) and average response time (R). This simple rule is shown in Equation 3-4.

Equation 3–4

$$N = X \times R$$

There are several ways to prove this rule formally and visually (consult Neil Gunther's book , *The Practical Performance Analyst*, for a visual proof). Intuitively, the rule states that increasing the throughput or the response time of a system will increase the number of customers in the system, also known as the *queue length*. Little's Law is applicable to any system in a steady state that preserves customers. In other words, the system does not eliminate customers or introduce new ones.

When applied to a single queuing center in steady state, Little's Law can be expressed as shown in Equation 3-5. Queue length is equal to the product of the arrival rate and the response time.

Equation 3–5

$$Q = \gamma \times R$$

You can use Little's Law to verify experimental performance data. If you know two of the three variables — the number of customers (N), the throughput rate (X), or the response time (R) — you can compute or verify the third variable by using the equation $N = X \times R$.

Example 3-1 illustrates the usage of Little's Law for computing the average number of customers (or the queue length) using experimental throughput and response time data.

Example 3-1: Applying Little's Law

The following table shows the measurement results for eight tests. During each test, after the system reaches a steady state, 30-second long observations are performed. The number of inputs (arrivals, A) to the system and the average time to pass through the system (R) are noted. Using Little's Law, you can compute the average customer population (queue length) in the system.

Observation Time (T)	Number of Arrivals (A)	Response Time (R)	Customer Population (N)
30	30	1.93	1.93
30	60	1.95	3.9
30	90	2.0	6
30	120	2.2	8.8
30	150	2.6	13
30	180	3.2	19.2
30	210	4.3	30.1
30	240	6.43	51.44

You can compute the arrival rates by dividing A by T. In steady state, the throughput (X) will be equal to arrival rate. Then, using Little's Law ($N = X \times R$), the customer population (N) can be computed as it was in the last column of the table above.

Figure 3-3 contains the performance metrics graphs obtained in Example 3-1. Note the exponential growth in the residence time and the number of customers as the arrival rate increases.

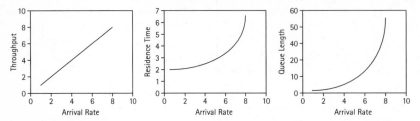

Figure 3-3: Throughput, residence (response) time, and queue length graphs for the tests given in Example 3-1

Utilization Law

B_i denotes the total time a service center is busy during an observation period of T. Consequently, the fraction of time the center is busy (the *utilization*) can be computed by dividing the busy time (B_i) by the total time (T). If you divide the busy time (B_i) by the number of completions (C_i), you can compute the average service time (S_i) for that center. Dividing the number of completions (C_i) by the observation period gives you the throughput (X_i) of that service center.

Equation 3-6 summarizes the equation known as the *Utilization Law*, which states that utilization is equal to the product of average service time and average throughput.

Equation 3-6

```
Utilization = U_i = B_i ÷ T = (B_i ÷ C_i) × (C_i ÷ T) = S_i × X_i
```

The Utilization Law is a special case of Little's Law. If you apply Little's Law to the service part of the service center, the response time is just the service time $(S)_i$. Then the utilization is the average number of customers serviced (not waiting) at the center.

Forced Flow Law

In a queuing network, a given transaction might need to travel to some service centers more than once before departing the network. V_i is used to denote the number of visits (*visit count*) each transaction makes to service center i before it is considered completed.

The Forced Flow Law, given in Equation 3-7, states that the throughput (X_i) of service center i is the product of the number of visits to that center (V_i) and the system throughput (X).

Equation 3-7

```
X_i = V_i × X
V_i = X_i ÷ X
```

Service Demand Law

If you multiply the number of visits (V_i) by the average service time (S_i) per visit, you get the *service demand* (D_i) that a single customer requires from service center i before exiting the system. Using Equations 3-6 and 3-7, the service demand at a service center can be calculated as in Equation 3-8, which is called the *Service Demand Law*. Intuitively, it states that if you know the utilization of a resource, you can calculate the per customer service demand by dividing the utilization by the system throughput.

Equation 3-8

$$D_i = V_i \times S_i = (X_i \div X) \times (U_i \div X_i) = U_i \div X$$

Introduction to Queuing Networks

Queuing networks are powerful tools for modeling the performance of computer systems and components. By modeling the computing systems using single queues or a network of queues and applying the fundamental performance laws, a variety of useful performance information can be obtained. Although in the past, a single queuing center was successfully used to model entire computing platforms, today's client-server architectures and networks require more complex modeling and greater detail. Next, an introduction to the queuing network models, with several varieties, will be provided. Once again, consult the references provided at the end of the chapter for more formal and complete treatment of these topics.

Symbols and Terminology

The basic queuing center model was previously shown in Figure 3-2. Customers (or transactions) arrive at the center, wait until the previous customers are serviced, receive their own service when the resource is free, and then depart the center. Besides this simple operation, many other detailed characteristics define the behavior of a queuing center. For example, the arrival policy defines how often and with what distribution the customers arrive at the center. The queuing policy defines which customers in the queue receive the service first — it does not have to be first-come-first-served. In addition, you must decide whether the queue length is limited or infinite (theoretically), and whether there is a single service resource (*server*) or multiple servers in parallel. Some queue characteristics that might be useful in modeling various scenarios follow.

Figure 3-4 shows a modified version of the queuing center in Figure 3-2. This queuing center has *m* servers instead of one. The customers in the single queue can be dispatched to any of the empty servers. There could be up to *m* customers that are active simultaneously. Think about the single queue with multiple tellers at the post office or bank, as opposed to multiple cashiers with their own queues in a department store.

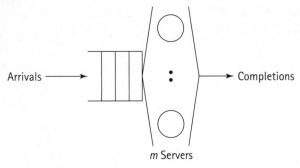

Figure 3-4: A queue with multiple servers

Similarly, Figure 3-5 provides another alternative queue representation that does not have a queue at all. The arriving customers advance to the servers without any queuing time. These types of queues are called *infinite servers* because they appear to have infinite resources to accommodate all incoming traffic. Each customer incurs some amount of delay at the server. Because of this, these service centers are sometimes called *delay centers*. Delay centers are generally used to represent terminals or clients of a server where the transactions wait a fixed amount of time before re-entering the system. In such cases, the delay is called the *think time*.

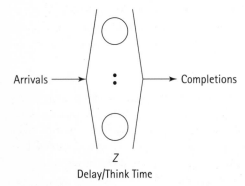

Figure 3-5: A delay center without a queue

A queuing center can be summarized by specifying the following characteristics:

✓ **Arrival Process** — The distribution of the inter-arrival times. Arrival process can be one of the following alternatives:

> **M** — Poisson arrivals. The number of arrivals in unit time has a Poisson distribution and the inter-arrival times have an exponential distribution. Because both of these distributions are *memoryless*, a fact that was discussed in Chapter 2, the derivations of many performance metrics are simplified.

> **D** — Deterministic. The arrival intervals are fixed and known deterministically.

> **G** — General distribution. The arrivals can have any type of distribution.

✓ **Service Time Distribution** — The probabilistic distribution of the service times. Service time distribution can have alternatives (M, D, G) similar to those discussed in the preceding arrival process.

✓ **Number of Servers** — A positive number designating the number of servers in the queuing center. Generally, 1 is used to denote a single server queue, and m is used to denote a queue with multiple servers.

✓ **Buffer Size** — The queuing center's storage capacity. In other words, the maximum allowed queue length (including the customers in service). Buffer size could be any positive number, but is generally assumed to be infinite (∞) for the sake of simplicity.

✓ **Population Size** — The size of the population source. Generally assumed to be infinite (∞) for the sake of simplicity.

✓ **Service Policy** — The service policy type. Determines who gets the service among the customers in the queue. The commonly used policy types include the following:

FCFS or FIFO — First-come-first-served or first-in-first-out.

LCFS or LIFO — Last-come-first-served or last-in-first-out.

RR — Round robin. The service is shared among the queued customers in a round-robin fashion using fixed time periods.

PS — Processor sharing. Ideal case of RR, where the time quantum is so small that each of Q customers in the queue receives $1 \div Q$ of the server's capacity.

Priority — The customers are served according to their priorities, where higher priority jobs preempt lower priority jobs.

The Kendall notation is used to summarize the above characteristics in order. For example, an M/M/m/10/100/RR queuing center has exponentially distributed inter-arrival times and service times, m number of servers, a buffer size of 10, a population size of 100, and a round robin service policy. Most of the queuing models are defined using infinite buffer sizes and population sizes, and FIFO service policy. In such cases, the last three specifications are dropped. For example, a M/G/1/∞/∞/FIFO queue is written as M/G/1.

Single Queue Calculations

For a single queuing center like that shown in Figure 3-2, the response time is the sum of the service time and the time spent in the queue, as shown in Equation 3-9. Here, the subscript i is dropped for the sake of simplicity, but it must be inserted if there is more than one queue.

Equation 3-9

$$R = S + W$$

For an M/M/1 queue, the waiting time (W) is a function of the queue length (Q). If an arriving job sees an average of Q jobs in front of it, it must wait until all of them complete, which takes QS time units. Note that for the previous statement to be valid, we are assuming the FIFO service policy and memoryless service time distribution of an M/M/1 queue. If you substitute $Q \times S$ for W, and then $X \times R$ for Q and U for $X \times S$, you can get the formula for the response time in terms of service time and utilization, as shown in Equation 3-10.

Equation 3-10

```
R = S ÷ (1 - X × S)
R = S ÷ (1 - U)
```

Examining Equation 3-10, you can see that the response time increases abruptly as the utilization (U) gets closer to 1, which is the saturation point. Multiplying both sides of Equation 3-10 by X and using Little's Law, you can get a formula for the queue length of an M/M/1 queue (see Equation 3-11).

Equation 3-11

```
Q = U ÷ (1 - U)
```

Similar derivations can be made for queues with multiple servers (M/M/m), parallel queues, and several other variations. These are beyond the scope of this book, however, and you should consult the queuing theory references provided at the end of this chapter. The queuing formulas provided in this chapter should suffice to understand the performance analysis presented in the rest of the book.

The next section discusses networks of queues, which are often studied in two categories — open queuing networks and closed queuing networks.

Open Queuing Networks

If the customers of a queuing network arrive from an infinite, external source, the resulting model is called an *open queuing network*. Open networks have no limitations on the number of customers that arrive in unit time or on the number of customers that exist in the system.

A typical transaction-processing system can be modeled using the open queuing network shown in Figure 3-6. External transactions arrive at the CPU. After some processing at the CPU, the transaction writes to Disk1, comes back to the CPU, and then writes to Disk2. After some final processing in the CPU, the transaction is considered completed and departs.

The response times in each service center can be computed depending on its type. If they are modeled as M/M/1 queues, you can use Equations 3-10 and 3-7 to find the response time of individual queues, as shown in Equation 3-12.

Equation 3-12

```
Rᵢ = Sᵢ ÷ (1 - X × Vᵢ × Sᵢ)
```

The response time in a queuing network is the sum of response times in all individual queues. The response time in an individual queue is the sum of response times over all the visits to that queue. The formula for the system response time is shown in Equation 3-13, also known as the *General Response Time Law*.

Equation 3–13

$$R = \Sigma_i \ (V_i \times R_i)$$

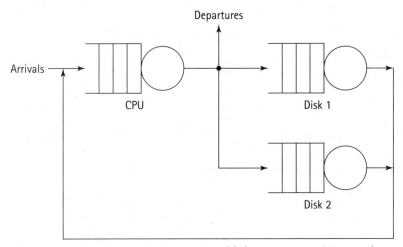

Figure 3-6: A transaction-processing system modeled as an open queuing network

With the Utilization and Forced Flow Laws, utilization of the individual centers can be computed in terms of the system throughput, as shown in Equation 3-14.

Equation 3–14

$$U_i = X_i \times S_i = X \times V_i \times S_i$$

Finally, you can compute the queue length of each center using Equation 3-11. The system queue length is the sum of all individual queue lengths, as shown in Equation 3-15.

Equation 3–15

$$Q = \Sigma_i \ Q_i$$

Example 3-2 shows the application of the open queuing network analysis to determine the performance metrics of the simple transaction-processing system shown in Figure 3-6.

Example 3-2: Open Queuing Network Analysis

Use queuing analysis to determine the performance metrics of the transaction-processing system in Figure 3-6. Assume an arrival rate of 60 transactions per second, and the following mean service times:

$$S_{cpu} = 0.002, \; S_{disk1} = 0.010, \; S_{disk2} = 0.010$$

From the description in the text, you can obtain the following visit counts:

$$V_{cpu} = 3, \; V_{disk1} = 1, \; V_{disk2} = 1$$

Using Equation 3-12 to determine center response times and Equation 3-13 to determine the system response time, you can obtain the following:

$$R = 3R_{cpu} + R_{disk1} + R_{disk2} = 0.007 + 0.025 + 0.025 = 0.057$$

The utilization of each center can be computed using Equation 3-14.

$$U_{cpu} = 0.36, \; U_{disk1} = 0.6, \; U_{disk2} = 0.6$$

The network's queue length can be computed using Equation 3-15.

$$Q = Q_{cpu} + Q_{disk1} + Q_{disk2} = 0.136 + 1.5 + 1.5 = 3.136$$

Therefore, at a 60 transactions per second (trans/sec) arrival rate, the average response time is 0.057 seconds, and the average queue length is 3.136.

Figure 3-7 shows the response time as a function of the arrival rate using the parameters given in Example 3-2.

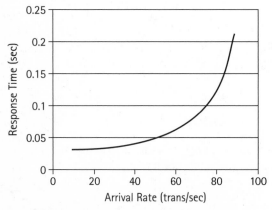

Figure 3-7: Response time versus arrival rate for the network shown in Figure 3-6

While calculating the performance metrics in an open queuing network, the arrival rate is the free variable. Other performance metrics depend on the arrival rate. The main purpose is to check how the response time changes depending on the arrival rate.

Closed Queuing Networks

A closed queuing network always contains a finite (constant) number of jobs (transactions). The jobs circulate through the network and reenter the system after they finish each cycle. This behavior is useful for modeling the throughput performance. In contrast, in open queuing networks the system's throughput is determined by the input rate and the number of jobs in the system is variable.

Figure 3-8 depicts a closed queuing network, which is very similar to the simple transaction-processing model shown in Figure 3-6. The only difference is the addition of the feedback loop at the top. The transactions go to a delay center after completing a round and reenter the system after some "think time." The number of transactions (customers) in the system is always constant and denoted by N. A closed network's throughput is the transaction rate at the outer loop where transactions pass through the delay center.

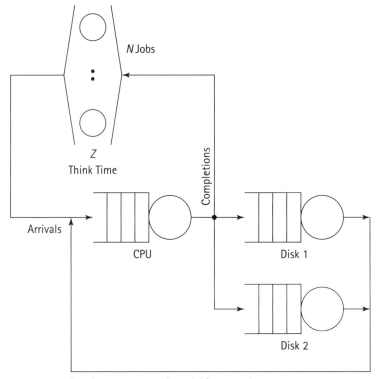

Figure 3-8: Closed queuing network model for a simple transaction-processing system

In a closed queuing network, response time, throughput, and queue lengths are all functions of the number of jobs (N) in the system. For example, R[N] is used to denote the response time when the population size is N.

The network's response time is the sum of all response times.

Equation 3-16

```
R[N] = Σᵢ (Vᵢ × Rᵢ[N])
```

The throughput for N jobs can be computed using Equation 3-17. Intuitively, it will take a think time plus the system response time for a transaction to complete a single round. When a transaction completes a round, every transaction in front of it will have also completed the system. Therefore, every Z + R[N] time period, N jobs are completed.

Equation 3-17

```
X[N] = N ÷ (Z + R[N])
```

Rewriting Equation 3-17, you can obtain the formula for the response time, as in Equation 3-18.

Equation 3-18

```
R[N] = (N ÷ X[N]) - Z
```

If you inspect the above formulas, response time is computed using the throughput, and the throughput is computed using the response time. Because of this circular dependency, there are no closed-form solutions for throughput in a closed queuing network. Generally, an iterative solution such as Mean Value Analysis (MVA) is used to compute the model outputs.

MEAN VALUE ANALYSIS

MVA is an iterative process and depends on the observation that a job arriving at a queue in a closed queuing network with n jobs (n changes from 1 to N), will see a queue length in front of it as if the system did not have that particular job (as if there are n-1 jobs). This property is known as the *arrival theorem.*

Using the arrival theorem, the response time at each service station in a closed queuing network with n jobs can be computed as in Equation 3-19, where Q_i [n-1] is the queue length at service station i when n-1 jobs are in the system:

Equation 3-19

```
Rᵢ[n] = Sᵢ (1 + Qᵢ[n-1])
```

Then, the new queue length at each station can be computed using Little's Law.

Equation 3-20

```
Qᵢ[n] = Vᵢ × X[n] × Rᵢ[n]
```

Starting from the fact that $Q_i[0] = 0$, you can compute X[N] by iterating over Equations 3-19, 3-17, and 3-20 for n from 1 to N. Listing 3-1 provides an example implementation of the MVA algorithm. It is written in Visual Basic and can be used as a Microsoft Excel macro.

Listing 3-1: MVA Implementation as a Microsoft Excel Macro (Visual Basic)

```
Private Sub ComputeVMA()
    Const MaxNumCustomers = 256
    Const MaxNumCenters = 256
    Dim Q(MaxNumCenters, MaxNumCustomers) 'Queue array
    Dim R(MaxNumCenters)                   'Response time array
    Dim S(MaxNumCenters)                   'Service time array
    Dim V(MaxNumCenters)                   'Visit counts array

    Z = 0.02                               'Think time
    NumCustomers = 30
    NumCenters = 3

    S(0) = 0.002                           'Service time examples
    S(1) = 0.01
    S(2) = 0.01
    V(0) = 3                               'Visit count examples
    V(1) = 1
    V(2) = 1

    For i = 0 To NumCenters                'Initialize empty queues
        Q(i, 0) = 0
    Next i

    For n = 1 To NumCustomers              'MVA loop
        RT = 0                             'Total response
        For i = 0 To NumCenters - 1        'Compute response times
            R(i) = S(i) + S(i) * Q(i, n - 1)
            RT = RT + V(i) * R(i)
        Next i

        X = n / (Z + RT)                   'System throughput

        For i = 0 To NumCenters - 1
            Q(i, n) = X * V(i) * R(i)      'Compute new queue lengths
        Next i
    Next n

    MsgBox ("Throughput is " + Str(X) + " Customers/sec")
    MsgBox ("Response time is " + Str(RT) + " sec")
End Sub
```

Example 3-3 illustrates the use of the MVA algorithm in the evaluation of the closed queuing network shown in Figure 3-8.

If Example 3-3 is repeated using different numbers of transactions from 1 to 100, the throughput and response time graphs shown in Figure 3-9 are obtained. Note that the throughput increases abruptly by the number of transactions, but flattens when it gets close to 100 trans/sec, which is the highest throughput this network can achieve. Response time increases linearly with the number of transactions because the queue lengths in the service centers increase linearly with the population number.

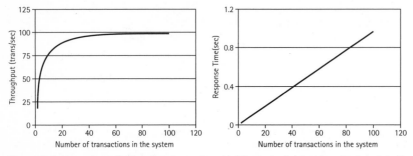

Figure 3-9: Throughput (left) and response time (right) graphs for the closed network in Figure 3-8

Example 3-3: Closed Queuing Network Analysis

For the closed queuing network model shown in Figure 3-8, assume a think time (Z) of 0.02 seconds and a population of 30 transactions. Also, assume the visit counts and service times given in Example 3-2.

Thus, the system parameters are as follows:

V_{cpu} = 3, V_{disk1} = 1, V_{disk2} = 1
S_{cpu} = 0.002, S_{disk1} = 0.010, S_{disk2} = 0.010
Z = 0.02

N = 30

If the above variables are used with the MVA algorithm in Listing 3-1, the following values for the response time and the throughput are obtained:

R = 0.291 seconds

X = 96.36 trans/sec

In this chapter, all the calculations are made assuming that the mean service time at a queuing center is the same for all transactions. This means that there is a single type of transaction. Such networks are called *single-class networks*. Queuing networks with more than one class of transaction are called *multi-class networks*. The MVA algorithm can be generalized to multi-class networks. Consult Raj Jain's *The Art of Computer Systems Performance Analysis* (John Wiley & Sons, 1991) for a discussion of multi-class networks.

Bottleneck Analysis and Performance Bounds

It is possible to find theoretical lower and upper bounds for a queuing network's throughput without solving the whole queuing system. Upper bounds can also be used to determine bottlenecks in the system.

Lower Bound for Throughput

In a closed queuing network with N-1 jobs, the queue length at a given station cannot be greater than N-1. This leads to the relation shown in Equation 3-21.

Equation 3-21

$$Q_i(N-1) \leq N-1$$

From Equations 3-19 and 3-21, you can find an upper bound for the response times at each station, as shown in Equation 3-22.

Equation 3-22

$$R_i(N) \leq S_i \times N$$

From Equations 3-16, 3-17, and 3-22, you can derive a lower bound for the throughput, as shown in Equation 3-23.

Equation 3-23

$$X(N) \geq N \div (Z + N \times \Sigma_i(V_i \times S_i))$$

This gives a closed-form approximation that can be used as a lower bound for the throughput without the iterative process of MVA. This lower bound is tight (close to actual throughput) for only small values of N (that is, N < 10). It underestimates the throughput considerably for large values of N.

Upper Bound for Throughput

The maximum possible throughput for a service station is $1/D_i$. In a queuing network, the service station with the smallest throughput will be a *bottleneck*. The system's overall throughput will be smaller than or equal to the throughput of the slowest station. This upper bound is valid for both closed and open networks, as shown in Equation 3-24.

Equation 3-24

$$X(N) \leq min_i \ (1/D_i)$$

In any configuration, one or more service stations with the slowest throughput constitute the bottleneck. If you remove one bottleneck, the service station with the next slowest throughput becomes the bottleneck. Because the maximum possible throughput ($1/D_i$) of a service station is inversely proportional to the demand of that station, the service station with the biggest service demand (D_i) is the bottleneck.

In a closed queuing network, the number of the customers also limits the throughput. From Equation 3-17, you can obtain the bound displayed in Equation 3-25.

Equation 3-25

$$X(N) \leq N \div Z$$

This is the upper bound on the throughput because of the delays and the number of customers in the system. It represents the maximum possible throughput (N/Z) of the delay station. One obvious result of this upper bound is the fact that the number of active jobs (N, or the queue depth) must be increased to overcome the throughput limitations due to the latencies (Z) in the system.

If you combine Equations 3-24 and 3-25, you can obtain a combined upper bound on transaction throughput, as shown in Equation 3-26.

Equation 3-26

$$X(N) \leq min \ (N \div Z, \ min_i \ 1/D_i)$$

This upper bound is tight and provides a close approximation of the throughput for large values of N. In Example 3-3, the disks have the highest service demands, 0.010 seconds (versus 0.006 seconds of the CPU). Therefore, the disks are the bottleneck. Their theoretical throughput of 100 transactions per second (1/0.010) is the maximum possible system throughput. Indeed, if you look at Figure 3-9, you can see that 100 trans/sec is the asymptote for the system throughput.

Summary

This chapter discussed the foundations of analytic modeling and demonstrated some of the relationships that can be garnered from mathematical equations.

Introduction to Analytic Modeling

- ✓ Analytic modeling is defined as the science of abstracting relations using mathematical formulas.

- ✓ Queuing networks have been the most successful analytic modeling tools for several decades.

- ✓ Analytic models are fast to define and evaluate compared to simulation and real-world experiments.

- ✓ Accuracy of the analytic models is low compared to that of the simulation models.

Fundamental Performance Laws

- ✓ Several useful performance metrics can be computed by simply observing the transaction arrivals and departures, which leads to operational performance laws.

- ✓ Little's Law is the most important operational law that can be applied in many contexts.

- ✓ Operational laws exist for utilization, throughput, and service demands.

Introduction to Queuing Networks

- ✓ Queuing networks are systems of queuing (service) centers.

- ✓ Queuing centers can be represented with a variety of arrival and service characteristics to enable modeling of various real-life scenarios.

- ✓ Open queuing networks have external arrivals and departures. They are used to model the system response time under various arrival rates.

- ✓ Closed queuing networks have a fixed number of customers circulating through the system. They are used to model the throughput of the systems for various population sizes.

Bottleneck Analysis and Performance Bounds

✓ The service center with the smallest throughput (highest service demand) is the bottleneck.

✓ There is always a bottleneck, which might move from one node to another depending on the service demands.

✓ Upper and lower bounds can be used to approximate the throughput without iterative solutions.

A summary of the queuing network modeling formulas is presented in Table 3-2 for your reference.

TABLE 3-2 Summary of Queuing Network Formulas

Little's Law	$N = X \times R, Q = \gamma \times R$
Utilization Law	$U_i = B_i \div T = S_i \times X_i$
Forced Flow Law	$X_i = V_i \times X$
Service Demand Law	$D_i = V_i \times S_i = U_i \div X$
M/M/1 Response Time	$R = S \div (1 - X \times S)$
M/M/1 Queue Length	$Q = U \div (1 - U)$
Open Network Response Time	$R = \sum_i (V_i \times R_i)$
Closed Network Response Time	$R[N] = (N \div X[N]) - Z$
Closed Network Throughput	$X[N] = N \div (Z + R[N])$
Throughput Lower Bound	$X(N) \geq N \div (Z + N \times \sum_i D_i)$
Throughput Upper Bound	$X(N) \leq \min (N \div Z, \min_i 1/D_i)$

References and Additional Resources

Denning, P.J. and J. P. Buzen. September 1977. "The Operational Analysis of Queuing Network Models," Computing Surveys, Vol. 9–3, pp. 223–252.

The seminal paper that introduced operational analysis.

Gelenbe, E. and G. Pujolle. June 1998. *Introduction to Queuing Networks*, 2nd Edition. John Wiley & Sons.

An updated book on queuing networks, with emphasis on the application of queuing network modeling to high-performance communication networks.

Gross, Donald and Carl M. Harris. December 1997. *Fundamentals of Queuing Theory*, 3rd Edition. Wiley-Interscience.

Provides rigorous proofs and explanations of queuing theory fundamentals. Includes Microsoft Excel examples.

Gunther, Neil J. October 2000. *The Practical Performance Analyst*. iUniverse.com.

A lively introduction to performance analysis, with lots of practical insights and examples.

Jain, Raj. April 1991. *The Art of Computer Systems Performance Analysis*. John Wiley & Sons.

The classic computer performance analysis reference. Unfortunately, it has not been updated lately, but author's notes and errata can be found at `http://www.cis.ohio-state.edu/~jain/books/perfbook.htm`.

Little, J.D.C. 1961. "A Proof of the Queueing Formula L = λW," *Operations Research*, Vol. 9, pp. 383–387.

The first proof of Little's Law, which is named after its author.

Chapter 4

Simulation Modeling

In This Chapter:
Simulation modeling provides you with an abstraction and analysis technique that does not require the restrictive assumptions of analytical models. This chapter introduces the following subjects on computer simulation:

- ✓ Discrete and continuous simulation types
- ✓ Advantages and disadvantages of simulation modeling compared to other modeling techniques
- ✓ Validation and verification of simulation models
- ✓ Sensitivity analysis of simulation models
- ✓ Software tools for simulation

ANALYTICAL AND SIMULATION MODELS are used in the rest of the book to analyze many aspects of storage networks, in alignment with the storage networking model introduced in Chapter 1.

Simulation Concepts

Simulations are representations of real-world entities in computer program form. In this most generic definition of simulation, the represented entities could be anything from social institutions to mechanical components. For the scope of this book, the interesting simulation projects involve models of computer systems, specifically, storage networks.

Like all other modeling work, the goal of computer system simulation is to capture the essential aspects of the system in a model and use it to analyze some metrics of merit. For example, simulation can be used to verify the functionality of a hardware design or the correctness of a communication protocol. This book concerns the simulation of system "performance." Therefore, the models in this book consist of components that directly impact performance. Still, this is not a very restrictive scope because performance can have a wide variety of interpretations in different contexts, as discussed in Chapter 1.

No matter how a simulation model is implemented, some common terms apply. *State variables* define the state of the system at a given moment. By saving and reloading the state variables, you can restart a simulation without losing information. An *event* is anything that causes a change in the state variables. If the state variables can take on continuous values, the model is called a *continuous-state model* or a *continuous-event model*. On the other hand, if the state variables only take discrete values, the model is called a *discrete-state model* or a *discrete-event model*. Continuous-event models are mostly used in physical sciences where the systems are generally continuous, as in a chemical process. Computer systems are generally modeled as discrete-event models because the states are generally discrete, like the number of jobs in a queue, available buffer size, and so on. If time is a variable in the model, it is called a *dynamic* model. Otherwise, it is a *static* model.

The storage network simulation models in this book are discrete-event, dynamic, performance models.

Model Correctness

Simulation models are used to make business decisions — for capacity planning, technology choices, product design, or tuning. The results of a simulation study may thus have far-reaching consequences. You must ensure that the model is reliable and serves its intended purpose. Simulation modeling result correctness is checked at two levels.

✓ **Model validation:** You must make sure that the conceptualized model is a valid representation of the real system. Modeling involves many assumptions that can make a model successful or useless. Always assume that your assumptions are wrong until they are validated. In addition to the assumptions, you must validate input parameter values and distributions and output results. For validation, you can refer to the judgments of experts in the area, check against measurement data, or compare with theoretical results if they are available. Any discussion on model validity inevitably ends up with the question of workload validity. The assumed workload must be representative of the real workload to which the system is subjected. The statistical distribution of the workload can be obtained from measurement data. Alternatively, captured traces of real workloads can be used to feed simulation executions. Such simulations are called *trace-driven simulations*.

✓ **Model verification:** After validating that the model reflects the real world correctly, you must check that the model is implemented as intended. Verification problems might arise from programming bugs or misinterpretation of the model. Most verification problems can be avoided with good software development practices, such as modular design. In addition, you can visually check the model outputs for degenerate cases. Specialized simulation packages will eliminate most of the implementation problems, especially packages with graphical design capabilities that perform most of the implementation tasks automatically so you can focus on model validation.

Models can be validated and verified in cycles many times during the model development stages.

You must convince others that your model has been validated and verified before your model can be considered reliable and useful.

When to Simulate?

If you are about to start a performance analysis project, you must decide which analysis method or methods to pursue — rely on intuition and expert knowledge, run real workloads or benchmarks on physical hardware, develop an analytical model, or implement a simulation model.

Each of these choices has its advantages and disadvantages. To help you decide whether to pursue the simulation path, the following sections list some advantages and disadvantages of simulation projects.

Advantages of Simulation

Simulation has been used to study system dynamics successfully for many decades because of the following advantages:

- ✓ **It is accurate.** Simulation enables modeling of very complex systems, which is very difficult with other modeling techniques. The more complex a model can get, the better it will represent the real system.

- ✓ **It can model dynamic behavior.** Simulation can be used to study time-dependent behavior of dynamic systems in contrast to the steady-state analysis of most analytic approaches.

- ✓ **It can model complex behavior.** Simultaneous resource usage, blocking, and parallelism can be easily modeled in simulation models, in contrast to analytic models, which cannot handle such scenarios without oversimplification.

- ✓ **It enables modular design.** Simulation models can start as a few high-level modules and be improved by introducing more detail into the modules that are deemed important.

- ✓ **It provides reasoning.** Similar to other modeling techniques, simulation can be used to explain the reasoning behind certain behavior by deconstructing the system. This cannot be done using real systems.

- ✓ **It provides alternatives.** If a base simulation model is available, you can easily try out alternative designs by modifying the model before making those changes in the real system.

- ✓ **It demonstrates the design is effective.** Rather than assuming that a system will work based on a design on paper, simulation demonstrates that it really will. This can be done visually, using the animation capabilities of many simulation packages, or through detailed simulation analysis.

- ✓ **It provides investment protection.** Because the cost of physical implementation is often more than the cost of the modeling study, simulation enables better investment decisions early in the process and prevents costly system modifications later.

Disadvantages of Simulation

Numerous simulation projects have been unsuccessful because the modelers or the project leaders make the following miscalculations:

✓ **It takes time to develop.** Developing simulation models requires considerable resources. Modelers must be trained in simulation techniques and simulation software. The actual model could require many development cycles to achieve the desired accuracy.

✓ **It takes time to execute.** Compared to the closed-form formulas of some analytical models, simulation models require considerable computation time to evaluate.

✓ **Garbage in, garbage out.** Many simulation inputs and outputs are essentially random variables. Without proper input and output analysis, distinguishing the effects of real system characteristics from the effects of randomness might be difficult.

Given all the advantages and disadvantages of simulation modeling, it is wise (and sometimes necessary) to include a mixture of expert knowledge, measurement, analytic models, and simulation in a performance analysis project.

Sensitivity Analysis and Model Outputs

Most computer systems behave in predictable ways. When the input workload changes slightly, the system performance also changes slightly. You should expect the same to hold true for a system model. When the inputs of a model change slightly, the outputs of the model should also change slightly — the model should not overreact to small changes. *Sensitivity analysis* studies the magnitude of output changes with respect to input changes.

Model sensitivity issues are illustrated in Figure 4-1. The two graphs in the figure show the mean response time outputs of a simulation model. The left side of the figure shows a typical arrival rate versus response time graph, which changes smoothly with increasing arrival rates. The response time increases considerably only when the system is saturated (utilization is close to 100 percent). On the right half of the figure, the output graph shows a response time curve for a sensitive system. An unexpected jump occurs in the middle of the curve. A small change in the arrival rate generates a big jump in response time long before the system is saturated. To the right of this jump, the response time decreases while the arrival rate increases, which is counterintuitive. Both of these behaviors point to problems with the model and/or its implementation. A modeling error might surface around those arrival rates. In the rare case that this is a genuine reflection of the real system — congratulations! You have found a bug in the design of the real system that should, and can, be prevented.

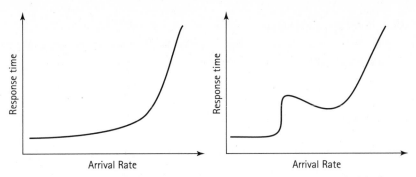

Figure 4-1: An expected response curve (left) and the response time output (right) of a sensitive model

To obtain representative model outputs, the simulation might need to execute for some time until its outputs settle down around a mean value. Until such *steady state* is achieved, the model outputs are in a *transient state* and may fluctuate randomly. For valid results, the outputs of the transient state must be removed. For example, Figure 4-2 shows the values of an output variable as the simulation progresses. Numerous techniques have been developed (see Raj Jain's book, *The Art of Computer Systems Performance Analysis*, further referenced at the end of this chapter, for a list) for the removal of the transient state effects so that the output is more representative. Example methods include long runs, initial data deletion, and batch means. Most simulation packages include methods for removing transient state effects automatically; therefore, this book omits the theory behind these methods.

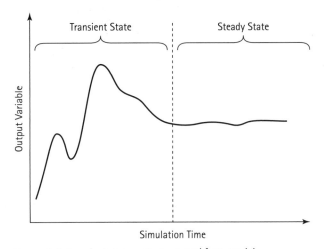

Figure 4-2: Transient state output removal from model

A related subject to transient output removal is *simulation termination*. You want to terminate a simulation after all the transient state effects diminish and the outputs are in the steady state. Most simulation packages include methods to ensure that the simulation is finished in a steady state.

Some simulation software packages have runtime options to set a confidence level that the outputs must achieve before the simulation ends. By setting this confidence level to a high value (for example, 95 percent), you can ensure that the simulation outputs are obtained in steady state.

Simulation Software Tools

The simulation software tools you use will determine what you can and cannot do. The choice of tools is therefore one of the most important decisions you make in a simulation project.

Simulation tools can be categorized as follows:

✓ **General-purpose programming languages.** You can implement a simulation model using programming languages such as C, C++, Java, and so on. If you decide to use a general-purpose language, it is a good idea to use an existing simulation library that you can link with your program for simulation constructs and methods, such as event schedulers, random number generators, data collectors, and so on. SMPL, SimPack, MOOSE, and CSIM18 are examples of simulation libraries that you can use with your own code.

✓ **Special simulation languages.** Specialized languages have been developed just for implementing simulation models. Languages such as SIMULA, SIMSCRIPT, and GPSS/H provide all the methods and constructs you need to develop discrete-event simulations.

✓ **Simulation packages.** Integrated simulation packages, like Hyperformix Workbench and OPNET Modeler, provide a simulation environment with graphical user interfaces, data analyzers, and animation tools. Special-purpose simulation packages, such as Ns (specialized for communication network simulation) and Arena (for business process simulation) are also available. Unfortunately, no specialized simulation tools for storage networks are yet available.

In addition, you can mix these tools together. For example, most simulation packages (such as Hyperformix Workbench) allow you to insert C code into simulation nodes, or link to external libraries. The Open Directory Project, available at `http://dmoz.org/Science/Software/Simulation`, provides a list of simulation projects and software tools.

Simulation Examples

This section contains examples of simulation models. The examples are kept simple to familiarize you with the concepts. You are encouraged to consult the references at the end of the chapter or the product manuals of simulation packages for detailed information on simulation techniques.

Figure 4-3 shows an implementation of the closed queuing network (previously discussed in Chapter 3, Figure 3-8 and Example 3-3). In this section, Hyperformix Workbench is used as an example simulation package. Hyperformix Workbench is a commercially available simulation environment that enables the design of simulation models using graphical symbols. On the right side of the figure, you see a palette containing the available simulation nodes.

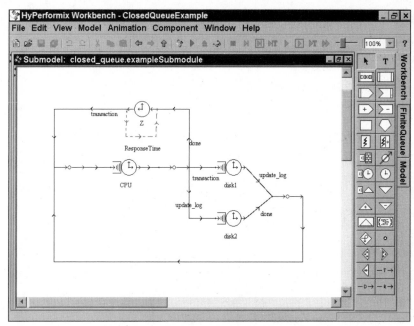

Figure 4-3: Closed queuing network example implemented as a simulation model

The simulated network contains a delay node at the top, generating transaction jobs. Three service nodes simulate the CPU and the two disks. Note that the delay node (Z) does not have a queue symbol preceding it, while the service nodes (CPU, disk1, and disk2) do. Delay nodes apply a specified delay time to pass jobs without queuing them, which is why they are sometimes called *infinite servers*. On the other hand, the service nodes (or service centers) maintain a queue of incoming jobs and apply service times to them according to a predetermined service specification.

Figure 4-4 shows the service node properties in Hyperformix Workbench for the CPU node and one of the disk nodes. The service time for the disk is set to an exponential distribution with a mean value of 0.010 seconds, and the service policy is set to first-come-first-served (FCFS). In simulation models, you are not restricted to any service distribution as you are with the analytical models. You can use any of the provided distributions, or you can write code to generate service times reflecting your modeled system. This makes simulation models more flexible.

Workbench allows you to assign categories to transactions, which can be changed while passing through the service nodes. This way, you can simulate various phases of a transaction's lifetime. For example, in Figure 4-3, a job starts in the "transaction" category at the delay node Z, passes through the CPU, and then through disk1. After disk1, it enters the "update_log" category, passes through the CPU, and goes to disk2. After disk2, it assumes the "done" category, passes through the CPU one last time, and retires to the delay node Z. This scenario implicitly models the visit counts that were assumed in the queuing model in Example 3-3 (see Chapter 3). For example, a transaction uses the CPU resource three times, which corresponds to $V_{CPU} = 3$.

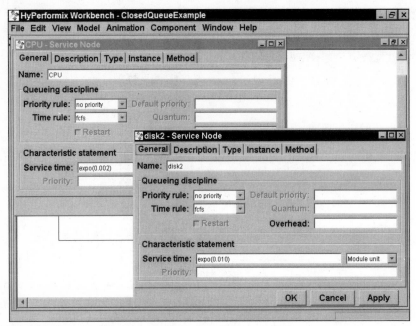

Figure 4-4: Service property specification for the service nodes

Simulation tools enable you to execute the model for any length of simulated time and collect various types of data that interest you. Figure 4-5 shows the statistical report generated by Workbench at the end of a run, which is 100 seconds long. Before the execution, you can specify what kind of statistics will be collected for each node.

In Figure 4-5, four types of statistics are shown for each service node. Sample count is the number of transactions that have passed through that node. The mean population (mean queue length), mean response time, and mean utilization are also shown. The last statistics line shows the mean response time (0.291), which is collected on the "Response Time" arc shown in Figure 4-3 and corresponds to the overall system response time. You can see that 9,630 transactions have completed in 100 simulated seconds. Therefore, the mean throughput is 96.3 transactions per second, which is equal to the mean throughput value obtained analytically in Example 3-3 (refer to Chapter 3). The difference with a simulation model is that you do not have to assume that the arrival rates and service times are exponentially distributed, even though this has been the case in the preceding figures to show the match between the analytical and simulation results.

Many simulation software packages provide simulation animation capabilities. With animation, you can visualize how the entities in the model are changing over time. This is useful for verifying the correctness of the model. In addition, visual displays are generally more intuitive and convincing than a table of statistics. Figure 4-6 is a screen snapshot taken during the animation of the closed queuing network example. Using animation, you can see the transactions circling around the model paths. You can specify break points (conditions that cause the simulation to pause) and inspection windows.

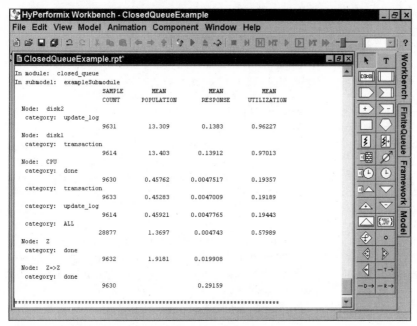

Figure 4-5: Statistics report for the closed queuing network

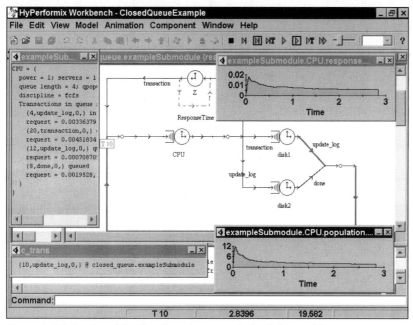

Figure 4-6: Animation of the closed queuing network simulation model

Dynamic graphs enable you to visualize statistics changing over time. Figure 4-6 shows time-based graphs for the CPU response time and CPU population (queue length). These two time graphs illustrate the transient and steady states discussed earlier in the chapter. Because most simulation executions change with time, the collected statistics depend on the initial values. The CPU response time and population graphs show that these values start from a zero value and quickly peak, then converge to a steady-state value over time. If you are interested in mean values, you are better off ignoring the transient values at the beginning of the simulation. Fortunately, most simulation packages, including Workbench, provide controls for removing these initial values automatically. On the other hand, you may at times be interested in these transient values. A simulation model can be used to verify that a system works as expected during start-up, shutdown, bursty arrivals, errors, and failures, all of which cause transient behavior. Analyzing these with analytic models is very difficult because analytic models tend be more inclined towards steady-state behavior.

You can easily model open queuing networks with simulation models. Figure 4-7 shows an implementation of the open queuing network in Figure 3-6 and Example 3-2 (refer to Chapter 3) using Hyperformix Workbench. Because, in an open network, jobs do not recirculate, you need a means of generating and destroying new jobs. For these purposes, Workbench provides source nodes and sink nodes, respectively. A source node can generate new jobs with specified time intervals. This corresponds to the inter-arrival time of an analytic queuing network.

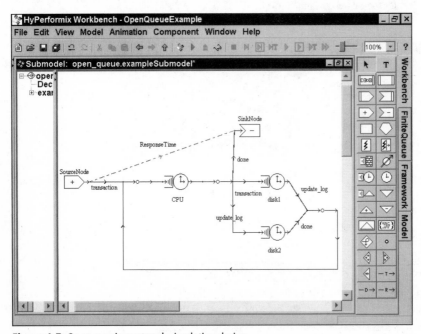

Figure 4-7: Open queuing network simulation design

Figure 4-8 shows the output statistics report for the open network example. The arrival time is set to generate 60 transactions per second. The simulation is executed for 100 simulated seconds. Note that the overall response time (0.059 seconds) corresponds to the results obtained in

Example 3-2 (see Chapter 3) using analytical solutions. Similarly, the utilization values match the analytic solution. With the simulation model, however, it is possible to see the response time and utilization breakdown for each transaction category. These transaction categories correspond to multi-class jobs, which are very complicated to handle with analytical solutions, if possible at all.

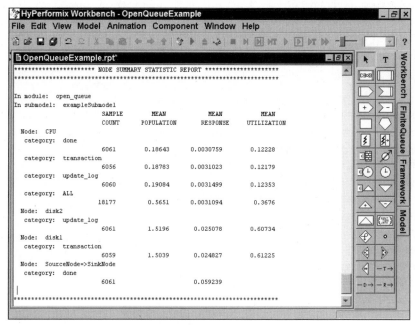

Figure 4-8: Statistics report for the open queuing network

Guidelines for Simulation Projects

If you decide to include simulation modeling in your performance analysis projects, remember the following guidelines for successful simulation modeling:

✓ **Get a good simulation software package.** You might be tempted to develop a homegrown simulation program using general-purpose programming languages. Even though this is a good exercise in and of itself, it's time-consuming and error-prone. A simulation package, whether a simulation language or an integrated simulation environment, will provide you with tested, pre-built event handlers, schedulers, and specialized modules. Especially good random number generators, essential to good simulation, are difficult to build yourself. Save yourself some time.

✓ **Know the goals of your simulation project.** A simulation can be implemented in many ways, and not all of them are appropriate for all purposes. If you know what you are building the model for, getting results will be much easier. You will be able to select the simulation parameters and level of detail accordingly, which leads to the next guideline.

✓ **Implement the right level of detail.** It is easy to get carried away with a simulation model. Over time, you will be tempted to introduce more and more detail, hoping it will provide better accuracy and more information. Even though this is partially true, you will also be introducing more complexity, errors, bugs, and uncertainty to your project, which might eventually backfire. If you know the project goals, you might be able to decide the appropriate level of detail.

✓ **Verify the model at every development stage.** This is just good software development practice. Verifying the system piece-by-piece, step-by-step, is easier than trying to fix a complex system as a whole. Verify that your implementation is correctly reflecting the model.

✓ **Validate the model at every development stage.** When you have a coarse level model, validate it using high-level measurement and theoretical data. When you have a detailed model, you can validate it against detailed data. Validation and verification are necessary if you want to obtain reliable, valid simulation results.

Summary

Simulation models are one of the crucial enablers in performance analysis. This chapter discussed the following key points in computer simulation:

Simulation Concepts

✓ Simulation models are computer programs representing real-world entities and processes for the purpose of analysis.

✓ State variables define the current state of the simulation, and anything that changes them is called an *event*.

✓ Discrete-event models have discrete (integer-valued) state variables.

Model Correctness

✓ Models are validated to make sure they represent the modeled system correctly.

✓ Models are verified to check that their implementation matches the intended model.

When to Simulate?

✓ Simulation models have numerous advantages over pure measurement or analytical studies. Simulation can be used to model dynamic, complex systems.

✓ Simulation models are time-consuming.

✓ The choice of the best performance analysis method depends on the project in hand. A mix of measurement, analytical, and simulation models could be the best choice.

Sensitivity Analysis and Model Outputs

✓ Model outputs should change proportional to the input changes. A behavior to the contrary may point to modeling and/or implementation problems.

✓ The final model outputs should be obtained when the simulation is in a steady state, and the initial transient state data should be discarded.

Simulation Software Tools

✓ The choice of simulation software is important because it dictates what you can eventually model.

✓ A mix of general programming languages, special simulation languages, and simulation packages can be used.

Simulation Examples

✓ Examples showed that the analytical models can be converted to simulation models and easily expanded.

✓ Simulation packages provide automatic output statistics reports.

Guidelines for Simulation Projects

✓ Obtain the right simulation software for your project.

✓ Determine the goals of the simulation study and choose the level of detail accordingly.

✓ Validate and verify the model at every development stage.

References and Additional Resources

Banks, Jerry (Editor). September 1998. *Handbook of Simulation: Principles, Methodology, Advances, Applications, and Practice*, Wiley-Interscience.

A collection of research papers that present a range of introductory to advanced-level simulation techniques.

Breslau, Lee, Deborah Estrin, Kevin Fall, Sally Floyd, John Heidemann, Ahmed Helmy, Polly Huang, Steven McCanne, Kannan Varadhan, Ya Xu, and Haobo Yu. May 2000. *Advances in Network Simulation*, IEEE Computer, 33 (5), pp. 59–67.

An overview of research on computer networks using simulation approaches, especially the Ns simulation tool. Similar research papers on network simulation, as well as additional information about Ns, can be found at www.isi.edu/nsnam/ns/.

Jain, Raj. April 1991. *The Art of Computer Systems Performance Analysis*. John Wiley & Sons.

This classic computer performance analysis reference contains information on simulation modeling.

Law, Averill M. and W. David Kelton S. December 1999. *Simulation Modeling and Analysis*, 3rd Edition. McGraw-Hill College Division.

Provides the fundamental theories behind simulation and statistical analysis.

Zeigler, Bernard P., Herbert Praehofer, and Tag Gon Kim. January 2000. *A Theory of Modeling and Simulation: Integrating Discrete Event and Continuous Complex Dynamic Systems*. Academic Press.

A newly updated version of a classic book on the theory behind most modeling techniques, including simulation.

Chapter 5

Experimental Analysis

In This Chapter

Experimentation is the ultimate test for your computing system designs (including storage networks). However, when you start experimentation, you must try an enormous number of combinations. This is true for real system experiments, as well as simulation runs. Simulation makes the combinatorial space explosion even worse. You can literally come up with several million different things to try. This chapter explains a systematic approach to planning and analyzing experiments. The discussion includes the following topics:

✓ The need for experimental analysis in computer science

✓ Proper design of experiments

✓ Determining the most important variables in an experimental study

✓ Software for automatic design of experiments and usage examples

✓ Analyzing experimental results

Introduction to Experimental Analysis

Experiments are a vital part of the study of computer systems. More often than not, random variables affect system performance. Probabilistic behavior cannot be understood using deterministic models. You must experiment with the system to determine these complex interactions. The reasons for experimentation can vary, but this section focuses on experiments for the verification of models or hypotheses. Performance experiments do one or more of the following:

✓ Determine which variables most affect system performance.

✓ Verify an analytic or simulation model against experimental results.

✓ Build a simple model of the interactions between input parameters and output results.

✓ Get rid of unimportant detail in a model and refine it.

✓ Find optimum, minimum, or maximum values for parameters.

Claims or assertions about the performance of any computer system must be verified with rigorous experimental data. Unfortunately, computing literature is full of publications (academic or commercial) without any substantial experimental verification. Most of the claims are based on limited "demonstrations," a far cry from any scientific method. Most of these results would alarm skeptics in any other scientific field—but not in computer science or computer technology. A survey of computer science publications (Tichy, 1995) found that 55 percent of papers that required empirical evidence lacked proper experimental results—if they had any at all.

The fast pace of computer (and/or information) science and technology, which marked much of the second half of the 20th century, caused computer scientists to race for one breakthrough after another. The competitive nature of information systems business also caused similar problems in academic circles. The result was a lack of proper scientific methodology and scrutiny—the foundation of most other "natural" sciences. No matter what the debate, experiments are necessary to achieve the outcomes previously listed.

Experimental study is problematic because you can experiment with so many alternatives. The number of experiments you can potentially undertake increases exponentially (multiplicatively) with the number of variables and their possible values. This problem was mitigated many decades ago when Design of Experiments (DOE) techniques were introduced. These techniques are the subject of study for the rest of this chapter.

Design of Experiments

Contrary to what the name implies, Design of Experiments (DOE) is a purely theoretical branch of statistical mathematics. It aims to construct combinations of experiment inputs that provide statistically the most significant results. The idea is to avoid insignificant experiments if their results could be predicted with other significant experiments.

Statisticians use special terminology that may or may not always match the usage in computer science. The following is a list of DOE-related terms and their explanations.

- ✓ **Response**—The system and model output variable or variables that are deemed important for the study in hand. Example system responses include response time, throughput, queue depth, mean time between failures, and so on.

- ✓ **Factor, control variable**—Input variables that are expected to affect the output responses. The response is assumed to be a function of the factors. The number of disks, CPU speed, and network type could be some example factors.

- ✓ **Level**—One of several possible values for a particular factor. For example, a CPU speed factor might have two levels at 1.2 GHz and 2.0 GHz.

- ✓ **Design**—A table where each row contains a particular combination of factor levels. Each row represents an experimental setting. A design tells you which experiments to perform.

- ✓ **Regression model**—In calculus, a variable y is a function of another variable x. If x and y are random variables (statistics), random variable y is regressed upon random variable x. Alternatively, you can say there is a regression model of y using x.

- ✓ **Term**—The variables used in a regression model. Terms can be the main factors (A, B, C, and so on) or their combinations (AB, BC, ABC, and so on).

- ✓ **Fit**—The degree to which a regression model is able to explain experimental results.

✓ **Residual** — The difference between the experimental measurement and the regression model output.

✓ **Effect** — The degree of a term's contribution to the outcome of the regression model. A term with a high coefficient multiplier in the regression formula will have a high effect on the output variable.

✓ **Confounding, aliasing** — If the effects of two terms are not discernible individually, those two terms are confounded, or aliased. For example, if A and BCD are confounded, the effect of A is blended with the effect of the interactions between the factors B, C, and D.

Even though several DOE techniques exist, the two most popular are full factorial designs and fractional factorial designs, which are discussed in the next two sections.

Full Factorial Designs

The easiest experimental design is to test every possibility. Such a design is called a *full factorial design*. For example, if an experiment has three factors (A, B, and C), and 3, 2, and 5 levels for the factors, respectively, a full factorial design specifies $3 \times 2 \times 5 = 30$ experiments.

Even though each factor can have many levels, an often-used simplification is to assume they have only two levels. A general rule-of-thumb is to take the minimum and maximum values of a factor as its two levels. Note that if the response is a monotonic function of the factor (that is, it either increases or decreases), using the two extreme points provides most of the effect information. Designs with two levels are called *two-level*, *bi-level*, or 2^k *factorial designs*. For simplicity, the two levels of all factors are coded as −1 and +1.

Two-level experimental designs are generally used for *screening* studies. These are the preliminary experiments to determine the factors that have significant effects. Later, more detailed experiments can be based on the information obtained from these screening analyses.

The design and analysis of full factorial designs is similar to that of fractional factorial designs, which will be discussed (including specific examples) next.

Fractional Factorial Designs

Because of time or resource constraints, it may not be possible to use a full factorial design. You might know or expect that the effect of higher order interactions between factors is not important. In such cases, you can reduce the number of experiments. *Fractional factorial designs* use only one half, one fourth, one eighth, and so on of the number of experiments generated by a full factorial design.

Almost all statistical software packages have some form of DOE functionality. Examples of statistical packages with DOE capabilities include the following:

✓ Umetrics MODDE

✓ SAS JMP

✓ Grabitech MultiSimplex

✓ RSD Matrex

In this chapter, Minitab Release 13 is used to illustrate the examples. Minitab provides an array of DOE techniques, besides other standard statistical formulations. Figure 5-1 shows the factorial designs available in Minitab.

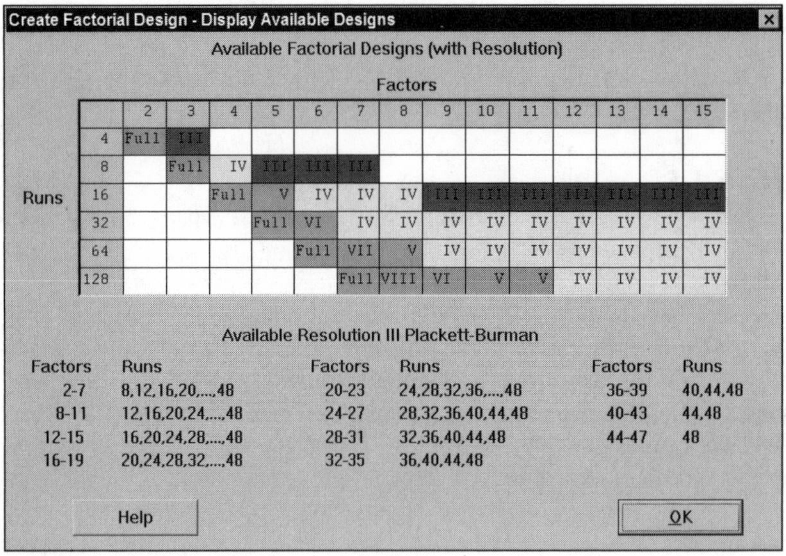

Create Factorial Design - Display Available Designs

Available Factorial Designs (with Resolution)

Factors

Runs	2	3	4	5	6	7	8	9	10	11	12	13	14	15
4	Full	III												
8		Full	IV	III	III	III								
16			Full	V	IV	IV	IV	III	III	III	III	III	III	III
32				Full	VI	IV	IV	IV	IV	IV	IV	IV	IV	IV
64					Full	VII	V	IV	IV	IV	IV	IV	IV	IV
128						Full	VIII	VI	V	V	IV	IV	IV	IV

Available Resolution III Plackett-Burman

Factors	Runs		Factors	Runs		Factors	Runs
2-7	8,12,16,20,...,48		20-23	24,28,32,36,...,48		36-39	40,44,48
8-11	12,16,20,24,...,48		24-27	28,32,36,40,44,48		40-43	44,48
12-15	16,20,24,28,...,48		28-31	32,36,40,44,48		44-47	48
16-19	20,24,28,32,...,48		32-35	36,40,44,48			

Help   OK

Figure 5-1: Available factorial designs in Minitab

The top of Figure 5-1 is a detailed look at the designs up to 15 factors. The vertical axis shows the number of experiment runs required for each design. Besides full factorial designs, fractional factorial designs with different resolutions are shown. The design's *resolution* is a measure of its accuracy and is generally shown by Roman numerals (for example, III, IV, and so on). It should suffice to know that higher resolutions can find more interactions between the factors and give you more accuracy. However, as Figure 5-1 shows, higher resolution designs cost more — they require more runs. For more detail, you can consult Minitab's user guide (Minitab [a], 2000).

As an example of an experimental analysis, assume that you need to find out the factors that determine a file server's performance. This file server might be a Network Attached Storage (NAS) appliance. The response variable is the file server's bandwidth, as measured by a network file system benchmark. You want to determine the relative effects of the following four factors on the file server's performance:

✓ CPU speed

✓ Main memory size

✓ Number of network interface cards (NICs)

✓ The file system type

Everything else should be kept constant as much as possible across experiments. Because you are trying to find the relative effects of factors, rather than detailed optimization, a two-level factorial design should suffice. For the system in hand, you decide that the levels given in Table 5-1 represent the minimum and maximum choices.

TABLE 5-1 Factors for the File Server Experiment

Factor	Name	Low	High	Coded Low Level	Coded High Level
A	CPU	1.2 GHz	2 GHz	-1	+1
B	Memory	2 GB	8 GB	-1	+1
C	NICs	2	4	-1	+1
D	File System	Ext2	Ext3	-1	+1

File system type is not a numerical choice. In this example, it can be either Ext2, the native Linux file system, or Ext3, an enhanced version of Ext2. A full factorial design requires $2^4 = 16$ experiments to test all possible combinations. For statistical significance, each experiment (measurement) should be repeated at least three times to account for experimental errors. This makes the total number of experiments $16 \times 3 = 48$.

Because completing all 48 experiments would take too long, you decide to do a fractional factorial design. A fractional design with a ½ fraction would require only $16 \div 2 = 8$ experiments. If each experiment is repeated (replicated) three times, you need $8 \times 3 = 24$ measurements. For the sake of simplicity, I will assume you use only a single replication for the rest of this example. There will be eight runs overall.

In Minitab, you can use the menu item Stat, DOE, Factorial, Create Factorial Design to generate tables for factorial designs. After entering the factors, as in Table 1-5, and choosing a fractional factorial design, Minitab prints the design information shown in Figure 5-2 and the design table shown in Figure 5-3.

The output in Figure 5-2 includes some useful information. You can see that the mean term (I) is aliased with ABCD, which is a four-way interaction. Therefore, this is a resolution IV design. Secondly, the main factors, A, B, C, and D, are confounded with three-way interactions. For example, the effect of A (which is CPU) will be indistinguishable from the effect resulting from the interactions between B, C, and D (which are memory, NICs, and file system). Because you know that the probability of this three-way interaction affecting the outcome is much smaller than the probability of CPU affecting the outcome, this confounding is not important and it is safe.

The worksheet in Figure 5-3 contains the eight experiments required for the fractional factorial design. Each row of factors is pre-filled by Minitab, and you must fill out the Bandwidth column as you finish the experiments. Because there are no replications, each experiment appears only once. If consecutive experiments can affect each other's outcome, you can tell Minitab to randomize the order of the experiments for statistical significance, in which case the columns StdOrder and RunOrder will be different. If you clean up the caches and file systems properly after each experiment, the order of tests will not make any difference in the file server experiments. The run order is not randomized in this case.

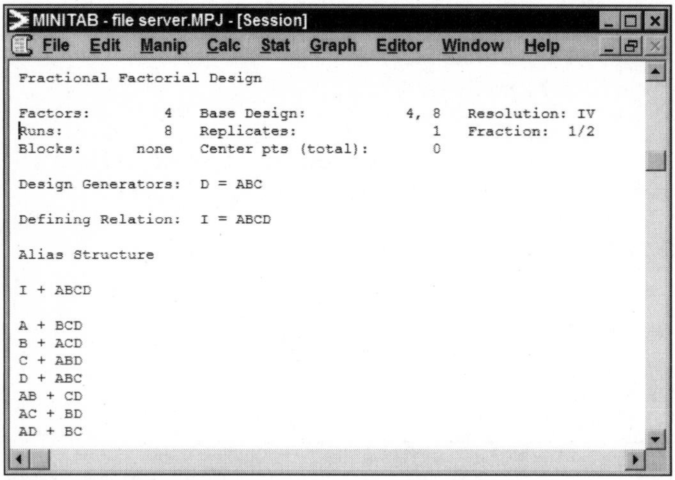

```
MINITAB - file server.MPJ - [Session]                          _ □ ×
  File  Edit  Manip  Calc  Stat  Graph  Editor  Window  Help    _ 日 ×

Fractional Factorial Design

Factors:        4    Base Design:         4, 8   Resolution: IV
Runs:           8    Replicates:            1    Fraction:   1/2
Blocks:      none    Center pts (total):    0

Design Generators:   D = ABC

Defining Relation:   I = ABCD

Alias Structure

I + ABCD

A + BCD
B + ACD
C + ABD
D + ABC
AB + CD
AC + BD
AD + BC
```

Figure 5-2: Design information for the file server experiment

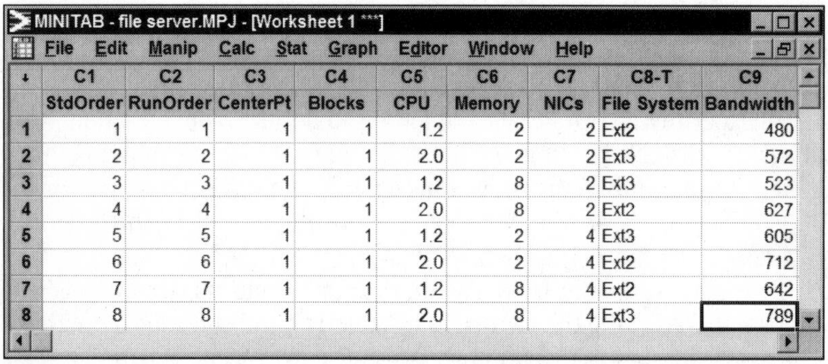

```
MINITAB - file server.MPJ - [Worksheet 1 ***]                      _ □ ×
  File  Edit  Manip  Calc  Stat  Graph  Editor  Window  Help        _ 日 ×
```

	C1	C2	C3	C4	C5	C6	C7	C8-T	C9
	StdOrder	RunOrder	CenterPt	Blocks	CPU	Memory	NICs	File System	Bandwidth
1	1	1	1	1	1.2	2	2	Ext2	480
2	2	2	1	1	2.0	2	2	Ext3	572
3	3	3	1	1	1.2	8	2	Ext3	523
4	4	4	1	1	2.0	8	2	Ext2	627
5	5	5	1	1	1.2	2	4	Ext3	605
6	6	6	1	1	2.0	2	4	Ext2	712
7	7	7	1	1	1.2	8	4	Ext2	642
8	8	8	1	1	2.0	8	4	Ext3	789

Figure 5-3: The design worksheet for the file server example

After executing the experiments and putting bandwidth results into the worksheet, you can use Minitab to analyze the relationship between the factors and the response. In Minitab, using the menu item Stat, DOE, Factorial, Analyze Factorial Design, you can generate several different statistical graphs to check the effects of factors. One type of graph, *Pareto chart*, plots the effects of each term on the response variable. The Pareto chart of the effects given in Figure 5-4 shows the importance of each factor for the file server experiments. The number of network interfaces (C) has the largest effect, followed by the CPU speed (A). Among the main factors, the file system type (D) has the least effect.

The vertical dotted line in the Pareto chart shows the effect value that a factor must pass to have a significance level denoted by alpha. For example, an alpha value of 0.10 denotes that within a 90 percent confidence interval, the effect is significant.

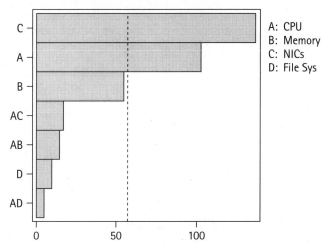

Figure 5-4: Pareto chart of effects for the file server example

Removing terms that do not have a significant effect is usually a good idea. After removing the terms involving the file system type (D) and repeating the analysis, you can get the refined Pareto chart shown in Figure 5-5. In this final analysis, you can see that the number of interfaces, the CPU speed, and the memory size have significant effects, in that order. Even though the interaction between the CPU speed and the interfaces and between the CPU speed and the memory size has some effect, it is less than the significance level.

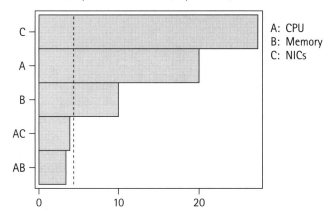

Figure 5-5: Pareto chart for the file server experiments

Regression Analysis

Figure 5-6 shows the Minitab design analysis output. An analysis of an experimental design actually fits a regression model to the experimental data. The model tries to approximate the response variable as a function of the factors. For example, the mathematical model for the bandwidth can be obtained from the coefficients given in Figure 5-6, as in Equation 5-1.

Equation 5-1

```
Bandwidth = 618.75 + 56.25 CPU + 26.5 Memory + 68.25 NICs + 6.5 CPU*Memory +
            7.25 CPU*NICs
```

The terms in Equation 5-1 are in coded units; that is, they are scaled to be between -1 and +1 using Table 5-1. For example, a memory size of 8GB is denoted by Memory = +1.

```
 MINITAB - file server.MPJ - [Session]                              _ 🗗 ×
  File   Edit   Manip   Calc   Stat   Graph   Editor   Window   Help      _ 🗗 ×

Fractional Factorial Fit: Bandwidth versus CPU, Memory, NICs

Estimated Effects and Coefficients for Bandwidt (coded units)

Term           Effect      Coef     SE Coef       T       P
Constant                 618.750      2.850   217.07   0.000
CPU           112.500     56.250      2.850    19.73   0.003
Memory         53.000     26.500      2.850     9.30   0.011
NICs          136.500     68.250      2.850    23.94   0.002
CPU*Memory     13.000      6.500      2.850     2.28   0.150
CPU*NICs       14.500      7.250      2.850     2.54   0.126

Analysis of Variance for Bandwidt (coded units)

Source               DF      Seq SS     Adj SS     Adj MS      F        P
Main Effects          3     68195.0    68195.0    22731.7  349.72   0.003
2-Way Interactions    2       758.5      758.5      379.3    5.83   0.146
Residual Error        2       130.0      130.0       65.0
Total                 7     69083.5

Observations for Bandwidt

Obs   Bandwidt       Fit   SE Fit   Residual   St Resid
 1     480.000   481.500    6.982     -1.500      -0.37
 2     572.000   566.500    6.982      5.500       1.36
 3     523.000   521.500    6.982      1.500       0.37
 4     627.000   632.500    6.982     -5.500      -1.36
 5     605.000   603.500    6.982      1.500       0.37
 6     712.000   717.500    6.982     -5.500      -1.36
```

Figure 5-6: Analysis output for the file server experiments

The bottom portion of Figure 5-6 also shows the fitted values obtained by the regression model given in Equation 5-1. The difference between the measured response variable (Bandwidth) and the computed approximation (Fit) is shown under the Residual column. These residual values and their distributions are crucial for model validity. Regression analysis depends on the assumptions that the residuals are independent and identically distributed (IID), and that they come from a normal distribution. These two assumptions can be visually tested using the two graphs shown in Figures 5-7 and 5-8, which are generated as part of the DOE analysis in Minitab.

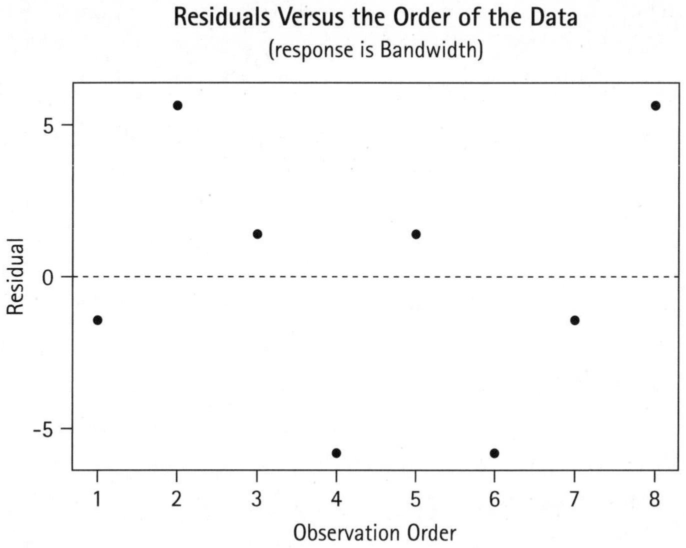

Residuals Versus the Order of the Data
(response is Bandwidth)

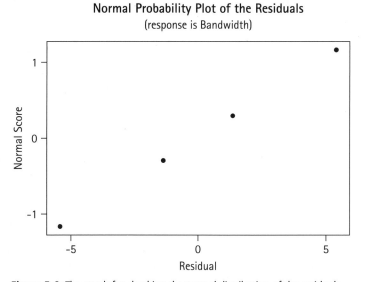

Figure 5-7: Residuals chart showing the distribution of residuals versus the observations

Figure 5-7 plots the residuals for each observation. You can see that the residuals are evenly distributed around zero; no bias towards any one side is evident. This is a strong indication that the residuals are independent. They satisfy the requirement of a valid regression analysis.

Normal Probability Plot of the Residuals
(response is Bandwidth)

Figure 5-8: The graph for checking the normal distribution of the residuals

Secondly, you must check whether the residuals are from a normal distribution population. Make a visual check using the residuals' normal probability plot shown in Figure 5-8, which is also generated as part of the factorial analysis in Minitab. In such a graph, the values are normally distributed if all the data points lie on the diagonal line or in close proximity to it. In Figure 5-8, all the points are almost on the diagonal, and you can thus conclude that the residuals are from a normally distributed population, and that the regression analysis is valid. For details on this normal probability plot, which is sometimes called a *normal-normal quantile plot*, see Minitab documentation (Minitab [a], 2000) or the references on the DOE given at the end of this chapter (Box, 1978; Jain, 1991; Montgomery, 2000).

Regression analysis in statistics has a different (and almost unrelated) meaning than the regression tests in quality engineering, where regression tests are repeated after each product improvement to make sure other working parts did not break. Regression analysis in statistics fits a mathematical relation to empirical data.

What can you do if one of the assumptions about residuals is not validated? First, check the Pareto chart of effects to see if there are other terms with low effects that can be removed from the model. Removing extra, ineffective terms generally produces a valid model.

If you are still not able to get a satisfactory model, you can try other, more general DOE techniques. For example, Minitab provides response surface, mixture, and Taguchi designs in addition to factorial designs. See the Minitab documentation (Minitab [b], 2000) for these DOE alternatives.

Regression analysis is not specific to DOE. You can use regression analysis to study relations in any kind of experimental data.

Summary

This chapter explains a systematic approach to planning and analyzing experiments, including the following points:

Introduction to Experimental Analysis

✓ Experiments can be used to verify a model, to find the variables that most affect system performance, and to find optimum parameter values.

✓ Computer science lacks the proper experimental validation tradition often found in other scientific fields.

Design of Experiments

✓ Design of Experiments (DOE) is a field in mathematical statistics.

✓ DOE is used to design experiments that provide maximum information with the least number of trials.

✓ Factors are the free (control) variables and responses are the system outputs.

✓ Full factorial designs use all available factor combinations and may require a lot of experiments.

✓ Fractional factorial designs reduce the number of experiments by neglecting some combinations that are expected to be unimportant and using the combinations that are expected to be important.

✓ Two-level designs use only two values for each factor and can be used to find out which factors have the greatest effects. Then, more detailed experiments, using more levels, can be conducted.

✓ Most statistical software packages enable automatic design of experiments using user-supplied parameters.

Regression Analysis

✓ Regression fits a mathematical model to experimental data, between the factors and the system response values.

✓ The goodness of the fit is measured by the residual between the model outputs and the measured values.

✓ The residuals should be checked for independence and normal distribution for the validity of the regression analysis, which might require removal of ineffective terms.

References and Additional Resources

Box, George E. P., J. Stuart Hunter, and William G. Hunter. June 1978. *Statistics for Experimenters: An Introduction to Design, Data Analysis, and Model Building.* John Wiley & Sons.

A classic reference book for experimental design by authors who have contributed much to this field.

Jain, Raj. April 1991. *The Art of Computer Systems Performance Analysis*. John Wiley & Sons.

This classic computer performance analysis reference contains extensive information on the design of experiments.

Kleijnen, Jack P.C. September 1998. "Experimental Design for Sensitivity Analysis, Optimization, and Validation of Simulation Models," in *Handbook of Simulation: Principles, Methodology, Advances, Applications, and Practice*, Jerry Banks (Editor), Wiley-Interscience, pp. 173–223.

Kleijnen discusses the special treatment of Design of Experiments topics as they are applied to simulation studies.

Minitab Inc. (a) 2000. *Meet MINITAB, Release 13 for Windows*.

An introductory guide for MINITAB, available at www.minitab.com.

Minitab Inc. (b) 2000. *MINITAB User's Guide, Release 13 for Windows*.

User's guide for MINITAB, available at www.minitab.com.

Montgomery, Douglas C. June 2000. *Design and Analysis of Experiments*, 5th Edition. John Wiley & Sons.

An in-depth textbook about the theory and application of experimental design in engineering fields.

Tichy, Walter F. 1998. *Should Computer Scientists Experiment More?* IEEE Computer, 31(5), pp. 32–40.

Lists 16 reasons why computer scientists refrain from experimentation. Provides an anti-thesis for each of these reasons.

Tichy, F., Paul Lukowicz, Lutz Prechelt, and Ernst A. Heinz. January 1995. *Experimental Evaluation in Computer Science: A Quantitative Study,* Journal of Systems and Software, (28)1, pp. 9–18.

Argues that computer science has a higher percentage of design papers without empirical validation (35 to 55 percent) compared to other sciences (less than 15 percent).

Part II

Performance Analysis and Modeling of Storage System Components

Chapter 6

Modeling Storage Devices

In This Chapter

Devices that contain the medium where the data is stored are the foundation of storage networks. The capacity and speed of these storage elements, and the interactions between them, determine how the other layers of the storage network behave and perform. This chapter presents descriptions and performance models of baseline storage devices, including the following subjects:

- ✓ A data hierarchy model that predicts the cost of data access in a multi-tier storage system

- ✓ Hard-disk drive performance models that incorporate physical and logical drive characteristics

- ✓ Disk array architectures that provide capacity, performance, and reliability improvements

- ✓ Magnetic tape and optical disc drives

Introduction to Data Storage Devices

No matter where data travels in a storage network, it must be stored at some place when it reaches the end of its path, temporarily or permanently. The four most popular storage mediums are as follows:

- ✓ Random access memory (RAM)

- ✓ Magnetic disk drive

- ✓ Magnetic tape drive

- ✓ Optical disks

In a storage network, it is possible to find various configurations and combinations of storage devices. Figure 6-1 illustrates an example of storage device stacking in a storage network. The data is cached at the edge and mid-level hosts and resides permanently on the storage medium at the bottom.

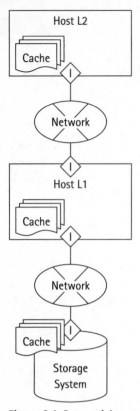

Figure 6-1: Data path in a storage network

All the devices on this path contribute to the storage network's performance characteristics. The following sections in this chapter focus on the performance characteristics of storage medium devices. Chapters 7 and 8 will discuss storage interconnects and networks.

Random Access Memory

Before any manipulation can be done, data must be brought into the main memory. The memory architecture directly affects the performance of computing systems. Main memories have evolved through many generations of technologies — including mechanical switches, mercury acoustic delay lines, Williams-Kilburn cathode-ray tubes, transistor-based memories, and the modern-day Extended Data Out RAM (EDO RAM), Dynamic RAM (DRAM), Synchronous Dynamic RAM (SDRAM), RAMBUS Dynamic RAM (RDRAM), and Double Data Rate SDRAM (DDR- SDRAM. This chapter uses DRAM to refer to all semiconductor memory technologies.

Figure 6-2 shows the historical and extrapolated trends in DRAM technology between the years 1984 and 2004. The three lines represent the bandwidth, latency, and chip capacity over the years. The graphs show a 10,000-fold increase in capacity and an almost 1,000-fold increase in memory bandwidth. Interestingly enough, only a 10-fold decrease in access latency occurred.

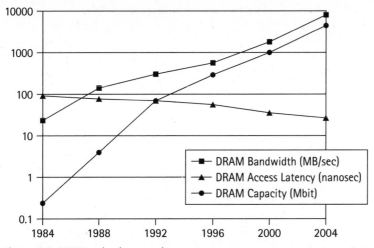

Figure 6-2: DRAM technology trends

The discrepancy between capacity/bandwidth and access latency is reminiscent of the access density problem discussed in Chapter 1. The access density problem for DRAM memory is illustrated in Figure 6-3. The figure shows the number of accesses that can be accomplished in a second (as input/output operations per second, IOPS). A second line shows the number of accesses per Mbit of memory (as IOPS/Mbit). Because memory capacity is increasing at a much faster pace than memory access times, the access density is decreasing year after year.

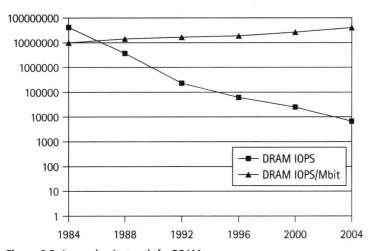

Figure 6-3: Access density trends for DRAM memory

A similar relation can be derived between processor speeds (which also increase exponentially) and memory access speeds. When left unsolved, this problem causes the high-speed processors to starve for data. One solution is the utilization of several layers of fast cache memory. The layers closest to the processor are faster, smaller, and more expensive. They are backed up by slower, cheaper, and larger memory layers. The objective is to utilize the locality in the memory references so that the most-used data fits into the faster and smaller caches.

You can combine the processor cache layers and storage network data layers into a single storage hierarchy, as shown in Figure 6-4.

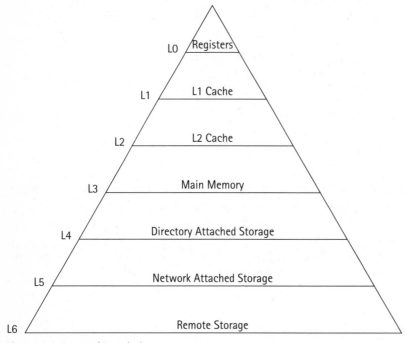

Figure 6-4: Storage hierarchy layers

In this data hierarchy, the processor works on the data in the registers. If the data is not in the registers, it is brought from the level-one cache (L1 cache). If it is not there either, it is brought from the level-two cache (L2 cache), and so on. As you go down the hierarchy, the storage devices become larger, slower, and cheaper. The devices at the bottom have the highest capacity and cheapest cost per byte.

Figure 6-5 shows the effects of cache sizes on memory access bandwidth. The tests were conducted using SiSoftware's Sandra benchmarks on two different Intel Pentium 4 machines. Both of the machines have 8KB L1 caches, and you can see that the tests with block sizes 8KB or less have the highest bandwidth because all the data resides in the L1 cache. The middle plateau in the figure denotes where the data resides in the L2 cache. The two machines have 512KB and 256KB L2 caches, respectively, and this is easily noticeable from where the L2 plateau ends for each machine. Above 1MB, all data is in the main memory. There, you can see the bandwidth difference between the faster RDRAM (RAMBUS) and relatively slower DDR-SDRAM.

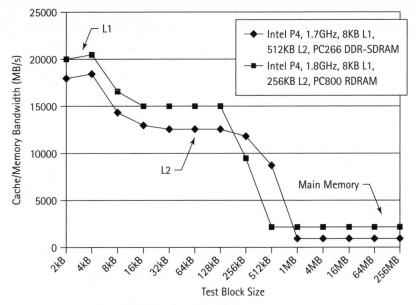

Figure 6-5: Memory bandwidth benchmark results

For a given memory hierarchy, you can compute the average time required to satisfy a data reference.

Here are some cache-specific terms:

- ✓ **Cache hit** — When the data resides in the accessed level, it is a cache hit.

- ✓ **Cache hit ratio (h_i)** — The ratio of the number of accesses that are cache hits to the number of all accesses at level i.

- ✓ **Cache miss** — When the data cannot be found at the accessed level, it is a cache miss.

- ✓ **Cache miss ratio (m_i)** — The ratio of the number of accesses that are cache misses to the number of all accesses at level i.

- ✓ **Line size** — The size of the data unit that is accessed at a particular level. The data is always kept in cache lines of this size.

- ✓ **Access time (t_i)** — The total time needed to access one line of data from level i.

- ✓ **Access probability (P_i)** — The probability that a given data reference will require access to level i.

The average time for a data reference can be computed as the sum of the average times spent at each level. The average time spent at each level is the product of the access time and the access probability at that level (Jacob, 1996). The average access time (T) in the entire hierarchy can be formulated as shown in Equation 6-1.

Equation 6-1

$$T = \Sigma_i \ P_i t_i$$

The probability that a level will need to be accessed can be computed using the miss ratios of the levels above it. Namely, P_i is equal to the probability that the level above it (l_{i-1}) will be accessed (P_{i-1}) and missed (m_i). This recursive formula is shown in Equation 6-2.

Equation 6-2

$$P_i = P_{i-1}m_{i-1}$$

Together with the fact that level 0 will always be accessed ($P_0 = 1$), Equation 6-2 can be used to compute all P_i values, which in turn will allow the computation of the average access time using Equation 6-1. Example 6-1 illustrates these computation steps.

Example 6-1 Average Access Time in a Data Hierarchy

The following table shows the access times (in processor cycles) and cache hit rates for seven layers of a data hierarchy. Compute the average access time of a data reference in this hierarchy.

Level	Device	Access Time (cycles)	Hit Rate
L0	Registers	1	0.9
L1	L1 Cache	1	0.95
L2	L2 Cache	8	0.98
L3	Main Memory	100	0.9
L4	Local Disk	10,000,000	0.98
L5	Network Server	50,000,000	0.98
L6	Remote Server	400,000,000	1

The miss ratio is the reciprocal of the hit ratio.

$$m_i = 1 - h_i$$

Given that $P_0 = 1$, the access probabilities for each level can be computed using Equation 6-2. Then, the average time at level i is $P_i t_i$. The results of these computations are shown in the following table.

Level	Miss Rate	Access Probability	Cost Per Access (cycles)
L0	0.1	1	1
L1	0.05	0.1	0.1
L2	0.02	0.005	0.04
L3	0.1	0.0001	0.01
L4	0.02	0.00001	100
L5	0.02	0.0000002	10
L6	0	4E-09	1.6
			Total = 112.75

Finally, the average access time for the entire hierarchy is the sum of the average times at each level (as shown in Equation 6-1). The average access time is computed as 112.75 cycles for the data given above.

An interpretation of this result is as follows. Although a majority (99.5 percent) of data references at the register and L1 cache level requires only one processor cycle, the small percentage of cache misses causes the average access time to increase because of slow access at the lower levels.

Note that the results in this example depend on the given hit rates and access times. However, the general pattern holds true for almost all data hierarchies.

The computations for the access time can be started at any level in the hierarchy, not necessarily at level 0. For example, accesses to main memory can be taken as the baseline (level 0), and the access time can be computed from there on.

In storage network performance analysis, the memory effects can be handled from two perspectives:

✓ **Memory performance in a data hierarchy**—As shown in Example 6-1, the memory layers' performance (speed) can be factored into the analysis. However, the response time of DRAM memory will almost always be negligible compared to that of other storage mediums. For example, in Example 6-1, the majority of the access time belongs to layers 4, 5, and 6.

✓ **Throughput limiting factor of memory**—The amount of available memory is almost always a constraint on the number of active jobs, or active IO operations, that can be handled simultaneously. Consequently, the system's throughput is limited. In queuing network terms discussed in Chapter 3, memory restricts the number of customers (multiprogramming level) in a closed queuing network, which directly affects the throughput. In practice, memory constraints can be found at the client or server in the following areas:

- Main memory
- Cache buffers
- Network protocol buffers
- Network interface card or host bus adapter buffers
- Switch forwarding buffers
- Disk caches, and so on

Hard-Disk Drives

Hard-disk drives are the workhorse of data storage. A majority of personal and business information is stored on these rotating, rigid, magnetic substance-coated platters.

The disk drive industry has come a long way. When IBM introduced the first magnetic hard-disk drive in 1956, it stored only 5MB of data—impressive for its time. The drive contained 50 24-inch diameter platters stacked in a cabinet. It was called Random Access Method of Accounting and Control 305 (RAMAC 305, for short). In 2002, a 2.5-inch mobile hard drive can store 40GB and weighs a mere 8 ounces. With the rapid increase in storage demand and the advent of storage networks, there is little doubt that the importance of hard-disk drives will continue into the foreseeable future.

Disk Drive Mechanics and Operations

The mechanical components of a typical hard-disk drive are shown in Figure 6-6. The drive consists of a set of *platters* (disks) rotating together around a *spindle*. The spindle's rotational speed (angular velocity) is constant. It is measured in *revolutions per minute (RPM)*. Typical RPM values are 5400, 7200, 10K, and 15K. Both sides of each platter (*disk surfaces*) are coated with magnetic substrates that retain data bits written by *read/write heads*. A read/write head is suspended on an arm for each surface. The arms (and heads) move over the surfaces horizontally. Arms are connected to a single *actuator* that moves all the arms together.

In the storage industry, it is customary to refer to a hard-disk drive as a "spindle." This reflects the fact that all the platters on a spindle rotate together, and constitute a single access time domain. A common saying is "if you want more speed, you need more spindles."

The external connection to the disk drive could be one of a dozen different storage interfaces (discussed in detail in Chapter 7). The inner works of a disk drive are almost independent of the external interface. In fact, you can find the same disk drive sold with different external interfaces. This section discusses the performance characteristics that are related to the inside of the disk drive.

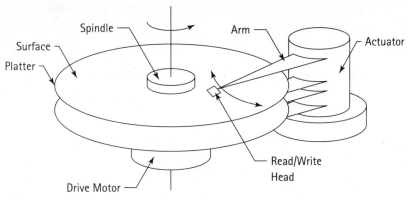

Figure 6-6: Physical components of a hard-disk drive

A hard-disk drive's logical data layout is shown in Figure 6-7. The data is written on each surface using concentric tracks. Corresponding tracks over all surfaces constitute a *cylinder* vertically. Each track is further divided into *sectors*. A sector is the minimum amount of data that can be read from or written to a disk drive.

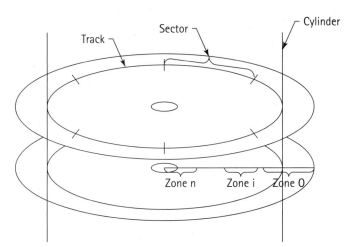

Figure 6-7: Logical view of a hard-disk drive

Note that the outer tracks are physically longer than the inner tracks. If all the tracks had the same number of sectors, space would be wasted on the outer tracks. To cope with this, the modern drives divide tracks into *zones*. Tracks in an outer zone have more sectors than the tracks in an inner zone. For example, an IBM Ultrastar 36XP drive has 16 zones. The outermost zone has 4112 cylinders and 360 sectors per track. The innermost zone has 235 cylinders and 216 sectors per track.

Generally, a single read/write channel is connected to all the heads. Therefore, the data is accessed through a single head at a time. The time to change between heads is called the *head switch time* and is generally around 0.8msec. The actual read/write occurs when the data sectors rotate under the read/write head. Consequently, the speed of data transfer is equal to the speed with which sectors travel under the head. Because there are more sectors on the outer tracks, read/write can occur more quickly on the outer zones.

A common optimization technique is to place data that must be quickly accessed on the outer zones, which have faster linear velocity (hence, faster read/write speed) than the inner zones.

When the head is on a target track, it must wait until the target sector rotates under the head before it can read or write data. This time period is called the *rotational latency*. Because the target sector could be at any place on the track, the rotational latency will equal, on average, one half of the rotation time, as shown in Equation 6-3.

Equation 6-3

```
average_rotational_latency = 1/2 × full_rotation_time
```

Another important contributor to the access time is the time required to position the head over the target track. This is referred to as *seek time*, and is governed by the power of the actuator and the stiffness of the arm. To change between two distant tracks, the disk arm must accelerate, cruise over tracks for some time, and then decelerate when it gets closer to the target track. The head must *stabilize* directly over the track. For a read operation, exact positioning is not crucial. The data layout contains enough information to indicate an erroneous read operation. On the other hand, the positioning for a write operation must be almost perfect so as not to damage neighboring data bits. Thus, the average seek times for write operations are always slightly greater than the average seek times for read operations.

Figure 6-8 shows the seek profile of a Seagate Cheetah X15-36LP disk drive. Such profiles can be experimentally obtained using disk parameter extraction software (Worthington, 1995). In Figure 6-8, the seek time is plotted as a function of the seek distance, which is denoted in number of tracks. The figure shows that for short seeks, the seek time rises more rapidly because most of the time is spent in acceleration and deceleration phases. For long seek distances, most of the seek time is spent in the constant, high-speed cruise. Therefore, the seek time is a linear function of the seek distance for long seeks.

Seek time can be approximated using Equation 6-4, where d is the seek distance in number of tracks. For very short distances, the seek time is best approximated as a function of $\sqrt{d}$. For medium and long seeks, two different linear functions can be used. The coefficients and the distinction between short and long seeks depend on the particular hard-disk type.

Equation 6-4

```
Seek time = 0              if d = 0
          = a₁ + b₁√d      if 0  < d ≤ Q₁
          = a₂ + b₂d       if Q₁ < d ≤ Q₂
          = a₃ + b₃d       if Q₂ ≤ d
```

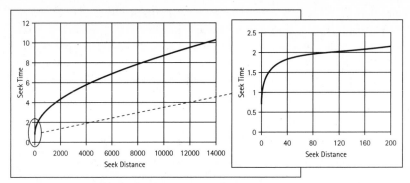

Figure 6-8: Seek profile for a Seagate Cheetah X15-36LP disk drive

Figure 6-9 shows the seek profile given in Figure 6-8, together with two linear functions that closely approximate the seek time. In fact, each disk drive contains lookup tables for seek profiles, which are updated dynamically. These profiles are used when the disk controller must make optimization decisions on where to seek next.

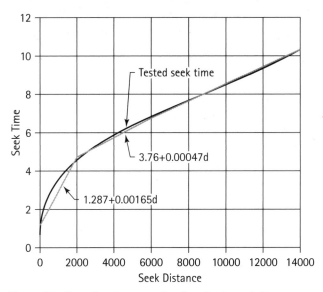

Figure 6-9: Linear function approximations for the seek time

The seek time plus the rotational latency constitutes the *disk access latency*, which is practically the average time to retrieve the first byte for a disk operation. Historically, access latency has been the one hard-disk drive characteristic to improve most slowly because it involves mechanical movement. Capacity and transfer bandwidth, on the other hand, have seen tremendous increases since the advent of the disk drive. This situation results in an access density problem similar to the memory access density problem discussed previously in this chapter. Basically, the possible number of operations per second per gigabyte of disk data is decreasing continually (Evaluator, 2001).

Figures 6-10 and 6-11 illustrate the access density problem. Figure 6-10 shows the historical trends for disk drive bandwidth, access latency, and capacity. Between 1984 and 2004, disk capacity and bandwidth will increase more than a 100-fold. On the other hand, disk access latency improvement is around 10-fold.

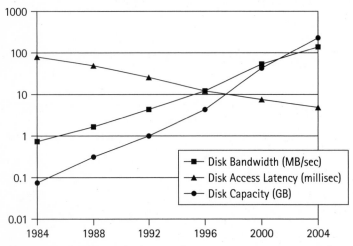

Figure 6-10: Disk drive technology trends

The access latency limits the number of possible IO operations per unit time. Figure 6-11 plots the improvements in terms of disk IOs per second (IOPS). However, when compared with the improvements in disk capacity, the access density (IOPS/GB) is decreasing with every generation of disk drives.

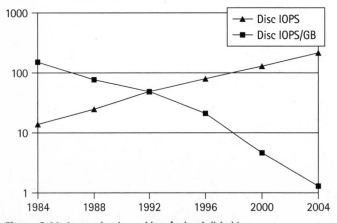

Figure 6-11: Access density problem for hard-disk drives

The access density problem has several possible remedies. First, the number of read/write channels and/or disk actuators can be increased inside a single disk drive to increase the disk IOPS. These improvements are not feasible right now because of the mechanical complexity of multiple actuators and electronic cross-talk problems. Another straightforward solution is the use of more and more disk drives in parallel. By spreading the operations across multiple disk drives, you can increase the total disk IOPS. Arrays with multiple disks are discussed later in this chapter. Another approach is to use intelligent caches all over the IO path to increase IOPS potential. Also, deep queuing and queue reordering has the potential to hide most of the access latency.

Modeling Disk Drives

This section discusses models for disk drives. A queuing network model or a simulation model of a single disk drive can be incorporated into system-level models to study the effects of individual disk characteristics on overall system performance.

Table 6-1 shows the notations that will be used for disk modeling.

TABLE 6-1 Disk Drive Modeling Parameters

Variable	Definition
r	Full-disk rotation time (s)
f	Full-stroke seek time (s)
t	Size of disk track (blocks)
h	Disk controller overhead (s)
i	Interface transfer time (s/block)
l	Mean request size (blocks)
λ	Request arrival rate (requests/s)
X	Throughput (requests/s)
R	Response time (s)
S	Service time (s)

The disk service time consists of the following components:

✓ Seek time

✓ Rotational latency

✓ Media transfer time

✓ Controller overhead

✓ Interface transfer time

To maintain a tractable analysis, assume that all of these service time components are non-overlapping. Therefore, the service time is equal to the sum of all of the preceding factors.

If the time for a full rotation is r seconds, the rotational latency is uniformly distributed on the interval [0, r]. The expected rotational latency is then r/2 seconds, with a variance of $c^2/12$.

As seen in Figure 6-8, a considerable portion of the seek profile is a linear function of seek distance and spans from 0 to the full-stroke seek time. This enables the simplifying assumption that the seek time is uniformly distributed on the interval [0, f], where f is the full-stroke seek. The expected seek time will then be f/2 seconds, with a variance of $f^2/12$. Another commonly used seek time approximation uses one-third of the full-stroke seek time as the average seek time. The choice really depends on the randomness of the modeled workload.

In addition, for simplicity's sake, assume that the data density on the disks is constant. Ignore zoned layout by assuming an average number of blocks per track (t). For a fixed request size (l), the media transfer time is a function of the disk rotation time (r) and the portion of the track accessed (l/t), as shown in Equation 6-5.

Equation 6-5

```
media_transfer_time = r(l/t)
```

For each IO operation, there will be h seconds of disk controller overhead, and for each block, i seconds of external interface transfer time. The disk interface's bandwidth depends on the particulars of the connection type and will be discussed in detail in Chapter 7.

If the arrival of requests to the disk drive are approximated as a Poisson arrival (exponential inter-arrival time), the disk drive can be modeled as an open queuing network with a single M/G/1 queuing center, as shown in Figure 6-12.

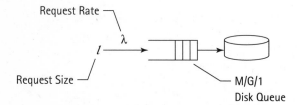

Figure 6-12: Queuing model for a single disk drive

The resulting service time for each IO request of size l can be computed as in Equation 6-6.

Equation 6-6

```
S = f/2 + r/2 + r(l/t) + h + il
```

In the service time equation, only seek and rotational latency are assumed to be random variables. Therefore, the variance of the service time is the sum of the variances of these two quantities, as shown in Equation 6-7.

Equation 6-7

$$(\sigma_s)^2 = (f^2 + r^2) \div 12$$

For an M/G/1 queue, queuing time (W) can be computed in terms of arrival rate λ, service time S, and the variance of service time $(\sigma_s)^2$, as in Equation 6-8.

Equation 6-8

$$W = \lambda((\sigma_s)^2 + S^2) \div 2(1 - \lambda S)$$

The response time is the sum of the waiting time and service time. The resulting formula for the response time is given in Equation 6-9.

Equation 6-9

$$R = S + W = S + (\lambda((\sigma_s)^2 + S^2) \div 2(1 - \lambda S))$$

As an example, the physical characteristics of a modern disk drive (Seagate Cheetah X15-36LP) are shown in Table 6-2.

TABLE 6-2 Specifications of a Seagate Cheetah X15-36LP Disk Drive

Capacity	36GB
Rotational speed	15000 RPM
Interfaces	Ultra160, Ultra320, 2 Gbit FC
Heads/disks	8/4
Tracks/surface	18,479
Average read seek	3.6msec
Average write seek	4.2msec
Adjacent track read seek	0.3msec
Adjacent track write seek	0.4msec
Full-stroke write seek	10.1msec
Internal formatted transfer rate	51–69 MB/s
Sustained transfer rate	42–58 MB/s
Cache buffer	8MB
Mean Time Between Failures (MTBF)	1,200,000 hours

Example 6-2 uses the disk drive specifications given in Table 6-2 to compute disk response times.

Example 6-2 Single Disk Drive Response Time

Compute the expected response time of the disk drive given in Table 6-2 for 128KB write operations with an arrival rate of 60 requests/sec. Assume the disk has Ultra160 interface and ignore host and interface-related delays, head switch overheads, and zoned data layout. Assume the disk controller overhead per request is 2msec.

Because there are 512 bytes in a block, the write request length in blocks is as follows:

```
l = 256 blocks
```

The arrival rate is given as follows:

```
λ = 60 requests/sec
```

The controller overhead is as follows:

```
h = 0.002 sec
```

The interface transfer time per block can be computed as follows:

```
i = 1 / (160MB/s × 2048blocks/MB) = 0. 0.000003 sec/block
```

From Table 6-2, using the number of surfaces, tracks per surface, and total disk capacity, you can find the average number of sectors for X15-36LP as follows:

```
t = 487 sectors/track
```

Because you know that the rotational speed is 15K, you can compute the revolution time as follows:

```
r = (60 sec/min) ÷ (15,000 rev/min) = 0.004 sec/rev
```

Also, from the table:

```
f = 0.0101 sec
```

The service time can then be computed as follows:

```
S = f/2 + r/2 + r(l/t) + h + il
  = 0.0101/2 + 0.004/2 + 0.004(256/487) + 0.002 + (0.000003)256

  = 0.0119 sec
```

So, the service time is 11.9msec.

The variance of the service time is as follows:

```
(σs)² = (f² + r²) ÷ 12

      = (0.0101² + 0.004²) ÷ 12 = 9.83417E-06
```

Assuming the disk is modeled as an M/G/1 queue, the mean waiting time can be computed as follows:

```
W = λ((σ_s)² + S²) ÷ 2(1 - λS)
  = 60(9.83417E-06 + 0.0119²) ÷ 2(1-60(0.0119))
  = 0.0159 s
```

The response time is the sum of the service time and the waiting time.

```
R = S + W =0.0119 + 0.0159 = 0.0278 s
```

The response time is about 27.8msec.

caution

It is clear from the discussion and examples that a disk drive's analytic models require various simplifying assumptions for mathematical tractability, most of which may not reflect real implementations. Therefore, analytic results should be used with caution, and only for preliminary assessments and relative performance comparisons. For detailed analysis, a simulation model will provide results that are more accurate by removing most of the assumptions.

Disk Arrays

The capacity and throughput of a single disk drive is limited. Using many disk drives together is often necessary to satisfy high-performance application requirements. *Disk arrays* are an organized collection of multiple hard-disk drives that provide various performance and reliability features.

Architecturally, you can implement disk arrays at various levels of the storage hierarchy. Arrays can be found on the storage bus inside a server, or as an external disk box, or as a complete external storage subsystem. Fundamentally, all of these use the same performance and reliability features, which are discussed next.

Disk Array Architectures

Distributing storage data over multiple disks enables one to:

✓ Combine the capacity of multiple disks into a large pool.

✓ Present this storage pool as multiple Logical Units (LUs).

✓ Load balance storage workload by distributing it over multiple disks.

✓ Utilize multiple disks in parallel to serve a single request.

✓ Increase reliability by replicating data on multiple disks.

The preceding list parallels the list given in Chapter 1 for storage virtualization benefits. This is not coincidental. Disk arrays "virtualize" the underlying disk drives.

Currently, the most popular strategy for distributing data over multiple devices is disk striping. Figure 6-13 illustrates stripe mapping. In this example, the first *stripe unit* (two file blocks) goes to the first disk; the second stripe unit goes to the second disk, and the nth stripe unit goes to the $((n-1 \bmod m)+1)^{th}$ disk, where m is the number of total disks used for striping. *Stripe width* (which is four in Figure 6-13) denotes the number of disks an LU is striped upon. The *stripe depth* denotes the size of the stripe unit, which is two blocks in Figure 6-13.

Although striping can decrease transfer time for large requests (by allowing parallel access), it must be balanced against the need to make multiple, independent transfers. For example, if a request uses all the available disks at the same time, it will block all other requests from using those disks. If each request uses half of the available disks, two requests can be served simultaneously. However, these requests will potentially be served more slowly because they are now using half the number of disks. The best choice for the stripe depth depends on a host of interrelated factors, including the access pattern, the system load, and hardware characteristics. A model for these interactions is presented in the next section. Optimization techniques for striping are discussed in Chapter 16, together with other subsystem-level optimizations.

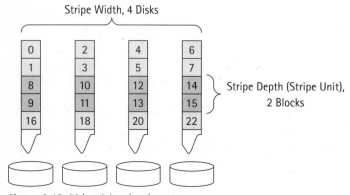

Figure 6-13: Disk striping data layout

A drawback exists to using multiple drives. Drives do fail. In addition, multiple drives are more likely to fail. Currently, the most reliable, state-of-the-art disk drive has an *Annualized Failure Rate (AFR)* of 0.73 percent. If m number of disks are used together, the failure rate will be proportional to the number of disks, as shown in Equation 6-10.

Equation 6-10

$$AFR(m) = m \times AFR_{disk}$$

For the above-mentioned drive, 100 drives have an AFR of 73 percent. This is only for independent disk failures and does not account for system failures.

When the stored data is important (and most data is very important), any failure rate is unacceptable. One solution is replicating the data twice. If one copy fails, the other copy can be used. The replicated disks constitute a *mirror set,* as shown in Figure 6-14. The downside of mirroring is that the space usage and the number of write operations doubles. Read operations might be faster by distributing them on two copies.

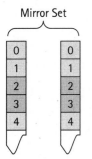

Figure 6-14: Disk mirroring

You can also mix striping with mirroring, as illustrated in Figure 6-15. The data is first striped on half of the disks. Those disks are then mirrored to the remaining half of the disks. Such a layout has the advantages of both mirroring and striping — load balancing and full redundancy. However, it still doubles the amount of required space.

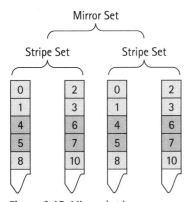

Figure 6-15: Mirrored stripes

You can introduce redundancy without requiring a full mirror. Error Correcting Codes (ECCs) and parity protection are two partial redundancy methods. ECC is mostly used for RAM memory. Disk arrays generally employ parity protection. One possible implementation is shown in Figure 6-16. Here, one of the disks is reserved as a parity disk, and the remaining disks contain data blocks. The parity is computed by applying the exclusive OR (XOR) function to all the data blocks in a stripe. If one of the disks fails, it can be regenerated by XORing all the remaining disks, including the parity disk. Parity protection can recover from a single disk failure. A second disk failure would cause data loss. The effect of this single-level data redundancy on the AFR computation can be formulated as shown in Equation 6-11, where $MTTR_{disk}$ is Mean Time To Replace (or Repair) a single failed disk.

Equation 6-11

$$AFR_{redundant} = AFR(m) \times MTTR_{disk} \times AFR(m-1)$$

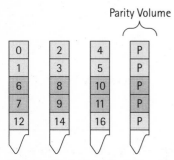

Figure 6-16: Partial redundancy with parity volume

One problem with parity protection is that every write operation requires a corresponding parity update write on the parity disk. Under a heavy load, the parity disk easily becomes the bottleneck. One solution is distributing the parity over all disks, as shown in Figure 6-17. The parity block location is shifted (rotated) over to a different disk for each stripe. This way, parity updates will be load-balanced over all the disks.

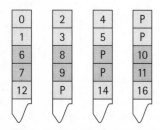

Figure 6-17: Parity protection with rotated parity blocks

Disk array data layouts and corresponding redundancy protection is classified by a Berkeley project (Patterson, 1988). There, disk arrays were termed *Redundant Array of Inexpensive Disks*

(RAID). Later, the word "inexpensive" was dropped from the acronym in favor of "independent." The original paper defined levels of RAID, which are basically different redundancy implementation categories. The currently accepted RAID levels are as follows:

- ✓ RAID0 — striping, no redundancy
- ✓ RAID1 — mirroring, full redundancy
- ✓ RAID10 — mirrored stripes, full redundancy
- ✓ RAID2 — ECC protection, not used
- ✓ RAID3 — byte-interleaved parity, single parity disk
- ✓ RAID4 — block-interleaved parity, single parity disk
- ✓ RAID5 — block-interleaved parity, rotated parity blocks
- ✓ RAID5DP — RAID5 with double parity blocks per stripe

Introducing full or partial redundancy in RAID systems has many performance implications. These RAID-related performance issues are discussed in Chapter 16.

Modeling Disk Arrays

This section presents an analytic queuing model for disk arrays. The model considers disk striping. Extensions for mirroring and parity protection are addressed at the end of this section.

TABLE 6-3 Disk Array Modeling Parameters

Variable	Definition
m	Number of available disks
j	Mean array controller service time
D	Request width (disks)
λ_A	Request arrival rate for the array

In addition to the single disk modeling parameters given in Table 6-1, disk array–specific parameters are defined in Table 6-3. The number of available disks is denoted by m. The arrival rate of requests to the array is denoted by λ_A. The requests arriving to the array are called *main requests,* and the requests arriving to individual disks are called *sub-requests*. Each main request is divided into D sub-requests, which are distributed across D disks. D is referred to as the *request width* because it is the number of disks serving a request. The relationship between the request width and the stripe depth is shown in Equation 6-12, where *ceiling* refers to the integer round-up function.

Equation 6-12

```
D = ceiling(request_length ÷ stripe_depth)
```

The disk array model is summarized in Figure 6-18. Main requests of size l blocks arrive with an arrival rate of λ_A. The arrival process is assumed to be memoryless, so the inter-arrival times are exponentially distributed. Main requests first queue at the array controller. The controller is assumed to have an average overhead of j seconds with an exponential distribution. These assumptions allow modeling of the controller queue as an M/M/1 service center. Then, the main request is divided into D sub-requests. The arrival rate for individual disks can be computed as in Equation 6-13, which assumes that the sub-requests are distributed among m disks uniformly.

Equation 6-13

$$\lambda_{disk} = (\lambda_A D)/m$$

The queuing model for the individual disks is the same as that given previously in this chapter. The only difference is that the disks serve the sub-requests instead of the main requests. The disks are modeled as M/G/1 queuing centers. In the array, the size of the sub-requests is l/D.

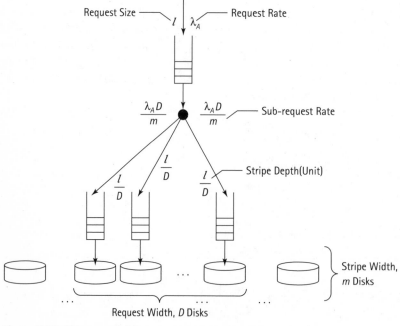

Figure 6-18: Disk array model

Because the uniform distribution assumes there are no access hot spots, the model results in a lower bound on the actual response time. In other words, assume that all disks are equally congested if multiple requests are arriving to them.

The model's solution is accomplished in two steps. First, individual disk queues are solved for their response times using the previously discussed M/G/1 model. The expected maximum of the sub-request response times is the striping response time. A main request is assumed to be finished when all of its sub-requests are finished. That's why the maximum sub-request response time is calculated.

The second step is the addition of a sub-request response to the array controller response time to find the overall main request response time, as shown in Equation 6-14.

Equation 6–14

$$R_{array} = R_{controller} + \gamma_D\, R_{disk}$$

In this equation, γ_D denotes a scaling factor that is used to approximate the maximum of D disk response times, R_{disk}. The scaling factor depends on the distribution of the disk response times. Kim and Tantawi (Kim, 1991) provide approximations for the scaling factor for various distribution functions. Equation 6-15 summarizes these scaling factors.

Equation 6–15

```
γD = 2D ÷ (D+1)          ,uniform distribution
   = 0.5772 + ln(D)      ,exponential distribution
   = 1 + CV ≤ (2log(D)),normal distribution with coefficient variation CV
```

Figure 6-19 compares simulation results obtained for various distribution assumptions with the preceding scaling factor for normal distribution. The simulation model is executed with exponential, deterministic, and normal distribution disk service times. A composite response time like the disk response time, which is the sum of various independent random variables, is expected to have a normal distribution. In Figure 6-19, the scaling factor computed for a normal distribution of R_{disk}, with a coefficient of variation equal to 1, is very close to the scaling factors obtained from the simulation of various disk service time distributions.

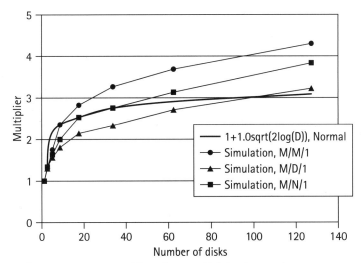

Figure 6-19: Scaling factors for the main request response times

The remaining array response time component is the controller response time, and it can be computed using the M/M/1 queue response time formula, as in Equation 6-16.

Equation 6–16

$$R_{controller} = j \div (1 - \lambda_A j)$$

Figure 6-20 illustrates the effect of the request width on workloads with various request sizes using the preceding array response time formula. The arrival rate (which is equal to throughput for an open queuing model) is set to 30 requests per second for all workloads. Note that in all cases shown in the figure, the striping always uses 64 disks. The question in hand here is the number of disks used in parallel for each request (that is the request width) to optimize the response time.

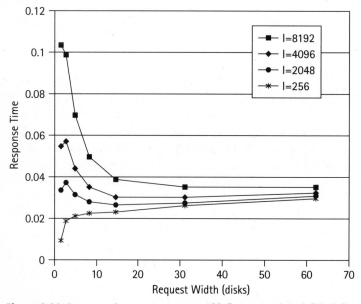

Figure 6-20: Response time versus request width (l = request length [blocks])

You can see from the figure that workloads with relatively small request sizes (l = 256 blocks) do not benefit from request widths greater than one disk. For small requests, distribution to multiple disks increases the response time. On the other hand, requests with big sizes benefit from larger request widths because of the parallel processing. Although it is not apparent in this figure, in workloads with high arrival rates, using a request width greater than an optimum value will increase the response time for all request sizes.

Request width is not a directly controllable parameter in any array system. However, stripe depth (stripe unit size) is settable in almost every disk array. It provides a means to match the striping behavior to workloads. You will find more on this in Chapter 16.

The disk array model discussed ignores redundancy, and is only applicable to disk striping (RAID0). A straightforward extension to mirroring or mirrored striping can be obtained by doubling the write operation request widths (D), which effectively doubles the arrival rate at individual disks. Read operations in mirrored arrays will be implicitly handled when the number of disks is factored in (double the number of disks compared with RAID0). Modeling arrays with parity protection is a more involved task. Chen and Towsley (Chen, 1996) provide analytic models for disk arrays with parity protection. For a detailed discussion of disk array modeling, see the references at the end of the chapter.

Magnetic Tapes

Magnetic tapes have been the storage medium of choice for backup applications ever since their introduction in the early 1950s. The tape provides the best cost/capacity alternative. The advances in hard-disk drive capacities caused people to think that disk drives might replace tape as the backup medium several times during past decades. Each time, however, tape drive manufacturers improved tape capacities and speeds to conserve the cost/capacity advantage. This is not at all surprising because tapes and hard-disk drives use very similar magnetic recording technologies.

Magnetic tapes are manufactured in various formats and with various recording technologies. The good thing about the tape "standards" is that because there are so many of them, you can choose whatever suits your application.

The three most popular recording technologies are as follows:

- ✓ **Longitudinal (linear) recording** — The tracks run in parallel, along the length of the tape.

- ✓ **Traverse recording** — The tracks are perpendicular to the length of the tape.

- ✓ **Helical scan recording** — The tracks are laid in diagonal stripes, with a 6-degree angle, in a helical fashion.

The tapes are almost always accessed sequentially. The access time components of a tape drive include the following:

- ✓ **Mount time** — Time required to grab and insert a particular tape cartridge into the tape drive. Applicable mostly to tape libraries with robotic tape mounting arms.

- ✓ **Load time** — Time for the drive mechanism to wrap the tape around the head and get ready for tape movement.

- ✓ **Positioning time** — Time to seek to the start of the data on the tape.

✓ **Data transfer time** — Time to read/write data sequentially. Governed by the tape drive bandwidth.

✓ **Rewind time** — Time to rewind the tape to the beginning so that the next time, it starts from a known position.

Tape drives are accessed with forward searches and forward reads/writes only. Most tape drives will not allow backward seeks because stop, start, and rewind cause too much wear on the tape. Therefore, the most optimal access for tapes is large, sequential read/write operations with enough input/output bandwidth to sustain the tape in full speed. Table 6-4 contains the characteristics of some popular tape standards.

TABLE 6-4 Some Recent Tape Standards

	DLT8000	Super DLT 220	LTO Ultrium 1	AIT-3
Data transfer rate (MB/s)	6	11	16	12
Capacity (GB)	40	110	100	100
Recording technology	Linear	Linear	Linear	Helical Scan
Load time (sec)	40	40	15	10

It is customary among tape manufacturers to publish their capacity and sustained data rate with a 2 to 1 data compression ratio assumption. For example, an Advanced Intelligent Tape 3 (AIT-3) tape that is advertised as having 200GB capacity and 24 MB/s bandwidth has 100GB of native (actual) capacity and 12 MB/s native transfer bandwidth.

A discussion of tape drive performance is best conducted in the context of back-up applications. More detailed analysis of tape backup performance accompanies the data backup in storage networks discussion in Chapter 15.

Optical Disks

Optical disk drives utilize a low-power laser to manipulate and sense the physical characteristics of storage media to perform write and read operations. For many years, Compact Discs (CDs) and

Magneto-optical (MO) discs have been in widespread use. Today, a Digital Versatile/Video Disc (DVD) can hold 4.7GB of digital data. Research continues to enable 36GB optical disks by 2005 that will be able to store 4 hours of High-Definition TV (HDTV) quality video.

Optical disk drives' behavior is very similar to that of hard-disk drives. The access time components are almost the same. The laser head has to seek to the target track and wait for the target sector, which are analogous to seek and rotational latencies in hard-disk drives. However, these latencies are much higher for optical disks, making them inefficient for random access. A typical optical disk has around 100–300msec seek time.

One notable difference between optical disks and hard disks is the layout of the tracks. Hard disks have concentric, circular tracks. Most optical disks have a single spiral track that extends all the way from the outer ream of the disk to the inner end. While the hard disks have a constant angular velocity (rotation speed), optical disks have a constant linear velocity. Optical heads travel over the sectors at a constant speed. This is achieved by changing the rotation speed according to the track positioned under the head. While accessing the inner tracks, the disk spins faster, and while accessing the outer tracks, the disk spins slower.

An optimization used by optical drives for short seeks is to divert the laser to the neighboring tracks optically without moving the head itself. Then, the head is moved to the target track while the read/write operation is going on. To divert the laser, the target track and the current track must be within a *proximal window size*.

The constant linear velocity of optical disks enables them to keep a constant read/write bandwidth when the access pattern is sequential. This makes optical disks appropriate for multimedia and backup/restore operations, which have almost all sequential patterns. CD drives are rated against a 1X disk speed, which has 150 KB/s bandwidth. For example, a CD drive with 24X speed would have 3.6 MB/s bandwidth.

Optical drives have a speed disadvantage when compared to hard-disk drives. Nevertheless, their cheaper price makes them appealing for some capacity-hungry applications. The constant improvement in hard-disk price, capacity, and speed makes optical disks less appealing in many cases. The development of DVDs provided a capacity boost to optical disks, but DVD applications are still very limited, except in the consumer market applications and digital libraries. Still, the vast majority of business and scientific data is stored on tapes and hard disks.

Summary

This chapter presented descriptions and performance models of baseline storage devices, and included the following topics:

Data Storage Devices

✓ The data path in storage networks contains a hierarchy of various storage devices.

✓ The most popular storage devices are RAM, hard-disk drive, magnetic tape, and optical disks.

Random Access Memory

✓ Memory capacity is doubling every generation.

✓ Memory access time lags behind capacity, causing a memory access density problem.

✓ Memory hierarchies with several cache levels are used to improve memory access times.

✓ A model of memory hierarchies can be extended to include the layers in the storage network.

✓ An important effect of memory (and buffers) in storage network models is its throughput-limiting factor.

Hard-Disk Drives

✓ A disk drive's logical layout contains zones, cylinders, tracks, and sectors.

✓ Similar to main memory, disk drives suffer from the access density problem because of the discrepancy between capacity and access time improvements.

✓ Access time components for disk drives include seek time, rotational latency, media transfer, controller overhead, and interface transfer times.

✓ Disk drive performance can be approximated using M/G/1 queuing models that incorporate the above access time components.

Disk Arrays

✓ Multiple disk drives can be used together as an array to provide larger capacity, capacity sharing, load balancing, parallel access, and improved reliability.

✓ Disk striping improves performance by spreading the accesses over many disks, but using multiple disks increases failure probability.

✓ Disk mirroring provides full redundancy against data loss, but decreases usable disk space.

✓ Parity protection provides resiliency against data loss in cases of single disk loss.

✓ RAID levels are used to classify several combinations of striping, mirroring, and parity protection architectures.

✓ Disk striping performance can be studied using models of individual disk drives, and by scaling the disk response times to account for the distributed nature of the disk array accesses.

Magnetic Tapes

✓ Magnetic tapes are most appropriate for large sequential accesses such as backup applications.

✓ Tape drives' performance characteristics mostly stem from the sequential nature of the access.

✓ Tape access time components are the mount, load, positioning, data transfer, and rewind times.

Optical Disks

✓ Optical disks provide high-density, cheap, versatile storage.

✓ Relative to magnetic disk drives, optical drives have poor random access performance.

✓ Optical disks are useful for consumer markets and special applications such as digital libraries.

References and Additional Resources

Chen, S. and D. Towsley. October 1996. *Performance Evaluation of RAID Architectures*. IEEE Transactions on Computers, 45(10), pp. 116–1130.

Presents queuing models for RAID architectures with mirroring and parity protection.

Evaluator Group, Inc. February 2001. *High Capacity Disks and Access Density*. WP-0003-1.

A detailed look at the access density problem in disk drives.

Jacob, Bruce, Peter Chen, Seth Silverman, and Trevor Mudge. October 1996. *An Analytical Model for Designing Memory Hierarchies*. IEEE Transactions on Computers, 45(10), 1180–1193.

Provides analytic models for determining the size of memory hierarchy levels using cost/performance optimizations.

Kim, Michelle Y. and Asser N. Tantawi. July 1991. *Asynchronous Disk Interleaving: Approximating Access Delays*. IEEE Transactions on Computers, 40(7), pp. 801–810.

Provides response time approximations for disk arrays. Shows that average access delay on each disk can be approximated with a normal distribution.

Lee, Edward K. and Randy H. Katz. *An Analytic Performance Model of Disk Arrays*. May 1993. Proceedings of the ACM Sigmetrics Conference on Measurement and Modeling of Computer Systems, Performance Evaluation Review, ACM Press, 21(1), pp. 98–109.

Presents analytic models for disk arrays and uses them for striping optimizations.

Menasc'e, Daniel A., Odyseas I. Pentakalos, and Yelena Yesha. May 1996. *An Analytic Model of Hierarchical Mass Storage Systems with Network-Attached Storage Devices*. SIGMETRICS 96, Philadelphia, PA, pp. 180–189.

Presents queuing models for storage hierarchies with disks and tapes.

Patterson, David A., Garth Gibson, and Randy H. Katz. June 1988. *A Case for Redundant Arrays of Inexpensive Disks (RAID)*. Proceedings of the ACM Conference on Management of Data (SIGMOD), Chicago, IL, pp. 109–116.

The original RAID classification paper.

Ruemmler, Chris and John Wilkes. March 1994. *An Introduction to Disk Drive Modeling*. Computer, 27(3), pp. 17–28.

Introduces a detailed disk drive simulation model.

Schindler, Jiri, John Linwood Griffin, Christopher R. Lumb, and Gregory R. Ganger. January 2002. *Track-Aligned Extents: Matching Access Patterns to Disk Drive Characteristics*. Proceedings of the Conference on File and Storage Technologies (FAST-02), USENIX Association, Berkeley, CA, pp. 259–274.

Introduces a technique to improve disk performance by matching the access patterns to the disk drive track layout.

Shriver, Elizabeth A.M., Arif Merchant, and John Wilkes. June 1998. *An Analytic Behavior Model for Disk Drives with Readahead Caches and Request Reordering*. SIGMETRICS 98, Madison, WI.

Detailed analytic models of disk drives with caches and command reordering.

Simitci, Huseyin and Daniel A. Reed. 1999. *Adaptive Disk Striping for Parallel Input/Output*. Proceedings of the Seventh NASA Goddard Conference on Mass Storage Systems, San Diego, CA, pp. 88–102.

Includes analytic queuing models of disk striping, which are used to drive optimization algorithms for striping parameter optimizations.

Varki, Elizabeth. *Response Time Analysis of Parallel Computer and Storage Systems*. November 2001. IEEE Transactions on Parallel and Distributed Systems, 12(11), pp. 1146–1161.

Presents an approximation of response time in fork-join queuing models that are applicable to parallel systems and storage arrays.

Worthington, B.L., G.R. Ganger, Y.N. Patt, and J. Wilkes. May 1995. *On-Line Extraction of SCSI Disk Drive Parameters*. SIGMETRICS 95, Ottawa, Canada, pp.146–156.

Presents microbenchmarks and similar online techniques for obtaining physical and logical characteristics of disk drives.

Chapter 7

Modeling Storage Interconnects

In This Chapter

The technology inside the storage devices changes incrementally, but the interfaces to storage devices (and IO devices in general) change more radically. You can transfer data more ways than you can store it. This chapter discusses IO interconnects that constitute the IO path from the compute elements to the storage elements. Discussion topics include the following:

- ✓ Classification and modeling of IO interconnects

- ✓ Host-side IO interconnects — PCI, PCI-Express, InfiniBand

- ✓ IO interconnects for accessing storage data — Advanced Technology Attachment (ATA), Serial ATA, Small Computer System Interface (SCSI), parallel SCSI, Serial-Attached SCSI, and Fibre Channel

- ✓ Storage performance implications of the aforementioned alternative technologies

IO Interconnects

As discussed several times in previous chapters, input/output in computing systems occurs on a hierarchical IO path. Each layer on this hierarchy is connected to layers above and below it using one of several possible IO interconnect technologies with various topologies and functionalities.

Figure 7-1 shows an example IO path and interconnect points. The first level of IO occurs at the system bus (the top), which connects the processor and memory modules. This is generally the highest speed and lowest latency interconnect on the IO path. The system bus is connected to a second level network, where all the external IO traffic converges. In the figure, the host interconnect is called the host bus with respect to the PCI bus, which is the prevalent IO interconnect today. However, as you will see later in the chapter, the host interconnect does not need to be a bus — other possibilities exist. The external IO paths are connected to the host IO bus using host bus adapters (HBAs). These specific devices translate the external IO traffic into local IO traffic.

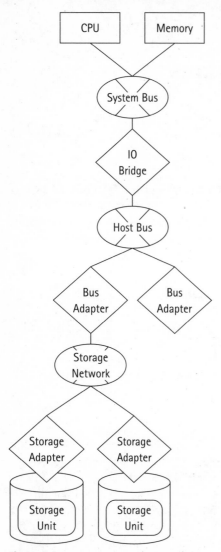

Figure 7-1: Interconnects on the IO path

The third-level IO interconnects are connected to the HBAs and constitute the external IO network. In the context of this book, the most important external IO network is the storage network. Note that although it is called a "network" here, the actual topology can take several different forms. Figure 7-2 contains four commonly used interconnect topologies — point-to-point, bus, loop, and switched network. Theoretically, all the layers in the IO path shown in Figure 7-1 can have any of the mentioned topologies.

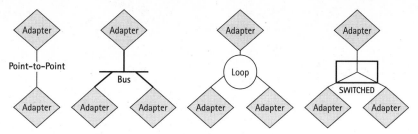

Figure 7-2: Common interconnect topologies

If the hosts are directly connected to storage devices, the storage network reduces to a simple device interconnect. Alternatively, the storage network could be a complex network with several layers. This chapter discusses alternatives for host interconnects and storage device interconnects. System (processor) buses are proprietary in nature, and will not be discussed here. Storage networks in general will be discussed in Chapter 8.

Modeling Interconnects

Modeling the interconnects that connect multiple end-nodes exhibiting complex behavior is a difficult task. However, interconnects can be classified into two high-level categories.

✓ **Shared interconnects** — If access to the interconnect requires some kind of arbitration between the connected end-points, it will be modeled as a shared interconnect.

✓ **Switched network** — If the end-nodes can send messages through the interconnect regardless of the other end-points, the resulting network will be modeled as a switched network.

Figure 7-3 depicts a shared interconnect model. A simplex (one-way) point-to-point connection, a bus, and a loop can all be modeled as shared interconnects because they require arbitration to access the connection medium. Shared resources are very difficult to model with analytic models. If you assume uniform access, you might be able to obtain simplified analytic models. The figure illustrates a simulation model for a communication bus, and includes three new symbols that are borrowed from the Hyperformix Workbench simulation tool. The triangle represents a shared resource. In the bus model, a bus transfer must obtain a bus token before it can use the bus.

N number of end-nodes generates transfer requests and queues them to obtain the bus token. Transfer requests wait at the "Obtain Bus Token" queue until it is their turn to claim the token. By using different service policies at this queue, various arbitration policies (for example, FCFS, priority, and so on) can be implemented. Because only one request can be active beyond this point, the other two service nodes do not have queues. The request that wins the arbitration (the token) spends some time in the "Arbitration Overhead" service station to account for the time needed for arbitration excluding the waiting time. Then, the transfer time on the bus is computed depending on the message length and the bus bandwidth. Finally, the request releases the bus token and proceeds to its destination node. Note again that this shared resource simulation model can be modified to include all shared medium networks.

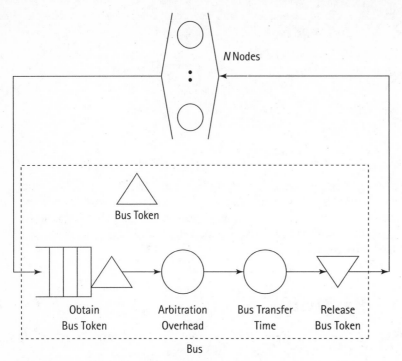

Figure 7-3: A model for shared interconnects

Figure 7-4 shows a model for a switched network. For simplicity's sake, a single switch connected to N nodes is shown. It can be easily extended to include multiple cascaded switches.

In the model, each port is modeled with two queues representing the port's input and output links. The service time at the queues are assigned according to the average routing (switching) delay at the switch and the transmission time at the link. In the middle of the switch, a non-blocking crossbar connection allows the assumption of independent access to each port.

The above model assumes there are no buffering constraints in the switch. Real network switches have limited memory buffers, and if they are connected to links with long delays and high bandwidths, buffer space becomes a constraint. In such a case, each queue in the switch model can actually be replaced with the shared interconnect model previously shown in Figure 7-3. In this case, the number of tokens is determined according to the number of available frame buffers on that link. Then, before a message can continue on a link, it must obtain an appropriate number of tokens (that is, frame buffers).

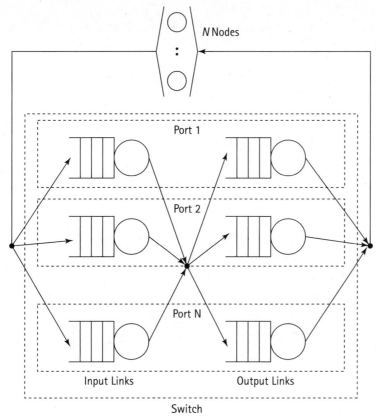

Figure 7-4: A switched network model

Host Connections

Host connections (host interconnects, or local IO buses) are the junction points where all the external IO traffic enters the system. Advances in network and processor performance put a strain on the host interconnects from both sides, making their performance critically important. The next three sections discuss current and emerging host interconnect technologies.

PCI

Peripheral Component Interconnect (PCI) became a standard in 1993 and provided a leapfrog performance improvement over the bus architectures it replaced, namely ISA and Extended Industry-Standard Architecture (EISA). The original PCI bus carried 32-bit data over a 33-MHz connection, providing 133 MB/s data bandwidth. In one bus cycle, a memory address is put on the bus, followed by the data in the next cycle. In the burst mode, longer data can be accessed per address cycle.

PCI defines an architecture where a hierarchy of buses creates a tree-like system topology. Figure 7-5 illustrates a PCI tree with two buses. You must have a single root controller at the root of the tree to map out the rest of the topology. The whole PCI system defines a single address domain. PCI defines a memory load/store architecture where the end-nodes can read or write anywhere in the memory space defined by PCI. Multiple PCI buses are connected using PCI-to-PCI bridges.

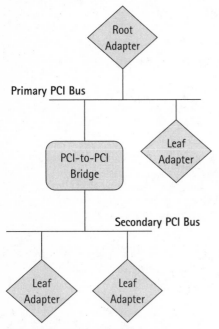

Figure 7-5: PCI tree topology

PCI chipsets contain buffers to match the speed of faster buses with slower buses. A single active transfer can occur in the PCI tree. This significantly limits the bus's scalability. The bus's bandwidth is shared among all connected devices. 133 MB/s might seem sufficient for many applications. However, when Symmetric Multi-Processing (SMP) systems with multiple central processing units (CPUs), multiple gigabit network cards, clustering interconnect cards, and storage controllers are considered, the host IO bus quickly becomes the performance and scalability bottleneck.

PCI has been updated many times. Bus width has increased to 64 bits from 32 bits. And bus frequency has increased to 66 MHz from 33 MHz. Each of these increases effectively doubles the bandwidth. Recently, PCI-X standard increased the frequency to 133 MHz, providing roughly 1 GB/s bus bandwidth.

The problem with width and frequency increases in buses like PCI is that these updates shorten the maximum possible bus length. Components must be packed closely together to eliminate signal skew between the lines. The result is a reduced number of slots in successive PCI generations. The latest PCI-X standard allows only one slot per PCI controller—hardly a bus configuration.

One other potential problem with PCI IO buses is the single fault domain. If one of the devices on the PCI tree locks up or exhibits another faulty behavior, it affects the whole bus and possibly the whole system.

System vendors and device manufacturers proposed several replacements for PCI. A serial, switched interconnect named PCI-Express (formerly third-generation IO or 3GIO) is promising to alleviate host IO problems.

PCI-Express

PCI-Express is a high-speed, packetized, chip-to-chip IO interconnect. It is being promoted as an upgrade/replacement to the PCI bus (PCI-SIG, 2002). PCI-Express reflects the move to serial interconnects in other interconnect technologies (for example, Serial ATA, InfiniBand, Serial-Attached SCSI, and so on).

Serial interface of PCI-Express reduces the pin count considerably compared to parallel buses. Full-duplex communication in PCI-Express can be achieved over four lines. Serial interface also enables much higher link frequencies. High-speed and switched networks also increase the scalability in terms of performance and connectivity. By cascading switching elements, almost any number of devices can be connected. The packet-switched network isolates the devices for better fault containment. If a device fails, it will not affect other devices.

Two other high-speed, chip-to-chip interconnects compete with PCI-Express: Hyper-transport and RapidIO. They are also being used to connect components on a motherboard at speeds much faster than PCI. However, these two interconnects are expected to stay strictly on the motherboards or backplanes, and do not allow you to attach external devices. They are more appropriate for embedded, special applications. Thus, they are not direct competitors to PCI-Express in the host IO bus expansions arena.

One other related key technology that is expected to have an impact on host IO interconnects is InfiniBand.

InfiniBand

Among all the interconnect technologies, InfiniBand's role is the most difficult to define. This stems from the fact that this high-speed, comprehensive network technology can play various roles on the IO path (InfiniBand, 2001).

InfiniBand can be used as a chip-to-chip interconnect on the motherboards, just like PCI-Express, Hyper-transport, and RapidIO. It can be used to replace the current host IO buses to allow external IO devices. It can also extend beyond a single host, and create a system area network where all compute nodes, communication nodes, and storage nodes are connected. It is in this last role that InfiniBand will have the most impact (Mellanox Technologies, 2001).

Figure 7-6 depicts a typical InfiniBand deployment. The channel adapters are central to the operations of the InfiniBand network. These are the end-node connection points. To indicate where they reside, they are referred to as Host Channel Adapter (HCA) or Target Channel Adapter (TCA). However, the functionalities are almost the same. On the host side, HCAs are connected to a system bus through system chipsets. Until chipsets are able to support InfiniBand natively, adapter cards that connect to other host IO buses are available.

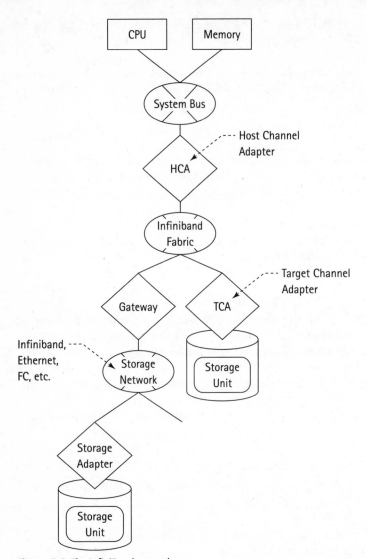

Figure 7-6: The InfiniBand network

Target devices are connected to the InfiniBand network (IB fabric) using TCAs. The described network structure is not radically different from many other networks. What makes InfiniBand unique is that it combines all sorts of IO networks and enables sharing of IO resources (TCAs) among many hosts. For example, in the IB fabric, there could be TCAs for storage devices, LAN and WAN connections over Ethernet, video displays, backup devices, and so on. In addition, these IO targets can be shared among many hosts that are connected to the IB fabric through HCAs. This enables all sorts of new form factor innovations for server platforms.

The IB fabric is expected to play an important role in server farms that are constructed with many *blade-servers*. Blade-servers are specialized, single-board computers that are mounted vertically to racks in large quantities to provide space efficiency and high performance. Blade-servers can be plugged into an InfiniBand backplane to share all other IO resources available in the system. InfiniBand specification defines the semantics of how this sharing will occur in great detail. The fabric is partitioned into subnets, which define the access domains. Access permissions are enforced at the transport level.

Several factors enable high-performance transmission in the IB fabric:

✓ IB is a packet-switched network as opposed to having shared buses.

✓ The links can be trunked (combined) together to create higher-speed links. The original link speed (1X) is defined at 2.5 Gb/s, which can carry 2 Gb/s after signal encoding is accounted for. IB devices are expected to support 4X (10 Gb/s), and 12X (30 Gb/s) speeds. Full-duplex communication will effectively double these bandwidths.

✓ Most of the protocol stack is implemented in hardware inside HCAs or TCAs. A comparison with the ISO network layers shows that network layers 1 through 4 (physical, data link, network, and transport) are executing in hardware. This implementation is much faster than if these functionalities were required from software running on the host platform. This also reduces the host CPU's load.

✓ InfiniBand communication is based on the Remote Direct Memory Access (RDMA)-based communication methods that are used directly by the application software. These methods are borrowed from Virtual Interface Architecture (VIA) (Buonadonna, 1998). The messages are sent from and received directly by the user space memory locations. This eliminates costly memory copy operations between user space and kernel space memory, which are generally necessary in other communication methods such as TCP/IP/Ethernet. User space communication also eliminates many context switches between user threads and operating system threads. The end result is low-latency communication.

Besides IO sharing, InfiniBand is expected to be important in server clustering implementations. Low-latency communication is essential for the Interprocessor Communication (IPC) messages exchanged between clustered servers.

InfiniBand supports four communication models:

✓ **Reliable Connection (RC)** — Establishes a connection between the end-points and sends messages reliably. The messages are checked for correctness and the receiver end-point acknowledges the receipt.

✓ **Unreliable Datagram (UD)** — Without establishing a connection, a single datagram can be sent to any end-point without any transmission guarantees.

✓ **Reliable Datagram (RD)** — Without establishing a connection, a single datagram can be sent to any end-point reliably, with receipt acknowledgements.

✓ **Unreliable Connection (UC)** — Establishes a connection between the end-points, but the transmission is not guaranteed.

The primary advantage (a radical approach to eliminating IO bottleneck) of InfiniBand is also its biggest drawback. IB requires an ecosystem where system, network, device, operating system, and application software vendors cooperate. Therefore, IB deployments will be gradual, and IB will coexist with all other IO methods rather than replacing any.

Table 7-1 summarizes the features of the popular host IO interconnects.

TABLE 7-1 IO Interconnect Features

Feature	PCI-X	PCI-Express (3GIO)	RapidIO	Hyper-Transport	InfiniBand
Bandwidth	8.5 Gb/s	2.5, 5, 10, 20 Gb/s	16, 32 Gb/s	12.8, 25.6, 51.2 Gb/s	2.5, 10, 30 Gb/s
Pin count	90	4, 8, 16, 32	40, 76	55, 103, 197	4, 16, 48
Physical media	PCB	PCB, connectors	PCB	PCB	PCB, Fiber, Copper
Packet size	N/A	256B	256B	64B	Up to 4KB
Flow control	N/A	End-to-end	End-to-end	End-to-end	End-to-end
Link length	Inches	30 inches	Inches	Inches	30in (PCB), 17m (Copper)

It took almost ten years for PCI to replace all the ISA slots in the servers. Therefore, you can expect PCI, PCI-X, PCI-Express, and InfiniBand to co-exist on server motherboards for some time to come and the changes to occur gradually.

Major server and processor vendors indicate that they position PCI-Express as an upgrade to the traditional PCI interconnects, and InfiniBand as an out-of-the-box interconnect for server clustering applications.

Storage Device Connections

Storage device connections evolve together with the rest of the computing technology. For balanced system performance, every new generation of computers requires new generations of storage interconnects. Storage device interconnects can have topologies like buses, loops, and networks just like the rest of an IO network. Making the distinction between device interfaces and storage networks is difficult when the same interface type is actually used to create the entire storage network.

Currently, Advanced Technology Attachment (ATA), parallel Small Computer System Interface (SCSI), Fibre Channel (FC), and their several variants are the most established storage device interconnects for open systems. Figure 7-7 shows the recent history of the storage interconnect advances and some projections for the near future. FC started with a very high bandwidth at the time of its inception and 200 MB/s FC (full duplex) is expected to satisfy most storage network demands for a while. (Future performance target speeds at 10Gb/s are on the horizon.) Parallel SCSI continues to double its bandwidth. However, its shared bus topology restricts the actual sustainable performance. ATA, driven by its cost and performance improvements, will be utilized in storage networks more and more.

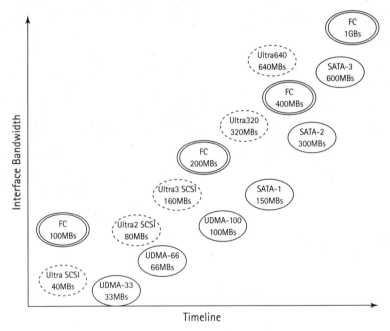

Figure 7-7: Storage interconnect bandwidth timeline

The next couple sections discuss these storage interconnects.

ATA

The Integrated Device Electronics (IDE) interface was developed by PC and disk drive manufacturers around 1986 to connect disk drives to motherboards. When it was standardized by the American National Standards Institute (ANSI) X3T10 group, it was renamed *Advanced Technology Attachment*. When the standard was enhanced later as ATA-2, it was also called *Enhanced IDE (EIDE)*.

ATA is based on the 16-bit IBM ISA (Industry Standard Architecture) bus. Later versions (ATA-2, -3, and -4) use a 32-bit bus. An ATA bus can accommodate only two devices (master and slave), which severely limits its scalability in high-performance systems. Starting with ATA-2, ATA controllers began to support Direct Memory Access (DMA) transfers. ATA-4 supported synchronous

DMA transfers at a 33 MB/s burst rate, so it was also called *UltraDMA-33*. UltraDMA controllers were later enhanced to support 66 MB/s and 100 MB/s burst rates.

ATA cables are parallel, ribbon cables with limited lengths restricted to the system chassis. The restrictions on cable length and the number of devices led to the development of a serial interface for ATA drives.

Serial ATA

Since serial interfaces do not have to worry about synchronization between multiple data lines, they can execute at a much higher signal rate and for a much longer cable length than the corresponding parallel interfaces. Reduced cable clutter is another advantage of serial interfaces such as serial ATA (SATA) (SerialATA, 2001). Speed and connectivity alone would not make serial ATA preferable to FC in any configuration. What makes serial ATA drives attractive for some markets is the price advantage of ATA disk drives.

The vast majority of disk drives are ATA drives, and their market is expected to grow in the future. The economies of scale enable the amortization of the development costs over millions of drives and reduce the cost per megabyte of data stored on ATA drives. Together with the improvements enabled by serial ATA, ATA drives became attractive for some storage networking environments, which is traditionally dominated by high-end SCSI and FC disk drives. Disk arrays with SATA drives and FC or SCSI front-end connections can create cost-effective solutions for online backup or data mirroring applications.

The cost/performance advantage of ATA drives led some vendors to design disk-to-disk backup solutions, which enable reduced backup windows and faster restores. These disk-based backup systems can be used as a staging layer in front of the traditional tape-based backup systems. Such performance optimizations are discussed later in the book.

Initial SATA interfaces are compatible with extant operating system software and ATA device drivers, without any modification. Future SATA implementation improvements will utilize special host-side device drivers to provide advanced command management capabilities, which are generally associated with SCSI drives. For example, SATA drives will be able to queue commands and deliver results out of order using queues and buffers resident in the host memory. This is in contrast to the parallel ATA interface, which does not allow multiple pending commands at the device.

SCSI Architecture

Small Computer System Interface was developed by Shugart Associates (which later became Seagate). It was originally called Shugart Associates System Interface. When it was standardized as ANSI X3.131-1986, it was called SCSI-1. SCSI-1 defined a parallel bus for interfacing computers with intelligent peripheral devices, such as hard-disk drives, CD-ROM, printers, and scanners. SCSI's popularity resulted in successive additions to the standard, and it evolved as an interface over many types of physical connections. SCSI standards started defining a framework where SCSI is used as a protocol for communicating storage information over numerous transport and physical layers.

It is necessary to distinguish the SCSI architecture from its specific implementations, like parallel SCSI interface. This section discusses the general SCSI architecture, which encapsulates almost all of the modern storage interfaces. The most well known SCSI implementation, the parallel SCSI interface, is discussed in the next section.

In literature, it is customary to use the term SCSI to refer to parallel SCSI implementations. However, SCSI is more than that.

SCSI architecture defines several layers and several standards at each level, as shown in Figure 7-8 (INCITS, 2002).

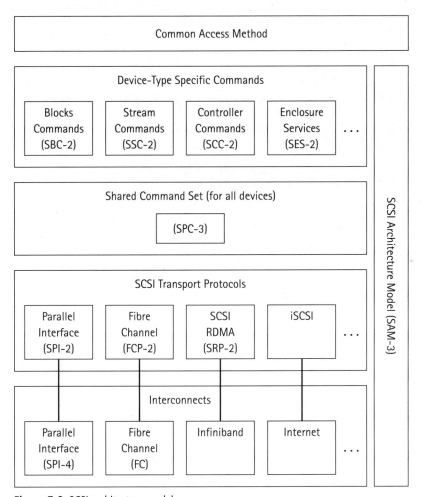

Figure 7-8: SCSI architecture model

SCSI layers start from the host access APIs and extend to several physical implementation standards. The functionality of each layer can be summarized as follows:

✓ **Common Access Method** — Defines a host software architecture and common interface for access to all SCSI devices. An implementation example is the Advanced SCSI Peripheral Interface (ASPI), which provides a common interface for accessing SCSI devices under Windows operating systems. Advanced Technology Attachment Packet Interface (ATAPI) enables Integrated Drive Electronics (IDE) devices to look like SCSI devices and to be accessed through ASPI.

✓ **Device-Type Specific Commands** — Define device models and commands for specific devices. Specify required command/response behavior for initiators/targets of the same type. For example, SCSI Block Commands 2 (SBC-2) standardizes the access to block-oriented devices such as hard-disk drives. Similarly, SCSI Stream Commands 2 (SSC-2) is for streaming devices such as tape devices.

✓ **Shared Command Set** — Defines the commands and behavior common to all SCSI devices.

✓ **SCSI Transport Protocols** — Define the requirements for exchanging information (commands, responses, and so on) between SCSI devices. Transport protocol examples include SCSI Parallel Interface 2 (SPI-2), Fibre Channel Protocol 2 (FCP-2), SCSI RDMA Protocol (SRP-2), and Internet SCSI (iSCSI).

✓ **Interconnects** — Standards defining the underlying communication channels between SCSI devices. These standards generally define the electrical and signaling requirements for device interoperability. Most of the time, a one-to-one correspondence exists between transport protocols and interconnects. For example, FCP-2 is designed to communicate over Fibre Channel (FC) networks. There are notable exceptions to this — for example, Internet Fibre Channel Protocol (iFCP) will be discussed later in the book.

In summary, SCSI is the storage systems' workhorse, and almost all of the current and future envisioned storage protocols implement or inherit from SCSI.

Parallel SCSI

The original SCSI standard, SCSI-1, defined a parallel, 8-bit data bus, and 5 MB/s bandwidth, that can connect eight storage devices including the host adapter. Successive generations doubled the data rate (10, 20, 40, 80, 160, 320, and 640 MB/s), either by doubling the number of data bits or by doubling the bus frequency. Although the earlier versions of SCSI devices experienced compatibility problems, later versions provided compatibility between different manufacturers' products, as well as backward and forward compatibility between successive SCSI versions.

When people talk about SCSI without any qualifiers, they generally mean parallel SCSI as opposed to the SCSI architecture, which encapsulates all sorts of transport and physical networks.

The main problem with parallel SCSI is the large number of different cable types that are not compatible. SCSI connections with *single-ended* drivers and cables support up to 6-meter lengths as opposed to *differential* drivers and cables, which extend up to 25 meters.

Figure 7-9 illustrates the logical components of an SCSI bus. The bus is constructed by daisy-chaining the devices as a string. On the bus, there must be at least one *initiator* and one *target*. Initiators are able to send IO commands to targets. SCSI host bus adapters (HBAs) are the most prevalent form of initiators. Some devices can have dual roles as both targets and initiators. Targets are the peripheral devices, most prominently storage devices such as hard disks or tape drives. The target could be a complete storage subsystem that hides behind a huge number of other storage devices. In such a case, a target can present multiple Logical Units (LUs) to the SCSI bus as separate devices, accessed through that particular subsystem.

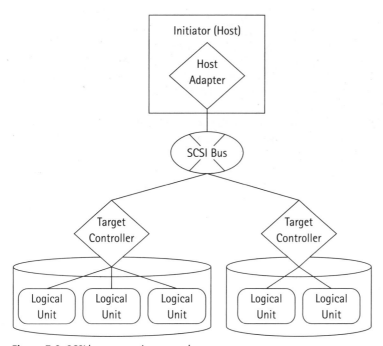

Figure 7-9: SCSI bus connection example

An SCSI bus and connected devices work like a big state machine, moving from state to state with a tightly controlled logic. In SCSI, these states are called *bus phases*. Figure 7-10 depicts the bus phases required for a typical SCSI command. The transitions through the phases occur as follows:

1. If nothing else is going on, the bus is in the Bus Free state.

2. The initiator puts a signal on the bus to indicate that it wants to use the bus. This is called the Arbitration state. If multiple nodes are arbitrating for the bus at the same time, the node with the highest SCSI ID wins the arbitration.

3. In the select phase, the initiator puts the address of the target with which it wants to communicate on the SCSI bus.

4. The command is sent on the bus.

5. The data is communicated in the data in/out phase.

6. After command completion, status information is sent.

7. The optional message in/out phases are mostly for exchanging exception information and might be absent for a given command.

8. Finally, the bus is released and goes back to the Bus Free phase.

9. The cycle starts again.

In SCSI, data exchanges use one of two transfer modes — asynchronous or synchronous. In asynchronous mode, each data exchange requires a complete handshake between the source and the destination depending on whether the target or initiator is sending the data. Request (REQ) and ACK signals determine the pace of the transfer. In synchronous mode, the data is transferred without any handshakes up to a pre-negotiated period of time. Because of the reduced overhead and latency, synchronous transfers are much faster.

The SCSI Ultra320 standard introduced *paced transfers,* where a parity line is used as a free-running clock, and the data transfers can continue without any handshakes. Paced transfers reduce the overhead and improve the useable bus bandwidth. Ultra320 also introduced *packetized transfers,* where command, status, and data are transferred in packets called *information units*. Multiple commands and responses can be transferred in a single communication.

Until Ultra320, all the previous SCSI standards transferred command and status information in 8-bit, asynchronous mode. This created a latency bottleneck and prevented the full utilization of the SCSI bus bandwidth, which has actually doubled with every new SCSI generation. In Ultra320, command and status are also exchanged as information units using paced or synchronous transfers. This reduces the command overhead that impaired earlier versions of SCSI. Another performance improvement introduced by Ultra320 is *quick arbitration and selection*, which enables the transition of bus ownership from one target to another without the Bus Free state. This way, transfers to and from multiple targets can progress back-to-back.

Serial-Attached SCSI

The parallel physical layer of SCSI plagues the advancements in SCSI technology as much as it plagues parallel ATA. Parallel interfaces have speed, configuration, and distance limitations. SCSI Trade Association (STA) started working on a serial physical layer for SCSI that will use physical connections of Serial ATA, the SCSI protocol set, and Fibre Channel framing (INCITS, 2002b).

Serial-Attached SCSI (SAS) will allow point-to-point connections like other serial interfaces and will allow scaling up to 128 devices. Parallel SCSI interfaces are expected to have serious challenges at 640 MB/s (Ultra640), and SAS is positioned as a natural extension to the SCSI line. Because Serial-Attached SCSI shares the same physical layer as Serial ATA, system designers will be able to provide systems that support both interfaces on the same platform. This will allow customers to configure their systems with cheaper and lower-performing ATA drives, or more costly, but high-performing SCSI drives, depending on their needs and budgets.

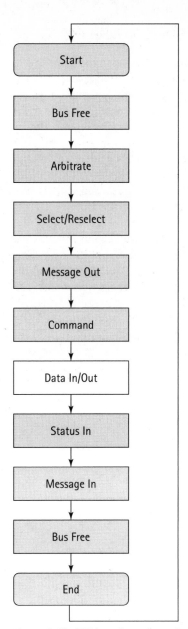

Figure 7-10: SCSI bus phases for a single command

Fibre Channel

Fibre Channel (FC) was introduced to overcome the limitations of parallel SCSI storage interconnects. FC allows you to attach more devices, using serial links over copper and fiber cables. FC can
be used in point-to-point, loop, and fabric topologies. FC fabrics are the backbone of storage
networks; they will be discussed in Chapter 8. FC arbitrated loops (FC-AL) are generally used for

attaching storage devices to hosts, FC hubs, or switches. FC-AL, as a storage interconnect, is discussed in this section.

Fibre Channel devices use two addressing schemes. Device manufacturers assign a 64-bit name to each device, commonly known as World Wide Name (WWN). This name is unique and assigned from a pool provided to the manufacturer by IEEE. In addition, FC devices have dynamic addresses. Port addresses are assigned according to the topology. 24-bit addresses are assigned by FC switches if the device is part of a fabric. This enables 16 million addresses. On an arbitrated-loop, the devices themselves choose the loop addresses, which are 8 bits long, during loop initialization. Because only addresses with certain bit patterns are allowed, you have 127 usable addresses on an arbitrated-loop.

Private devices can communicate with only those devices on their own arbitrated-loop. Public devices can communicate with devices outside of the loop using the fabric connections.

Figure 7-11 illustrates a dual-loop architecture. The loops contain five storage devices and a host with two ports each. Each closed loop creates a chain of ports where data can be transmitted unidirectionally. A port that needs to transmit data must obtain the ownership of the loop. This process is called *arbitration*. The sending port waits until the loop is idle, and then transmits an arbitration request around the loop. If the arbitration request returns to the original port, the arbitration is won and the loop is owned by that port. The source port can then send an OPEN request to any port on the loop to start communicating. After the communication is finished, the origin port closes the target, releases the loop, and another arbitration cycle begins.

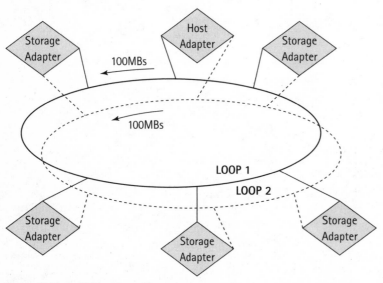

Figure 7-11: Dual FC arbitrated loops

Each port on the loop has a priority defined by its port address. Higher port numbers have higher priorities. In an arbitration cycle, a higher-priority port can replace the arbitration message of a lower-priority port with its own arbitration message. It is possible to use a fairness algorithm on an FC loop, such that in a predetermined period every port on the loop has a chance of winning the arbitration. Even though this seems to avoid starvation problems, it might cause performance problems when a single host adapter accesses several storage devices simultaneously. The best performance is obtained when the host completes command send operations to all the devices before receiving any data back. If, because of a fairness algorithm, a device obtains the loop and starts sending/receiving data before other devices have received their commands, the possibility of command processing and communication overlap is reduced and performance may degrade. A similar behavior is observed for SCSI buses (Barve, 1999).

When a single host initiator port is connected to multiple storage target ports on a single FC arbitrated-loop, the host port must be set to the highest priority and the access fairness algorithm must be disabled. This increases the possibility of overlap between command processing and data communication and improves performance.

The mapping of the SCSI command set onto the FC physical layer enables storage access on an FC network (loop or fabric). The resulting high-level mapping is called *SCSI Fibre Channel Protocol* (FCP) (NCITS, 2001). Effectively, FC is substituted for the parallel SCSI bus.

In FC, a single cycle of communication between the initiator and target (between the OPEN and CLOSE requests) is called an *exchange*. Each exchange is divided into *sequences* that correspond to the phases of a single IO operation. Finally, each sequence consists of *frames,* which are the units of data exchange in FC.

In FCP, each SCSI command is mapped onto an *exchange*. For each SCSI command, the initiator starts an exchange with the target. This exchange is used to transmit the command, data, and responses. FCP allows multiple commands to be active using multiple, simultaneously active exchanges, practically enabling command queuing in a target.

A loop can be used as a full-duplex connection, allowing data sends on the output ports and data receives on the input ports simultaneously. Using a loop where one half of the loop transmits from the initiator to the target and the other half of the loop transmits from the target back to the initiator is termed *spatial reuse*, and effectively doubles the useable bandwidth. Unfortunately, current disk drives do not allow simultaneous data in and out. However, advanced FC drives allow data transfers in one direction while receiving commands in the other direction. This enables overlapping between command and data transmission phases of consecutive IO operations between the same initiator and target pair.

Media access time and data transfer time are not always additive for FC attached storage devices (Du, 1998). Consider the example given in Figure 7-12. The storage device response time starts with some initial sequential overhead. In the case of a disk drive, this period is the initial command processing time and disk latency. Storage devices, such as disk drives, generally have two functionally separate hardware modules, one of which reads/writes from/to the storage medium into/from a staging buffer. The second module transmits to/from the staging buffer from/to the external interface. The work of these two modules can potentially overlap. After some amount of media read, the loop interface starts the arbitration and transfers the available data at the same time another piece of the stored data is read from the medium. This can work in a pipelined fashion. When the loop is busy or the media access is slow, stalls can occur between successive transfers. However, for a long transfer and an uncongested loop, the device response time is determined by the media access time.

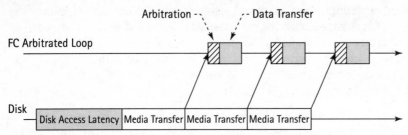

Figure 7-12: Overlapping disk media transfers and loop data transfers

Summary

This chapter discussed the IO interconnects that make up the IO paths from compute elements to storage elements, and included the following observations:

IO Interconnects

✓ An IO path consists of several layers connected through various communication interconnects.

✓ The IO interconnects can be classified as system (processor) interconnects, host IO interconnects, and the external network interconnects.

✓ The most popular interconnect topologies include point-to-point, bus, loop, and switched networks. Each layer of the IO hierarchy can have any of these topologies.

Modeling Interconnects

✓ Point-to-point, bus, and loop interfaces can be modeled as shared interconnects. Sharing (resource contention) is difficult to model with analytic models. Simulation techniques with resource models can be used to study shared interconnects.

✓ Switched networks can be modeled with routing queue models.

✓ Network switches with buffer constraints can be modeled using shared resources.

Host Connections

✓ PCI has evolved for several generations to provide higher bandwidth as a host IO bus. However, it is a shared bus, which limits the number of devices that can be connected efficiently. In addition, because PCI is a single fault domain, it makes fault-tolerant solutions difficult to implement. Any faulty device can take the bus down.

✓ PCI-Express provides a hardware upgrade to PCI bus while preserving software compatibility with the legacy PCI software. PCI-Express provides packetized communication between system components over serial links.

✓ Technically, InfiniBand can be deployed at all levels of the IO path. However, it is expected to play a significant role as a systems area network in data centers with large numbers of clustered servers and IO subsystems.

Storage Device Connections

✓ More ATA drives exist than any other storage device. Economies of scale make ATA drives cost-effective. However, ATA drives are slow. The Serial-ATA interface will provide higher bandwidths and better potential for later bandwidth upgrades, giving ATA a performance boost.

✓ SCSI architecture defines a layered model for storage access over standardized interfaces. Device-specific commands, transport protocols, and physical interconnects are independently defined.

✓ Parallel SCSI interface's performance has doubled several times in the past decade with every new SCSI generation. Parallel SCSI interface has configuration and cabling difficulties. Because it is a shared bus, it does not scale well to higher number of devices. Serial-Attached SCSI borrows SATA's physical layer and provides an upgrade path for SCSI.

✓ Fibre Channel implements the SCSI command set over serial interfaces (copper or fiber optic). FC can connect many more devices than parallel SCSI, and can be dynamically configured (is hot pluggable). FC storage communication streams are divided into exchanges, sequences, and frames.

References and Additional Resources

Barve, Rakesh, Phillip B. Gibbons, Bruce K. Hillyer, Yossi Matias, Elizabeth Shriver, and Jeffrey Scott Vitter. May 1999. *Round-Like Behavior in Multiple Disks on a Bus*, Proceedings of the Sixth Workshop on Input/Output in Parallel and Distributed Systems. ACM Press, pp. 1–9.

A good example for "unintended consequences." Shows that a fairness algorithm in the operating system causes a convoy (round) behavior of the disks on a SCSI bus. Presents an analytic model to predict performance.

Buonadonna, P., A. Geweke, and D. Culler. November 1998. *An Implementation and Analysis of the Virtual Interface Architecture*. Supercomputing '98, Orlando, FL.

A report on an early implementation (over Myrinet) of Virtual Interface Architecture (VIA), discussing the mechanisms for user-level communication implementations.

Du, David H. C., Tai-Sheng Chang, Jenwei Hsieh, Yuewei Wang, and Sangyup Shim. April–June 1998. *Interface Comparisons: SSA versus FC-AL*. IEEE Concurrency, 6(2), pp. 55–70.

Compares FC-AL with Serial Storage Architecture (SSA), another serial interface. Includes descriptions of their trace-based simulation models.

InfiniBand Trade Association. June 19, 2001. *InfiniBand Architecture Specification Volume 1&2*, Release 1.0.a.

All the standards documents about InfiniBand can be found at InfiniBand TA's Web site, www.infinibandta.org. IO in InfiniBand is defined in a separate annex to the standard.

Mellanox Technologies. December 10, 2001. *Understanding PCI Bus, 3GIO and InfiniBand Architecture*, Doc. Num. WP120501100.

A white paper by an InfiniBand vendor on the relative features and positions of these three technologies. Available at www.mellanox.com.

NCITS T10 Committee. November 1, 2001. *SCSI Fibre Channel Protocol-2 (FCP-2)*, Project: 1144-D, Rev: 07a.

T10 is the technical committee that proposes all SCSI protocol draft standards. This document contains the second generation Fibre Channel Protocol. It is available at www.t10.org.

INCITS T10 Committee. July 7, 2002. *SCSI Architecture Model-3 (SAM-3)*, Project: 1561-D, Rev: 01.

This working draft describes the third-generation SCSI Architecture Model. It is available at www.t10.org.

INCITS T10 Committee. July 24, 2002. *Serial Attached SCSI (SAS)*, Project: 1562-D, Rev: 01.

This working draft describes a physical interface for SAS that is compatible with Serial ATA. In addition, it describes protocols for transporting SCSI commands to SAS devices and transporting ATA commands to SATA devices. It is available at www.t10.org.

PCI-SIG. July 2002. *PCI-Express Specification 1.0*.

Details about PCI-Express (formerly 3GIO) can be found at PCI Special Interest Group's Web site, www.pcisig.com, and Intel's Web site, www.intel.com.

SerialATA Workgroup. August 29, 2001. *Serial ATA: High Speed Serialized AT Attachment*, Revision 1.0.

This SATA specification and other information about SATA is available at www.t10.org.

Chapter 8

Modeling Storage Networks

In This Chapter

Networking topics, which were traditionally tied to data communication networks, abound in storage discussions as well. With the advent of storage networks, understanding networking concepts is a necessity even for storage applications. This chapter contains introductory descriptions and performance modeling concepts of networking topics related to storage. The discussion includes the following topics:

- ✓ The network layers model, which facilitates an understanding of networking concepts

- ✓ Fibre Channel networking concepts, including fabrics, port types, service classes, and flow control

- ✓ IP storage networking proposals, including Internet Small Computer System Interface (iSCSI), Internet Fibre Channel Protocol (iFCP), Fibre Channel over TCP/IP (FCIP)

- ✓ Gigabit Ethernet and TCP/IP performance concepts, including CPU utilization and protocol offloading, jumbo frames, and buffer sizes

- ✓ Wide area network (WAN) connections for extending storage networks

- ✓ Models for network switches, routers, and arbitrated loops

- ✓ Simulation and analytic modeling examples for storage networks

Storage Networks

This chapter discusses storage networks under two major categories. The incumbent storage networking technology is Fibre Channel. Over many years, Fibre Channel fabrics became the dominant technology for high-performance, shared, long-distance, highly available storage networking. Lately, a couple of storage networking protocols based on TCP/IP/Ethernet have begun to emerge that complement and, in some cases replace, FC fabrics. The market division between these storage networking technologies is yet to be seen. Storage networks are therefore discussed as *Fibre Channel storage networks* and *IP storage networks*.

The study of networking concepts has traditionally been based on layered models. The most widely used and copied networking model is the Open Systems Interconnect (OSI) model for networking. The OSI model contains seven network layers:

✓ **L7 (Application)** — Upper-layer protocols that add value to the network communication by providing specific services to the user.

✓ **L6 (Presentation)** — Enables applications to use different data formats over the network. Generally not implemented as a separate layer.

✓ **L5 (Session)** — Establishes, manages, and terminates communication (sessions) between cooperating applications. Presentation and session layers are often implemented as part of the application layer, or they are omitted.

✓ **L4 (Transport)** — Adds a layer on the network that provides reliable communication with end-to-end flow control and error recovery mechanisms.

✓ **L3 (Network)** — Contains protocols to route the data packets through the network using network layer addresses. Provides higher layers with a network-independent interface for data transmission.

✓ **L2 (Data Link)** — The protocols that govern the encoding and decoding of information on the physical layer constitute the data link layer. Can include controls for overflow protection, error detection, and correction. Packet routing is performed using physical layer addresses.

✓ **L1 (Physical)** — Includes the hardware medium for communication. The physical links (copper cable, optical cable, radio wave, and so on) and connectors are part of the physical layer.

This layering is a conceptual tool that aids the discussion of networking concepts. You will find many references to these layers in the following discussion.

Fibre Channel Storage Networks

Chapter 7 introduced Fibre Channel Arbitrated Loop (FC-AL) topology as a storage device interconnect. Although loop and point-to-point FC connections may be sufficient for small storage networks, a switched network topology enhances FC by providing better scalability, manageability, and performance. When FC devices are connected to several interconnected switches, the resulting network is an *FC fabric*. Loop devices can also participate in the fabric through special ports.

The devices (end-nodes and switching elements) connect to the fabric using these interface types:

✓ **N_Port (Node Port)** — FC ports on end-nodes. For example, the Host Bus Adapters (HBAs) on servers and storage subsystems have N_Ports.

✓ **NL_Port (Node Loop Port)** — End devices connect to an FC-AL chain using NL_Ports.

✓ **F_Port (Fabric Port)** — FC ports on FC switches that connect to N_Ports and provide fabric connectivity to the end-devices.

✓ **FL_Port (Fabric Loop Port)** — Ports on FC switches that provide fabric connectivity to NL_Ports on an FC loop.

✓ **E_Port (Extension Port)** — Multiple switches connect together using E_ports and allow extension of the fabric network. The link between two E_Ports is called an *Inter-Switch Link (ISL)*.

Figure 8-1 illustrates these port types on a simple FC fabric. In the figure, two switches are connected with E_Ports to form a single fabric.

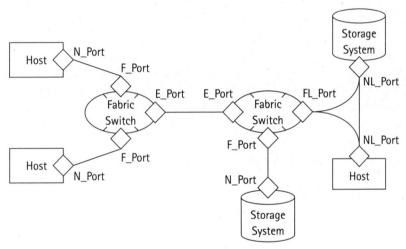

Figure 8-1: FC port types

FC hubs physically look like switches. However, they are used to form FC loops and do not perform any switching function. Hubs combine the loop connections centrally. When the loop is physically inside a hub, it is much easier to administer. In addition, if one part of the loop fails, FC-AL hubs have logic circuits to bypass the failed part via port by-pass technology and continue operations on the rest of the loop.

In the previous chapter, FC SCSI Protocol (FCP) was introduced as a mapping of the SCSI commands onto the FC physical links. This mapping is based on the FC layers, which define a protocol hierarchy similar to the OSI model. FC protocol layers enable communication of various protocols on top of the FC-compliant hardware. There are five FC layers:

✓ **FC-4** — Defines how upper-layer protocols (ULPs) are mapped onto the FC transport. Corresponds to the OSI application layer (L7). Even though there are ULP mappings for SCSI, Internet Protocol (IP), High Performance Parallel Interface (HIPPI), Asynchronous Transfer Mode (ATM), and so on, FC is almost exclusively used for SCSI storage traffic, which is defined by the FCP upper-layer protocol.

✓ **FC-3** — General services layer. Corresponds to the OSI presentation and session layers (L6 and L5). Although used infrequently, this layer can provide security, multicasting, and virtualization services.

✓ **FC-2** — Frame protocol and flow control. Corresponds to the OSI transport and network layers (L4 and L3). Most of the FC functionality resides in this layer. Fibre Channel Physical Standard (FC-PH) describes layers FC-2, FC-1, and FC-0. FC signaling, framing, sequence and exchange handling, flow control, and class of service are defined in FC-2. The FC frame structure defined by FC-2 contains the following:

  ■ Start-of-frame and end-of-frame fields

  ■ A 32-bit error checking code

  ■ A frame header with source and destination addresses

  ■ Control parameters

  ■ A 2,112-byte long data payload

✓ **FC-1** — Encode/decode layer. Corresponds to the OSI data link layer (L2). FC-1 defines the access control to the physical layer. For example, encoding/decoding, transmission protocol, and link maintenance are handled in FC-1. FC uses an 8-bit/10-bit coding (8B/10B) scheme, which transmits 10 bits for each 8 bits of data. 8B/10B coding provides frame delimiting, voltage balance, and error detection, and it is being used in most of the contemporary network technologies (for example, Gigabit Ethernet and InfiniBand).

✓ **FC-0** — FC physical layer. Corresponds to the OSI physical layer (L1). Defines the physical links and physical interactions in the system. For example, it includes mechanical, electrical, and optical specifications for copper and fiber links and connectors. 1Gbit FC physical layer transmits at a rate of 1.0625 Gb/s. However, after accounting for encoding overhead, the actual payload rate is 800 Mb/s or 100 MB/s. If a link is working in full-duplex mode, it might carry data at a rate of 200 MB/s. Similarly, 2Gbit FC transmits at 2.125 Gb/s and provides 200 MB/s and 400 MB/s payload data rates for half-duplex and full-duplex links, respectively.

Fibre Channel Flow Control

In network protocols, flow control limits the transmission rate so that the network or the receiver is not flooded with traffic beyond its capacity. If the transmission rate is too high, the excess frames will be lost (dropped) somewhere in the network or at the receiving end. This happens, for example, when the receiver does not have sufficiently available memory buffers to store the incoming traffic. If the transmission rate is too slow, you won't have an overflow problem. However, the capacity of the network and the receiver will not be used sufficiently, either. Flow control is an optimization problem, and by its nature, directly affects network performance.

FC uses a *credit-based flow control* mechanism where the transmitter needs some form of credit (permission) amount from the receiver before the transmission can take place. On the other hand, TCP, Ethernet, and ATM use *rate-based flow control*, in which the transmitter tries to estimate the sustainable rate using a feedback algorithm and transmits accordingly.

FC contains two different flow control mechanisms: *buffer-to-buffer* and *end-to-end*.

BUFFER-TO-BUFFER FLOW CONTROL

Buffer-to-buffer flow control is used between two directly connected FC ports. For example, two N_Ports in a point-to-point connection, or an N_Port and an F_Port in a fabric connection, use buffer-to-buffer credit (BB_Credit) values.

When the two end-nodes log in to the FC fabric, they inform each other of the number of frames they can accept without further acknowledgements. Every time the sending port sends a frame, it decrements the buffer credits. Every time the receiving port has freed buffer space for newer frames, it sends an R_RDY (Receiver Ready) signal to the sending port, which in turn increments its credits. In summary, the number of unacknowledged frames in the system is less than the value of BB_Credit. This limits the number of active jobs (that is, frames) in the system, which can be modeled with closed queuing network models.

END-TO-END FLOW CONTROL

End-to-end flow control is very similar to buffer-to-buffer flow control except that it concerns two communicating end-nodes, which may not be directly connected. The first time the two end-nodes log in to each other, they establish end-to-end buffer credits (EE_Credit).

The sending port decrements its credit for the particular receiving port by the number of frames it has sent. It increments the credit value every time the receiver acknowledges the frames by returning ACK link control frames. In contrast to the R_RDY signals in buffer-to-buffer flow control, ACK frames can acknowledge the receipt of multiple frames at once. End-to-end credits restrict the number of active (unacknowledged) frames in the fabric, so they can be modeled with closed queuing network models where the number of jobs corresponds to the value of EE_Credits.

No direct relationship between BB_Credits and EE_Credits exists in a system. Nevertheless, the network links must be balanced. The end-to-end communication's throughput will be restricted by the link with the smallest throughput. Therefore, links with high delays must employ high BB_Credits to compensate for the latency.

Most of the FC fabric switches have options to set higher buffer credits for long distance, long delay links. This option enables better throughput by pipelining the transmission of more frames simultaneously on those links. However, note that in some switch implementations, reserving more buffers for some ports may result in a reduced number of buffers to others.

Classes of Service in Fibre Channel

In FC, the manner of communication between two end-points is categorized into *service classes*. Many standard and non-standard service classes exist, but the first three are the most commonly observed.

- ✓ Class 1 — Connection-oriented, circuit-switched channel, with delivery acknowledgements. Forms a virtual, dedicated data path between the end-points and does not allow any other traffic to pass through the ports on this path. Requires all the elements (end-points and switches) on the path to support Class 1 service. Because the links on the path are dedicated, Class 1 does not require BB_Credit flow control. Flow control is performed using EE_Credit. Although this could be the dream connection type for a single communicating pair, because of the resources it requires in FC switches, actual products supporting Class 1 are very rare. Special applications that require low latency, guaranteed bandwidth connections are appropriate for Class 1 service.

✓ **Class 2** — Connectionless, frame-switched channel, with delivery acknowledgements. Does not require any reserved ports and can multiplex traffic from different sources at a port. Requires both BB_Credit and EE_Credit flow control. Some storage devices support Class 2 for critical applications that require immediate notification of transmission problems.

✓ **Class 3** — Connectionless, frame-switched channel, without acknowledgements. Corresponds to datagram traffic in general networks where the source does not know whether a frame is received at the other end. Uses only BB_Credit against buffer overruns. Because it does not use end-to-end flow control, lost frames can only be detected by higher-layer protocols. For example, in SCSI connections, if a command is lost in the fabric, the upper-layer protocol FCP will time out and initiate proper error-recovery procedures. Almost all storage network traffic is carried over Class 3 service.

In terms of error recovery, the difference between Class 2 and Class 3 services is the amount of time it takes to recognize an error. Class 2 recognizes errors faster, as they occur, because of the acknowledgement data or the lack of it. Class 3 leaves it to the upper-layer protocol to generate a time-out condition.

Although error detection might take longer, Class 3 provides higher throughput than Class 1 and Class 2 services because it does not require end-to-end acknowledgements that add latency.

IP Storage Networks

As a general communication infrastructure, IP-based technologies have experienced a widespread success that no other data communication technology, before and after it, has. Ethernet is another success story that made this technology the de facto standard for local area networks (LANs). With widespread use come economies of scale and the reduction of costs. In addition, Ethernet kept increasing its speed 10-fold in every generation. These two trends provide IP/Ethernet-based networks a cost/performance advantage that cannot be matched by any other data communication technology.

Because of IP/Ethernet's cost/performance advantage and widespread availability, it appealed to storage professionals as a means to construct and supplement storage networks (Clark, 2001). Work continues on several IP-based storage networking protocols, discussed in the next few sections.

iSCSI

Internet SCSI (iSCSI) provides a mapping of the SCSI command set to the Transmission Control Protocol/Internet Protocol (TCP/IP) protocol stack (IPSWG, 2002). With this mapping, it is possible to exchange SCSI commands and data over any network that supports TCP/IP protocols.

Several points on the IO path can handle this mapping. The easiest solution is to put iSCSI software drivers in target and initiator computers and handle all processing using the host CPUs. Although this is a low-cost solution, it will slow down the host processor. An alternative is offloading the iSCSI processing to special Network Interface Cards (NICs) that can understand the iSCSI protocol.

Several HBA vendors are working on developing iSCSI NICs, and some prototypes are now available. In a pure iSCSI network (see Figure 8-2), all traffic coming in and going out of the hosts and storage devices is carried over IP. iSCSI HBAs (NICs) take care of all storage to IP conversions. iSCSI NICs, by themselves, will not be able to connect to legacy FC storage networks. Therefore, converters for iSCSI to FC connectivity (in the form of standalone storage routers or multiprotocol switches) are required.

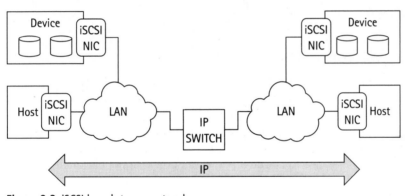

Figure 8-2: iSCSI-based storage network

iFCP and FCIP

Both Fibre Channel over TCP/IP (FCIP) and Internet Fibre Channel Protocol (iFCP) are IP storage proposals that try to leverage the existing dominance and availability of IP networks to transport Fibre Channel (FC) traffic and connect islands of FC SANs.

Many technical differences and similarities exist between these two approaches, but they also differ in their fundamental approach to the problem. FCIP is a tunneling protocol that connects existing FC SANs. iFCP's objectives are very similar to iSCSI's with regards to enabling a storage network mainly (natively) based on IP networks instead of just being a tunneling protocol between several FC networks.

iFCP is a gateway-to-gateway protocol. iFCP gateways have F_PORTs (fabric functionality ports) on one side where FC devices connect and IP ports on the other side where the IP network is connected. Figure 8-3 shows a storage network that combines FC, iFCP, iSCSI, and IP traffic using gateways.

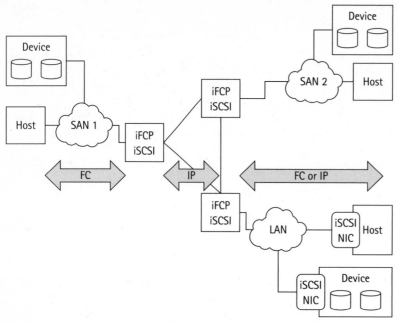

Figure 8-3: A storage network with iFCP/iSCSI/FC gateways

FCIP, in accordance with its FC investment preservation goal, connects two FC networks trans-parently, as shown in Figure 8-4. It carries (tunnels) FC-2 frames between two end-points. These end-points are most probably FC switches. FCIP has specifications for combinations of B_PORTs (bridge ports) and E_PORTs (switch ports). In this regard, an FCIP device is a "bridge" between FC and IP traffic. These specifications utilize and build on existing Fibre Channel Backbone (FC-BB) specifications for ATM (BBW_ATM) and SONET (BBW_SONET). Its limited scope and reliance on existing standards makes FCIP easier to implement than iFCP. FCIP requires the user to continue to keep and manage FC fabrics.

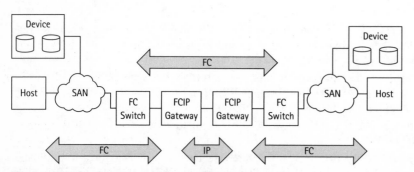

Figure 8-4: FCIP gateways connecting two SAN islands

iFCP can increase the number of fabric domains (239 in FC) and fabric devices by associating fabric addresses with IP addresses and port numbers locally in a gateway (similar to Network

Address Translation for IP networks). Then, the gateway must inspect each incoming and outgoing frame and substitute (translate) the appropriate destination ID (D_ID) and source ID (S_ID) fields.

FCIP creates a single contiguous naming space when two or more SAN fabrics are connected. The new extended fabric will elect a principle switch to reassign all the fabric addresses. If the tunneling connection between the SAN islands is disrupted due to problems in the IP infrastructure, there is the possibility of fabric segmentation. In such a case, each SAN island will choose its own principle switch and assign its own addresses. When the tunneling connection is restored, a disruptive reboot of the fabric may be required to reselect a principle switch and reconverge fabric addresses.

Because iFCP hides local addresses and names from the extended fabric, iFCP will not have the fabric segmentation problem in cases of IP infrastructure disruptions. When the IP connection is restored via IP routing protocols, iFCP fabric will continue to function as normal.

Both FCIP and iFCP have provisions for using multiple TCP connections between peer devices. An FCIP device looks like an FC switch to the connected FC devices, and the TCP connections between the FCIP devices are totally transparent to the connected FC devices. On the other hand, iFCP keeps track of connections between two end-points (FCP portals), and assigns one, and only one, TCP connection for a pair of connected FCP portals. This might allow iFCP to monitor and tune each FCP connection individually.

Like iSCSI, iFCP uses Internet Storage Name Service (iSNS) to associate, register, and discover storage target to TCP port mappings. FCIP currently does not specify any such mechanisms, and relies on existing mechanisms such as Lightweight Directory Access Protocol (LDAP), Dynamic Host Configuration Protocol (DHCP), and so on.

Gigabit Ethernet

Gigabit Ethernet (GbE) is the current generation of high-performance Ethernet. Although 10 Gigabit Ethernet devices are emerging, they are mainly used at the core networks of communication providers and are not as widespread as GbE.

GbE borrows much of its physical layer features from 1Gbit Fibre Channel. Except for a slight difference in frequency, both GbE and FC use the same cabling, interface, and signaling infrastructure.

The most apparent difference between GbE and FC networking is the way the network and transport layers are implemented (Fatoohi, 1995). In FC, the network and transport layers are defined in FC-2 and are actually implemented in FC hardware (FC HBAs). GbE is a physical and data link layer specification and does not specify any network/transport layers. Therefore, network/transport layers are separate implementations on top of GbE. The most prominent network and transport layers for GbE are IP and TCP/UDP, respectively. These layers are implemented as software drivers inside host operating systems, and consume considerable CPU time.

Gigabit Ethernet is more CPU-intensive than 100Mbit Ethernet, as shown in Figure 8-5. These tests are executed between two machines with 400 MHz Pentium II processors. On the sending node, over 60 percent of the CPU time is used for Gigabit transfers, while less than 10 percent of the CPU time is used for 100Mbit Ethernet transfers. For transfer sizes greater than 64KB, the CPU utilization starts to increase, due mostly to the extra buffer handling required by the kernel. The CPU usage on the receiving node (which is not shown here) is more significant. The utilization gets close to 100 percent for GbE and over 30 percent for 100Mbit Ethernet.

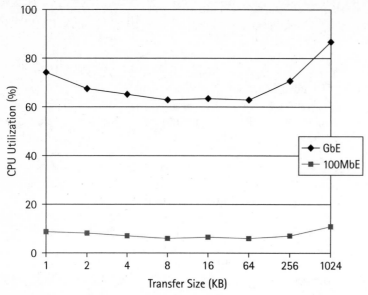

Figure 8-5: CPU utilization for GbE and 100Mbit Ethernet

The GbE's high throughput requires considerable CPU processing time, which might negatively affect the applications running on the host CPU. To elevate the load on the CPU caused by Gigabit transfers, some network adapter cards employ a technique called *checksum offloading*. Using this technique, the checksum computations of the TCP/IP protocol stack can be performed directly on the network adapter card instead of the host CPU.

However, checksum offloading is not sufficient by itself to reduce the CPU load. NICs that offload much of the TCP/IP protocol stack from the host CPU are required to elevate the burden of the Gigabit transfer processing. The same argument is true for IP storage protocols that execute on host CPUs. To achieve comparable performance against FC, these storage protocols must be executed on specialized host bus adapters. TCP offload engines (TOEs) that perform some or all of the TCP/IP stack operations in hardware are available. Similarly, there are prototype host bus adapters that offload most of the iSCSI stack execution from the host CPU.

Some Gigabit Ethernet implementations allow Maximum Transmission Unit (MTU) sizes bigger than the IEEE standard (802.3z) maximum value of 1,500 bytes. MTU defines the maximum amount of data that can be put into a single Ethernet frame. Jumbo frames defined by the Alteon Networks (an early GbE adapter vendor) can be up to 9,000 bytes long. In some cases, jumbo frames provide a 60 percent bandwidth increase over standard frames. In addition, the CPU utilization is smaller for jumbo frames because they generate a smaller number of frames and less overhead.

Although jumbo frames considerably increase the performance of the Gigabit connections, all devices on the transfer path (adapters, switches, and so on) must support this frame size. Otherwise, the path MTU will be set to the minimum of the MTUs on the path (most probably 1,500 bytes).

The socket programming interface allows the user to set receive and send buffer sizes. These parameters determine the maximum amount of inbound and outbound data that can be in transit in the network at a given moment (Padhye, 1998), which is analogous to FC end-to-end buffer credits. For high-speed networks like GbE, the operating system's default socket buffer size (generally 64KBs) will not be sufficient, and must be increased (Farrell, 2000). Chase, Gallatin, and Yocum, of Duke University, (Chase, 2000) discuss optimizations of the TCP/IP stack to reduce the load on the host CPUs. Their optimizations, which include the following items, result in near wire-speed TCP performance:

- ✓ Larger MTU sizes
- ✓ Interrupt suppression
- ✓ Copy avoidance by page remapping
- ✓ Integrated copy/checksum
- ✓ Hardware checksum computation

Other Storage Networks

Besides FC fabrics and IP storage networks, you should be aware of a couple of other important storage networking protocols.

The networks previously discussed perform block-level storage transfer. File-level storage data transfer and the storage networks based on this principle constitute a significant portion of the storage networking world.

Performance analysis of file-level storage networks will be discussed in Chapter 18.

InfiniBand has the potential to become an important IO network in data-center environments, or the back-end network of storage subsystems (Voruganti, 2001). InfiniBand and its potential as a storage network were previously discussed in Chapter 7.

Storage networks can be extended over long distances using WAN technologies. This creates new opportunities and challenges for storage networks.

Storage connections over WAN distances and performance models for them are discussed in Chapter 19.

Modeling Storage Networks

This section discusses performance models for storage networks. First, it presents descriptions and models of switches, routers, and arbitrated loops. Then it discusses simulation and analytic models of storage networks with FC fabrics.

 Performance models for network-attached storage (NAS) and similar file-based storage networks will be discussed in detail in Chapter 18.

Modeling Switches and Routers

Network switches and routers have very similar functions. Both of them take network packets from input ports, check the packets' addresses, and forward the packets to the output ports that have a path to the destination addresses.

The difference between switches and routers is the level of address detail they look for. For example, Ethernet switches look at the Media Access Control (MAC) address in the Ethernet frame and forward the frame to the port attached to the device with that MAC address. In terms of the OSI model, Ethernet switches are considered Layer 2 switches because the MAC addresses are valid in the data link layer. These switches do not need to know anything inside the frame payload other than the Ethernet device address. The switch keeps track of the address and interface mappings in a table. When a frame arrives with an unknown destination address mapping, the frame is broadcast on all interface ports. When a reply arrives for that frame, the source address and the interface on which it arrived will form a new mapping.

IP routers are called "Layer 3 devices," and sometimes even "Layer 3 switches," because they consider the Layer 3 addresses in the packets. Layer 3 is the network layer and contains the IP address. IP addresses can have worldwide validity, so keeping track of IP address-to-interface mappings compared to MAC addresses is a bit more complicated. Neighboring routers exchange their routing tables and similar network status information using routing protocols such as the following:

- ✓ Open Shortest Path First (OSPF)
- ✓ Border Gateway Protocol (BGP)
- ✓ Intermediate System-to-Intermediate System (IS-IS)
- ✓ Routing Information Protocol (RIP)

The preceding discussion about switches and routers is directly applicable to IP/Ethernet switches and routers. In FC, all the switching and routing functionality is performed at the FC-2 layer. There is no switch versus router distinction in FC. FC switches use the Fabric Shortest Path First (FSPF) routing protocol.

Although they have addressing differences, switches and routers have the same packet-forwarding job. Packet forwarding can occur in two ways, by *store-and-forward switching*, which stores the incoming packets in the switch's internal buffers and then forwards them to the interface, where the destination can be reached, and by *cut-through switching* (or *routing*). In cut-through routing, when the first part of a packet arrives, the switch looks at the destination address and starts forwarding the packet to the outgoing interface without storing it internally. Cut-through routers achieve higher throughput rates and lower latencies than store-and-forward routers, but they are more expensive to design and manufacture.

A central feature in modeling switches and routers relates to the internal switching capabilities of the switching device. Some switching/routing devices can sustain full-speed communication for all source/destination interface combinations. They are called *non-blocking switches* because a communication path inside the switch is not affected (blocked) by other communication occurring between other ports. If the communication within the switch is effected by other communication paths inside the switch; such switches are called *blocking switches*. Non-blocking switches require substantial resources inside the switch (the switching backplane) and cost a lot more than blocking switches.

A non-blocking switch can be modeled as shown in Figure 8-6. N ports on the switch each have an input (ingress) link and an output (outgress) link. Each link has its own queuing center. The connection between the input queues and output queues is a fully-connected mesh network without any shared sources that could become a bottleneck.

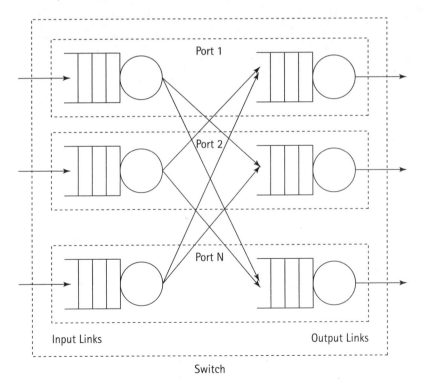

Figure 8-6: Non-blocking switch architecture model

A similar model is shown in Figure 8-7 for a blocking switch. The switching backplane in a blocking switch contains resources shared by all paths. Consequently, the overall throughput is limited by the throughput of this backplane. In the model, the shared resource (that is, the backplane) is shown as a queuing center with a service time computed as the reciprocal of its throughput.

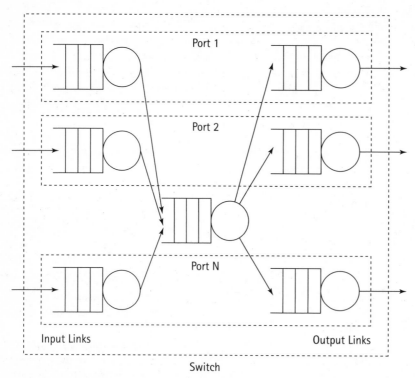

Figure 8-7: Blocking switch architecture model

Modeling Arbitrated Loops

Arbitrated loops (such as FC-AL) are essentially shared interconnects. Any model for loops should account for the fact that only a single pair of communicating end-points can use the loop.

A simulation model for an FC-AL is shown in Figure 8-8. The simulation model includes only a single loop resource, which must be obtained by the transactions that want to use the loop.

After a transaction obtains the loop (wins the arbitration), the arbitration overhead and loop transfer time are accounted for. Then, the transaction releases the loop and another arbitration occurs. Details of arbitration can be modeled at the "Obtain Loop" node's service scheduling policy or First-Come-First-Served (FCFS) scheduling can be used. Loop transfer time is computed using the transaction size and the loop bandwidth, which is 100 MB/s for a 1Gbit FC-AL.

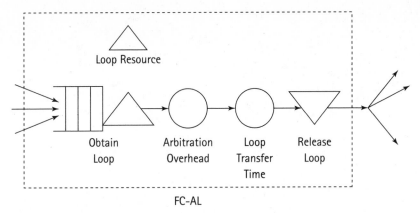

Figure 8-8: Simulation model for an FC arbitrated loop

 For a detailed analysis of loop length and number of devices on a loop, see Ruwart's works in the "References and Additional Resources" section at the end of this chapter..

A Simulation Model for Fibre Channel Storage Networks

This section combines previous component models to construct a simulation model for a Fibre Channel storage network. Figure 8-9 presents a closed queuing network that can be used as a basis for simulation.

The host computers are modeled with single queuing nodes; however, they can be replaced with more sophisticated host computer models. For this example, they are kept simple. The FC fabric is modeled with a single FC switch model. A blocking switch with a central processing unit is chosen, but you can use a non-blocking switch instead depending on the devices you are studying. In addition, more complicated fabrics can be modeled by cascading switches one after another and connecting more host computers and storage devices. Such an extension would also require the simulation of FC routing algorithms. For the sake of simplicity, a single target device (a disk array) is used here.

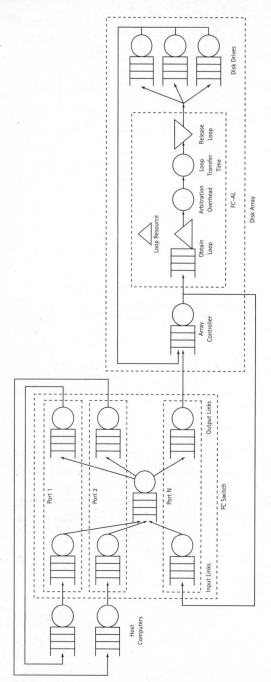

Figure 8-9: A simulation model for an FC attached disk array

The disk array is modeled by adapting the analytic disk array model discussed in Chapter 6, which included disk striping effects. Here, the back-end disks are assumed to be on an FC arbitrated loop. The loop is modeled using the simulation model introduced in the previous sections. The disks are modeled after the M/G/1 disk model in Chapter 6, and can be replaced with more refined models to account for on-disk components (disk controller, disk cache, mechanical components, and so on) explicitly.

The workload generated at the host computers is defined by the request type (read, write), request size, and the number of active (outstanding) IO requests per host computer. The performance results obtained from this simulation model will strongly depend on the modeled workload.

Workload generation is one of the most important aspects of performance modeling studies and is discussed in greater detail in Chapter 9.

An Analytic Model for Fibre Channel Storage Networks

The simulation model in Figure 8-9 must be simplified to obtain a tractable analytic model. Modeling the FC switch at the port level causes unnecessary complexity for an analytic model. Furthermore, FC loop sharing is difficult to model exactly in this type of model. A simplified, open queuing network model is shown in Figure 8-10.

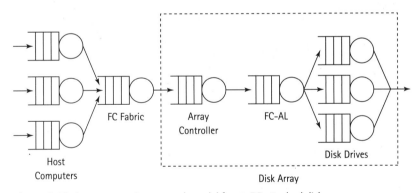

Figure 8-10: An open queuing network model for an FC attached disk array

In open queuing network models, the input (arrival) and output (departure) rates are assumed to be constant, and the system response time is computed as the summation of waiting and service times at each service node.

In Figure 8-10, the overall system throughput is equal to the sum of the host computer throughputs. Similarly, the FC switch's arrival rate is equal to the sum of the host request rates. The host computers and the FC fabric are modeled as single queuing centers with exponential arrival times and general service time distributions (M/G/1 service center). The service time for the host includes the operating system overhead (due to device driver layers) and the host bus overhead. The service time for the FC fabric includes the switching latency, the propagation delay on the FC link, and the transmission time on the link. For small (local) distances, the propagation delay is insignificant and can be omitted. For long distances, the propagation delay is governed by the speed of light in the fiberglass medium. The FC transmission time is a function of the request size and the FC link bandwidth.

The service time for FC-AL is the sum of the arbitration overhead and loop transmission time. The arrival rate for the FC-AL service center is equal to the arrival rate to the array controller multiplied by the request width (because of striping), as defined in Chapter 6. The disk drive arrival rates and their service time computations were also given in the disk array model in Chapter 6. As a result, the overall response time can be computed as the sum of response times at the host, in the fabric, and in the disk array.

The model can be easily extended to account for multiple layers of FC fabric (cascaded switches) and multiple disk arrays by inserting multiple queues for the fabric and distributing the load to multiple disk arrays. You can use models of other storage devices instead of disk arrays. In addition, you can extend the host model to account for the IO path components inside the host explicitly (for example, operating system, host IO bus, host bus adapter, and so on).

Zhu, Zhu, and Xiong, listed in the "References and Additional Resources" section at the end of this chapter presented a very similar analytic model for storage area networks and found that such a model has good accuracy against real experiments.

Summary

This chapter provided introductory descriptions and performance models relating to storage networks, and included the following topics:

Storage Networks

✓ Two major storage networking approaches (Fibre Channel and IP storage) complement each other.

✓ Fibre Channel fabrics are widely deployed, and IP storage networks are just emerging.

✓ Networks, in general, are studied using the seven layers of the OSI model for networking: the physical, data link, network, transport, session, presentation, and application layers.

Fibre Channel Storage Networks

✓ FC fabric combines end-devices using multiple FC switches. The port (interface) types determine where a port can connect in the fabric.

✓ FC layers are a set of protocols that define the physical and logical characteristics of FC fabrics and allow interoperability of FC devices. FCP maps SCSI protocol onto FC to allow storage traffic over the fabric.

✓ Flow control allows optimum usage of network resources. FC uses BB_Credits for buffer-to-buffer flow control and EE_Credits for end-to-end flow control.

✓ FC service classes determine the nature of communication between two end-points. Class-1 is connection-oriented with acknowledgements, Class-2 is connectionless with acknowledgements, and Class-3 is connectionless without acknowledgements. The main difference in these classes is the way they handle error conditions such as lost or out-of-order frames.

IP Storage Networks

✓ IP storage networks aim to utilize the cost/performance advantage of existing IP/Ethernet-based installations.

✓ iSCSI provides a mapping of the SCSI protocol onto the TCP/IP protocol stack. It is possible to implement iSCSI in NICs to offload processing from host CPUs.

✓ iFCP and FCIP enable the transport of FC traffic over IP networks. FCIP is a transparent, tunneling protocol between two distant FC SANs. iFCP is a gateway protocol between FC devices and IP networks and has more sophisticated management capabilities than FCIP.

✓ Gigabit Ethernet provides performance comparable to that of FC. However, GbE communication taxes the host CPU. Special HBAs to offload TCP/IP and iSCSI stack operations are required to decrease the load on host CPUs. In addition, frame sizes and receive buffer sizes must be set to high values to fully utilize GbE.

Modeling Storage Networks

✓ IP/Ethernet switches forward packets using Layer 2 (MAC) addresses. Routers forward packets using Layer 3 (IP) addresses. In FC, both functionalities are performed in the FC switch.

✓ Store-and-forward switching first stores the incoming packets in the switch memory and then forwards them. Cut-through switching forwards the packet without storing it.

✓ Non-blocking switches have enough internal bandwidth to enable full-speed communication between all pairs without any internal bottlenecks. Blocking switches have limited bandwidth that is shared by all of the internal paths.

✓ FC-AL can be modeled as a shared resource for which all connected devices must arbitrate to gain access.

✓ Simulation and analytic models for storage networks can be obtained by combining the component models discussed in Chapters 6, 7, and 8.

References and Additional Resources

Chase, J., A. Gallatin, and K. Yocum. June 2000. *End-System Optimizations for High-Speed TCP.* IEEE Communications, Special Issue on High-Speed TCP, Vol. 39, pp. 68–74.

Presents optimizations of the TCP/IP stack to reduce the load on host CPUs. The authors show that their optimizations result in near wire-speed TCP performance.

Clark, Tom. December 2001. *IP SANS: An Introduction to iSCSI, iFCP, and FCIP Protocols for Storage Area Networks.* Addison-Wesley.

A book that explains all of the current IP storage proposals in detail.

Farley, Marc. May 2001. *Building Storage Networks*, Second Edition. McGraw-Hill.

A comprehensive guide to everything related to storage networks.

Farrell, P. A. and H. Ong. 2000. *Communication Performance over a Gigabit Ethernet Network.* Proceedings of the IEEE International Performance, Computing, and Communications Conference.

Discusses the performance of GbE. The authors show that large MTU, socket buffer, and TCP window sizes are necessary to obtain sufficient bandwidth from GbE.

Fatoohi, R. September 1995. *Performance Evaluation of Communication Networks for Distributed Computing.* Proceedings of the Fourth International Conference on Computer Communications and Networks, pp. 456–459.

Compares several communication networks, including Ethernet and FC. The author finds the FC rate for small messages low compared to Ethernet.

IPSWG; IP Storage Working Group. September 5, 2002. *iSCSI.* Version 16.

Internet SCSI (iSCSI) is an IETF project that targets the mapping of the SCSI protocol over TCP/IP. This Internet-draft status document can be found at www.ietf.org.

Padhye, J., V. Firoiu, D. Towsley, and J. Kurose. September 1998. *Modeling TCP Throughput: A Simple Model and Its Empirical Validation.* ACMSIGCOMM 98, Vancouver, CA, pp. 303–314.

Presents analytic models for TCP throughput, considering such effects as TCP window sizes, loss rate, time-outs, round trip time, and so on.

Ruwart, T. M. March 1999. *Performance Characterization of Large and Long Fibre Channel Arbitrated Loops.* 16th IEEE Symposium on Mass Storage Systems, pp. 11–21.

Studies the performance of long Fibre Channel arbitrated loops. Discusses the cost of the several loop phases and finds that a request size of at least 256KB is required to fully utilize the FC-AL's available bandwidth.

Voruganti, Kaladhar and Prasenjit Sarkar. April 2001. *An Analysis of Three Gigabit Networking Protocols for Storage Area Networks*. Proceedings of the 20th IEEE International Performance, Computing, and Communications Conference (IPCCC 2001). Phoenix, Arizona.

Provides a protocol-level comparison for storage over FC, InfiniBand, and iSCSI. Points out the need for a framing mechanism for iSCSI, because TCP does not employ that concept. Argues, expectedly, that FC and InfiniBand would perform better in local networks and that iSCSI would perform well for WAN distances.

Zhu, Yao-Long, Shu-Yu Zhu, and Hui Xiong. April 2002. *Performance Analysis and Testing of the Storage Area Network*. Proceedings of Tenth NASA Goddard Conference on Mass Storage Systems and Technologies (MSS2002), Adelphi, Maryland. April 15–18, 2002.

Presents an analytic queuing model for simple storage area networks. This paper, and similar storage-related research papers, can be found at the conference Web page, `http://storageconference.org`.

Chapter 9

Modeling Storage Workloads

In This Chapter

You can obtain any targeted performance result from a system by applying a specially chosen workload. Workloads should be selected and described such that they reflect the applications a user will encounter in the real world. For proper performance modeling, benchmarking, and tuning, adequate workload characterization studies are required. This chapter discusses workload definition in both general and storage networking contexts, and includes the following topics:

✓ The importance of workload definitions and how they can make a difference

✓ Real workloads and their synthetic models

✓ Important aspects of workload specifications, and the parameters that define storage workloads

✓ Common storage workload descriptions

The Importance of a Workload Definition

Almost all conversations about performance studies follow these lines:

First Speaker: We obtained...performance of...on this system.
  Second Speaker: What was the experimental setup?
  First Speaker: We used...of...and...of...
  Second Speaker: What was the test workload?
  First Speaker: It was...for...
  Second Speaker: But, that is a very limited workload for...
  First Speaker: We obtained it by studying the...
  Second Speaker: It does not matter; it is not representative of real applications.

This leads to the question: "What is a representative workload?" You could be on either side of the preceding conversation, and you would still need an understanding of workloads in order to perform or review performance analysis.

To point out the importance of workload definitions, this chapter begins with a simple example of workload assumptions on a single service center. Figures 9-1 and 9-2 illustrate the fact that even seemingly subtle differences in workload assumptions can make big differences in performance measurements. Both figures contain statistical plots for a single queuing center. The service time of the queuing center is 7 ms and is constant (deterministic service time distribution). In addition, both cases assume that the mean arrival time is 10 ms. The two figures differ in their assumptions of arrival time distributions.

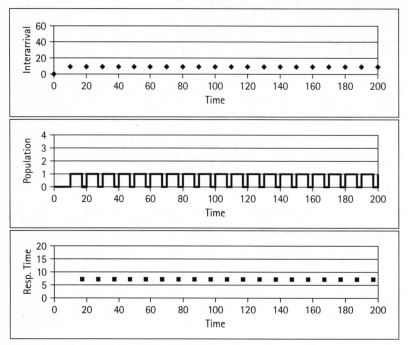

Figure 9-1: Interarrival time, queue population, and response time plots for constant interarrival distribution

In Figure 9-1, the interarrival time is assumed to be constant at 10 ms. Arrival to the service center is uniformly spaced in time. Because the service time is 7 ms, less than the interarrival time, there is absolutely no queuing (waiting) at the center, and the response time is 7 ms for all jobs. The figures show the interarrival time, queuing center population (waiting and in-service jobs), and response time data up to 200 ms.

Figure 9-2 also assumes that the mean interarrival time is 10 ms. However, in this case, the distribution is assumed to be exponential. Exponential distribution causes "bursty" arrivals. In other words, periods with little activity are followed by periods with intense arrivals. As the figure shows, during arrival bursts the queue length (population) and the response time go up. As a result, the two cases with the same mean interarrival times have very different mean response times. In the first case (Figure 9-1), the mean response time is constant at 7 ms. In the second case (Figure 9-2), the mean response time for the jobs is 10.6 ms. If the experiments are carried on longer, the effects of bursty arrival will actually cause the mean response time to be 15.17 ms in the long run. This response time can be computed using the formulas for an M/D/1 (exponential interarrival time, constant service time) queuing center (Jain, 1991).

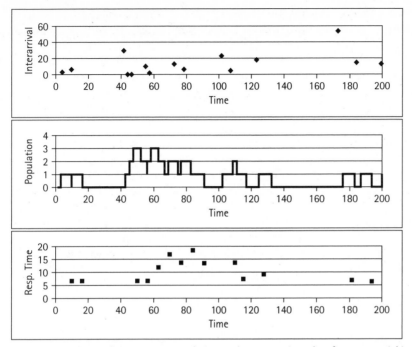

Figure 9-2: Interarrival time, queue population, and response time plots for exponential interarrival distribution

You can conclude from this example that defining workloads is a difficult task, and small omissions, or oversimplifications, can make a big difference.

A typical workload modeling study contains the following steps:

1. Choose the set of parameters that are essential to describe a given type of workload.

2. Choose workload data collection tools such as performance monitors and trace collection tools, or use existing workload data.

3. Collect workload data from a system under test.

4. Analyze the workload data to extract parameter information using data analysis techniques (introduced in Chapter 2) to find the averages, distributions, correlations, and so on.

5. Construct the workload model as a stochastic specification or an executable emulation.

The rest of the chapter discusses various aspects of the workload modeling process.

Types of Workloads

Real systems may exhibit very different performance behavior under different workloads. People are generally interested in some special application workload because it might be very critical for their business. For example, a database administrator will be interested in the performance of the servers under a database management system (DBMS) load. Although measuring the performance of real applications (workloads) on real systems provides the most reliable and direct performance information, it is problematic for several reasons. First, real workloads are mostly unrepeatable. Real applications are very complex, with time-varying inputs and outputs. Capturing a steady behavior is impossible. Furthermore, real systems are dedicated to production applications, which means they are seldom available for experimentation. In addition, dedicating a real system to performance studies could be expensive.

Synthetic workloads are used to capture the essence of real workloads in performance studies. What constitutes "the essence" of a real workload is highly dependent on the system under study. Generally, a synthetic workload must contain enough information to replicate the performance behavior of the real workload. Figure 9-3 illustrates this relation. When executed on the real system, a synthetic workload must produce the same kind of performance results as the real workload. In a performance study, the workload and/or system parameters are changed systematically to observe the resulting difference in the performance metrics (of which response time and throughput are typically the most important). The performance metrics for storage networks were introduced in Chapter 1.

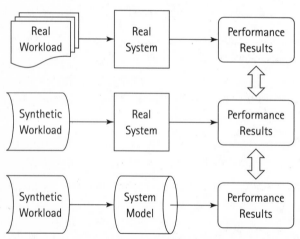

Figure 9-3: Verifying performance results for synthetic workloads

This relation can be continued through one more step. The synthetic workload on a real system and the same synthetic workload on a model of the system should produce comparable performance results.

In storage networks, the top level shown in Figure 9-3 represents the performance monitors that collect real-time performance data from production systems. The middle level represents storage performance benchmarks that execute synthetic workloads on real systems to obtain performance data. The bottom level represents the performance models that accept synthetic storage workload definitions and produce performance results. The rest of this chapter discusses techniques for workload description.

Performance monitors and benchmarks for storage networks will be studied in more detail in Chapters 12 and 13.

Describing Workloads

Workload descriptions can be classified into three categories, with increasing levels of detail:

- ✓ **Business Workload** — The highest level of workload definition is described in business-oriented terms. Examples include the number of sales points, the number of customers supported, and so on.

- ✓ **Functional Workload** — Functional descriptions include systems, programs, requests, and replies. Some example specifications are Online Transaction Processing (OLTP), data mining applications, Customer Relationship Management (CRM), number of purchases and/or invoices completed in unit time, and so on.

- ✓ **Operational Workload** — Describes the operations performed to complete the preceding functions. Examples include the types and rates of disk operations, processor cycle time, memory and cache usage, and so on.

Storage networks might be supporting many business and functional workload requirements. However, those definitions are highly subjective and do not allow in-depth technical study. The rest of the chapter thus concentrates on operational workload descriptions, which are referred to as "IO workload characterization" in most scientific contexts.

Open and Closed Workloads

As discussed in previous chapters, models and modeled systems can be studied in two classes: open models/systems and closed models/systems. In an open model (with an open queuing network) the arrival rate and system throughput is controlled by external factors. The system response time is the main performance metric, and it is a function of the request arrival rate. Therefore, a workload description for an open system defines the request arrival rate.

On the other hand, in a closed model the workload is defined by the number of active jobs circulating in the system. The system throughput and response time are a function of the number of active jobs. A workload description for a closed system defines the number of simultaneous jobs in the system.

There may or may not be a direct correspondence between open/closed systems and open/closed models. Some systems are natural candidates for either open or closed models. For example, communication systems with a limited number of message packets are natural candidates for closed models. And sometimes, the same system can be modeled with both open and closed models depending on the modeler's assumptions.

Throughput versus Response Time Workloads

Some types of applications require absolute maximum system throughput, even if this means increased response time for individual operations. These applications must have multiple simultaneous streams to keep up the throughput. Examples include OLTP applications, backup applications, multimedia processing systems, and so on. In these cases, the workload requirements are defined in terms of throughput, or requests completed in unit time.

Some applications require the minimum possible response time for individual operations, even if this means the total system throughput is suboptimal. These applications have few parallel streams and cannot submit the next operation until the previous ones are completed. Examples of response time-sensitive applications include database reconstruction, decision support systems, and so on. For these workloads, the performance requirements are described in terms of response time.

Stochastic versus Trace-Based Workloads

You can generate a synthetic workload in two general ways. First, you can generate it using stochastic (probabilistic) techniques. The workload must be defined (*parameterized*) with stochastic variables. (Parameters for storage workloads are discussed later in this chapter.) Then, the workloads are generated by applying algorithms to the parameters. This is generally in the form of a benchmark.

The second alternative is to generate *trace-based* workloads. The real workload is executed on the real system and traces of system operations (requests, replies, and so on) are collected. These traces are played back on the original system with modifications, on a different system, or on a model of the system.

Tools for performance data collection are discussed in Chapter 13.

Workload traces produce a more accurate representation of the real workload than stochastic parameters. However, obtaining and executing traces is difficult. Similar to the multiple levels of workload description (see Figure 9-3), there are multiple levels to collect workload traces. A trace might contain database operations as top-level commands, or it might contain the traces of the resulting disk IO operations.

Ousterhout (1985) and Heath (1996), listed in the "References and Additional Resources" section at the end of this chapter, both conducted trace-based studies that characterize the workloads of UNIX file systems and network file servers, respectively.

Self-Similar and Heavy-Tailed Workloads

Several workload types have been shown to repeat the same pattern on many scales. This is referred to as *self-similarity* because the data is correlated with its own component parts. Fractals that repeat a pattern at several levels are a good visual example of self-similarity. Internet and local area network (LAN) traffic, and file server and Web server traffic, are also known to be self-similar. For example, when you look at the access pattern on a monthly scale, you see a bursty pattern with several on/off periods. When you magnify the data to view it for a week, you again see a similar bursty pattern, and so on.

The problem with self-similar workloads is that they are difficult to model with simple statistical terms. While an exponentially distributed pattern will converge to an average behavior over time, self-similar data does not converge to a mean and is difficult to predict.

A related concept is the *heavy-tailed distribution* of workload data. Most workload data relating to network and file traffic exhibits skewed distributions, with a large number of data points at small sizes and a small number of data points for very large sizes — hence the term *heavy-tailed*. If just an average data point is used, neither the small sizes nor the large sizes will be modeled accurately. A small amount of large-sized data might have a big impact on the real system, which you will not be able to model using average data. You must be aware of this problem when characterizing the workload for storage networks. However, detailed treatment of this subject is beyond the scope of this book; you are therefore encouraged to consult other references on the subject (such as Feitelson, 2002).

Parameterizing Storage Workloads

The following section presents a (non-exhaustive) sampling of parameters that are generally used to describe a wide range of storage-related workloads. Note that a given workload characterization does not necessarily need all of these parameters defined.

Workload Type and the Number of Streams

The workload type defines the functionality of the work — whether it is a database workload, network file system workload, local file system workload, or block device level workload. For each workload type, you need to know the number of clients, processes, threads, or streams that generate the workload because this dictates the extent of the load on the system.

IO Type

The IO request type could be a read, write, or control operation. Most of the time, control operations are excluded from workload definitions because they constitute a very small portion of the IO stream and can usually be included either in the read operations or the write operations. For example, a Network File System (NFS)-level "get directory" command is basically a file read command.

The IO type is parameterized as either the percentage of reads or the percentage of writes in the workload.

Request Size

Request size is the amount of data transferred in a single data operation. Generally, IO response time is a direct function of request size. Defined in blocks, KB, or MB, request size will have different values for different workload levels. A file transfer command might be several GBs in size, while the underlying disk IOs are a few blocks each.

Queue Depth

Another parameter that directly impacts response time and throughput is *queue depth*. Although the term may have slightly different meanings in different contexts, it is generally used to define the number of outstanding requests that are active simultaneously.

Workloads that define a constant queue depth are defining a closed queuing network. Therefore, the queue depth corresponds to the number of jobs in the queuing network. Queuing theory says that the throughput and response time in a closed network are proportional to the queue depth. So, applications seeking high throughput should keep long queue depths, and applications seeking fast response times should keep short queue depths.

Reference Address

Workload parameters can include the address to which IO operations refer. Storage device performance is sensitive to the accessed data's address, in addition to other factors. Hard disk drives and magnetic tapes have latencies that depend on this *reference address*.

Although memory devices such as RAM have fixed latencies that do not change with the data address, inclusion of addresses in memory workloads is important, too. Memories are constructed as hierarchies of caches, which are very sensitive to access patterns. In such cases, the distribution of the addresses will define the cache miss and hit ratios, which directly affects performance.

Storage data addresses are generally expressed in logical block addresses (LBAs) or logical block numbers (LBNs). In case of Small Computer System Interface (SCSI) disks, one block corresponds to one sector, which is 512 bytes.

Locality

A workload has two types of data locality. If successive references in a data stream are close to each other, the workload has *spatial locality*. Such a workload is very suitable for devices with read-ahead caches that access data beyond the requested size in anticipation of future use. If several sets of data are repeatedly accessed together, the references have *temporal locality*. In other words, they are close in time.

Locality can be expressed in several ways. For the purposes of workload definition, you can use a histogram showing the distribution of the distance between successive reference addresses.

The most prevalent notion of address locality is *sequential access*, which refers to the fact that all addresses are consecutive. If no detectable correlation exists between the addresses, the workload contains *random access*. For storage devices, sequential access patterns have significant performance advantages over random access patterns.

An access pattern might contain portions that are sequential. The length of each sequential portion is called the *run length*. A histogram of run length distributions shows the workload's degree of sequentiality.

A special case of sequential access is the *strided access* pattern, as shown in Figure 9-4. Strided patterns are sequential access with regular gaps between successive references. Strided access patterns are common in scientific applications and database workloads, where a fixed portion of each successive record is accessed.

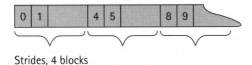

Strides, 4 blocks

Figure 9-4: A strided access pattern

When two sequential streams are combined (interleaved), the resulting pattern might look random, as seen in Figure 9-5. However, a close examination of the interleaved stream reveals two sequential streams. Actually, this behavior is quite common for disk drives, where two files accessed sequentially will look like random accesses at the disk controller level. To cope with this, disk drive caches are partitioned into several segments, where each segment tracks the accesses belonging to a particular sequential stream.

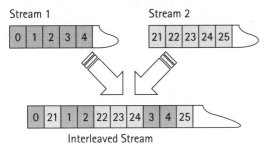

Figure 9-5: Interleaved sequential access pattern

Arrival Time and Rate

The time a request arrives at a system has several important effects on performance and must be captured in most workload descriptions. First, the distribution of arrival times on, say, an hourly, daily, or weekly basis might point to periodic patterns over time. Second, the distribution of inter-arrival times dictates the arrival rate to the system and directly affects the length of queues and utilization levels.

Although most network and file traffic arrivals have bursty, self-similar, and heavy-tailed distributions (as discussed previously in this chapter), most workload generation, simulation, and benchmark tools allow only the specification of standard distributions. If you want to model the above complex behavior, you will need to employ traces obtained from real systems.

Common Storage Workloads

This section presents examples of workload specifications for some common storage workloads. Such specifications can be used to configure workload generation tools such as IOmeter (Schmisseur, 2000), or can be used to obtain parameters for simulation and analytic models.

Workload generation tools (benchmarks) are discussed in Chapter 12.Transaction Processing Workload

Transaction processing typically represents a database server performing transactions. The workload defines the IO operations produced by such systems. Typically, the average request size is 4KB or 8KB. The accesses are 100 percent random with 67 percent read operations, and span a large disk space (GBs to TBs). The queue depth varies widely with the number and type of database activity.

Web Server Workload

A Web server performs read operations (100 percent read) almost exclusively. Small log file write operations occur, but they are negligible compared to the read load. Accesses are 100 percent random and span a large storage space. The queue depth can vary widely in relation to the number of Web-client accesses. The request sizes change from a single block (512B) to large sizes (1MB), where most of the accesses occur with small sizes (heavy-tailed distribution).

File Server Workload

A file server accesses its storage devices to serve files to clients. File accesses are 80 percent read and 100 percent random. File systems access storage devices using file system block sizes, which range from 4KB to 64KB. The workload spans a wide range, and the queue depth changes with the rate of file system accesses.

Video Server Workload

A video server exhibits streaming read operations (100 percent read), with large request sizes (greater than 64KB). Video files are accessed sequentially (100 percent sequential), and each file is around a few GBs (about 2GB). Each user corresponds to a job on the storage side, so the queue depth is proportional to the number of users.

Write Streaming Workload

Graphics and video editing software and computer-aided design (CAD) applications write to storage devices using large (greater than 64KB), streaming (100 percent sequential) write operations (100 percent write). A special case of streaming applications is the backup and data replication software where, on one side, the storage is accessed with streaming reads, and, on the other side, written using streaming writes.

Summary

This chapter examined the importance of defining a workload and listed some of the parameters that define workloads in storage networks. It included the following topics:

The Importance of a Workload Definition

✓ System performance is highly dependent on the choice of workload. Performance analysis studies must therefore include proper consideration when choosing workloads.

✓ Subtle differences in workload definition can have a huge impact on performance outcomes.

Types of Workloads

✓ Real workloads on real systems are highly dynamic and are difficult to use for performance studies directly.

✓ Synthetic workloads are used to model real workloads, and are more amenable to performance modeling. Synthetic workloads on real systems must produce performance results similar to that of real workloads.

Describing Workloads

✓ Workloads can be defined at several levels ranging from high-level specifications, such as business functions, to low-level specifications, such as IO operation details.

✓ Workloads that specify a constant job arrival rate can be used in open queuing network models to compute response time effects. Workloads that define a constant number of outstanding jobs (IOs) can be used in closed queuing models to obtain throughput results.

✓ Workloads can be generated based on statistical specifications, or by replaying trace data obtained from earlier executions of the workload.

✓ Self-similarity, heavy-tailed distributions, and bursty arrivals are common in network and storage data traffic patterns.

Parameterizing Storage Workloads

✓ Generally used parameters for storage workloads include the workload type, number of clients, IO type, request size, queue depth, address distribution, and interarrival time.

✓ Locality in the storage workload shows the closeness of data references and has important performance consequences for storage devices. Typical parameters to define locality include sequentiality, randomness, sequential run lengths, and stride lengths.

Common Storage Workloads

✓ Transaction processing and file server workloads contain small, random, and mostly read operations, while Web servers exclusively have read operations with occasional big sizes.

✓ Video servers generate large, sequential read operations. Write streaming workloads, such as video editing, generate large, sequential write operations.

References and Additional Resources

Feitelson, Dror G. 2002. "Workload Modeling for Performance Evaluation," in *Performance Evaluation of Complex Systems: Techniques and Tools*, editors M. C. Calzarossa and S. Tucci, Lect. Notes Comput. Sci., Vol. 2459, Springer Verlag, pp. 114–141.

A summary paper of workload modeling techniques, including statistical modeling, and the handling of self-similar and heavy-tailed distributions.

Heath, John R. and Stephen A.R. Houser. December 1996. *On the Relationship of Server Disk Workloads and Client File Requests*. CMG96, San Diego, CA.

This trace-based analysis shows that, in their test environment, most client operations are reads, while most server backend IO is write operations. Shows that most of the reads are absorbed by the server cache.

Jain, Raj. April 1991. *The Art of Computer Systems Performance Analysis*. John Wiley & Sons.

Contains sections on principal-component analysis and clustering that can be used to categorize experimental workload data into classes.

Ousterhout, John, Herve DaCosta, D. Harrison, John Kuntze, Mike Kupfer and James G. Thompson. December 1985. *A Trace Driven Analysis of the Unix 4.2BSD File System*. Proceedings of the Tenth Symposium on Operating System Principles, Orcas Island, Washington, pp. 15–24.

An early paper on UNIX file system traces. Showed that most new data is overwritten in a few minutes of creation, which increases the effectiveness of file system caches.

Schmisseur, Mark. June 2000. *RAID Benchmarking Workload Analysis*. InfoStor, 4(6).

Presents workloads that can be generated using the IOmeter tool to evaluate RAID subsystems.

Part III

Storage Performance Engineering

Chapter 10

Storage Quality of Service

In This Chapter

Not all data is created equal, and not all of it requires equal treatment. Some applications and data on the storage network require absolute best performance, while others do not. The resources on the storage network are limited, and providing the highest performance to all applications may not be possible. This leads to decisions about *Quality of Service (QoS)* levels, QoS monitoring, and QoS enforcement. This chapter discusses the following topics on storage network QoS:

- ✓ Definitions and requirements for QoS

- ✓ Storage network QoS problems

- ✓ QoS in IP networks and the architectures for specifying QoS

- ✓ Service Level Agreements and management and monitoring tools for storage QoS

Defining Quality and Service

Quality and service have different meanings in different contexts. In general, *service* can be defined as the expected behavior or outcome from a system. *Quality of service* (QoS) is thus the degree to which this expected outcome is realized. Quantifying and measuring QoS is also a context-dependent task.

For an Internet user who browses a news site, QoS might mean the responsiveness of the Web server. For a system administrator, QoS might mean the throughput and availability of the Web server, the network connection, and storage subsystem. In any case, QoS must be implemented end-to-end. To achieve a desired level of service, all the components on the end-to-end path must be able to deliver that level of service.

Some key concepts concerning QoS are as follows:

- ✓ **QoS Architecture** — The system must include the structures and interfaces to request, configure, and measure QoS. Furthermore, if the system's peak performance is below the desired level, no amount of management will be able to provide QoS.

- ✓ **Admission Policy** — Probably one of the most critical aspects of a QoS system. When a system accepts to serve (admit) a request, it must ensure that resources are available to achieve the requested QoS level. If there are not enough resources, or if using the existing resources will hamper the QoS guarantees of the previously admitted requests, the new arrivals should be rejected (or *dropped*, in networking terminology).

✓ **Resource Reservation** — After a request is admitted to the system, sufficient system resources must be reserved to provide QoS to that request.

✓ **Class of Service (CoS)** — Even though *CoS* is sometimes used interchangeably with *QoS*, technically it has a different meaning. CoS defines the type of service and does not indicate how well the service is performed. For example, a Fibre Channel (FC) class of service defines message delivery guarantees, which is different from any QoS guarantees of throughput, response time, and so on.

One way to quantify QoS is to compute the ratio of the QoS deficiency to the desired level, as shown in Equation 10-1 (Menascé, 2001).

Equation 10-1

```
QoS Deviation = ΔQoS = (Achieved QoS - Desired QoS) ÷ Desired QoS
```

In this equation, if the desired QoS level is greater than the achieved QoS, the result is a negative ratio indicating the extent of the deviation. A positive deviation denotes a QoS better than the one desired. If multiple parameters are used to measure QoS, a weighted sum can be used to summarize the achieved QoS level, as shown in Equation 10-2.

Equation 10-2

```
Total QoS Deviation = Σᵢ (wᵢ × ΔQoSᵢ)
```

For example, in an e-commerce site (Menascé, 2001), the parameters for QoS can be defined as the maximum response time, minimum throughput, and maximum rejection rate. Each of these parameters can be assigned a relative importance (weight, w_i). Then, Equation 10-2 can be used to track the overall QoS, dynamically.

Storage QoS

If all data and all applications required absolute best performance all the time, QoS would not be achievable. In reality, different data and different applications have varying performance needs. This allows for trade-offs in performance. While some applications have high QoS priorities, others can be delayed to make way for the high priority jobs.

QoS in storage systems, and in all systems for that matter, is an optimization problem. The optimization is achieved by trading one performance metric for another. For example, one trade-off occurs between throughput and response time. Previous chapters showed that increasing the number of active jobs (queue length) increases both the throughput and the response time. If an application requires low, bounded response time, it must be set to accept low, bounded throughput values.

Storage subsystems generally cannot make QoS guarantees. One reason for this is the fact that they are constructed to accept and queue all arriving IO commands. Still, you can achieve partial QoS indirectly with certain performance-tuning techniques. For example, the queues can be prioritized to favor some jobs over others. You can also assign more buffer/cache space and disk spindles to jobs with high priority. In any case, these optimizations will provide a best-effort service level without any explicit QoS guarantees.

Unlike their IP counterparts, FC fabrics do not yet have the QoS mechanisms. Currently, products that are advertised with QoS for FC networks mostly perform monitoring and configuration for best-effort performance.

QoS must be implemented and analyzed end-to-end. If the storage subsystem is able to achieve a service level but the storage network lacks the desired performance, end-to-end QoS is not achievable. Consider the IO path shown in Figure 10-1, which illustrates the path from the application level down to the storage device over a storage network. The number of components on the shown path is only a portion of the real number of levels that exist between these two end-points. For example, the operating system has file system, network stack, and kernel components, each of which affects the service level.

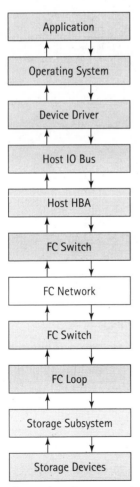

Figure 10-1: Components that affect QoS on the IO path

Unfortunately, you won't find any QoS architectures or tools to configure all the components on the IO path. Many management applications pick some components they have control over and treat the rest as black boxes.

As discussed in Chapter 9, while workload modeling was introduced, performance metrics depend on the workload characteristics as much as the system configuration. For example, specifying that a system should have R_{max} response time is pointless unless the workload type (write percentage, sequentiality, size distribution, and so on) is also specified. Figure 10-2 shows the essential components of a storage QoS analysis. Workload is a combination of the arriving jobs, while the performance (response time, utilization, and so on) of the storage network components are a result of the system components and the workload (Wilkes, 2001). An ideal QoS analysis requires the measurement, collection, and correlation of workload, performance, and QoS metrics.

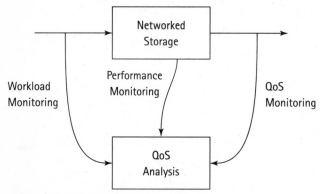

Figure 10-2: Requirements for a complete QoS analysis

IP Network QoS

Data communication networks, especially IP networks, have been the subject of QoS studies for many reasons (Aurrecoechea, 1998; Huston, 2000), including the following:

✓ Almost all business-critical applications require network connectivity.

✓ Because the communication networks are essentially distributed systems, they have significant performance variability.

✓ Because networks extend beyond the boundaries of a single organization, the network connections are almost always out-sourced to communication companies.

Thus, it is necessary to specify a level of performance guarantee (QoS) between the interfacing networks, generally in the form of a *Service Level Agreement (SLA)*.

The next two sections introduce two commonly used QoS specifications for IP networks.

Differentiated Services

Even though the original IP protocol specification contained *Type of Service (TOS)* information in the IP datagram header, in practice it was almost never used. This header information field was later used by the *Differentiated Services (DiffServ)* protocol (Blake, 1998) to specify service levels for IP packets (datagrams). This field (DS) contains a DiffServ Code Point value, which is assigned when the packet is entering a DiffServ network at an admission router. Each Code Point value is associated with a *Per Hop Behavior (PHB)*. The association between Code Points and PHBs is not dictated by the DiffServ specification and is decided by the network (and the network administrator) that supports DiffServ. By using specific PHBs, the network is supposed to provide several QoS levels.

Figure 10-3 illustrates a DiffServ network. The arriving IP packets' DS fields are assigned a Code Point value at the admission router. This value defines the PHB for the next network forwarding action. The next DiffServ router in the network can assign another Code Point and choose another PHB, and so on.

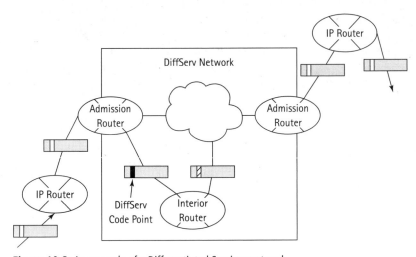

Figure 10-3: An example of a Differentiated Services network

PHBs define the following for a specific IP packet:

- ✓ Throughput
- ✓ Loss rate
- ✓ Latency
- ✓ Jitter allowed

A router can tune these metrics using different buffer management and packet scheduling alternatives. PHBs are negotiated between a customer and network provider using SLAs and *Traffic Conditioning Agreements (TCAs)*. When a customer network presents a packet to the provider network, the admission router "conditions" the traffic by classifying it into service classes and assigning DiffServ Code Points.

> DiffServ uses per network hop and per IP packet service specifications. It is not an end-to-end QoS specification. Still, by carefully planning SLAs and TCAs, and carefully assigning Code Points and PHBs, you can configure a DiffServ network with end-to-end QoS behavior.

Multiprotocol Label Switching

Network packet routing is a computationally daunting task. Each packet's address must be compared against thousands of network prefixes to find the network with the closest address. To expedite this task, label switching was invented. The idea is to decide the network path for a packet at the edge of the network and give the packet a unique label to denote the designated path. The routers inside the network (core routers) simply read the label to find the exact path the packet will take without any lengthy address comparisons.

Figure 10-4 illustrates a *Multiprotocol Label Switching (MPLS)* network (Rosen, 2001). Packets arriving at an MPLS edge router are stamped with labels that show their designated path inside the MPLS network. The label itself can change during each network hop. However, the path remains the same. While the packet is exiting from another MPLS edge router, the label is removed.

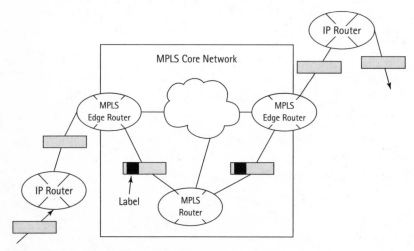

Figure 10-4: Label switching in an MPLS network

QoS in MPLS networks is achieved by the 3-bit Class of Service (CoS) field in the MPLS label. An edge router chooses this CoS field according to several criteria, which might include the TOS field in IP packets, source address, destination address, and so on. Packets with high CoS field values can be forwarded on a path with minimum latency or maximum throughput, while low CoS values can be forwarded in a best-effort fashion. This flexibility in path assignments enables network administrators to be creative about how QoS is achieved on their network.

Only the high-end network equipment (switches, routers) support MPLS. Thus, it has only been adapted so far in core networks with big-iron network equipment (and rightly so, because MPLS is geared towards heavy-duty routing tasks).

Label switching together with the CoS field in MPLS, provides an end-to-end specification for QoS between the MPLS network edges. The label actually dictates the path. This is in contrast to DiffServ, which allows intermediate routers to change the service levels and the path of the packets.

Because they are implemented differently, you can utilize MPLS and DiffServ in parallel, at the same time. In such a scenario, you can use MPLS to dictate the intermediate hops (paths) that a packet will pass and use DiffServ to dictate the forwarding behavior during each hop.

Performance Management for Storage QoS

Implementing QoS in storage networks requires the interplay of various management tasks, including (but not limited to) the following:

- ✓ Enterprise/storage capacity planning
- ✓ Enterprise/storage resource management
- ✓ QoS
- ✓ Performance monitoring

Storage Resource Management (SRM) is a prerequisite for wide adoption of storage networks and it is a newly established application segment. SRM tools are sometimes referred to as *Storage Network Management (SNM)* or *Storage Area Management (SAM)* tools.

SRM and performance monitoring techniques and available tools will be discussed in more detail in Chapter 13.

Service Level Agreements

QoS requirements are formally or informally documented by Service Level Agreements (SLAs) between customers and providers. In this context, a customer and a provider could mean a business and a service provider business, different units of a single organization, or just two computing platforms.

The SLAs for storage networks specify one or more of the following basic storage networking metrics:

✓ Minimum storage capacity

✓ System availability (uptime)

✓ Maximum downtime

✓ Mean and maximum latency

✓ Mean and maximum packet loss ratio

✓ Mean and minimum throughput

✓ Monetary penalties for missing the above QoS limits

QoS by Overengineering

The easiest way to ensure that storage network performance can sustain all QoS requirements is to build a system with a peak performance far beyond the total load it will ever encounter.

However strange this might sound, many communication networks have actually been built this way — with lots of access capacity. Unfortunately, you can't overengineer in every situation and many scarce (and expensive) resources can cause you to make trade-off decisions. Many storage networking equipment and subsystems are still expensive, and making best use of the equipment in hand is a good idea. This requires monitoring and management of storage network QoS.

Managing QoS

Diverse resource types on a storage network require a management framework that can handle a heterogonous pool of storage and networking equipment. Because no widely adapted management interface standard exists, the current SRM tools try to use a myriad set of proprietary management Application Programming Interfaces (APIs). Some candidates for universal SRM management will be discussed later in the book. SRM tools help in resource discovery, QoS configuration, and SLA monitoring and enforcement.

SRM tools that specialize in QoS monitoring and management can be grouped into two classes:

✓ In-band, on-the-loop monitoring/management tools

✓ Out-of-band, external monitoring/management tools

Figure 10-5 illustrates a generic example of an in-band QoS monitoring tool. The data collectors are actually devices that look like network switches. However, they pass the packets (frames in FC) directly between port pairs, while capturing performance statistics from each packet. They function like the Ethernet tap devices punctured into the coaxial cables. The data collector devices are transparent to the other devices on the network. They can understand and monitor end-to-end flows by checking the source and destination addresses of the packets passing through them. It is also possible to compute latency and throughput statistics by correlating crossing packets. These statistics can be interpreted at the network level (for example, FC frames) or at a higher-level protocol (for example, SCSI commands). An example of in-band monitoring tools is Finisar's SAN QoS Traffic Monitor.

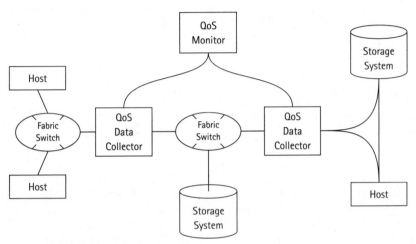

Figure 10-5: In-band QoS monitoring tool

Figure 10-6 shows an out-of-band QoS monitoring and management tool. The tool is not in the data path, so it requires access to devices that can collect statistical data on the tasks they perform. Because no management interfaces are generally accepted for storage networks and devices, out-of-band management tools depend on access to proprietary APIs of device vendors. A QoS monitoring device in a storage network might need to support hundreds of these proprietary interfaces to present a complete state of the storage network performance. Access to these management interfaces generally occurs through a secondary network, typically an IP network. Examples of out-of-band SRM tools include InterSAN's Pathline and TrueSAN's Cloudbreak.

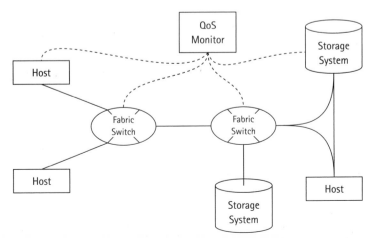

Figure 10-6: Out-of-band, QoS monitoring/management tool

The greatest concern voiced against in-band tools is that they might introduce extra delays into network traffic because they are on the data path. This might be true for some implementations, but in general, a device that passes a packet through without any manipulation will have negligible latency compared to the other sources of latency in a storage network. The greatest advantage of an in-band monitoring tool is that it is independent of the devices it monitors. It does not require access to the proprietary management interfaces.

Because an out-of-band monitoring tool is not on the data path, it will not introduce any latencies. However, it must support all the devices it monitors.

 Whether monitoring is performed in-band or out-of-band, management is almost always performed out-of-band, through the secondary network and through proprietary APIs.

FC switch vendors are working on adding QoS capabilities to their switches. Unfortunately, no QoS standards for FC currently exist. Vendors will initially define QoS between their own products, and like all things FC, this will cause initial incompatibility problems between devices. FC QoS is only part of the solution. As previously mentioned, FC QoS must be tied with application host and storage subsystem QoS specifications.

The newest SRM tools can discover the associations between the applications and the stored data and utilize these relations in their management decisions.

Summary

This chapter discussed issues and rules pertaining to storage Quality of Service, and included the following points:

Defining Quality and Service

- ✓ Quality of Service (QoS) is the degree to which a system realizes its expected service behavior.

- ✓ Admission policy and resource reservation are two critical requirements for implementing QoS architectures.

- ✓ The level of QoS can be quantified as the weighted sum of deviations of performance metrics from their expected value.

Storage QoS

✓ Applications and the data they put on storage networks have different priorities. This allows performance optimization through trade-offs between high- and low-priority tasks.

✓ QoS guarantees are harder to achieve in storage networks because, unlike their communication network counterparts, they cannot randomly drop packets.

✓ QoS in storage networks is a function of various components, including workload types and system architectures. A successful QoS analysis/implementation should consider all of these end-to-end effects.

Network QoS

✓ Data communication networks, and IP networks specifically, are the focus of many QoS studies because they exhibit widely varying performance behavior.

✓ Differentiated Services architecture classifies the incoming traffic into equivalency classes and assigns them Per Hop Behavior to approximate QoS guarantees over large Internet networks.

✓ Multiprotocol Label Switching inserts small labels into each packet and uses them to forward the packet through certain paths over the network to achieve QoS levels.

Performance Management for Storage QoS

✓ QoS for storage networks is defined using Service Level Agreements (SLAs) between users and providers. SLAs specify the mean, minimum, and/or maximum values for various performance metrics.

✓ Storage Resource Management tools that are specific to QoS use in-band or out-of-band performance data collection.

✓ In-band performance data collectors use special network hardware that sits on the data path transparently and collects statistical data from the traffic passing through the device.

✓ Out-of-band performance and QoS monitors use a secondary network to access the management interfaces of the devices in the storage network.

References and Additional Resources

Aurrecoechea, C., A. Cambell, and L. Hauw. May 1998. "A Survey of QoS Architectures," *Multimedia Systems Journal*, 6(3), pp. 138–151.

A survey of QoS architectures for distributed multimedia systems.

Blake, S., D. Black, M. Carlson, E. Davies, Z. Wang, and W. Weiss. December 1998. *An Architecture for Differentiated Services.* IETF RFC 2475.

Proposes DiffServ as a scalable QoS architecture for IP networks and defines two Per Hop Behavior mechanisms for achieving differentiated services.

Huston, Geoff. February 2000. *Internet Performance Survival Guide: QoS Strategies for Multiservice Networks*. John Wiley & Sons.

A comprehensive reference on QoS in IP networks.

Menascé, Daniel, Daniel Barbara, and R. Dodge. October 2001. *Preserving QoS of E-commerce Sites Through Self-Tuning: A Performance Model Approach*. Proceedings of the 2001 ACM Conference on E-commerce, Tampa, FL.

Presents a method to dynamically monitor and tune the QoS of an e-commerce site with Web server, application server, and database server tiers.

Rosen, E. C., A. Viswanathan, and R. Callon. January 2001. Multiprotocol Label Switching Architecture. RFC 3031.

Proposes the MPLS architecture for forwarding packets based on short labels that allow assignment of special paths to each class of service.

Wilkes, John. June 2001. *Traveling to Rome: QoS Specifications for Automated Storage System Management*. Proceedings of the International Workshop on Quality of Service, Lecture Notes in Computer Science, Volume 2092, Springer-Verlag.

Introduces the Rome specification language for storage QoS. Rome abstracts the storage system into streams and stores, and enables capacity and performance requirement definitions on them.

Chapter 11

Storage Capacity Planning

In This Chapter

Storage networks are complex systems with complex, and often unexpected, interactions. In general, planning the capacity of storage networks and storage systems is not an easy task. Most of the time, storage networks are over-provisioned, with lots of capacity to overcome design deficiencies. This can increase costs unnecessarily. Fortunately, guidelines and techniques are available for avoiding this pitfall. This chapter presents capacity planning concepts and includes the following subjects:

✓ A system-level look at the capacity problem and storage networks as part of the system

✓ Use of models, specifically queuing networks, in computing capacity limits and requirements

✓ Capacity management tools and research studies

Capacity Planning Concepts

Have interesting failures. If you need to have a personal crisis, have it now. Don't wait until midlife, when it will take longer to resolve. ~Garrison Keillor's advice to Macalester College's graduating class, May 19, 2002

A system's capacity can be defined as its ability to service increasing workloads without exhibiting unacceptable performance degradation. Capacity, workload, and performance are all relative and subjective terms and should be specified in measurable terms of Service Level Agreements (SLAs), Quality of Service (QoS) objectives, and performance metrics.

Capacity planning is the process of determining which workloads will saturate a given system and designing the system so that the required SLAs are met. *Capacity management* is the process of ensuring that the current capacity is adequate and used in the most effective way.

Figure 11-1 summarizes the steps involved in capacity planning. If the system exists and is available, one of the most important tasks is monitoring and measuring the performance data. This data is used to manage the existing capacity and to understand the workload to which the system is exposed. Analyzing the workload and checking the historical usage trends enables you to predict future workloads. Business plans, such as expansions and changes, can be incorporated into the workload prediction.

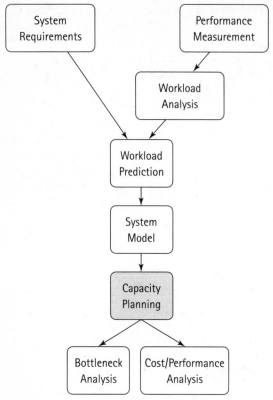

Figure 11-1: The capacity planning process

An approximate prediction of future capacity needs can be fed into a system model to identify specific architectural needs. You can apply the following information to the model to analyze cost and performance:

- ✓ Different system architectures
- ✓ Hardware and software elements
- ✓ Usage patterns
- ✓ Service levels
- ✓ Capacities

Generally, the objective is to find the least costly system design that will support all the requirements. If the analysis is being performed on an existing system, one capacity planning output is the identification of the current performance bottlenecks.

Bottlenecks are system components that cause system performance to saturate. Figure 11-2 illustrates the performance of a system for two capacity levels. Note that the performance metric in the example is assumed to have favorable values as it gets smaller (for example, response time).

The first (current) configuration violates the service level requirement above workload level W_1. After improving the bottleneck components that saturate the system, the capacity allows workloads up to W_2 before the performance metric violates the desired service level.

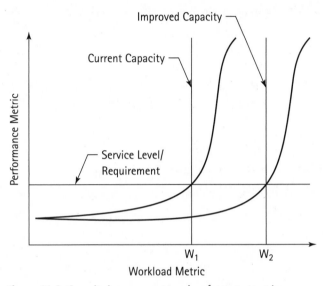

Figure 11-2: Capacity improvements and performance metrics

Performance is only one aspect of system capacity and capacity planning. For example, for storage systems and networks, storage space, system availability, and reliability are also important factors in capacity planning.

System Level Performance Analysis

Capacity planning is a system-level process. Even though individual components should be designed to support the required capacity, the overall system capacity could be different than the sum of the component capacities. This is true for storage space capacity, processing capacity, throughput, and response time. Complex systems require complex interactions between the components. Capacity planning activities should thus involve system-level models that embody system-level interactions.

The following list of questions identifies issues that must be considered when planning a computing system that involves storage networks:

✓ How many clients will the system support?

✓ How many servers are in the system? How many of them will be front-end servers, application servers, and database servers?

✓ What is the configuration of application servers?

✓ How large are the databases? What are the throughput and access time requirements?

✓ What are the reliability and availability requirements?

✓ Is database replication required? How? Are there backup requirements?

✓ What are the workload types at the front-end and at the storage network?

✓ What is the average size of IO access? What is the average file/database size?

✓ Are there any real-time requirements? Is there multimedia content?

✓ What are the requirements for the network service provider? What is the outside throughput and bandwidth?

✓ How many ports are required in the storage network?

✓ How many file access streams and how many block access streams are there?

✓ How many storage subsystems are there? Many small or a few large subsystems?

✓ What are the scalability requirements? Are there plans for growth? How much access storage and port capacity will be needed?

✓ What is the budget?

✓ What is the budget expectation for the next month? Next quarter? Next year?

✓ What is the Total Cost of Ownership? What are the administrative requirements, Service Level Agreements, and out-sourcing costs?

Capacity planning, like all other planning activities, is an iterative process. It must be repeated during the project design, development and testing, and production phases.

Cost/Performance Analysis

Adding more resources to an existing system often remedies capacity shortcomings. There are two problems with this approach, however. First, adding resources after the system is deployed can be cost-prohibitive. You might need to replace or upgrade older technology, which costs money. Second, upgrades may simply not be possible. A poorly designed system will prohibit future upgrades. Even if you add new resources, you might not be able to remove the bottleneck because it could be inherent to the architecture.

As the quote from Garrison Keillor at the beginning of this chapter suggests, most problems are best solved early in the development cycle, in the design phase. Fixing a system that has been around for a long time and accumulated several, undocumented processes and hardware is a daunting task—one that may not even be possible.

A capacity planning process must include identification and modeling of major cost sources (Chase, 2001; Menasce, 2002).

There are two major sources of cost:

✓ **Startup costs**—These beginning costs can include, but are not limited to, the following:

- Client and server machines

- Mainframe computers

- Storage subsystems

- Network switches

- Bridges

- Routers

- Cabling

- Operating systems

- System management and monitoring tools

- DBMS

- Office applications

- Network and storage network management tools

- Storage resource management tools

✓ **Operating costs**—Normal, ongoing costs in maintaining a system can include (but are not limited to) the following:

- System administrators' salaries and benefits

- Network and helpdesk support personnel

- WAN and Internet Service Provider (ISP) services

- Remote backup services

- Storage service provider services

- License and support fees

Incorporating all of these costs into cost/performance analysis provides the overall cost expectation, or the *Total Cost of Ownership (TCO)*.

Capacity Analysis with Queuing Network Models

After you construct a model of the storage system (analytical or simulation), it can be used to study the effects of several parameter changes on system behavior. For example, you can increase certain workload-defining parameters and check where the system saturates and what the expected performance is. This section provides examples of using simple queuing models to help in capacity planning. These examples can be extended in many complex ways as long as you have a model of the system under study.

The total time spent in a service node in an open queuing network is the sum of the response times of all visits to that node. Equation 3-12 given in Chapter 3 provides the formula, $R_i = S_i \div (1 - XV_iS_i)$ for the response time per visit at an M/M/1 service node. Then, by multiplying the per-visit response time (R_i) with the number of visits per job (V_i), the total response time (T_i) per job at service node i can be computed as in Equation 11-1.

Equation 11-1

$$T_i = V_i R_i = V_i S_i \div (1 - XV_i S_i)$$

The *service demand* on a service node is defined as the sum of service times over all visits of a certain job, and is computed as shown in Equation 11-2.

Equation 11-2

$$D_i = V_i S_i$$

Equation 11-1 can then be rewritten by substituting Equation 11-2, as in Equation 11-3.

Equation 11-3

$$T_i = D_i \div (1 - XD_i)$$

If the throughput value that causes a particular response time (T_i) on service node i is desired, it can be obtained by solving Equation 11-3 for throughput (X), as shown in Equation 11-4.

Equation 11-4

$$X = (1/D_i) - (1/T_i)$$

If a service-level requirement states that the response time (T_i) should be less than a maximum set value (T'), the throughput (consequently, the arrival rate) should be constrained. You can use Equation 11-4 to compute the maximum throughput X such that service node i's response time does not exceed T'. Equation 11-5 shows this relationship.

Equation 11-5

$$T_i \leq T' \rightarrow X \leq (1/D_i) - (1/T')$$

Note that Equation 11-5 considers the response time limit for a single service node. If the open queuing network has multiple service nodes, they must all be considered in computing the response time. You cannot drive a formula similar to Equation 11-5 for limiting the response time in a general open queuing network. Each network must be considered individually by driving the system's response time using Equation 3-13 ($R = \sum_i V_i R_i$), solving for the throughput, and computing the maximum throughput for a given response time limit.

If an SLA or QoS specification states that the utilization (U_i) of node i should be less than a maximum utilization U', Equation 3-14 ($U_i = X V_i S_i$) can be used to compute utilization of an M/M/1 service node. Utilization of service node i is the product of the system throughput X and the service demand D_i at node i, as shown in Equation 11-6.

Equation 11-6

$$U_i = X_i S_i = X V_i S_i = X D_i$$

Then, the maximum throughput (or the arrival rate) should be less than U'/D_i to keep utilization less than U'. Equation 11-7 shows these relationships.

Equation 11-7

$$U_i \leq U' \rightarrow X \leq U' \div D_i$$

There are no direct solutions for response time or throughput for closed queuing networks. Some iterative techniques, as shown in Chapter 3, or simulation runs, as shown in Chapter 4, are required. Therefore, you cannot find direct solutions for QoS limits. Instead, upper and lower bound approximations shown in Chapter 3 can be utilized for closed networks.

For example, Equation 11-8 states that the system's throughput will be less than the minimum $1/D_i$ value. $1/D_i$ represents the maximum throughput a service node can sustain, whether or not the node is in an open or closed queuing network. In addition, in a closed network, the throughput is bound by the number of jobs (N, queue length) divided by the think time (or the interarrival time), as shown in Equation 11-8.

Equation 11-8

$$X(N) \leq \min(N/Z, \min_i 1/D_i)$$

Figure 11-3 shows a simple transaction system with a single server and two storage subsystems. Examples 11-1 and 11-2 study this queuing network and show how the capacity limits can be computed.

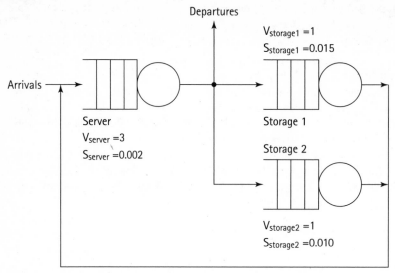

Figure 11-3: Queuing network model of a server and two storage subsystems

Example 11-1: Queuing Network Capacity Analysis

Consider the queuing network model given in Figure 11-3, which represents a transaction system. Assume the service nodes are modeled as M/M/1 queues. The service times and visit counts are as follows:

$$S_{server} = 0.002, \; S_{storage1} = 0.015, \; S_{storage2} = 0.010$$
$$V_{server} = 3, \; V_{storage1} = 1, \; V_{storage2} = 1$$

Find the maximum arrival rate such that the response time of the storage subsystems is less than 50 milliseconds and their utilization is less than 80 percent.

The service demands are computed as follows:

$$D_{server} = 0.006, \; D_{storage1} = 0.015, \; D_{storage2} = 0.010$$

The maximum possible throughput supported by each component is computed as follows.

$$1/D_{server} = 166, \; 1/D_{storage1} = 66, \; 1/D_{storage2} = 100$$

Therefore, storage subsystem 1 limits the system throughput by 66 transactions per second.

Using Equation 11-4, you can compute the throughput rate corresponding to 50 milliseconds response time given in the question.

$$X_{storage1} = (1/0.015) - (1/0.050) = 46$$
$$X_{storage2} = (1/0.010) - (1/0.050) = 80$$

This means that subsystem 1 can support up to 46 transactions per second and subsystem 2 can support 80 transactions per second before their response time passes 50 milliseconds.

The throughput limit for 80 percent utilization level can be computed using Equation 11-7.

$$U_{storage1} = 0.80 \div 0.015 = 53$$
$$U_{storage2} = 0.80 \div 0.010 = 80$$

So, subsystem 1 can support up to 53 transactions per second, and subsystem 2 can support up to 80 transactions per second before their utilizations exceed 80 percent.

As a result, the maximum arrival rate should be 46 transactions per second to have less than 50 milliseconds subsystem response time and less than 80 percent subsystem utilization.

Note that Equation 11-3 can be solved for the service demand and used to find the required service time to satisfy a given maximum response time and/or minimum throughput constraint.

This section considered QoS limits on individual components (storage subsystems). The next section provides a similar analysis for overall system performance.

Example 11-2: System Throughput Limits

Consider the transaction system given in Figure 11-3 and the preceding section, and compute the maximum possible system throughput. In addition, to have a maximum system response time of 100 milliseconds and a maximum queue length of ten transactions, what is the allowable arrival rate?

The following equations can be used to compute the response time corresponding to various throughput values.

$$R_i = S_i \div (1 - XV_iS_i)$$
$$R = \Sigma_i \ V_iR_i$$

Then, these response times can be plotted against the throughput values, as shown in the graph in Figure 11-4. An examination of the graph shows that the response time approaches 100 msec (0.1sec) as the arrival rate reaches 52 transactions per second.

Similarly, you can compute the system's queue length using the following equation, which is the sum of the queue lengths of all service nodes:

$$Q_i = X_iR_i$$
$$Q = \Sigma_i \ Q_i$$

The queue length is a function of the throughput and is plotted in the graph in Figure 11-5. As the graph shows, at around 60 transactions per second, the queue length surpasses ten transactions.

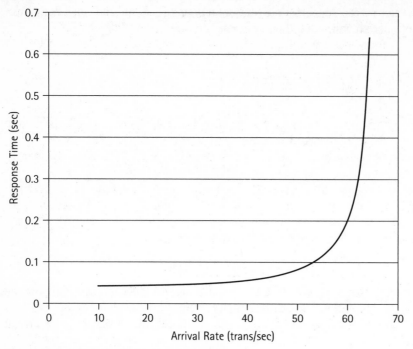

Figure 11-4: Arrival rate versus response time plot

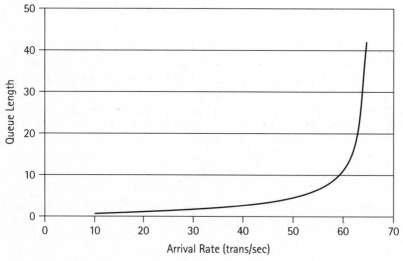

Figure 11-5: Arrival rate versus queue length plot

As a result, the arrival rate must be less than 52 transactions per second to have a response time less than 100 msec and a queue depth of ten transactions.

Capacity Planning Tools

In current practice, storage network design—including capacity planning—is a manual task performed by system experts and administrators who depend on intuition and rules of thumb (Gray, 2000). This is an error-prone approach that causes suboptimal designs. Most of the time, storage systems are over-provisioned to tolerate unexpected system growth, which causes idle resources that add unnecessarily to the TCO.

No commercially available, intelligent tools currently exist to help in the design and tuning of storage system and storage network capacity. Most storage management tools incorporate some capacity planning features. However, these are only intended for usage pattern analysis and trend analysis, and do not offer any architectural design changes. Commercial storage management tools such as the following do present the storage network with some level of abstraction:

- ✓ CA Unicenter
- ✓ Compaq StorageWorks
- ✓ HP OpenView
- ✓ IBM Tivoli
- ✓ EMC ControlCenter

These tools help the storage administrator implement the storage configuration in a more organized fashion. However, the administrator must still make almost all design and configuration decisions.

Block storage subsystems and network-attached storage (NAS) devices have proprietary management applications that keep track of capacity usage on that device and might include services to notify the administrator about the fill-rate and the need for additional storage space.

Some proof-of-concept, research tools aim at automating the storage system design. Minerva (Alvarez, 2001) and its successor, Ergastulum (Anderson, 2001), accept workload definitions and storage device models as input, and generate disk array configurations and workload to device mappings. The Appia tool (Ward, 2002) uses a similar approach to assign data flows to network arcs, and creates cost-effective network designs. SANTK (O'Keefe, 2002) is another tool that aids in Fibre Channel network topology decisions. All of these tools still require the user to understand all the workload requirements, to model the workload, and to model the devices that are included in the design space. These tools are promising advances, but in order to be applicable to commercial products, they require further development.

Summary

This chapter discussed the complexities of planning the capacity of storage networks and storage systems, and included the following subjects:

Capacity Planning Concepts

✓ Capacity planning is used to find the saturation points in a system to guide the design and tuning processes.

✓ The capacity planning process requires the study of past, current, and predicted workloads, system models, and cost/performance analysis.

✓ A system's capacity includes its storage capacity, performance capacity, reliability, and availability.

System-Level Performance Analysis

✓ Capacity planning is a system-level activity in which the interactions between all components must be considered.

✓ You should examine each storage network and consider its place in the overall computing system.

Cost/Performance Analysis

✓ Performance comes with a cost. Capacity planning is an optimization problem.

✓ Most capacity problems are more difficult to fix later in the design cycle or in the production phase.

✓ Include startup and operating costs in capacity planning.

Capacity Analysis with Queuing Network Models

✓ A model (analytical or simulation) can be used to analyze and predict a system's capacity requirements and limits.

✓ Response time, throughput, and utilization relationships in queuing network models are particularly useful for performance capacity analysis.

Capacity Planning Tools

✓ In current practice, capacity planning is mostly a manual task, one that is tedious and error-prone.

✓ Storage management applications provide partial capacity planning support by providing historical usage patterns.

✓ Promising research activities are underway, focusing on the development of intelligent tools for automatic design and the provisioning of storage systems and networks.

References and Additional Resources

Alvarez, Guillermo A., Elizabeth Borowsky, Susie Go, Theodore H. Romer, Ralph Becker-Szendy, Richard Golding, Arif Merchant, Mirjana Spasojevic, Alistair Veitch, and John Wilkes. November 2001. *Minerva: An Automated Resource Provisioning Tool for Large-Scale Storage Systems*. ACM Transactions on Computer Systems, 19(4), pp. 483–518.

Presents a tool that accepts workload definitions and storage device models as input, and generates disk array configurations and workload to device mappings.

Anderson, Eric, Mahesh Kallahalla, Susan Spence, Ram Swaminathan, and Qian Wang. 2001. *Ergastulum: An Approach to Solving the Workload and Device Configuration Problem*. HP Laboratories SSP Technical Memo, HPL-SSP-2001-05.

Describes a tool for automatic design and configuration of storage systems based on workload definitions and storage models.

Chase, J., D. Anderson, P. Thakar, and A. Vahdat. October 2001. *Managing Energy and Server Resources in Hosting Centers*. In 18th ACM Symposium on Operating System Principles (SOSP'01), pages 103–116. Chateau Lake Louise, Banff, Canada.

Proposes a framework for dynamically turning on/off Web servers in a hosting center according to cost and SLA constraints, with the objective of saving energy.

Gray, J. and P. Shenoy. 2000. *Rules of Thumb in Data Engineering*. In Proc. 16th International Conference on Data Engineering, pp. 3–12.

Presents price/performance comparisons of data caching and data fetching when data is reused over time.

Menasce, D. A. and V. A. F. Almeida. 2002. *Capacity Planning for Web Services: Metrics, Models, and Methods*. Prentice Hall, Upper Saddle River, NJ.

Provides performance analysis and capacity planning methods for e-business services.

O'Keefe, Matthew T. and University of Minnesota Fibre Channel Group. 2002. *Designing Fibre Channel Storage Area Networks, Development and Use of the SANTK*. Available at `http://www.borg.umn.edu/fc`.

Describes a tool (Storage Area Network Configuration Toolkit) that helps in the SAN design process.

Ward, Julie, Michael O'Sullivan, Troy Shahoumian, and John Wilkes. January 2002. *Appia: Automatic Storage Area Network Fabric Design*. In Conference on File and Storage Technologies (FAST'02), USENIX, pp. 203–217. Monterey, CA.

Presents two heuristic algorithms that design a Fibre Channel network using data-flow requirements, while minimizing the implementation cost.

Part IV

Storage Performance Tools

Chapter 12
Storage Benchmarks

Chapter 13
Performance Monitoring and Management Tools

Chapter 12

Storage Benchmarks

In This Chapter

If you cannot measure performance, you do not know how good (or bad) it is. Computer benchmarks are as old as computers themselves. They are useful tools for comparing different configuration alternatives for purchase or performance-tuning decisions. There is a large breadth of storage-related benchmarks. This chapter discusses the most popular ones, and includes the following topics:

✓ Benchmarking definitions, general tips, and guidelines

✓ Block I/O–based storage benchmarks

✓ File system–based storage benchmarks

✓ Application-based system benchmarks

Benchmarking Considerations

Why do we need artificial, over-simplified programs (known as benchmarks) to study performance? Because real applications and workloads are costly, hard to measure, impractical to set up, not repeatable, and made up of lots of unknown, complex interactions. Benchmarks overcome these limitations. They are a set of well-defined, representative workloads that can be executed on many systems to compare their performance.

Benchmarks should provide measurable, repeatable performance results. They are used for monitoring system performance, diagnosing problems, and comparing alternatives. Benchmarks are limited, by definition (they must be simple), providing only a partial picture. Consider them a complementary source of information to other studies involving cost, reliability, ease of use, and so on.

Benchmarks range from toy benchmarks that have simple kernel loops to large system benchmarks that simulate enterprise-level information processing. This chapter focuses on benchmarks that provide meaningful information about storage subsystems.

A good benchmark must provide understandable, relevant information for its domain. It must be scalable for testing a wide range of systems. In addition, it must be unbiased to be acceptable by a wide range of users and vendors.

Here is a list of items that you should consider when setting up a benchmark test-bed for storage. Further tips are discussed later in the chapter, as different benchmarking concepts are introduced.

✓ In multiple central processing unit (CPU) systems (*Symmetric Multi-Processing, or SMP*), the number of processors will affect the systems' performance. In addition, on these systems, assigning subsets of processors to specific processes and their threads will change execution performance. To utilize processor caches more effectively, threads could be assigned to a small subset of available processors. On many systems, this is accomplished through *processor affinity* system calls. Using affinity calls should be carefully considered.

✓ Caches change benchmark behavior in unexpected ways. Therefore, you must make sure that all caches are empty before each benchmark execution. Examples of caches to consider in storage benchmarks include the processor caches (L1, L2, and L3), file system buffer cache, network file system client and server caches. You may need to power-cycle client and server machines, or unmount and remount file systems in between benchmark runs to ensure that the caches have a *cold start*.

✓ In addition to the choice of using or not using a cache, the size and scheduling policies of caches profoundly affects execution profiles. Expanding or restricting cache sizes and cache policies are some of the first factors to try in a benchmarking study.

✓ In benchmarks that can execute on multiple machines simultaneously, you might need to synchronize the machine times and timings of events. *Network Time Protocol (NTP)* can be used to synchronize machine clocks. Distributed benchmark utilities generally have options that can be set to synchronize the benchmark events (such as start and stop execution) between multiple benchmark instances.

This chapter discusses storage benchmarks in three major categories: block I/O benchmarks, file system benchmarks, and application-level benchmarks.

Block I/O Benchmarks

Benchmarks that exercise and measure storage systems using block I/O interfaces are useful for obtaining the performance characteristics of storage layers below the file system level. These could be regarded as raw storage performance benchmarks. IOmeter and SPC-1 are the two most widely accepted benchmarks in this category.

IOmeter

IOmeter was developed by Intel Corp., and is currently distributed as an open-source project. It is a tool for generating tightly controlled I/O workloads and collecting performance data such as response time, throughput, and CPU usage.

It is best used for stress testing I/O systems to find system bottlenecks. Because it does not have any prescribed, real-world workload definitions, it cannot be used as an application performance predictor. However, it can easily be configured to generate almost any kind of I/O pattern through a graphical user interface.

Although IOmeter sometimes appears in literature for benchmarking file servers, it lacks the necessary capabilities to generate a proper file access workload. IOmeter generates reads and writes to volumes (raw or formatted). However, file server workloads are generally dominated by metadata-type operations such as directory searches and file attribute checks. When used to benchmark file systems, IOmeter is only useful for checking the read/write throughput of a file system.

IOmeter is more useful for testing the block devices directly (as raw devices, which bypass the file system). At the block device level, everything is a data read or a data write operation, no matter what the higher levels might be doing (for example, accessing file attributes).

IOmeter can be set to execute with any queue length. A device's queue length denotes the number of outstanding I/Os on that device at a given time. Deep queue lengths generally increase the throughput and the response time, as shown several times previously in this book.

Figure 12-1 contains sample throughput-response time curves obtained using IOmeter. In these experiments, four IOmeter "worker" processes are executed on four different client machines. These machines access a disk array as their back-end storage, using 16KB random write operations.

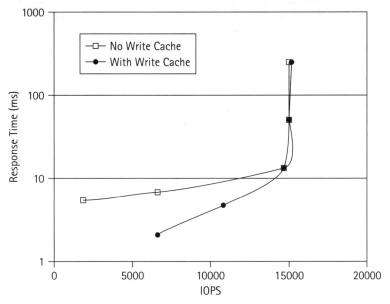

Figure 12-1: Sample throughput-response time curves obtained with IOmeter

In the figure, the two curves represent tests with write caching enabled and disabled on the disk array, respectively. Successive data points on each curve are obtained by setting the client queue depths at values of 2, 8, 32, 128, and 512. The figure shows the range where write caching significantly reduces the response time. The figures are obtained from spreadsheet outputs of IOmeter runs. This example shows the usefulness of IOmeter as a stress test tool.

Storage Performance Council Benchmarks

Storage Performance Council (SPC) is a group comprised of companies that are predominantly in the data storage and server business. SPC was formed to develop industry-standard benchmarks for storage networks. By overseeing the development and publication of benchmark results, the group aims to provide a level playing field for storage system vendors.

SPC plans to release a series of benchmarks, each intended for use in a different environment. The first benchmark, SPC-1 (SPC, 2002; McNutt, 2001), represents a workload that is both throughput- and response time-sensitive. It was developed by studying the workload of transaction processing systems that require small, mostly random, read and write operations (for example, database systems, OLTP systems, and mail servers).

SPC started working on the SPC-2 benchmark, which will represent workloads with large I/O sizes and mostly sequential access. It is intended to emulate video on-demand servers, film rendering applications, and backup/restore operations.

SPC benchmark source code is controlled by the member companies, and SPC has put an audit structure in place to authenticate test results. After a test sponsor (a member company) submits benchmark results in the form of a *Full Disclosure Report (FDR)*, auditors assigned by SPC review the results and post them for peer-review for 60 days, at the end of which time the results are assumed to be official.

SPC-1 reports two main performance metrics. *SPC-1 IOs per second (IOPS)* represents the highest IOPS rate achieved during the benchmark. Any reported SPC-1 IOPS result should not have a response time greater than 30ms. The second reported metric is the *SPC-1 LRT (Least Response Time)*, which is obtained at 10 percent of the load level of the reported SPC-1 IOPS rate. Figure 12-2 illustrates these two metrics.

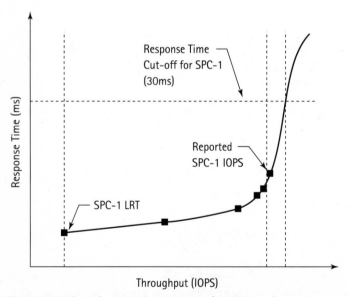

Figure 12-2: Throughput-response time curve for SPC-1 results

An FDR is supposed to contain the throughput-response time curve, as shown in Figure 12-2, and the IOPS rate and LRT. In addition, sponsors who want to publish SPC-1 results are supposed to disclose the total price of their Tested Storage Configuration (TSC), as defined later in this chapter. An FDR contains a cost/performance value in the form of dollars per SPC-1 IOPS.

Table 12-1 presents a summary of public SPC-1 results currently available. Test sponsors are also supposed to disclose the data capacity and the data protection level they have used in the tests, as shown in Table 12-1.

TABLE 12-1 SPC-1 Results Submitted as of October 2002

Tested Storage Configuration	SPC-1 IOPS	SPC-1 LRT	ASU Capacity (GB)	$/IOPS	Data Protection Level	FDR Submission Date
3PAR InServ S800 Storage Server	47,001	2.34	4,444.44	$34.65	Mirroring	10-Oct-02
Dell Corp., PERC3/ QC SCSI RAID Controller	7,650	3.10	440.00	$4.48	Mirroring	19-Jun-02
HP StorageWorks Enterprise Virtual Array Model 2C12D	24,006	2.29	2596.3	$22.00	Mirroring	2-Oct-02
IBM Enterprise Storage Server F20	8,009	2.99	1,259.85	$44.58	RAID5	20-May-02
LSI E4600 FC Storage System	15,708	1.64	400.00	$16.01	Mirroring	20-May-02
Sun StorEdge 9910	8,404	2.07	343.51	$74.29	Mirroring	20-May-02

In SPC-1, all host computers involved in the test, the storage network, and the storage subsystems comprise the *Benchmark Configuration (BC)*, as shown in Figure 12-3. All the storage-related items, including the host adapters, cables, network switches, and hubs, constitute the *Tested Storage Configuration (TSC)*. This is significant because the reported system cost involves everything in the TSC.

The workload generator in SPC-1 is based on *Business Scaling Units (BSUs)*. One BSU represents a group of users collectively generating a prescribed I/O demand. Each BSU demands 50 IO operations per second. These are generated through eight streams. Five streams generate random reads and writes. Two of the streams generate sequential reads. The final stream generates sequential writes. The streams are assigned to *Application Storage Units (ASUs)*, as shown in Figure 12-4.

Benchmark Configuration (BC)

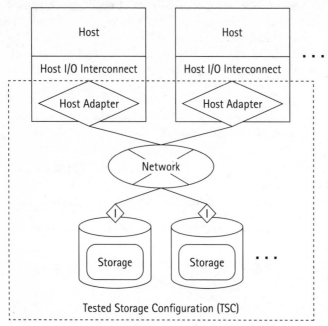

Figure 12-3: BC and TSC definitions for SPC-1

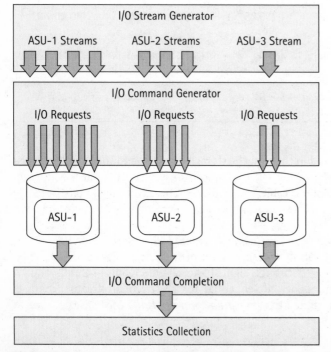

Figure 12-4: Streams and Application Storage Units in SPC-1

There are three ASUs. ASU-1 is the data store that holds the raw data for the applications. It contains 45 percent of the total ASU capacity. ASU-2 is the user store that holds an organized, secure store for user files. It contains 45 percent of the total ASU capacity. ASU-3 is the log that provides information consistency for the data in the ASU-1 and ASU-2. It contains 10 percent of the total ASU capacity.

An official SPC-1 test, which can be submitted to SPC, comprises several mandatory phases. Figure 12-5 shows the progress of the test in time (not drawn to scale). Changing the number of simulated BSUs controls the load in SPC-1. To increase the throughput, more BSUs are added, and to decrease the load, fewer BSUs are used. The primary metrics (IOPS and LRT) are measured only in the stable states (shown as plateaus in the figure).

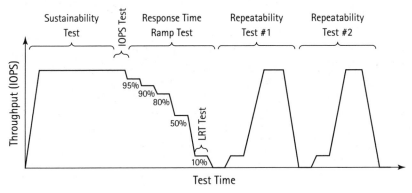

Figure 12-5: SPC-1 test phases for a complete benchmark execution

The first phase is the sustainability test, which executes at the highest BSU load for a long period. The intention is to ensure that the highest throughput can be sustained over time. Through the end of the sustainability test, a measurement is taken to obtain the official SPC-1 IOPS rate. Then, in the response time ramp test, the load is decreased gradually to obtain a response time-throughput graph. At the end of the ramp, at the 10 percent load level, SPC-1 LRT is recorded.

IOPS and LRT measurements are repeated twice to check the repeatability of the test results after system shutdowns. SPC-1 IOPS and SPC-1 LRT results must be within 5 percent of the values obtained in the sustainability and repeatability tests to be valid for official submittal.

SPC-1 is the first and only industry benchmark applicable to storage networking environments. Although SPC-1 has a narrow workload scope, SPC is working on additional benchmarks to broaden the covered workload types.

File System Benchmarks

File systems add another layer above the block I/O interface, and they change the storage workload coming down to the storage devices. File system caching and metadata handling cause a unique type of workload that must be tested with special benchmarks. This category includes Bonnie, IOzone, NetBench, PostMark, and SPEC SFS.

File System Benchmarking Considerations

File system performance is sensitive to many system configuration parameters, and benchmarking file systems can be a tricky task.

The following is a short list of tips to consider when setting up file systems for benchmarking:

✓ File systems (local or network-mounted) buffer write operations in buffer caches before committing them to stable storage (such as hard disks). This data destaging can happen immediately before the write call returns, or later at a synchronization time or at the file close time. Applications that require absolute reliability can use the synchronous write operations, which force all data to stable storage before an acknowledgement is generated. In most systems, this is done through the O_SYNC option at the file open time. You should be aware of the method your benchmark is using. Using synchronous write operations will prohibit any gains from write buffering. If asynchronous operations are allowed, the benchmark developer or user must decide whether to include file destaging overhead (*fsynch* and *fflush* system calls) in the benchmark timings.

✓ File locking keeps data consistent when multiple readers/writers are operating on the file. Files can be locked on local or network-mounted file systems. In both cases, locking files might disable file caching. Check your benchmark options for allowing or disallowing file locks.

✓ Memory-mapped files effectively cache the entire file on the client computer's memory. This eliminates almost all disk I/O until the file is closed or a synchronization system call is made. Performance and reliability implications of this behavior are obvious and should be considered in file system benchmarks.

The following list contains tips that are especially useful when benchmarking network file systems:

✓ Decide where the benchmark program, data files, and output files will reside. When benchmarking network file systems, executing the benchmark programs from local file systems while the data files reside on the remote mounted directories is advisable.

✓ Network File System (NFS) client caches must be cleared by unmounting and remounting the remote directories between test runs. This guarantees that the performance of later benchmark runs are not tainted with the cached data of previous runs.

✓ Server write commit times must be included in the execution time. Any outstanding write operations on the server side are committed to the disk storage at file close time. This could have a large impact on the performance of small files that are entirely in the server cache.

✓ While benchmarking networked storage, the parameters used to set up the network connection will directly impact performance. NFS, for example, can execute over Transmission Control Protocol (TCP) and User Datagram Protocol (UDP) sockets. The choice between the two protocols will determine where data error handling is performed (in the network stack in the case of TCP, and in upper-layer protocols with UDP).

✓ Socket buffer sizes and TCP window sizes determine the amount of in-transit data over the network. These can be changed by changing the registry keys in MS Windows-based machines, and by manipulating the system parameters in the /proc file system on Linux machines.

✓ NFS allows the user to set the granularity of the read and write data exchange (*rsize* and *wsize*). You will need to experiment with multiple values to find the optimum settings for your environment.

✓ Operational parameters of Ethernet connections are important as well. Full-duplex connections will eliminate contention at the wire level. Many older Ethernet adapter cards might be set to half-duplex connections by default. In addition, a larger Maximum Transmission Unit (MTU) size (*jumbo frames*) will reduce the network packets' fragmentation.

✓ Network file system performance is proportional to the number of clients accessing the file server. The throughput, as well as the response time, will increase by the number of clients.

✓ The number of NFS daemons on the client (*biod*) and server (*nfsd*) affects the throughput. The number of daemons determines the number of operations that can be served simultaneously.

✓ Besides data, file system metadata (*inodes* and *vnodes*) is cached on both the client side and the server side. Metadata caches allow fast access to file attributes, and they will eliminate disk accesses as long as the data is in the cache. Therefore, the inode cache size is important.

Bonnie

Bonnie and its variants (for example, Bonnie++) are simple file system workload generators that can be used to quickly test a file system's throughput on UNIX machines. You can use it for quick comparisons. However, the benchmark results do not have a real-world correspondence.

Bonnie uses standard C library calls, which are portable to many platforms. The benchmark performs a series of operations on a large file. A sample output looks like this:

```
        -------Sequential Output-------- ---Sequential Input-- --Random--
        -Per Char- --Block--- -Rewrite-- -Per Char- --Block--- --Seeks---
Machine  MB K/sec %CPU K/sec %CPU K/sec %CPU K/sec %CPU K/sec %CPU  /sec %CPU
testsys  500  4332 13.7  4722 .3.3  1413 .2.8  4674 10.3  4744 .5.6  52.0  1.0
```

One of the useful outputs is the CPU utilization percentage that can be used to check whether CPU is a bottleneck.

IOzone

IOzone is a free, open-source file system benchmark. It enables the study of system configurations on file system performance. The user can set IOzone to generate a wide variety of access patterns and to collect statistics on performance. Rather than being an application-specific benchmark, IOzone is a tool for generating a large number of access patterns.

The source code is in ANSI C and can be compiled on a large number of platforms, including many Microsoft Windows and UNIX-based machines. The parameters can be set to generate the following:

✓ Read

✓ Write

✓ Re-read

✓ Re-write

✓ Read/write backwards/strided

✓ Random read/write

✓ Memory-mapped read/write

✓ Asynchronous read/write

On a single machine, the benchmark can use multiple processes or threads. On multiple machines, IOzone can execute as a distributed file system benchmark.

IOzone can purge processor caches and mount/unmount file systems to remove dirty cache effects. It can generate Microsoft Excel output data that can be used to draw surface plots showing the interactions between file sizes, access sizes, and performance metrics. IOzone can be configured to generate synchronous or asynchronous I/O operations.

IOzone has useful parameters for benchmarking both local file systems and network mounted file systems. A typical invocation of IOzone for a network mounted file system would look like this:

```
./iozone -acR -U /mnt/test -f /mnt/test/testfile -b output.xls > logfile
```

In this example, -a is used to let IOzone test all file sizes between 64KB and 512MB and record sizes from 4KB to 16MB. The parameter -c is used to tell IOzone to include write commit times at the end of an NFS V3 file close. The -R option generates output data as Excel spreadsheets. The -U option causes IOzone to unmount the file system between tests. The next two parameters denote the directory and file name to use for data accesses. -b denotes the Excel output filename. The standard outputs are piped to a local file.

Figure 12-6 shows the results of file system performance data obtained using IOzone. Here, two file systems (fs1 and fs2) are compared for two file sizes (16MB and 1GB) and various buffer sizes (4KB to 16MB).

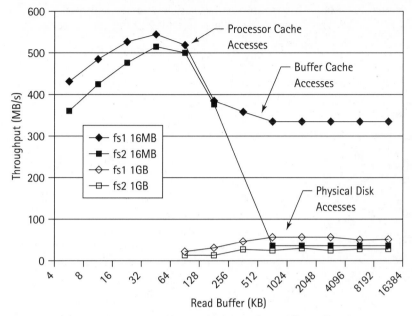

Figure 12-6: IOzone data comparing the performance of two different file systems

The figure clearly shows the effects of various caches on the data path. For small-sized reads from a small file, most of the data is in the processor cache, which yields a very high throughput. The data for the large file size comes directly from the physical disks, causing a big drop in throughput. The point that differentiates the two file systems is the use of the buffer cache for the small file size. The first file system (fs1) effectively uses the buffer cache, while the second one (fs2) bypasses the buffer cache and causes poor performances. These results were obtained on Linux servers using two commercially available journaling file systems.

Although IOzone results cannot be used to predict the performance of a particular application on a particular platform, its wide variety of configuration parameters and ease of use make it an excellent tool for diagnosing and debugging the performance pitfalls in file system–based storage networks.

NetBench

NetBench is a network file system benchmark for *Common Internet File System (CIFS)* clients and servers. CIFS is a network file system protocol based on Microsoft's *Server Message Block (SMB)*, and is the native resource-sharing protocol for Microsoft Windows platforms.

Although NetBench is freely available, the source code is controlled by Ziff-Davis, Inc. NetBench accepts workload definition files and replays these workloads on client machines. In standard NetBench practice, the "disk-mix" workload definition file provided as part of the distribution is used. This workload was obtained by collecting traces of popular desktop applications.

Figure 12-7 shows a breakdown of SMB operations generated between a client machine running NetBench and a CIFS server. The figure shows that a vast majority of the operations are writes and metadata access (get attribute, open, close) operations.

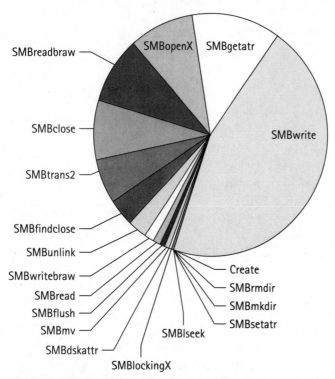

Figure 12-7: NetBench disk-mix workload breakdown

As discussed earlier in this book, the workload has a profound effect on performance outcomes. For example, a home-directory server, which keeps and serves user files, will have a very different operation distribution than the one shown in Figure 12-7. A home-directory server will face mostly metadata-type operations (such as directory opens, closes, searches, and file attribute checks). One study shows that actual read and writes in a home-directory server are less than 25 percent of all operations (Ramany, 2001).

Figure 12-8 shows the distribution of operation sizes generated by the NetBench disk-mix workload. While most of the write operations (updates) are less than 1KB, read operations center around 4KB.

Another important factor determining workload is the place where the workload is defined in the storage network. In NetBench, CIFS workload is defined from the perspective of end-user desktops. However, network-attached storage (NAS) devices are increasingly being used as back-end storage for file servers, Web servers, or database servers. Therefore, the client traffic is filtered and transformed into server traffic before it reaches a CIFS server (for example, a NAS device).

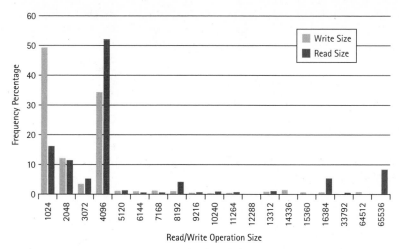

Figure 12-8: Read/write operation size distribution for NetBench disk-mix workload

Previous studies showed that file servers generate exclusively write-dominant traffic because almost all read and metadata traffic is captured by the large caches on the servers.

NetBench executes workload generators on multiple clients (Windows 95/98/NT/2000), which are controlled through a control station (Windows NT/2000). It incorporates a GUI-based control program, which enables the easy launch of the benchmark and generation of output files. The output is in the form of Excel spreadsheets that contain total bandwidth (throughput, in NetBench terms) in Mb/s and average response time in milliseconds. A single setup can be repeated for different numbers of clients.

A sample result is shown in Figure 12-9. The figure combines the NetBench results obtained for two different server file systems. The objective is to study the effect of the server's local file system on overall network file access performance. In this example, the first file system scaled better to a high number of clients and consistently provided better response time.

As the figure shows, NetBench performance depends on the number of clients. A high-end file server or a NAS device might require 60 clients before it is saturated. This makes NetBench impractical if you do not have access to a large test-bed.

Another concern with NetBench is the small footprint of the accessed data. This causes most of the data to be served from client and/or server caches and makes the benchmark insensitive to back-end stable storage (disk) performance. The server's processing and communication power becomes the key factor for higher NetBench results. To remove the effects of various caches, the caches must be enabled/disabled using separate system configuration manipulations.

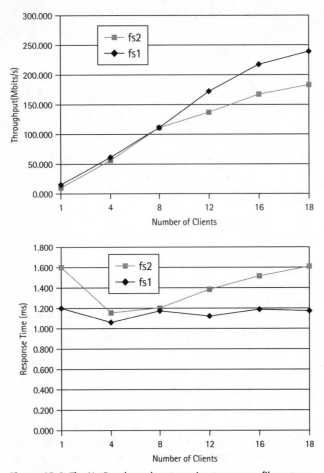

Figure 12-9: The NetBench results comparing two server file systems

PostMark

PostMark is a very specialized file system workload generation tool. It is intended for testing small file, high-throughput environments such as e-mail and netnews servers. It generates a large pool of small files and performs opens, closes, reads, and updates on that pool. The results are very specific to that environment and are not generally applicable to other workloads. PostMark can exercise local file systems and both CIFS- and NFS-mounted file systems.

SPEC SFS

Standard Performance Evaluation Corporation (SPEC) is an industry consortium that develops and publishes a broad range of benchmarks—from CPU to Web server benchmarks—for the evaluation of computing systems.

System File Server (SFS) is SPEC's benchmark for the performance of NFS servers. It is based on two earlier benchmarks, LADDIS and Nhfsstone. The latest version is SPEC SFS97_R1 V3.0. It supports both NFS V2 and NFS V3, as well as TCP and UDP as transport protocols.

Newer versions are updated to include workload specifications for modern NFS servers. SFS executes on client computers (which must be UNIX-based) and can access any server that supports NFS. The primary outputs include a table of throughput versus response time. The single figure of merit is the highest throughput obtained at a response time less than 50ms.

SPEC SFS is storage throughput–sensitive, and using more spindles will provide better SFS numbers. Instead of using the newer, bigger disk drives, using a larger number of older, smaller drives is more advantageous. Although this might be seen as a benchmark anomaly, it is a fact of throughput performance.

Application-Level Benchmarks

Application-level benchmarks stress the system end to end, from the CPU to network, to storage devices. These benchmarks emulate business application loads, and their results are more meaningful in their application domains. This category includes TPC and SPEC benchmarks.

TPC Benchmarks

The Transaction Processing Performance Council (TPC) is a group of companies that produces benchmarks for transaction processing and database applications. Most of the TPC benchmarks are system-level, end-to-end benchmarks that exercise almost all parts of the computing system, including the clients, the network, the servers, and the storage subsystems.

The current flagship TPC benchmark is TPC-C, which simulates an Online Transaction Processing (OLTP) environment with multiple terminal sessions in a warehouse-based distribution operation (TPC, 1998). It contains read-only and read/write operation mixes that simulate new-order, payment, order-status, stock-level, and delivery transactions. TPC-C can be scaled quite well by increasing the number of warehouses and the users.

The TPC-C metrics include throughput (new-order transactions per minute, tpmC) and price/performance ($/tpmC). TPC-C is a widely accepted benchmark with results submitted from all major systems companies. Because it stresses all components, it is hard to tell the effect of storage subsystems on TPC-C results directly, unless the storage subsystem is the bottleneck. One obvious expectation from storage subsystems is a high throughput rate, rather than high data bandwidth.

TPC-H and TPC-R benchmarks simulate Decision Support System (DSS) environments. However, they are not as popular as TPC-C, and most of the time vendors ignore them.

TPC-W is one of the latest benchmarks from TPC (TPC, 2000). TPC-W simulates a transactional Web environment such as that seen with e-commerce sites. It provides performance and price/performance metrics. It is modeled after a Web bookstore. Primary transactions include browsing, shopping, ordering, and business-to-business transactions.

TPC-W's primary metrics are Web Interactions per Second (WIPS), dollars per WIPS ($/WIPS), and Web Interaction Response Time (WIRT). TPC-W improves over TPC-C/H/R by requiring a very detailed system performance disclosure that includes the CPU utilizations, database logical and physical I/O activity, and network and storage I/O rates.

SPEC Web

SPEC produced a series of Web server benchmarks over the years (Eigenmann, 2001). The latest version, SPECWeb99, is based on Web workloads obtained from logs of large Web installations and agreed upon by major server vendors. A companion benchmark, SPECWeb99_SSL, measures the performance of Web servers using secure communication protocols.

Newer versions reflect the latest developments in Web technology, including dynamic HTTP, rotating ads, cookies, and so on Similar to SPEC SFS, SPECWeb99 is a client-based benchmark and supports any Web server capable of serving HTTP.

The benchmark's primary outputs are a table of requested load and response times. The peak throughput is the single figure of merit, with no limits on response time. Web servers generate mostly read, random, small-size storage I/O operations. Therefore, SPECWeb99 will be sensitive to the throughput of the storage system for such I/O patterns.

Real Applications as Benchmarks

General wisdom says that the best benchmark for testing alternative systems is the real application that will be used on these systems in the production phase. Although there is truth in this argument, there are some pitfalls as well.

The problem with real applications is that their workload is very difficult to control. The real workloads are mostly dynamic, time- and input-sensitive, which makes repeating the same execution twice almost impossible. Without repeatability, comparing two configurations in a meaningful way is difficult. Real applications are also difficult, costly, and time-consuming to set up.

Therefore, the application under study is the best benchmark for a purchase decision or performance tuning only if it enables the generation of repeatable workloads.

Performance results obtained from applications will not be publishable because they will not be repeatable out of the test-bed in which they are obtained.

Summary

This chapter discussed the most popular storage benchmarks, and included the following topics:

Benchmarking Considerations

- ✓ Benchmarks are simple programs with well-defined workloads that simulate the behavior of real applications in a specific domain.

- ✓ Benchmarks must be representative, repeatable, and scalable, with easy-to-interpret results.

- ✓ When preparing a benchmark test-bed, carefully consider processor architectures, cache hierarchies, and time synchronization issues.

Block I/O Benchmarks

- ✓ Block I/O benchmarks provide raw storage performance without the added cost of file systems or database applications.

- ✓ IOmeter is a simple-to-use tool for benchmarking multiple storage targets from multiple client machines. It can be configured to generate a wide range of workloads for stress testing and bottleneck analysis. It does not provide any industry standard workloads.

- ✓ SPC-1 is the first benchmark developed by SPC and simulates the storage load of transaction-oriented workloads with lots of random, small I/O operations. It provides peak throughput and least response time measurements.

File System Benchmarks

- ✓ File system benchmarks simulate the workloads of standard file system interfaces. They include the file system overhead on the client and server systems.

- ✓ Bonnie, IOzone, and PostMark are simple, configurable benchmarks for testing the performance of a wide range of file system workloads.

- ✓ NetBench and SPEC SFS have standard workload definitions, which can be used to obtain file system performance metrics that are comparable across different systems.

Application-Level Benchmarks

✓ Application-level benchmarks emulate real application workloads in an effort to approximate the performance of systems under such workloads.

✓ TPC produced a series of benchmarks, TPC-C/H/R/W, that emulate a complete transaction system, decision support system, or Web transaction system. TPC results are affected by all system layers, including the storage subsystems.

✓ SPECWeb99 is a benchmark for studying the performance of Web servers.

Real Applications as Benchmarks

✓ Real applications are hard to use as benchmarks because of their complexity and cost.

✓ Applications can be used as benchmarks inside an organization if generating repeatable workloads and performance results is possible.

References and Additional Resources

Eigenmann, Rudolf. 2001. *Performance Evaluation and Benchmarking with Realistic Applications*. MIT Press.

Contains a collection of research papers on realistic benchmarking, with an emphasis on SPEC benchmarks.

McNutt, Bruce and Steve Johnson. 2001. *A Standard Test of I/O Cache*. International CMG Conference 2001, pp. 327–332.

Explains the hierarchical reuse algorithm used in SPC-1 to generate workloads appropriate for cache hierarchies.

Ramany, Swaminathan. 2001. *A Case for a New CIFS Benchmark*. Int. CMG Conference 2001, pp. 639–648.

Presents workload characterizations for CIFS servers, and critiques current CIFS benchmarks, including NetBench.

Storage Performance Council. 2002. *SPC Benchmark-1 (SPC-1) Official Specification, Revision 1.5.0*.

Available at www.storageperformance.org.

Transaction Processing Performance Council. April 16, 1998. *TPC Benchmark C, TPC Benchmark C Standard Specification*, Revision 3.3.3.

Transaction Processing Performance Council. June 27, 2000. *TPC Benchmark W (Web Commerce) Specification*, Version 1.1.

The following are Web links to benchmarks discussed in this chapter:

IOmeter (Intel)
http://sourceforge.net/projects/iometer/

SPC-1 (SPC)
www.storageperformance.org

Bonnie
www.textuality.com/bonnie/

IOzone
www.iozone.org

NetBench (Ziff Davis)
www.netbench.com/benchmarks/

PostMark
www.netapp.com/tech_library/3022.html

SPEC SFS, SPECWeb99 (SPEC)
www.spec.org

TPC-C/H/R/W (TPC)
www.tpc.org

Chapter 13

Performance Management and Monitoring Tools

In This Chapter

It's a well-known fact (especially in the storage networking realm) that the cost of management far outweighs the cost of the hardware acquisition. Numerous existing tools and emerging standards aim at reducing storage management complexity by automating most of the tasks that are currently performed manually by expert administrators. This chapter discusses enterprise-wide storage resource management tools, and includes the following topics:

- ✓ The definition of performance management and the need for automated management in storage networks

- ✓ Enterprise management tools and protocols

- ✓ Standards-based storage management using the emerging Bluefin standard

- ✓ An overview of existing storage management tools

- ✓ Performance monitoring tools for systems, networks, and storage networks

Introduction to Performance Management

The purchase of high-performance equipment does not guarantee realizable performance. Performance must be designed for, configured, monitored, and fixed. Performance management consists of several activities (Lipovich, 2000):

- ✓ Performance data collection

- ✓ Real-time monitoring

- ✓ Problem detection and diagnosis

- ✓ Automated policy enforcement

- ✓ Historical performance data retention

- ✓ Performance and trend reporting

- ✓ Performance analysis and modeling

- ✓ Capacity planning

Although all these activities are essential to successful performance management, finding comprehensive tools or knowledgeable administrative personnel to perform all these tasks together is difficult. Currently, most of these tasks are performed using specialized, individual tools and require manual control and intervention.

Even the tools that promise automated management require you to manually configure policies and some threshold values. How would you know where to set the threshold value? Setting performance thresholds requires an understanding of expected or normal system behavior. Unfortunately, normal behavior is a relative term that changes from system to system, and from application to application. In addition, the expected performance differs depending on the time period. For example, the expected response time during the weekends or holidays may be different than it is during business days. Setting thresholds based on average behavior might cause false alarms that could waste administrative resources.

Performance management in storage networks starts with *storage provisioning*, which is the process of assigning storage resources to the users and applications, as needed. This seemingly simple task can become almost impossible in a relatively complex storage area network (SAN). This task includes the following steps:

1. The storage administrator must know the type of storage that the application needs.

2. The size of storage, performance, availability, and backup requirements must be determined.

3. A storage resource matching these requirements must be located in the current SAN, or it must be configured from scratch.

4. To support the availability requirements, multiple paths from the application to the data store must be set up. The switches and host bus adapters (HBAs) must be zoned to provide the path. This step must be repeated for each redundant fabric connection and each HBA on the end-points.

5. The storage device must be configured for logical unit number (LUN) mappings and for the required storage layouts.

6. All these configurations must be tested and recorded so that the changes can be tracked back when needed.

These operations might be simple to perform for an expert administrator in a simple SAN environment. However, in a storage network with hundreds of servers, switches, disk arrays, tape libraries, and application types, the complexity is beyond the capability of manual configuration. Automated management tools based on policy rules are required for such complex tasks. Policy-based management is used to differentiate service according to resource and demand attributes. The policies should include the following:

✓ Application type

✓ Storage type

✓ Performance and availability requirements

✓ Cost

✓ Security constraints

These tools must present the end-points (the application and the storage) to the user and hide all the complexities in between, while still allowing the administrators to drill down to the level they need in case of problems.

The rest of the chapter discusses enterprise management and management protocols. Enterprise management is not specific to storage; however, storage and networks constitute an important (if not the most important) part of the overall enterprise computing management. An overview of storage management tools and performance monitoring tools is also included.

Enterprise Management

Managing an enterprise computing system is the process of ensuring that the expectations (for example, Service Level Agreements, or SLAs) are met, while satisfying day-to-day business activities. This process requires careful planning, execution, and improvement at several layers. The management activities for achieving service levels in an enterprise environment (Lewis, 2001) can be summarized as follows:

- ✓ **Infrastructure Management** — The computing systems, the network, and the applications must all be in working condition and configured for best performance. Most of the "managed" components have their own management interface.

- ✓ **Fault Management** — If any of the infrastructure components fail to provide service, the fault must be detected and, if possible, alternative service nodes or paths must be established. Servers or applications that crash, or network switches or ports that go down, are typical examples. Successful tools must be able to drill down to the root cause of the problem, such as running out of memory, CPU or network overload, and so on.

- ✓ **Resource Management** — This level consists of several tools that manage the resources. Asset management tools keep track of devices and their configuration and license information. Maintenance tools make sure routine maintenance tasks are scheduled on time. Problem management tools inform proper administrative personnel about faults received from infrastructure components and keep track of the problem until it is resolved. Resource provisioning tools assign available resources to services to obtain desirable service levels.

- ✓ **Performance and Capacity Management** — Performance and capacity tools measure component performances and are used to determine whether any particular resource is the bottleneck. Advanced tools include predictive trend analysis such that performance and capacity problems are detected before they happen to enable proactive responses.

- ✓ **Service Level Policies** — The tools at this layer are used to group infrastructure components (physical or logical) into "services." These services are then configured and monitored for service level compliance according to set policies. Ideally, the service level policies should correlate performance with the business impact.

- ✓ **Service Level Management** — Using the tools of all the previous levels, this layer makes sure all the service levels are met and makes necessary modifications to the infrastructure or the service policies to maximize business benefits and minimize business interruptions.

A discussion of the current enterprise management protocols and management tools follows.

Enterprise Management Protocols

There have been several attempts at standardizing the interfaces and protocols for enterprise infrastructure management. The most prominent protocols are discussed below.

SNMP

Simple Network Management Protocol (SNMP) is an Internet standard protocol defined in RFC 1157 to manage nodes in an IP network. There is no restriction on what the nodes should be. The monitored nodes can be computers, switches, routers, software objects, and so on. In addition, SNMP's architecture is applicable to networks other than IP.

The managed nodes in SNMP contain *SNMP agents*, which are accessed from the *SNMP management station*. The agents have *Management Information Base (MIB)* data structures, which are sets of parameters used to query or set management information. Many standard MIBs have been defined, and hardware and software vendors continue to develop their private MIBs. With a standard complaint MIB, any SNMP agent should be able to interact with any SNMP manager. SNMP agents can generate *traps* to the SNMP managers to signify important events.

SNMP has widespread use in networking equipment today. However, it is generally used for monitoring purposes only. SNMP has limited support for active device control (that is, management).

DMI

Desktop Management Interface (DMI) was developed by *Distributed Management Task Force (DMTF)*, formerly *Desktop Management Task Force*, to standardize the management of networked computers. DMI found widespread acceptance from PC and server hardware and operating system vendors.

DMI's focus is enabling local area network (LAN) and desktop support personnel to access hardware and software inventory information easily. For example, using DMI interfaces you can get a list of hardware resources (processor, memory, fans, and so on) and software programs. Although DMI can co-exist with SNMP, the two do not interoperate. However, you can easily convert DMI information to other network management protocols, including SNMP.

DMI information is kept in text files using the *Management Information Format (MIF)*. Hardware and software vendors develop their own MIFs specific to their components. The components publish their information using the *Component Interface (CI)* and the *Service Layer*, which resides in the operating system. The management software communicates with the Service Layer using the *Management Interface (MI)*. The access primitives (built-in basic operators) are Get, Set, and List.

DMI components come with most PC and server hardware and are freely available on the Internet. Intel's LANDesk Client Manager (LDCM) is based on DMI, and supports SNMP and most enterprise management applications.

CIM/WBEM

Web Based Enterprise Management (WBEM) is an initiative developed by a group of companies to standardize access to management information over the Web. The standard is currently governed by DMTF. WBEM defines the interfaces and access methods for the software agents and management applications that comprise the enterprise management framework. WBEM utilizes emerging Web technologies, while providing access to traditional management stacks such as SNMP.

Figure 13-1 illustrates WBEM's usage in a storage network. All the components (hardware or software) on the storage network can have software agents that define managed objects. The agents are monitored and controlled by a management application that resides on a central management console. In this example, the host desktop, file system, IP network switch, NAS appliance, FC HBA, FC switch, and storage subsystems all have agents that can be managed in the WBEM framework.

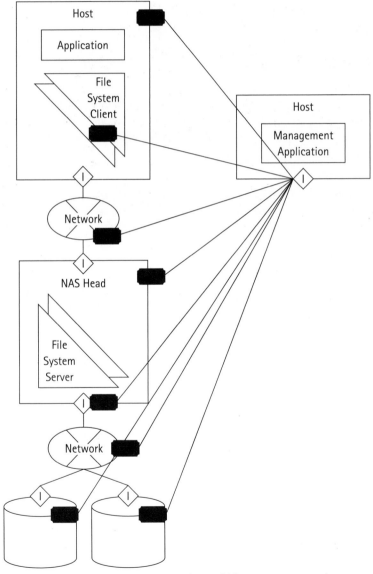

Figure 13-1: WBEM management agents in a multi-layer storage network

WBEM uses *Common Information Model (CIM)* as a standard way to define management information. CIM is an object-oriented information description language and methodology that enables the definition of component properties, methods, and relationships in an organized, standardized manner. CIM models are independent of encoding and transportation methods. They can be expressed visually using the *Unified Modeling Language (UML)*, or in textual form using *Managed Object Format (MOF)*. The core set of models defined by DMTF includes Systems, Applications, Networks, and Devices. Standardizing the information model enables different applications developed by different vendors to interoperate.

XmlCIM defines a standard way of encoding CIM models in *Extensible Markup Language (XML)* and transporting them over *Hypertext Transfer Protocol (HTTP)*. Any medium of communication that supports HTTP can be used for WBEM access.

SNMP and DMI information can be easily converted to CIM/WBEM using converters (SNIA, 2002). The software components for a CIM/WBEM framework are shown in Figure 13-2. In the example, managed objects publish their CIM information using CIM providers to *CIM Object Managers (CIMOMs)*. CIMOMs communicate with the Management Application (the client) over HTTP using XmlCIM. CIMOM is a service layer that functions as a collection point for CIM models. SNMP MIB and DMI MIF information are converted to CIM and treated similarly to other native CIM providers.

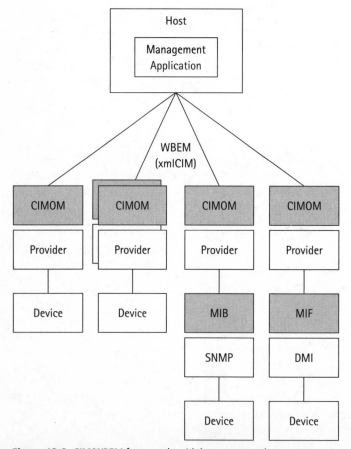

Figure 13-2: CIM/WBEM framework, with legacy protocols

Enterprise Management Tools

The major enterprise management frameworks are Hewlett Packard OpenView, BMC Patrol, Computer Associates Unicenter, and IBM Tivoli. With various add-ons and combinations, all of these tools look very similar. They depend on both proprietary and open systems management protocols to provide a centralized management console that can control various enterprise systems.

The enterprise management tools include the following components:

✓ Configurations and operations management

✓ Performance and availability management

✓ Security management

✓ Network management

✓ Storage management

Some tools include automated distributed management according to predefined policies and rules.

Bluefin, Standards-Based Storage Management

A storage network consists of devices and applications from a heterogeneous mix of vendors. Managing such a complex system requires the utilization of many proprietary, device-specific, and vendor-specific management interfaces. However, this management complexity is completely contrary to the promise of storage networks — centralized management and utilization of diverse storage resources.

A couple of impediments exist to centralized management of storage resources:

✓ **Vendor Lock-In** — Vendors might find it more profitable to hinder interoperability to force the customer to purchase their own equipment.

✓ **Lack of Standards** — In the absence of standardized management interfaces for unifying the control of storage resources, vendors feel free to develop their own.

✓ **Inadequacy of Standards** — Existing standards such as SNMP lack the necessary functionality to provide a full set of management features for complex systems like storage networks.

Most storage device vendors have some SNMP support, which is insufficient for management purposes, as a "check-off" integration with enterprise management applications. The devices have built-in Web servers for management, which do not integrate with SNMP or constitute a management application programming interface (API).

Storage Network Industry Association (SNIA) promotes interoperability between storage vendors and has programs and processes to develop storage industry standards. One of the projects, called Bluefin (SNIA, 2002), aims to provide standard protocols and mechanisms for storage system management interoperability.

Bluefin is based on CIM/WBEM and extends these to include storage resources. New CIM models have been defined to include storage resources. The models are detailed enough to include various physical and logical storage layout topologies. Several vendors have already demonstrated the use of Bluefin to monitor the physical (disk drives, cache, ports, and so on) and logical (LUNs, volumes, and so on) storage resources. SNIA's current work focuses on extending the functionality to include control functions (such as volume management and LUN mapping) in addition to monitoring. As the only standards-based, open storage management framework, Bluefin holds great promise.

Bluefin links distributed management applications (clients) with device management agents. The management agents can be directly embedded into the storage devices or accessed through a proxy server.

On top of CIM/WBEM, Bluefin adds device discovery and distributed locking mechanisms. Discovery is based on *Service Location Protocol (SLP)*. Distributed locking service coordinates the management operations that might originate from multiple management clients or are targeted at multiple providers.

Having a common management interface across multiple storage devices allows the management software developers to focus on higher-level functionality such as automation rather than the details of individual device management. Currently, each device has its own proprietary access method (API) for management. The management software vendors are forced to work with (or deal with) multiple vendors in order to provide network-wide manageability.

Storage Management Tools

Managing storage resources is an essential part of enterprise resource management. Storage management tools provide the following:

- ✓ Discovery
- ✓ Provisioning
- ✓ Monitoring
- ✓ Automation
- ✓ Reporting of storage resources (capacity, performance, and so on)

With vendor-supplied, device-specific management tools, it is easy to discover and manage individual components such as HBAs, switches, and logical disks. Some component management tool examples include Emulex LightPulse, Brocade FabricManager, and Hitachi Data Systems HiCommand Device Manager. However, understanding the end-to-end data path and all the associated performance implications using point products is difficult. As Figure 13-3 shows, data passes through various components and layers before it reaches the application layer. Visualizing, controlling, and optimizing this path is essential to provide any service level guarantees.

After you identify where the data enters and exits in each storage network element, it must be tied to a specific application to obtain a complete path. Then, the data must be tracked during its life cycle through generation, replication, backup, and deletion. Knowledge of the data's life cycle is a powerful management tool. This way, for example, you can understand the impact of performance degradation or loss of a network switch on a particular business application.

Gathering and updating this complex information manually is almost impossible. New attempts have been made to do this job automatically and dynamically with intelligent, comprehensive tools. This new generation of storage network management tools will be essential as storage networks continue to get more complex.

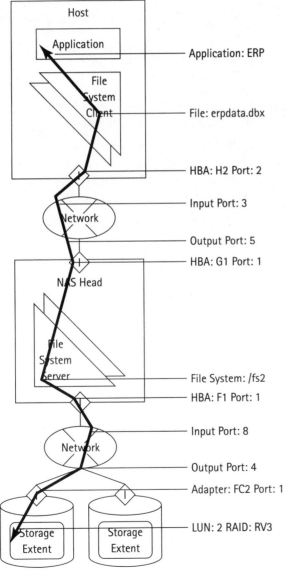

Figure 13-3: Data-flow path in a multi-layer storage network

You can categorize the current generation of storage management tools into four groups:

- ✓ **Storage Component Management Tools** — Almost all storage network components have vendor-supplied management tools. Most of these are accessible through Web browsers, and some have command-line interfaces. A poor man's storage network management tool can be obtained by manually inserting links to all device management pages into a single Web page for easy access.

- ✓ **Storage Network Management (SNM) Tools** — These tools can access multiple vendor devices and manage the network resources. They possess features for setting network paths, including zone information and path fail-over. Some tools might include virtualization functions at the network layer.

- ✓ **Storage Resource Management (SRM) Tools** — Resource management tools assign resources to specific computers, applications, or users. The most widely used tool in this category is the storage capacity management, which keeps track of storage space usage according to preset policies. SRM tools are also used to provision storage when they are first inserted into the system and make logical volume to LUN mappings.

- ✓ **Storage Area Management (SAM) Tools** — SAM tools combine all the previous tools into a single, central management application for an end-to-end view of all the storage resources. The resources are managed using policy-based, automated tools. System performance is managed according to SLAs, and proactive actions are performed to optimize current and future usage.

SAM tools consider detailed application, file system, and database information in their decisions, which are not generally included in SNM or SRM tools.

As previously discussed in Chapter 11 about capacity planning, the easiest solution is to assign excess capacity to everything by over-engineering every component. However, this is not a cost-efficient solution. It is better to track resource usage continuously and make additions dynamically. Considering the fact that the cost of increasing storage capacity reduces every year, it is more cost-efficient to grow dynamically.

An overview of the current storage management products follows.

EMC ControlCenter/Open Edition is an integrated SAN management tool that depends on the proprietary WideSky interface to manage multiple array types. It includes a Workload Analyzer that collects historical performance data and can be used in performance planning. StorageScope monitors capacity usage based on user groups or business units. ControlCenter integrates with third-party enterprise management frameworks using SNMP interfaces.

Hitachi Data Systems (HDS) provides an add-on management tool called Dynamic Optimizer. It includes a workload analyzer that runs in the disk array firmware and monitors all incoming and outgoing data. It monitors the storage device for any performance "hot spots" (storage devices that are more heavily used than others), and dynamically moves data to remove the hot spot. For example, it can move a slow RAID5 volume to a RAID10 volume while the applications are online. It can also be set to do the optimizations automatically, or to generate alerts to the administrator when hot spots are discovered.

InterSAN PATHLINE is one of the emerging SAM tools that tries to manage the entire storage network infrastructure end-to-end. In PATHLINE, the connection between the applications and the data store is abstracted with Virtual Private DataPath. PATHLINE uses policy-based automation, based on the following:

- ✓ Number of physical connections

- ✓ Number of fabrics

- ✓ Type and class of storage devices

- ✓ Bandwidth

- ✓ Security requirements

- ✓ Availability requirements

caution

The problem with the current generation of SAM tools is that the initial configuration still requires considerable manual input. The definition of policies is a manual task. In addition, the administrator must input where each application resides and the type of storage it needs. These are not trivial tasks, and more advanced SAM tools should automate the initial configuration and discovery processes as much as possible.

Veritas SANPoint Control provides automatic discovery of and integration with hosts that run Veritas Volume Manager software. It can also discover Oracle and Exchange applications.

Many startup companies (for example, CreekPath Systems, ProvisionSoft, Invio Software, TeraCloud, and so on) are developing management tools that automatically discover the path between the applications and the data store. Some of these tools and some research projects (Alvarez, 2001; Anderson, 2001) try to generate synthetic policies automatically based on the storage environment and usage patterns.

Besides the storage network–specific management tools from independent vendors, almost all of the enterprise management frameworks have add-on products for storage. Examples include BMC Patrol Storage Network Manager, Computer Associates SANITI Framework, HP OpenView Storage Manager, and Tivoli Storage Network Manager.

Performance Monitoring Tools

This section discusses tools that are specifically designed to capture performance information, first covering the most widely available operating system level tool, Windows System Monitor, and then performance tools for networks in general and storage networks.

Windows System Monitor

Microsoft operating systems (Windows XP/Windows Server 2003) include Microsoft Management Console (MMC) System Monitor (formerly Performance Monitor) (Edmead, 1998). Windows operating systems are heavily instrumented for performance data collection. Almost all operating system components (objects) publish performance data to the Management Console. Third-party applications (such as database management systems) can also use this interface to put out performance data for users.

The performance data in the System Monitor is centered around objects (System, Processor, Network, LogicalDisk, PhysicalDisk, Memory, Cache, and so on) (Friedman, 2002). Under each object, it is possible to monitor several performance counters. Table 13-1 shows the most useful performance counters for the Processor, Network Interface, and Logical/Physical Disk objects.

TABLE 13-1 Windows System Monitor Performance Counters

Object Name	Counter Name
Processor	% Processor Time
	% User Time
	% Privileged Time
	Interrupts/sec
	% Interrupt Time
Network Interface	Total Bytes Received/sec
	Total Bytes Sent/sec
	Packets Received/sec
	Packets Sent/sec
	Current Bandwidth
Logical Disk, Physical Disk	Avg. Disk sec/Read
	Avg. Disk sec/Write
	Avg. Disk sec/Transfer
	Disk Reads/sec
	Disk Writes/sec
	Disk Transfers/sec
	Avg. Disk Queue Length
	Avg. Disk Read Queue Length
	Avg. Disk Write Queue Length

Object Name	Counter Name
Logical Disk, Physical Disk	Current Disk Queue Length
	% Disk Read Time
	% Disk Write Time
	% Idle Time
	Disk Read Bytes/sec
	Disk Write Bytes/sec
	Avg. Disk Bytes/Read
	Avg. Disk Bytes/Write

The data collection period and interval are configurable. In addition, you can direct the performance data to a log file for post-processing. This is useful for comparing the performance before and after a system configuration change.

To illustrate the use of System Monitor in storage network performance analysis, consider the NetBench (see Chapter 12) benchmark execution shown in Figure 13-4. In this example, a file server is serving 16, 4, and 1 client computer(s) in sequence. The figure shows the average response time as seen by the client machines.

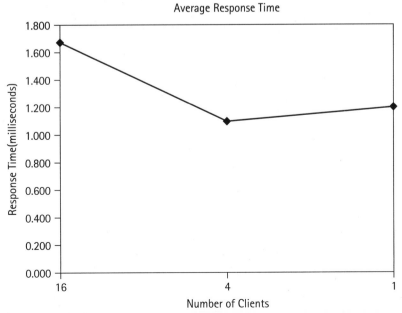

Figure 13-4: NetBench average response time results for 16, 4, and 1 client(s)

While these three NetBench iterations are run, the System Monitor on the file server computer is set to record performance data. Figure 13-5 shows the processor utilization and the network bandwidth usage as a function of time. The server has dual processors and each processor can be monitored separately. As is typical for most Windows operating systems, the processors have very close loads. The figure clearly shows the utilization levels for 16, 4, and 1 client(s) loads. The processing power does not seem to be a bottleneck for this server. Note that the network bandwidth is scaled to 1/1,000,000 to fit into the same graph.

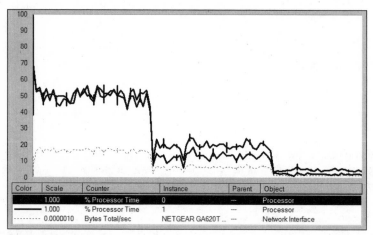

Color	Scale	Counter	Instance	Parent	Object
	1.000	% Processor Time	0	---	Processor
	1.000	% Processor Time	1	---	Processor
	0.0000010	Bytes Total/sec	NETGEAR GA620T ...	---	Network Interface

Figure 13-5: Server processor utilization and network bandwidth during NetBench execution

Figure 13-6 shows the physical disk performance for the same set of benchmark executions. The darker line shows the average write response time in milliseconds. The average time is 45 ms for 16 clients, 20 ms for 4 clients, and 15 ms for 1 client. The other line shows the average physical write operation size, which increases from around 8KB to 24KB.

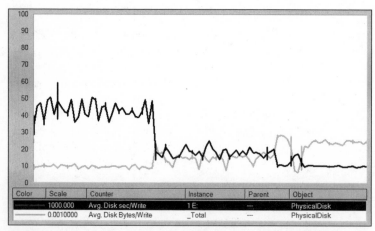

Color	Scale	Counter	Instance	Parent	Object
	1000.000	Avg. Disk sec/Write	1 E:	---	PhysicalDisk
	0.0010000	Avg. Disk Bytes/Write	_Total	---	PhysicalDisk

Figure 13-6: Server physical disk response time and operation size for write operations during NetBench execution

These graphs show that neither the server nor the disks are the bottleneck. The setup will be able to serve more clients if more clients are added. The number of clients is the performance-limiting factor. It is possible to use System Monitor on the client computers to understand why the clients are not pushing more load to the server.

This example can be easily extended to more complex storage network topologies. The Windows server will abstract a SAN-attached storage LUN as a physical disk and, for all practical purposes, the treatment of the two will be the same at the application layer (and for System Monitor). System Monitor will provide you with the performance profile at the end-nodes — it is up to you to find the correlation between the performance data of different end-nodes (servers/clients).

Windows System Monitor allows performance data collection from remote computers, which can be useful in a complex storage network with numerous servers and clients.

Network Monitoring Tools

Some performance monitoring tools are specifically designed to measure network performance. Application layer monitors are independent of the underlying network protocols, while others are specific to a network infrastructure (such as IP).

Mercury Interactive Corporation's LoadRunner is a comprehensive enterprise application-testing tool that includes network-testing capabilities. LoadRunner can perform load testing on business applications by generating thousands of virtual clients. During the tests, real-time monitors capture performance data across many tiers (servers, networks, clients). LoadRunner includes WAN emulation modules to test the impact of wide area networks on application reliability and performance by introducing bandwidth limits, latency, and errors.

HP MeasureWare is another enterprise IT infrastructure monitoring tool. It collects application and process-level performance data in real time and displays it using the PerfView management console that integrates with HP OpenView. Metrics are defined for and data can be collected from servers, clients, applications, databases, and networks.

Network emulation and monitoring tools from Spirent Communications and Shundra Software Ltd. enable network administrators to test their network for the effects of network errors, latencies, and congestion. These software or hardware tools sit in between network nodes and emulate the aforementioned network problems while monitoring the traffic passing through them.

NetIQ provides a simple, free tool named Qcheck that can be used to measure the bandwidth and latency between network end-points. It can test several different protocols, including Transmission Control Protocol (TCP) and User Datagram Protocol (UDP). The tool can also be used to execute ping and traceroute commands for one-way diagnostics.

Storage Network Monitoring Tools

Almost all of the SRM, SNM, and SAM tools discussed previously in this chapter contain capabilities for monitoring the performance of storage networks. Besides these, tools specifically designed to monitor storage networking performance are available.

Some of the storage networking monitoring tools were discussed in Chapter 10. These tools are used to manage the quality of service (QoS) in the storage network. They can be in-band, hardware-based monitors (for example, Finisar's SAN QoS Traffic Monitor), which sit on the data path and capture performance data from the passing traffic. They can also be out-of-band tools that use the APIs of individual network devices to extract performance data. Examples in this category are InterSAN's PATHLINE and TrueSAN's Cloudbreak.

Numerous types and brands of FC monitors capture individual FC frames based on filters. These tools enable very low-level, detailed FC traffic analysis. They are useful as diagnosis tools; however, the data is too detailed for general performance study. Some of these monitors have software post-processors that extract high-level protocol operations (for example, FCP) from the raw data and show event correlations.

Summary

This chapter discussed enterprise-wide storage resource management tools used to automate system analysis tasks, and included the following topics:

Introduction to Performance Management

✓ Performance must be designed for, configured, monitored, and fixed. Changing environments require dynamic adjustments for continuous performance availability.

✓ Currently, performance management is mostly a manual task, with some help from administrative tools.

✓ Policy-based, automated management tools are required to ensure performance SLAs in large, complex storage networks.

Enterprise Management

✓ Managing the computing resources in an enterprise environment is a multi-layer task ranging from the management of the individual devices, to the management of applications and service level policies.

✓ Simple Network Management Protocol (SNMP) and Desktop Management Interface (DMI) are legacy management protocols that are useful for monitoring but lack control semantics. Common Information Model (CIM) and Web Based Enterprise Management (WBEM) are emerging technologies that have the potential to create a standard, interoperable, extensible management infrastructure.

✓ Current enterprise management tools (OpenView, Patrol, Unicenter, Tivoli, and so on) use a mix of proprietary interfaces as well as open standards (SNMP, CIM) for centrally managing enterprise resources.

Bluefin, Standards-Based Storage Management

✓ Lack of standards in storage management leads to point solutions that are incompatible, causing replication of development and management efforts.

✓ Bluefin is a proposed storage management framework based on CIM and WBEM.

✓ Bluefin adds a discovery method and distributed locking mechanism on top of CIM/WBEM.

Storage Management Tools

✓ Almost all storage devices come with a command-line interface and a Web server interface for management. However, these are not interoperable and do not constitute any basis for enterprise-wide storage management.

✓ Storage management software can be categorized into Storage Network Management (SNM), Storage Resource Management (SRM), and Storage Area Management (SAM), in increasing order of functionality.

✓ All of the large storage vendors have their own SRM tools, with differing levels of functionality. In addition, numerous start-up companies are developing policy-based, automated storage management applications. These management software solutions are expected to support management standards (like Bluefin) when they are available.

Performance Monitoring Tools

✓ Enterprise management tools and storage resource/network/area management tools have functionalities for monitoring performance at several layers (server, application, network, and so on).

✓ Windows System Monitor provides a rich interface to the performance counters in the Windows operating system. It is useful for measuring end-node performance on storage networks.

✓ Network monitoring tools specialize in assessing the effects of network behavior on application-level performance. Network emulators can be used to simulate network degradation and outages.

✓ Storage network monitoring tools keep track of storage traffic using in-band or out-of-band hardware/software tools to ensure storage QoS.

References and Additional Resources

Alvarez, Guillermo A., Elizabeth Borowsky, Susie Go, Theodore H. Romer, Ralph Becker-Szendy, Richard Golding, Arif Merchant, Mirjana Spasojevic, Alistair Veitch and John Wilkes. November 2001. *Minerva: An Automated Resource Provisioning Tool for Large-Scale Storage Systems*, ACM Transactions on Computer Systems, 19(4), pp. 483–518.

Presents a tool that accepts workload definitions and storage device models as input, and generates disk array configurations and workload to device mappings. Anderson, Eric, Mahesh Kallahalla, Susan Spence, Ram Swaminathan, and Qian Wang. 2001. *Ergastulum: An Approach to Solving the Workload and Device Configuration Problem.* HP Laboratories SSP Technical Memo, HPL-SSP-2001-05.

Describes a tool for automatic design and configuration of storage systems based on workload definitions and storage models.

Edmead, Mark T. and Paul Hinsberg. November 1998. *Windows NT Performance Monitoring, Benchmarking, and Tuning.* New Riders Publishing.

Contains in-depth coverage of Windows Performance Monitor configuration, test cases, and explanations of various counters.

Friedman, Mark and Odysseas Pentakalos. January 2002. *Windows 2000 Performance Guide.* O'Reilly & Associates.

Provides Windows 2000 performance tuning and monitoring techniques, including details on Performance Monitor.

Lewis, Steve R. 2001. *Implementing Web-Based Performance and Capacity Management Tools: A View from the Trenches.* 27th International Computer Measurement Group Conference (CMG 2001), pp. 87–92.

Describes the experience of implementing Service Level Management in a global IT infrastructure.

Lipovich, G. Jay. 2000. *Integrated Performance Management: Twelve Elements of the New Performance Imperative.* 26th International Computer Measurement Group Conference (CMG 2000).

Reviews the benefits of an integrated performance management framework in the context of S/390 architectures.

Storage Networking Industry Association. 2002. *SNIA Storage Management Initiative, CIM/WBEM Technology Backgrounder.* Available at `http://www.SNIA.org/SMI`.

A short introduction to CIM/WBEM technologies.

Storage Networking Industry Association. August 2002. *"Bluefin" A Common Interface for SAN Management.* Available at `http://www.SNIA.org/SMI`.

An introduction to the Bluefin SAN management protocol.

Part V

Storage Performance Tuning

Chapter 14

Host System Tuning

In This Chapter

If the host systems that use the storage network resources are slow, performance improvements in the storage network components will not result in any realizable outcomes. End-systems have several software and hardware components that affect the storage IO performance. This chapter discusses optimization techniques for host systems as they relate to storage, and includes the following topics:

✓ Elements of the host system architecture that affect the IO path

✓ Analyzing and tuning host system hardware bottlenecks

✓ File system optimization techniques

✓ Network interface and protocol tuning

Host System Architecture

In a storage network with external storage devices, considerable IO path overhead is still incurred inside the host systems (end clients). If the host systems' IO path is not configured for optimum performance, having a fast storage network will not help.

Figure 14-1 illustrates the IO path components on the end-nodes that are connected to storage networks.

The figure's left side contains the software components, while the right side shows the hardware components on the IO path. For an optimum storage IO performance, you need all of these components to work optimally.

If you notice a slowdown or cannot obtain the desired performance, there are a few common suspects:

✓ The systems do not have enough processor or IO bus power.

✓ Disks, storage systems, or the storage network are not able to sustain the desired workload.

✓ Because of insufficient memory, the system is continuously swapping memory pages in and out of disk storage.

✓ The network interface or the network itself is overloaded, causing dropped packets.

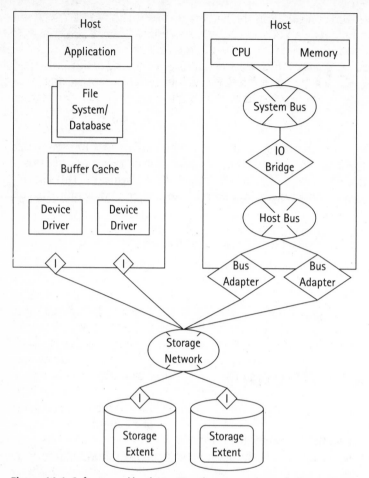

Figure 14-1: Software and hardware IO path components on the host computers

 One rule of thumb to keep in mind is that *a bottleneck always exists*. The slowest component determines the network's performance. If the system is fast enough to serve the required workload, the workload is not hard enough. Then the workload is the bottleneck. Workload is generated by another computer outside of your system or by a human using the system. The workload source may not be fast enough to use the full potential of your system. An apparent example of this behavior is the lack of sufficient queue depth in the workload.

Chapters 6 through 9 discussed performance modeling and analysis techniques. Chapters 10 through 13 introduced performance monitoring and management methods. By using some or all of this knowledge, you can detect which system resources are the bottleneck and need further improvement.

You can easily solve a bottleneck by upgrading the bottleneck component with a faster one (although this may not always be possible because of cost or technical issues). However, you might be able to get further performance out of the existing components.

The following sections discuss performance tuning issues under three general topics: processor, file system, and network tuning. The text points out possible analysis and optimization strategies. However, you should consult the references given at the end of the chapter for implementation details.

Processor Tuning

Computing system performance is generally identified with the speed of the processor (central processing unit) in the system. Systems with faster processors are regarded as superior. Although this belief is not always substantiated, given the fact that the computer architects try to balance their systems by designing equally fast components throughout the system, you could expect a system with a fast processor to also have a fast IO bus, fast memory, and so on. If this is not the case, you have an imbalanced system to begin with, and simple tuning methods will not be able to fix it.

Many system bottlenecks show themselves as (or are perceived as) central processing unit (CPU) bottlenecks. When a system's performance degrades due to increased load, the suspect is generally the "slow" CPU. However, many other system resources are exhausted before the CPU. For example, the IO bus, storage devices, storage network, and host memory are first candidates for being bottlenecks. Although the CPU utilization might seem very high, this may be a side effect of another bottleneck. For example, excessive page file activity (so-called *trashing*) due to lack of adequate memory will cause CPU utilization to go up. In such a situation, adding more memory rather than a faster CPU will improve performance.

Some system implementations waste CPU cycles more than others. For example, *Programmed Input Output (PIO)* uses the host CPU to transfer data between the main memory and IO devices. *Direct Memory Access (DMA)* can be used to offload this work from the CPU to the IO controllers. DMA transfers reduce the CPU utilization considerably. A similar difference exists between Small Computer System Interface (SCSI) disk drives and Integrated Drive Electronics (IDE) attached drives. The SCSI command set provides an interface where most of the command processing and almost all of the low-level details are handled within the peripheral devices. On the other hand, the IDE interface still requires the host operating system and, consequently, the host CPU to get involved in many IO transfer details.

Like most things in computing, a tradeoff exists between DMA and PIO. DMA is not always more efficient than PIO. DMA requires the programming of DMA controllers, which adds some setup latency. This overhead is compensated for over long data transfers. For short messages though, PIO might be faster.

Some file systems and system utilities automatically store data in a compressed format and decompress it when it is read back. Compression is a CPU-intensive task and increases latency for storage accesses. It is not recommended for IO-intensive workloads. One scenario where compression really helps in improving performance is the replication of data to remote sites over long delay links. These links generally have less bandwidth compared to their local counterparts, and reducing the amount of data shipped (by compression) enables faster transfers.

CPU load changes over time and among different applications. Usually, system load exhibits a cyclical pattern. For example, nights and weekends are less loaded in many business IT organizations. These patterns in time enable some scheduling optimizations. Storage backups and batch program executions can be performed during otherwise idle periods. Even during normal execution hours, carefully distributing and scheduling applications among multiple CPUs and systems will improve performance.

Scheduling in multiple CPU systems (*Symmetric Multi-Processing,* or *SMP*) is performed by assigning execution threads to each CPU. Always assigning a group of threads to the same CPU ("*processor affinity*") to utilize processor caches more efficiently might be beneficial. Large enterprise computing platforms have specialized software for scheduling and assigning applications according to time and resource availability.

Table 14-1 summarizes the activity levels of various system components under five exemplary application types. One apparent result is that memory and storage are almost always active. Memory and storage are the two ends of the IO path and they have direct performance consequences.

TABLE 14-1 Resource Usage Activity Levels of Various Application Types

Application	Processor	Memory	Storage	Network
File server	Light	Medium	Active	Active
Database server	Active	Active	Active	Light
Web server	Medium	Active	Active	Active
Domain controller	Light	Active	Medium	Medium
E-mail server	Medium	Active	Active	Medium

File System Optimizations

As illustrated in Figure 14-1, a file system is a layer between applications and storage device drivers. File systems are on the path of any IO activity and have significant impact on IO performance.

File systems are represented as *logical volumes* in Windows operating systems and *mount points* in UNIX systems. You can obtain file system–specific performance information by utilizing the logical disk performance counters in Windows (Aubley, 1998) and `iostat` and `fstat` commands in UNIX systems (Musumeci, 2002). If the utilization of a particular file system increases above 60 to 70 percent, the response time starts to increase significantly. Such a file system is a candidate for improvement. You might be able to distribute the load of that particular file system to other file systems or on more physical drives.

If physical disk drives are directly connected to the host, only one logical drive should be assigned to each physical drive. This should eliminate the constant movement of the disk arm between regions belonging to multiple logical drives. Some journaling file systems (for example, VxFS, XFS, and so on) recommend separating their log partition from the main data partition to eliminate seek penalties.

File systems allocate disk storage in chunks called *Allocation Units (ALUs)*. Most file system formatting utilities allow you to set ALU sizes explicitly. If the applications that use that particular file system have a common access size, making the ALU size match the application request size will streamline the accesses and prevent a lot of indexing overhead in the file system. For example, if a database workload consists of 4KB accesses, the file system can be formatted at that size. If there is a video streaming workload, a larger ALU (64KB, for example) will give better performance.

As discussed previously in this book, certain storage configurations are more appropriate for certain workloads. For example, while RAID5 layout might be fast for read-intensive accesses, RAID10 is faster for write accesses. If you can analyze the applications' workload requirements, grouping applications with similar workloads and assigning them to the appropriate storage will improve performance. You could tune a storage volume for large sequential accesses and another one for small random accesses. Then, you can group applications or files to use these specific resources.

Host-based RAID functions are implemented in *Logical Volume Managers (LVMs)*. Although LVM has many other management advantages, it also implements RAID algorithms using host resources (CPU, IO bus, memory, and so on). While this is a simple, cost-efficient way of achieving RAID availability and performance, the resource consumption on the host system restricts its usefulness. Disk mirroring (RAID1) is appropriate for host-based implementations, but the parity calculations in RAID5 are prohibitive and must be implemented on a separate RAID controller that is optimized for this task. In addition, host-based LVM does not easily lend itself to storage sharing. While a hardware-based storage system can be easily shared among multiple hosts, host-based LVM requires the installation and coordination of distributed LVM software on all involved hosts.

File systems use host RAM for caching disk data. Windows NT and Linux, for example, try to use all of the available memory for caching file blocks. Adding more memory, in many cases, increases the performance of hosts that perform considerable file operations. Windows Server operating systems have knobs for tuning the amount of memory available for caching, which should be set to maximum for hosts used for file serving. In Solaris, UNIX File System (UFS) write throttle parameters (`ufs_WRITES`, `ufs_HW`, and `ufs_LW`) can be used to set the amount of buffer cache allocated for each file.

Remember that having multiple outstanding SCSI commands will improve the throughput. The ability to queue multiple commands simultaneously is termed *Command Tag Queuing (CTQ)*. SCSI and FC host bus adapters have parameters to dictate the length of the SCSI command queues. In Windows, you will generally find a registry key specific to the device driver to denote the length. In Linux, it is a compile time constant. In many operating systems, the default behavior is not to allow command queuing, which is clearly not optimal, and must be checked after the installation.

The type of file system is another important determinant in system performance. Other factors besides performance determine your choice of file system. For example, you would want to consider the following:

- ✓ Cost
- ✓ Availability
- ✓ Robustness
- ✓ Scalability
- ✓ Security

Log-based (or journaling) file systems provide some performance increase for small-sized random IO by collecting and writing all the write updates into the log part of the file system. Later, the log is cleared and the updates are moved to their original locations when the system is idle. Other log-based file systems only log metadata changes, rather than the file data, to increase system stability in case of system crashes.

File system fragmentation occurs after the file system is used for a long period with various file deletions and insertions. After these operations, the file system on the storage devices becomes fragmented with many small, disconnected regions. It becomes harder to find continuous space to put newer files. Defragmentation software goes over the file layouts and moves and combines the fragments. This provides a dual advantage: it improves read performance by creating long consecutive regions, and it makes new write operations faster because finding consecutive blocks is easier.

SCSI buses and FC links are constructed to run at a speed that is the least common denominator of all the connected devices. This is done for backward compatibility with the older, slower devices. Therefore, slow and fast devices should not be mixed on the same SCSI bus or FC loop.

Solid state disks (SSDs) are used to cache storage data using nonvolatile RAM (NVRAM) devices. Most of the SSDs are implemented as battery-backed DRAM memory. Although most nonvolatile memory caches reside inside storage subsystems or as a stand-alone device on the storage network, some SSDs can be inserted inside host systems. For example, Sun StorEdge Fast Write Cache contains battery-backed memories that are used to improve write performance in file servers. The application types that are good candidates for write caching include small, write-intensive workloads such as database logs, OLTP data, and writes to RAID5 volumes. Workloads that will not benefit from write caching include read-only accesses and large asynchronous writes.

Other file system optimization techniques were previously introduced in Chapter 12 while discussing file system benchmarking techniques. Please refer to that chapter for additional optimization tips.

Windows Volume Shadow Copy Service

Volume Shadow Copy Service (VSS) is introduced by the Windows XP and Windows Server 2003 operating systems. VSS is designed to make backup operations easier by always providing consistent file system copies without the need for backup windows.

VSS creates copy-on-write snapshots (shadow copies) of data volumes. When a backup operation starts, it can use a shadow copy and continue even if the original file system keeps changing. In this way, backup operations are not hindered because of open files, and applications can continue to execute during the backups. The copy-on-write data is kept on a portion of the original volume, so there must be enough free space on the volume to hold dynamic data during the backup. Windows Server 2003 also allows user access to shadow copies for faster file restores.

VSS has application program interfaces (APIs) for applications and storage arrays to coordinate the shadow copies and backup operations. Applications ("writers" in VSS) can be queried and instructed to flush their internal buffers to create a consistent copy of their data. In addition, VSS storage interfaces can be used to instruct storage devices ("providers" in VSS) to create shadow copies using their own, internal, optimized methods. For example, a hardware VSS provider can use copy-on-write, or mirror-break to replicate a volume without operating system involvement.

When combined with VSS-aware applications (for example, Microsoft Exchange Server, or SQL Server, and so on) and VSS-aware storage subsystems, VSS will provide faster, easier backup operations without the need for backup windows.

Windows Virtual Disk Service

Another storage management interface introduced by Windows Server 2003 is the *Virtual Disk Service (VDS)*. VDS provides a unified management interface to multiple-vendor storage subsystems.

VDS is a middle-layer software sitting between hardware VDS providers and management applications. Using VDS, a single management console will be able to discover, configure, and monitor storage subsystems from different vendors. Without VDS, such a task requires access to multiple management consoles and increases the management burden.

One of VDS's targets is to provide storage devices more autonomous management capabilities. For example, storage devices are expected to handle hot-spare insertion and hot-spot removal automatically ("automagically" in VDS). The need for such automatic storage management functionality has long been anticipated in projects such as attribute-based (or attribute-managed) storage (Golding, 1995).

In addition, management or production applications can use the VDS interface to give management hints to the storage layers for improving the services they get. For example, an application might request from a specific device a new volume for large, sequential, read accesses and the underlying storage provider configures a RAID volume optimized for such accesses.

Because VDS provides a unified interface for applications, file systems, and storage devices, it becomes easier to coordinate file system expansion and truncation. For example, when an application decides that it needs additional storage space, it uses VDS to request additional space from the underlying storage subsystems, which in turn notify the file system to make the necessary adjustments to the file system structures.

Similarly, VSS can be integrated into VDS for easier, faster, consistent backup operations initiated directly from applications and handled automatically by the hardware providers.

Direct Access File System Protocol

Direct Access File System (DAFS) Protocol was developed by a consortium of companies led by Network Appliance (the notable NAS appliance vendor). DAFS intends to improve network file system performance by eliminating operating system and network stack overheads (Magoutis, 2002).

DAFS utilizes *Remote Direct Memory Access (RDMA)* methods to transfer file data directly between application buffers and file server buffers. RDMA is defined by the *Virtual Interface Architecture (VIA)*. VIA is supported by Ethernet and Fibre Channel standards. In addition, InfiniBand uses VIA as its native transport protocol. VIA enables communication end-points to exchange data directly at the application space without copying the data to the operating system buffers. This eliminates the memory copies and the associated interrupt and network stack overheads.

DAFS file access components are illustrated in Figure 14-2. The most notable difference between DAFS and a standard network file system client-server architecture is the elimination of the file system components from the client (among other improvements). In DAFS, almost all file system processing is offloaded to the DAFS file server.

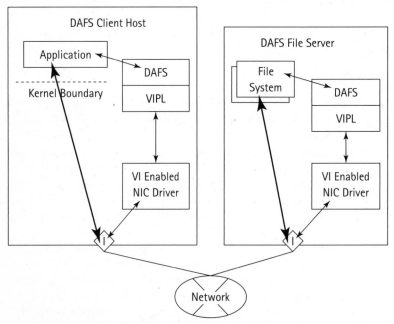

Figure 14-2: DAFS file access architecture

On the client side, the DAFS layer and the *VI Provider Layer (VIPL)* can be implemented in the user space or the kernel space. If the application is DAFS-aware and uses DAFS APIs to access data, full advantage of RDMA can be achieved by using the application buffers for transmission. On the other hand, if the application is not DAFS-aware, it can still use the normal file system call mechanisms to the operating system, and a layer inside the operating system can utilize DAFS. Testing has shown that kernel layer DAFS implementations are as fast as direct-attached disk storage, while application layer DAFS implementations provide significantly better performance improvements.

The biggest obstacle for DAFS is the lack of applications that use DAFS APIs directly. In addition, network interface cards (NICs) that support VIA are not in common use right now and cost more than the commodity NICs. DAFS is a natural fit for InfiniBand transport semantics and, if InfiniBand is able to penetrate the data centers, DAFS could prevail as a high-performance network file system protocol. DAFS shares many common features with NFSv4; expect these two standards to merge or be mutually compatible in the near future.

Network Interface Optimizations

Network interface performance is a complex function of the following:

- ✓ Application design
- ✓ Network device drivers
- ✓ NICs
- ✓ Physical network
- ✓ Network protocols

A problem in any of these components may hinder performance.

Network tuning issues pertaining to the physical network design and operations are discussed in Chapter 17. This section discusses ideas and tips about tuning the network end-points. End-node optimizations include the operating system and device driver tuning, protocol optimizations, and protocol offload.

If a host's network load is considerable, utilizing multiple network cards and distributing the load among them might be a good idea. You can achieve this by putting each card in a different network subnet.

Limiting the number of protocols supported on a network connection will eliminate unnecessary operating system overhead. For example, in Windows operating systems, you can remove the protocol and redirector bindings from interfaces that do not use those particular protocols.

Do not assume that default NIC settings are good or even correct. For example, network speed auto-sensing can hide a network design or implementation mistake. While you are assuming the interface is working at 1 Gb/s speed, it might be negotiated as 100 Mb/s half-duplex. Set the NIC parameters to the highest expectation, and let the problems surface early rather than letting them hide.

The next three sections discuss tuning options for protocol parameters and protocol implementations.

TCP/IP Network Protocol Optimizations

Transmission Control Protocol/Internet Protocol (TCP/IP) network stacks provide many user-tunable and self-tuning protocol parameters (Dunigan, 2002). On links with long delays and high bandwidth, the single most important factor determining the sustained bandwidth is *TCP window size*. TCP employs an adaptive algorithm to determine the amount of in-transit data that can exist on the links. As a result, the sustained bandwidth is bound, as shown in Equation 14-1, where RTT denotes the *Roundtrip Time* of the link.

Equation 14-1

```
Sustained TCP Bandwidth ≤ TCP Window Size / RTT
```

Example 14-1 illustrates how the end-node buffer sizes limit the achievable bandwidth in TCP/IP connections.

Several factors determine the TCP sliding window size (Huston, 2000). The send and receive buffer sizes on the sender and receiver ends determine the amount of memory that can be used to store retransmission and out-of-order data. At the start of a TCP session, both sides advertise their receive buffer sizes. TCP also employs a *slow-start algorithm* and gradually increments the window size to find the available bandwidth dynamically. Figure 14-3 illustrates the sliding window on a TCP stream.

When the TCP stack determines (or suspects) network congestion through lost packets, the window size is reduced to half. Then the window is increased gradually again, until another congestion point is reached. The congestion window algorithms are mostly built into the operating system software and you can't generally tune them directly. Still, the send and receive buffer sizes are settable through the socket programming interfaces. Most operating systems restrict the maximum buffer size to 64KB. This limit can be changed by overriding the parameters in the Windows registry (Friedman, 2002) or by changing the parameters in the /proc file system in Linux (Fink, 2001).

TCP acknowledges the successful transmissions cumulatively using the last successful segment's sequence ID in the ACK control field in the TCP header. If a TCP frame is lost in the middle of a stream, all the segments after that point must be retransmitted. Enabling the *TCP Selective Acknowledgement (SACK)* mechanism allows TCP to notify the sender of all the received segments, even if they are after a lost segment. This increases the bandwidth in congested networks with some frame losses or drops.

You can also increase TCP bandwidth by letting the slow-start algorithm proceed at a higher rate than the current one *Maximum Segment Size (MSS)* per RTT. In addition, the initial window size can be increased to two or more MSS sizes to start with a higher burst of data.

Example 14-1 TCP Bandwidth Bound

A long-haul link has 40ms roundtrip time (RTT) and a physical link bandwidth of 622 Mbit/s (OC-12). If a single TCP session over this link has a maximum receiver buffer size of 64KB, what is the maximum achievable bandwidth over a single TCP connection?

Receiver buffer size limits the TCP sliding window size to 64KB. Using Equation 14-1, the limit on sustained TCP bandwidth can be computed as follows:

```
Sustained TCP Bandwidth ≤ 64 KB ÷ 40 ms

Sustained TCP Bandwidth ≤ 13.1 Mb/s
```

Therefore, even if the physical link bandwidth is far greater (622 Mb/s), only 13.1 Mb/s of the available bandwidth will be used because of the limited receiver buffer size.

To utilize the full link bandwidth, you must have 622 ÷ 13.1 ~= 48 simultaneous TCP sessions in parallel. Or, the receiver (and sender) buffer sizes will need to be increased 48 times (64KB × 48 = 3MB).

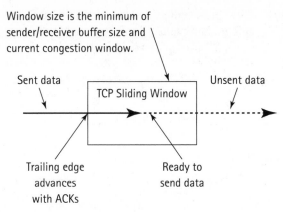

Window size is the minimum of sender/receiver buffer size and current congestion window.

Sent data

TCP Sliding Window

Unsent data

Trailing edge advances with ACKs

Ready to send data

Figure 14-3: TCP sliding window mechanism

Almost all the TCP optimizations mentioned can be performed on the end-nodes, at the edges of a network, without any modification to the network itself (Chase, 2001). This is one of the reasons why TCP is so successful and prominent in the networking world.

Protocol Offload Hardware

TCP/IP processing requires considerable processing power. As discussed in Chapter 8, at gigabit speeds the TCP stack might overwhelm even the most powerful processor.

NICs generate interrupts every time data arrives at a port. The CPU must reply to this interrupt and move the data to the IP stack buffers. The data is then moved to the TCP level and checked for data order and consistency. The TCP checksum is computed and compared with the checksum in the TCP header. If there is a mismatch, the segment is discarded, causing a retransmission. All these interrupts and data movements generate considerable processor overhead. You can alleviate this burden by offloading some of the processing to specialized devices.

Network processing offloading is not a new concept. The checksum computations have been offloaded to NICs for a long time now. The current generation of advanced NICs are offloading more or all of the TCP/IP stack from the main CPU. These *TCP/IP Offload Engines (TOEs)* implement the TCP/IP stack in hardware in the network cards. They differ by how much of the stack is offloaded. Generally, TCP connection establishment, tear-down, and error handling is performed in the host system's CPU, while normal data transmission is handled at the TOE. With storage interfaces such as iSCSI, NICs are expected to execute the entire TCP/IP stack, including the application layer (iSCSI) in hardware. This is not an easy task. At gigabit and 10-gigabit speeds, the amount of IO bus, memory bus, and processing power required is beyond the capability of most of today's technologies.

Zero-Copy Network Stack

One partial solution to the problem of network stack processing requirements is to optimize the stack to do less work. For example, with careful software design, you can eliminate most of the memory copy operations occurring when data is moved between TCP/IP stack layers.

In a traditional network stack, the data is copied from the application space to the operating system space. Then, TCP headers are added and the resulting data is copied to IP frames. After IP headers are added, the data is copied to network device driver buffers and, from there, sent to the NIC. All these copy operations consume considerable memory and IO bus resources, as well as CPU time. Several research projects explored the idea that the data could be moved from the application space directly to the network interface buffers (and vice versa for receive). Some of these studies were able to reduce the software overhead considerably and achieved near line-speed performance (Chase, 2001).

Summary

This chapter discussed optimization techniques for host systems as they relate to storage, and included the following topics:

Host System Architecture

✓ Ultimately, it is the host systems that utilize the storage network resources. If they are not configured optimally, the storage systems' performance advantages will be lost.

✓ Hosts have many software and hardware components that sit on the IO path. Any of these components could be the bottleneck that restricts the realizable performance.

✓ The usual bottleneck suspects are the processor, storage subsystem, memory, and network interface. Performance analysis and monitoring techniques introduced in previous chapters can be used to identify system bottlenecks.

Processor Tuning

✓ Although the processor's speed is always emphasized, other resources in the system must be well-balanced, performance-wise.

✓ Some other bottleneck, such as lack of memory, might surface as a CPU over-utilization.

✓ You can decrease processor load by using techniques that offload processor tasks. For example, DMA instead of programmed IO, SCSI instead of IDE, and multiple CPUs instead of a single one.

✓ CPU load changes with time and type of application. Scheduling tasks accordingly will improve CPU utilization.

File System Optimizations

✓ All operating systems have some kind of performance utility to track the performance of the individual file systems. These utilities can be used to find the load distribution among different file systems.

✓ Setting the file system block sizes and storage layouts according to application work-loads will improve access performance and reduce processing overhead.

✓ Buffer caches and Solid State Disks are used to cache file system data. The size of the cache is one of the first factors to consider when tuning.

✓ Windows Volume Shadow Copy Service and Windows Virtual Disk Service are two new interfaces that can be used by host-side applications to configure storage devices more efficiently. Direct Access File System protocol is designed to streamline network file access over networks that support Remote DMA.

Network Interface Optimizations

✓ Work enters and leaves a computing system at the network interface. Therefore, the performance of this interface is essential to overall system performance.

✓ TCP/IP protocol has many user-tunable parameters that affect performance. Operating systems have interfaces to tune these parameters. The most notable parameter is the TCP receive buffer size, which eventually determines the sustainable bandwidth.

✓ Newer NICs incorporate more and more TCP/IP stack operations. By offloading these tasks from the host processor, you can sustain line-speed network performance.

References and Additional Resources

Aubley, Curt. July 1998. *Tuning & Sizing NT Server*. Prentice Hall.

Although this book is somewhat out-dated now, the performance tuning strategies discussed are valid for most Windows systems, and even for other platforms.

Chase, J. S., A. J. Gallatin, and K. G. Yocum. April 2001. *End System Optimizations for High-Speed TCP*. IEEE Communications, Special Issue on TCP Performance in Future Networking Environments, 39(4), pp. 68–74.

Presents tuning techniques for reducing the host overhead in processing TCP/IP communications.

Dunigan, Tom, Matt Mathis, and Brian Tierney. November 2002. *A TCP Tuning Daemon*. Proceedings of High Performance Networking and Computing 2002 (SC2002), IEEE. Baltimore, Maryland.

Presents an automatic method for tuning the TCP session performance using kernel-level instrumentation data. Available at www.sc2002.org.

Edmead, Mark T. and Paul Hinsberg. November 1998. *Windows NT Performance Monitoring, Benchmarking, and Tuning*. New Riders Publishing.

Presents performance tuning topics on network, CPU, memory, and disk in NT servers.

Fink, Jason R. and Matthew D. Sherer. August 2001. *Linux Performance Tuning and Capacity Planning*. Sams.

A general overview of performance tuning techniques in UNIX environments with some special tips for Linux.

Friedman, Mark and Odysseas Pentakalos. January 2002. *Windows 2000 Performance Guide*. O'Reilly & Associates.

Includes Windows 2000 performance tuning and monitoring techniques, including details on Performance Monitor.

Golding, Richard, Elizabeth Shriver, Tim Sullivan, and John Wilkes. October 1995. *Attribute-Managed Storage*. In Proceedings of the Workshop on Modeling and Specification of I/O, San Antonio, Texas.

Discusses the need for managing storage arrays automatically based on workload access patterns and storage system performance attributes.

Huston, Geoff. June 2000. *TCP Performance*. The Internet Protocol Journal, Cisco Publications, Volume 3(2).

Discusses the performance effects of various TCP algorithms and parameters. Back issues can be downloaded at `www.cisco.com/ipj`.

Magoutis, K., S. Addetia, A. Fedorova, M. Seltzer, J. Chase, A. Gallatin, R. Kisley, R. Wickremesinghe, and E. Gabber. June 2002. *Structure and Performance of the Direct Access File System*. Proceedings of USENIX 2002 Annual Technical Conference, pp. 1–14, Monterey, CA.

Musumeci, Gian-Paolo D. and Mike Loukides. February 2002. *System Performance Tuning*, 2nd Edition. O'Reilly & Associates.

A guide for performance tuning in UNIX systems with emphasis on Solaris 8. Updated considerably from the first edition to include recent advances in computing systems.

Chapter 15

Application Tuning

In This Chapter

A storage network's characteristics should match the characteristics of the applications that use it, and vice versa. You can configure application software to make best use of the underlying storage IO devices. This chapter presents application-level storage IO tuning opportunities, including the following topics:

✓ Relationship of application, system, and storage IO traffic

✓ Optimizing database systems for best storage performance

✓ Backup optimizations using storage networks and point-in-time copies

✓ Network backup performance modeling tips

Optimizing Applications for Storage

A complete IO performance tuning effort requires that you study the hardware, the systems software, and the application software. Complex interactions occur between all the layers. If these interactions are not tuned to match each other's requirements, the resulting performance may be disappointing even if the components alone are fast enough.

An analysis of the applications should yield the requirements for the IO subsystem. For example, capacity and performance requirements dictate the size and the number of storage devices. Transaction IO size and IO type and availability requirements dictate the RAID levels of the underlying storage (Kreiser, 2000).

The IO request sizes at the application level, the file system level, the device driver level, and the storage controller level should align nicely. They do not need to be the same. However, if you can make these sizes even multiples of each other, you can prevent unnecessary splitting of IO requests and reduce latency. The type of IO dictates the caching and buffering of data at various levels. Write-intensive workloads can take advantage of battery-backed memory buffers, while read-intensive workloads can take advantage of large memory caches. Applications with multiple threads of execution can utilize command tag queuing at the Small Computer System Interface (SCSI) levels by having multiple outstanding commands simultaneously.

These and other storage-related tuning topics are presented in this chapter. Databases and backups are probably the flagship applications of storage networks. Therefore, this chapter uses these two application types as examples to discuss several optimization topics.

Optimizing Database Systems

Business runs on databases. Almost all critical applications rely on some sort of database technology to store and retrieve information. Examples of business functions that depend on database technology include the following:

- ✓ **Online Transaction Processing (OLTP)** — Execution of business transactions in real-time. OLTP uses database systems for the consistency, availability, and security of transactions.

- ✓ **Online Analytical Processing (OLAP)** — A class of business software used to extract relationships, trends, patterns, and exceptions in data. Might use a data warehouse as the underlying database.

- ✓ **Customer Relationship Management (CRM)** — Manages all aspects of relationships between businesses and customers. Collects and stores information from marketing, sales, and customer support in databases. Uses the database to perform data-mining operations for opportunity detection.

- ✓ **Data Warehouse** — Used to denote a remote, centralized, large database that contains images of all enterprise databases. Used by planners and researchers to detect trends and categories. A data-mart is generally a subset of a data warehouse specialized to specific functions or departments.

- ✓ **Database Management System (DBMS)** — A suite of software programs that manage the storage of large, persistent business data. DBMS ensures the security and integrity of the stored data while allowing dynamic updates and queries.

Besides the preceding database software, other information technology products, such as Web servers, mail servers, messaging services, and e-commerce applications, might use databases as their backend storage.

The explosion in the size and complexity of databases has put a lot of pressure on the storage systems that host these databases. The storage systems are expected to have high throughput and bandwidth rates as well as high availability characteristics, yet still be cost-effective. The high performance, scalability, and distance properties of storage networks are appealing for large, enterprise databases. Over the short period of storage networks' history, database systems have become the main application that uses the storage networks.

Databases exact demanding IO requirements. If the storage devices are not tuned to work well with databases, they can quickly become the bottleneck. The optimizations that are directly storage subsystem- and network-related are the subject of Chapters 16 and 17. If the database is not designed and tuned to work well with storage, it will not achieve the expected performance. The following list details topics on tuning database systems for better storage performance:

- ✓ **Optimize transaction and query design** — If database queries are poorly designed, no amount of storage systems optimization can sustain performance. For example, frequent full table scans or high amounts of recursive SQL (the standard database query/update language) statements will saturate the storage system as well as the database server. Optimizing the SQL and database design is beyond the scope of this book. Consult your database language and software documents for details.

✓ **The more spindles the better** — Each given disk drive has a limited amount of IO throughput. A database workload should be distributed over as many spindles (disk drives) necessary to sustain the required performance. Oracle's Stripe and Mirror Everything (SAME) strategy (Minhas) stresses this fact by urging Database Administrators (DBAs) to distribute load on all available disks.

✓ **Spend cash on cache** — Database software is designed to take advantage of caches residing in server memories to eliminate physical IO accesses. Many database operations (for example, table sorts) can work effectively with memory caches. Database server machines are designed with the highest RAM that can possibly be put within cost constraints.

✓ **Coordinate database block size, file system block size, and stripe unit size** — To eliminate partial, split IO operations, the block size that the database uses for IO must match the block size used by the file system. Similarly, stripe unit size on storage arrays must be equal to or an even multiple of the file system block size. If detailed analysis is not possible, use a large stripe unit like 1MB to balance between disk positioning time and transfer time.

✓ **Use large database block sizes** — Database block size should match the particular database's dominant access pattern. For example, for an OLTP system, a block size of 4KB could be appropriate. However, an OLAP system is probably performing large sequential sweeps of the database. In that case, a large block size (up to 32KB in Oracle) might be a better choice. While a larger block size might waste IO bandwidth, a smaller size might cause extra latency.

✓ **Mirror for high availability** — Mirrored volumes (RAID1 or RAID10) provide better write performance than parity-protected (RAID3 or RAID5) volumes. If performance is not critical for some of the database files, those files can be stored on RAID5 to save space. When in doubt, RAID10 is the safe choice. It provides good performance and availability.

✓ **Remove hot spots** — A non-tuned data layout might create access hot spots that cause contention for a few physical disks. Oracle's SAME strategy recommends distributing everything on every disk, in hopes of eliminating hot spots. Although this might be a good choice as a default layout that does not require much management work, it is not guaranteed to eliminate congestion. A better strategy would be separating the workload across databases and inside a database. Servers, storage network paths, and storage devices should not be shared between multiple databases. Inside a database, the data files (tablespaces) should be separated from indexes and redo (transaction) logs.

✓ **Put transaction logs on faster storage** — In many database systems, most of the write traffic is observed by the redo logs. Dedicating some fast (for example, 15K rpm disk drives in a RAID10 configuration) storage solely for redo logs is a good idea.

✓ **Separate tables and indexes** — OLAP systems sweep database tables and indexes in parallel. Therefore, in those configurations, putting tables and indexes on separate physical devices provides faster IO performance.

✓ **Eliminate file system overheads** — File systems keep track of last access times for each file, after each access. This can cause doubling of IO accesses in some situations. For databases, knowing when the database was last read is probably not important. You can turn this file system feature off by setting the `noatime` file attribute (in Linux, and similar attributes in Windows NT/2000). Several other ways to optimize file systems were discussed in previous chapters.

✓ **Use direct IO interfaces** — Database systems can work on raw partitions or file system (formatted) volumes. Raw partitions are accessed directly by the database applications without the involvement of any file systems. Because raw IO bypasses the file system cache, it generally has less latency. However, raw IO partitions cause some management problems. They must be explicitly handled by the database administrator. On the other hand, a file system relieves many management duties. For example, most advanced file systems (and volume managers) provide dynamic expansion, mirroring, snapshots, and remote replication, which are difficult with raw partitions. Fortunately, these advanced file systems also provide a *direct IO* mode, which bypasses the buffer cache and copies database data directly to the physical storage interface. In real systems, direct IO provides performance very close to that of raw IO.

Some of these database optimizations require direct control over the placement of files on physical devices. However, given the current state of storage networks with multiple levels of virtualization, it is hard, if not impossible, to control physical data placement. After passing through the host volume manager, storage routers, and the storage subsystem controller, the data's location is anybody's guess. Still, some new storage management tools do show the data path between the applications and the storage devices — end-to-end. These tools might prove useful in data placement optimizations.

Some vendors argue that the user should not be concerned with the physical layout of the data. Some of these vendors provide capabilities in their storage subsystems to detect, distribute, and eliminate hot spots automatically. However, under heavy and dynamic load, the performance advantages of these tools are yet to be tested. The main concern is the latency in the removal of hot spots, which could be significant in an already saturated system.

Designing for Backups

When digital data is at the center of the business operations, proper backup of the data becomes critical for business functions. Data backups (and restores) are required for operational, business, and legal reasons. However, backups consume resources (money, time, effort, and so on) that could otherwise be used for revenue-generating tasks.

This trade-off calls for optimized backup configurations. Backups must be reliable, cost-effective, and undisruptive. When designed properly, storage networks can be utilized for performing optimized backups. The following sections discuss the problems with current backup practices and then introduce backup alternatives utilizing storage networks. Several topics on optimizing backups over storage networks will also be presented.

Problems with Conventional Network Backup

The traditional backup strategy for networked computers is to install backup software agents on all computers that contain data to be backed up. Then, the data is sent over a local area network (LAN) connection to a central backup server, which collects the backup data from all the connected clients and writes it onto direct-attached storage devices (mostly tape devices). This scenario is illustrated in Figure 15-1.

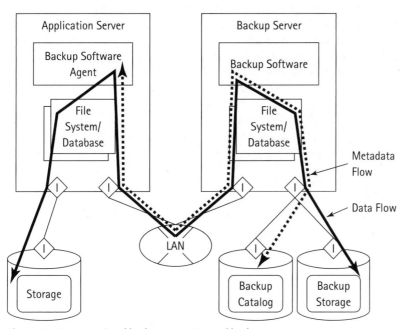

Figure 15-1: Conventional backup over LANs and backup servers

The backup server also keeps track of all the files that have been backed up and logs the information in a backup catalog for easy restores later (Chervenak, 1998). Backup data and catalog can be on the same device. All data and metadata traffic is carried over the LAN links. In a network with hundreds of host computers to be backed up, LAN bandwidth capacity can easily become a performance bottleneck. In addition, because all the traffic is targeted at the backup server, the server's resources could be overwhelmed by the backup tasks. The IO bus on the server must take in the data from all the clients and push the data out to the backup storage devices.

Such a backup setup requires large backup windows to complete the tasks. While the backup window is up, the applications on the clients cannot execute. If the applications do execute, the backup data will be inconsistent or incomplete. All the updates to the data must happen either before the backup starts or after the backup ends.

Another potential problem with the traditional network backup configurations is the software components' availability. The agents might not be available for all the operating systems that the backup clients are supposed to run.

LAN-Free Network Backup

LANs are not designed or optimized for high-volume storage data traffic. Sending backup traffic over LAN links uses up considerable link capacity. If other critical business applications use these links, those applications will face considerable service degradation during backup operations.

Storage networks (whether SAN-based or IP-based) provide an extra network just for storage traffic. In addition, storage networks enable storage device sharing between multiple hosts. These capabilities are very handy for backups. First, the backup traffic can be handled in the storage network alone, outside of the LAN. Second, because the application servers and backup servers can access the same storage devices, backup servers can access the storage devices directly, and the application servers (clients) are not on the data path.

Such network backup setups, where backups are performed on a storage network, are called *LAN-free backup*. Figure 15-2 illustrates a LAN-free backup scenario.

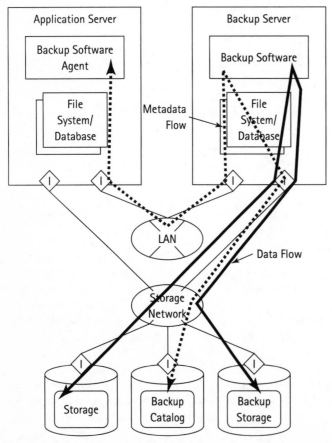

Figure 15-2: LAN-free backup using storage networks and backup servers

The control information (metadata) about the files that must be backed up is exchanged between the backup server and the application servers (backup clients) over the LAN. In this regard, LAN-free backup is not completely LAN-free. However, the size of the information that describes the files and the file locations (that is, the metadata) is insignificant compared to the size of the data.

In Figure 15-2, both types of flow are shown. Metadata flow occurs between the backup agents and the main backup application. At the end of the backup, the backup applications write a log of all the backup files into the backup catalog. The catalog identifies file locations in case they need to be restored. The main data flow occurs between the source volume and the backup device (typically a tape). However, because these two target devices cannot exchange data directly, the backup server is required to read and write the data as an initiator. Computers, devices, or software entities that mainly move data between two targets, without much processing, are generally called *data-movers*.

Because all backup traffic passes through the backup server, it can easily become a bottleneck point in large systems with large volumes of backup data.

Server-Free Network Backup

Backup (or restore) data must move between two storage devices, from disk to tape or similar storage device combinations. In addition, a data-mover must be responsible for the move (read, then write). The data-mover can take many forms. The previous section discussed that in LAN-free backup, backup servers act as data-movers. If storage subsystems (disk arrays, tape libraries, and so on) have enough intelligence and compute capability, they can exchange data among themselves. The current generation of storage network switches and hardware virtualization devices have the capability to act as data-movers. *Storage routers* that connect two different storage interconnect types can also have such capability.

Figure 15-3 shows a backup system where the data flows through a storage router. The storage router in the example connects the backup device (tape library) to the storage network. For example, such a router could be a FC-to-parallel-SCSI converter. Most of these storage routers can act as data-movers.

A setup where the backup data flow occurs outside of the application server, backup server, and LAN is called a *server-free backup*. You can't eliminate the role of the backup server, but the duties can be offloaded. For example, in Figure 15-3, the data-moving task is offloaded to the storage router. Because a data-mover can be a specialized device that performs a limited set of tasks extremely fast, it provides higher performance than general server hardware used as a backup server would. In addition, multiple data-movers can be controlled by a single, central backup server.

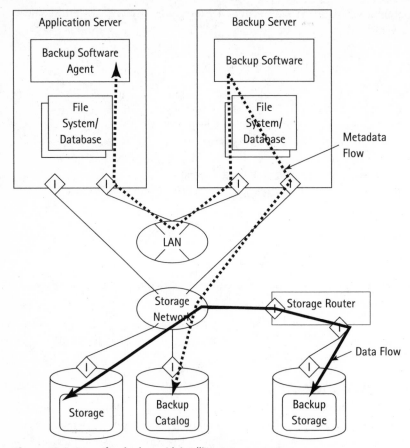

Figure 15-3: Server-free backup with intelligent storage routers

Offloading data-moving functionality is accomplished using techniques that can be referred to as *third-party copy*. The most well-known and widely available third-party copy technique is SCSI-3 *extended copy operation (XCOPY)* (INCITS, 2002). With SCSI extended copy, a host can build a complex data transfer command and send it to target devices that actually perform the data transfer among themselves without the host's involvement. Because XCOPY is part of the SCSI standard, it can be used over any SCSI transport (including parallel SCSI, FC SANs, and so on).

Alternatively, you can construct the metadata for data movement in table form and send it to special data-mover devices using means other than SCSI. For example, metadata can be sent over a LAN connection to a special backup device, which actually moves the blocks pointed by the metadata. Such third-party transfers are called *off-host backups* (just another term for server-free backup).

Network Data Management Protocol

A particular problem exists with backing up network-attached storage (NAS) appliances and certain file servers. Most NAS devices contain their own direct-attached storage devices. Even if there is a backend storage network behind the NAS device, it is generally controlled and accessed solely by the NAS device, and is not accessible from outside. This causes problems for backup operations. The only way to back up these devices is to use the device vendor's proprietary backup solutions. For example, the appliance might include a dedicated tape device, and the appliance management console can be used to perform backups locally. This can create a management problem in a network with many heterogeneous NAS devices. Each device must be accessed and backed up individually.

Network Data Management Protocol (NDMP) is a new network-based backup protocol, proposed by Network Appliance and Intelliguard (now Legato). NDMP tries to remedy the drawbacks of traditional backup configurations with an architecture that offloads the backup responsibility to several devices.

NDMP consists of three main components:

- ✓ **NDMP Data Server** — Contains the data that will be backed up (for example, the NAS appliance). Sends the data to the tape server.

- ✓ **NDMP Tape Server** — Contains the backup storage devices (for example, the tape library). Receives the data from the data servers and writes it to the tape.

- ✓ **NDMP Client** — The main backup software. Coordinates the data movement between the data servers and tape servers. Receives metadata information from the data servers about the files that have been backed up.

NDMP servers and clients communicate over standardized interfaces. Therefore, NDMP implementations of different vendors are supposed to interoperate. For example, NDMP-compliant backup software can configure an NDMP-compliant NAS device to back up its data on an NDMP-compliant tape library.

Figure 15-4 illustrates the NDMP components and the data and metadata traffic paths. The standard interface eliminates the need for proprietary backup agents at the data servers specific to each backup software. As shown in the figure, the backup is performed between the data server and the tape server. The NDMP client receives only the results of the backup operation for cataloging and error reporting.

NDMP's three components do not need to reside on different computers. Several configurations are possible. For example, Figure 15-5 shows an NDMP system where the NDMP server has both the data sources and the backup devices. This could be a NAS device with an integrated tape drive.

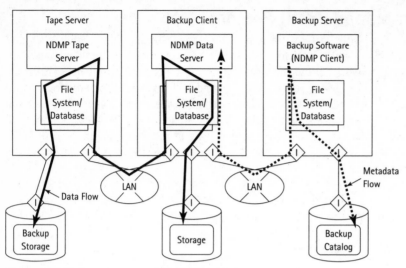

Figure 15-4: Three components of the NDMP backup setup

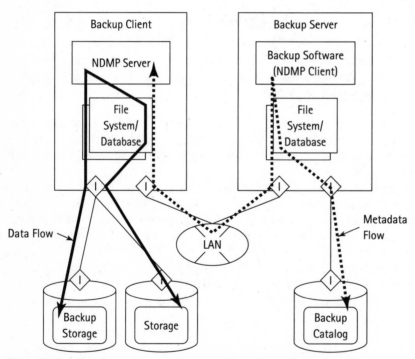

Figure 15-5: NDMP data and tape servers can reside on the same server

Accelerating Backups Using Point-in-Time Copy

The data volumes to be backed up must be stable. During the backup operation, the data should not be allowed to change. If this is not enforced, inconsistent or corrupt data can result. For example, in an image-level backup, the resulting (restored) file system might contain corrupt file tables because of incomplete metadata updates. In a file system level backup, the data in the files or across several files might be inconsistent.

You can use a couple of techniques to obtain consistent backups. First, the application servers must be told to empty their buffers and pause their data updates at a consistent state. To support this, database applications have a special backup mode. Then, a quick, point-in-time copy of the data must be performed. After this point-in-time copy is captured, the application servers can be released to perform normal IO operations. The backup can be performed using the point-in-time copy (Azagury, 2002).

Two main techniques for performing point-in-time copies are *split-mirror* copies and *copy-on-write* snapshots.

BACKUPS USING SPLIT-MIRRORS

Split-mirror functionality is generally provided by the disk array subsystems. In addition, split-mirroring is possible using logical volume manager software in the hosts or somewhere in the storage network. However, subsystem-based split-mirror copies are the most efficient.

Figure 15-6 illustrates the steps involved in a typical split-mirror operation.

1. A mirror copy of the source volume is created.

2. After the mirror is started, every update to the original volume is also reflected to the mirror volume.

3. Just before the backup is started, the application servers are quiesced (paused), and the mirror between the two copies is broken.

4. After the two mirrors are split, the servers are free to use and update the original volume. The backup operation can be performed using the mirror copy.

5. After the backup operation is completed, the mirror copy should be resynchronized with the original volume. This means that the write operations must be logged during the mirror is broken and the writes must be applied to the mirror copy after the mirror is reestablished. Data structures must be in place to denote which blocks are different between the two copies. In some implementations, it is also possible to perform the synchronization from the mirror copy back to the original volume.

6. Finally, after the resynchronization, the mirror operations continue normally until the next mirror split operation.

Besides being a backup source, mirrors are useful as a high-availability or disaster recovery tool. However, after the mirror split, the original volume is not protected. To solve this problem, *three-way mirroring* is sometimes used. When one of the mirrors is split, at least two synchronized copies will exist at all times.

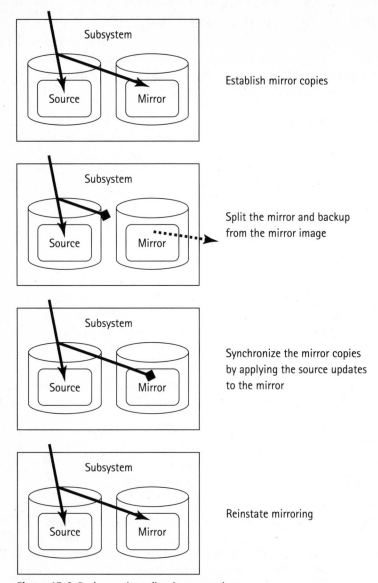

Establish mirror copies

Split the mirror and backup from the mirror image

Synchronize the mirror copies by applying the source updates to the mirror

Reinstate mirroring

Figure 15-6: Backups using split-mirror operations

BACKUPS USING SNAPSHOTS

Another point-in-time copy generation technique makes use of software snapshots. Snapshots create almost instant copies of the source volume at a virtual level. When the data is updated in the original volume, special algorithms are used to preserve the data in the snapshot copy (Brown).

One such technique is called *copy-on-write*. As the name implies, the original data is copied to the snapshot volume only if portions of the original data are overwritten. This mechanism is shown in Figure 15-7.

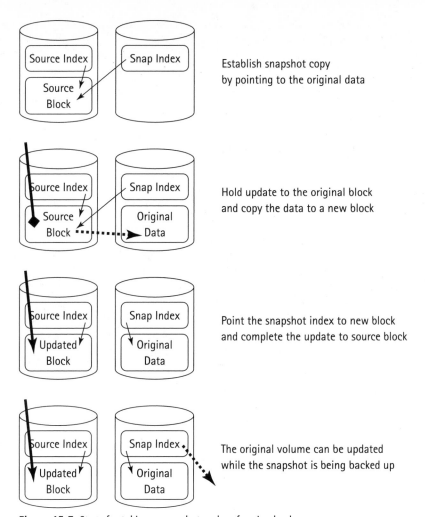

Figure 15-7: Steps for taking a snapshot and performing backup

Before the snapshot is taken, the servers are quiesced for a short time and a snapshot index is generated. At this point, both the original volume and the snapshot volume have pointers to the original data blocks. Thus, the copies are exactly the same — as expected. This operation is generally fast, and server operations can resume immediately.

When a write operation is pending, that operation waits until the original data is copied to a new block. Then, the snapshot pointers are updated to point to the new block with the original data. After the copy, the write operation is allowed to complete, changing the original block, as shown in the third step in Figure 15-7. These operations ensure that the data pointed to by the snapshot indexes is always the data that existed at the point of the snapshot.

Instead of copy-on-write, you can use a technique called *redirect-on-write*, where the original block is left in the snapshot copy and a new block is used for the updated data. This removes the copy delay required by the copy-on-write method. However, redirect-on-write changes the layout of the original file blocks. When the snapshot is removed, the blocks should be copied back to their original locations. So, copy-on-write is not really eliminated; it is just deferred.

When a backup is required, it can safely use the snapshot copy, which is guaranteed to be consistent. After the backup operation is completed, the snapshot volume and the blocks in it can be removed without affecting the original volume. Alternatively, the snapshot copy can be reserved as an online backup copy.

Several snapshot implementations allow multiple, scheduled snapshots. You can restore the volume to any of the saved snapshots, allowing instant recovery without going to the backup tapes.

A snapshot volume still depends on the original volume for most of its data blocks. The snapshot space only contains the blocks that have been updated since the snapshot time. The blocks that are not updated are still in the original volume. Therefore, depending on snapshots instead of regular backups to tape is not a good idea. Snapshots can be used to recover earlier versions of files and deleted files. They cannot recover corrupt or lost file systems.

The space required for snapshots is proportional to the amount of data that has been updated since the snapshot time. If this ratio is small, the space used for snapshots is insignificant.

As discussed in Chapter 14, Virtual Disk Service (VDS) and Virtual Shadow Copy Service (VSS) are two new Microsoft features that streamline the process of application quiescing, taking snapshots, and backing up data. These interfaces provide hooks to coordinate the applications, the file system, and the array subsystems.

File-Level Backup versus Image Backup

Backups can be performed on raw storage volume by making an exact, block-by-block image of the original volume. Alternatively, a file system can be used to locate file blocks and a file-level backup can be performed.

An image backup does not know anything about the file layout and blindly copies everything in the volume to the backup media. This is a fast operation because the volume can be read sequentially and streamed to the backup device. However, if the file system on the volume is only 10 percent full, image-level backup will still back up the entire volume—100 percent of it.

Files can be scattered throughout the storage device, and accessing them might require lots of random, mechanical seek operations, which are inherently slow. On the other hand, a file system knows where the used blocks are and transfers only the blocks with data during a backup. In addition, a file system can locate the files that have been changed since the last full backup, and only the changed files are backed up instead of the entire file system. This significantly reduces the backup time and the backup-window. In addition, the size and number of the files are factors in file-level backups. A few large files can be read and backed up sequentially, while many small files require lots of seeks and cause interruption of the backup streams.

In summary, image backups are fast because of sequential access and slow because of the amount of data. File-level backups are slow because of random accesses, and fast because of the reduced amount of data. The optimum backup method depends on the particular system. If the volumes are almost full, an image backup will be faster. If the volumes are almost empty, a file-level backup will be faster. If the volumes are half full, you have an optimization problem.

Modeling Network Backups

The blueprints given in the previous sections about LAN-free, server-free, NDMP-based, and snapshot-based backups can be used as a basis for modeling backups over storage networks.

Backup performance models have four main levels:

- ✓ The servers that generate the backup traffic

- ✓ The storage network (the fabric and the ports) that carry the traffic

- ✓ The storage routers that move the traffic

- ✓ The backup devices (the tapes) that absorb the backup traffic

To model backup performance, you must account for the number and performance of the elements in each level. The server backup size depends on the activity in the server applications. Storage network and router performance is mostly defined by the hardware implementation and the number and type of available ports and paths.

Multiple tape devices can be combined by striping the backup data to increase backup speed. The striping might involve parity to increase reliability in case one tape goes bad in the stripe group. The tape devices perform best when the input traffic comes in a streaming mode and fills the tape buffers. The tape head can continue writing at full speed without any pauses or rewinds. Tape drives also have built-in compression capabilities. They are generally expected to obtain a compression ratio of 2 to 1. However, this depends on the data type. Compression increases the need for high-speed streaming input.

Most backup software and devices can interleave streams from multiple sources. A single server's backup throughput will generally not be enough to saturate high-speed backup tape devices. In such cases, you can combine the backup traffic from multiple servers into a single backup stream that can be written to the tape in streaming mode. Conversely, the restores from a single tape can be performed in an interleaved fashion to multiple targets, simultaneously.

One technique that can be used to improve backup performance is staging the backups utilizing multiple storage technologies configured as hierarchies. For example, by using an array of disk drives that emulate a tape library, the first stage of backups can be performed at disk speeds, which are generally faster than tapes. Restores from disks are also faster. Later, old data can be destaged to bigger, cheaper (but slower) tape libraries.

The expected end result of a backup performance modeling study is the assurance that backup operations can be completed in a given backup window dictated by business schedule requirements, and the assurance that the data can be restored rapidly enough to meet service level agreements that are dictated by business availability requirements.

Summary

This chapter presented application-level storage IO tuning opportunities, and included the following topics:

Optimizing Applications for Storage

✓ Storage IO characteristics of applications, systems software, and storage network devices should be considered and optimized together.

✓ The IO type, size, frequency, and the number of IO streams at the application layer guide the storage networks' design.

✓ Database systems and backup applications are the flagship applications for storage networks.

Optimizing Database Systems

✓ Databases are used in almost all business functionalities as the underlying storage interface for data integrity and security characteristics.

✓ Placement of database files, the configuration of database block sizes, database caches, and raw versus direct IO access are the major tuning points for database IO performance.

✓ File placement optimizations require the visualization of the entire path from the application to the spindles. Some storage management software and storage subsystems have automatic data placement and hot-spot removal functionalities.

Designing for Backups

✓ Backups are essential for operational, business, and legal reasons. They must be reliable, cost-effective, and undisruptive.

✓ Storage networks are a natural fit for optimized backup operations. Design techniques, such as LAN-free backups, server-free backups, and standards-based (NDMP) backup, can eliminate many of the problems faced by traditional network-based backups.

✓ Backups can be accelerated using point-in-time copy techniques such as split-mirrors and snapshots. Point-in-time copies significantly reduce or eliminate the need for backup windows.

Modeling Network Backups

✓ Servers, network ports (paths), storage routers, and storage devices are the main elements for modeling the performance of backup applications over storage networks.

✓ Bandwidth and throughput characteristics at the underlying layers should be able to satisfy the backup traffic generated at the server layer.

✓ Backup devices use interleaving of multiple streams and compression to improve backup performance.

References and Additional Resources

Azagury, Alain, Michael E Factor, and Julian Satran. April 2002. *Point-in-Time Copy: Yesterday, Today and Tomorrow*. In Proceedings of Joint NASA and IEEE Mass Storage Conference.

Discusses the state of the point-in-time capabilities in current commercial products, and states that point-in-time copy can essentially be done in near zero time.

Brown, K., J. Katcher, R. Walters, and A. Watson. *SnapMirror and SnapRestore: Advances in Snapshot Technology*. Network Appliance Inc., Technical Report TR3043.

Available at www.netapp.com.

Chervenak, Ann, Vivekenand Vellanki, and Zachary Kurmas. March 1998. *Protecting File Systems: A Survey of Backup Techniques*. In Proceedings of Joint NASA and IEEE Mass Storage Conference.

Survey of backup concepts such as device- and file-based backup, snapshots, compression, full and incremental backups, and so on.

Gimarc, Richard L. and Amy Spellmann. December 1998. *Modeling Microsoft SQL Server 7.0*. In Proceedings of CMG 98.

Presents a simulation model of SQL Server and tests it using TPC-C workloads.

INCITS T10 Committee. November 10, 2002. *SCSI Primary Commands-3 (SPC3)*, Project: 1416-D, Rev: 10.

This working draft introduces the third-generation SCSI primary commands. Section 7.3 describes the extended copy operations. Available at www.t10.org.

Kreiser, Randy. 2000. *I/O and Storage Tuning: An Introduction to I/O and Storage Tuning Tips and Techniques*. IEEE Symposium on Mass Storage Systems 2000, pp. 25–30.

Contains tips on tuning applications, system software, and storage for IO performance.

Minhas, Mughees A. *ORACLE9i Database Administration Best Practices*. Oracle Corporation, Doc #452.

Available at `http://otn.oracle.com`.

Chapter 16

Storage Subsystem Tuning

In This Chapter

Storage subsystems are the backbones of any storage network. For high performance and high availability, these building blocks must be designed and configured optimally. However, optimal configuration of storage subsystems depends on the workload to which they will be subjected. In addition, workloads are often dynamic and change over time, requiring continuous, adaptive system tuning. This chapter discusses storage subsystem configuration and tuning, including the following topics:

✓ A general architectural model for current, state-of-the-art storage subsystems

✓ Data layout optimizations, including the choice of RAID levels and striping parameters

✓ Advanced techniques for improving RAID performance using disk-based XOR

✓ Research on new storage architectures that incorporate more functionality into storage devices

Storage Subsystem Architectures

Any sufficiently complex storage subsystem that can be part of a storage network is composed of the following basic building blocks:

✓ Front-end interfaces that connect the subsystem to the host computers over the front-end storage network. These may be Fibre Channel (FC) ports in block-based devices and Ethernet in file-based devices.

✓ Subsystem controller(s) that has the logic and processing elements to move data from the storage elements to the front-end connections. The controller is responsible for virtualization, RAID, access control, and availability tasks.

✓ Cache memory, which can be part of the controller or a separate device used to accelerate read/write operations.

✓ Back-end interfaces that connect the controllers to the back-end storage devices (disk/tape drives) over a back-end storage network, which is most likely an FC loop/fabric or a parallel Small Computer System Interface (SCSI) bus.

✓ Back-end storage devices that actually contain stored data. Commonly, SCSI, FC, or Advanced Technology Attachment (ATA) disk drives or tape drives.

The subsystem's main task is to present several back-end storage devices as a single, manageable, highly-available, high-performance storage device to the outside world. As such, it provides storage virtualization in its most general interpretation.

Figure 16-1 depicts the current practice in the design of mid-range to enterprise-level storage subsystems. Most of the current commercially available storage subsystems (for example, HP Enterprise Virtual Array, EMC Clarion, BlueArc SiliconServer, and so on) are variations of the architecture shown in the figure. The differences are as follows:

✓ Type of front- and back-end interfaces

✓ Number of front- and back-end interfaces

✓ Number of back-end devices

✓ The amount of available cache

✓ The type of storage processors in each controller

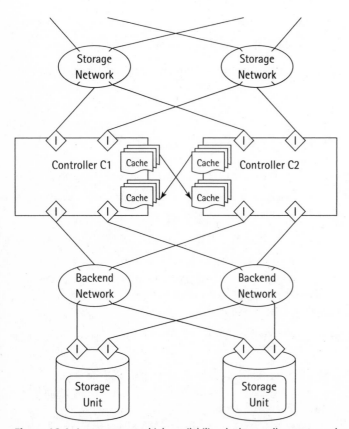

Figure 16-1: A contemporary, high-availability, dual-controller storage subsystem

The subsystem architecture in Figure 16-1 has high-availability features. All elements are dual-ported. And, there are always at least two paths (dual-pathed) between any two elements. The caches are mirrored between the two controllers. The controllers should be architected to fail-over and assume each other's tasks in case of failures. All these precautions ensure that no *single point of failure* exists in the data path.

A common joke about high availability solutions is that "*single point of failure is better than multiple points of failure.*" As entertaining as this notion sounds, it ignores the fact that even a single point of failure, by definition, is enough to take the system down.

A glimpse at the subsystem architecture in Figure 16-1 reveals the following storage performance factors:

✓ **Front-End Network** — The number and speed of the front-end interfaces determine how much data can be transferred in and out of the system. Multiple interfaces can be used in an active-active fashion to enable load balancing, or they can be configured as active-passive for only availability.

✓ **Storage Controller** — Because the controllers act as data-movers, their performance characteristics are critical. The controllers generally incorporate specialized IO processors or Application-Specific Integrated Circuits (ASICS), which are optimized for moving data quickly. Controllers must have fast IO buses that connect the storage processors to the front- and back-end interfaces. Mid-range systems contain some generation of the Peripheral Component Interconnect (PCI) bus. However, enterprise-level systems incorporate specialized buses or fabrics inside the controller for high throughput.

✓ **Cache** — Speed, size, and policies determine the cache's effectiveness. Caches can be used as read and read-ahead caches for access patterns that have data locality, or they can be used as write buffers to improve write performance. In the case of writes, the cache must be backed up by auxiliary batteries to save data that is not committed to stable storage (disk) in the event of system failures. Most subsystems with caches also mirror the cache information to a second cache before acknowledging the end of the write operation to the host. This extra cache mirroring has its own overhead and must be weighed against the benefit of caching.

✓ **Back-End Network** — Data must pass through the back-end network to arrive at the stable storage. The speed and number of back-end interfaces could be performance bottlenecks. RAID algorithms, such as mirroring, striping, and parity generation, increase the bandwidth and throughput requirements of the original data stream while it is being transferred at the back-end. For example, mirroring doubles the number and bandwidth usage of the write operations.

✓ **Back-End Storage** — Eventually, all data must be stored or retrieved from the stable storage (disks, tapes). Under heavy load, the overall system throughput could quite possibly be defined by the back-end storage performance (this is another way of saying that the back-end will be the bottleneck).

Even if the subsystem components are designed to exhibit very good performance, the achievable performance still depends on how they are used by the applications. The following sections discuss data layout optimizations for storage subsystem performance.

Data Layout Optimizations

Subsystems incorporate hundreds of back-end storage devices. Utilizing the performance and capacity of all these devices requires data striping (Ganger, 1993). However, the greater the number of devices, the greater the risk of system failures or data loss. Therefore, data must be guarded by mirroring or parity protection. As shown earlier in Chapter 6, Redundant Array of Independent/ Inexpensive Disks (RAID) is a technique that combines striping, mirroring, and parity protection. Remember that several RAID levels have different performance and availability features.

Choosing a RAID Level

After a storage subsystem's hardware requirements and capacity have been decided, the next most important configuration decision is the distribution of the application data onto the available devices. This must be done according to the applications' performance, capacity, and availability requirements. Data layout decisions here are discussed in terms of the choice of RAID levels (Patterson, 1988).

Table 16-1 summarizes the performance and availability features of various RAID levels, as well as their advantages and disadvantages.

TABLE 16-1 Characteristics of Various RAID Levels

RAID Level	Performance	Availability	Advantages	Disadvantages
RAID0	Best	Bad	High performance	No redundancy
RAID1	Good	Best	Full redundancy	Full redundancy (cost)
RAID3	Good	Good	High bandwidth, low write penalty	Low throughput
RAID4	Bad	Good	Concurrent IO	Requires battery-backed caching for good performance
RAID5	Good	Good	Concurrent IO	Write penalty
RAID6	Good	Good/Best	Better availability than RAID5	Requires another parity dimension
RAID10	Best	Best	Full redundancy and high performance	Full redundancy (cost)|

RAID0 is pure striping. It is vulnerable to data loss when a single disk failure occurs. RAID1 duplicates all data to two disks and can survive even if one of the disks fails. RAID10 combines striping and mirroring. RAID1 and RAID10 require duplication of every write and may slow down the write performance. On the other hand, reads can be sent to either of the two destinations and might see some response time improvement.

RAID3 uses rotationally synchronized disks (Kim, 1986) to stripe data at the byte level and contains a single parity disk. All read and write operations access every disk in the stripe group. Because the disks are rotationally synchronized, they access a given stripe at the same point in time. Such a striping technique combines the bandwidth of all the disks and is suitable for access patterns that require high bandwidth (for example, video editing). On the other hand, because all the disks are kept busy for each operation, only one active operation can occur at a time. The stripe group's throughput rate is almost equal to the throughput rate of a single disk. Hence, RAID3 is not appropriate for applications that require a high throughput rate (for example, transaction-processing systems).

RAID4 is similar to RAID3 in terms of striping and in having a parity disk. However, RAID4 disks are not rotationally synchronized, and multiple operations can access disks of a stripe group at the same time. Because portions of a stripe can be accessed independently, care must be taken to keep the parity data up-to-date at all times. This requires reading the old parity and old data blocks and updating the parity. Therefore, the parity disk is accessed twice for each and every write operation. The single parity disk in RAID4 can quite easily become the performance bottleneck. Some implementations use battery-backed cache buffers to accumulate write operations and commit them in big chunks to reduce or eliminate the parity calculation overhead. Parity overhead, and ways to decrease it, are discussed in more detail later in this chapter.

RAID5 is very similar to RAID4. However, in RAID5, the parity information is distributed to all disks, so accesses to the parity information do not concentrate on a single disk. Still, RAID5 requires the retrieval, calculation, and update of the parity information and may not be suitable for access patterns with considerable write operations. Because it uses striping, it is a good choice for read-intensive workloads with few or no write operations.

RAID3 does not suffer from the parity update penalties observed in RAID4 and RAID5. In RAID3, all write operations access all of the disks in the stripe (including the parity disk) at the same time, and can generate the new parity without accessing the old parity.

RAID6 (also referred to as RAID Double Parity, Advanced Data Guarding, or any number of other proprietary names) is RAID5 implemented in two dimensions. For each stripe, RAID6 keeps two parity blocks. RAID6 can survive two disk failures without data loss. The algorithms (equations) used to generate the two parity blocks must be independent; they should allow the solution of two equations (parity equations) to find two unknown variables (two missing disk blocks) in case of disk failures.

A fine line exists between fault-tolerance and high-availability. Fault-tolerance assumes the system survives and keeps running even in cases of multiple failures. RAID systems can be part of a high-availability solution. However, for fault-tolerance, everything in the system must be duplicated, including the application hosts, adapters, IO paths, power and cooling systems, and system administrators, not just the data. If you cannot use the data, having it safely stored somewhere will not help you.

Automatic RAID Level Tuning

HP AutoRAID (Wilkes, 2001) and Hitachi Data Systems (HDS) Dynamic Optimizer have facilities to move stored data automatically between RAID levels depending on the access pattern.

RAID5 provides a good cost/performance ratio for read-intensive workloads. However, it is slow for write-intensive workloads. RAID10 requires almost twice the disk space of RAID5, and has good read and write performance. You can optimize cost/performance by migrating data between RAID5 and RAID10, depending on the percentage of the writes in the access pattern.

For automatic tuning to work, the workload must be observed continuously to classify it as read-intensive or write-intensive. In addition, changing RAID levels for existing data has its own overhead and cannot be performed instantaneously. To perform the move, the tuning method must wait until the system is idle. If the system is busy, it might be a while before the correct level is configured. This is not a problem if the changes in the access pattern are gradual over time. However, if the change occurs while the system is busy, the system might be stuck in a state of suboptimal data layout for some time.

Stripe Unit Size Tuning

Besides the RAID level, the next most important factor in RAID performance tuning is the determination of the striping unit size (striping depth). Several research studies have shown that the optimal stripe unit depends on the workload (Simitci, 1999; Chen, 1990).

Rotationally synchronized disks under heavy load, with lots of incoming requests, require a large striping unit to limit the number of disks used for each request. This, in turn, increases the number of requests served concurrently. If the system is lightly loaded, the striping unit must be small to allow the utilization of multiple disks for each request.

If the disks are not synchronized, intrarequest parallelism (that is, using multiple disks for a single request) is not helpful. In such a case, having a stripe unit large enough to contain an entire request is more favorable.

Several researchers proposed using the striping unit for disk striping performance optimization. Simitci and Reed (Simitci, 1999) used the arrival rate per unit time to gauge the system load and drives models of striping based on the system load. Details of the striping model were discussed previously in Chapter 6. Chen and Patterson (Chen, 1990) used the number of concurrent accesses as a measure of system load. They then concluded that the formula shown in Equation 16-1 is a heuristic approximation of the optimal stripe unit for synchronized, block striped arrays.

Equation 16-1

```
Stripe Unit = S × average positioning time × average data transfer rate
              × (concurrency-1) + 0.5KB
```

This formula depends on three parameters and points to the fact that the stripe unit must increase linearly with the increasing disk positioning time, disk transfer rate, and command concurrency. The constant S in the formula is estimated to be 1/4 (Chen, 1990). However, for today's high data bandwidth disks, a smaller constant multiplier (for example, S = 1/16) provides more meaningful results.

For unsynchronized RAID arrays commonly found today, a simple rule of thumb is to use small (4KB to 64KB) stripe units for transaction-oriented workloads with lots of small, concurrent accesses, and large (128KB to 1MB) stripe units for workloads with a small number of large, sequential accesses.

RAID Controller Implementation

RAID functionality can be implemented in four places on the IO path:

- ✓ **Host System Processor** — RAID can be implemented as a software function in the operating system or in a volume manager application.

- ✓ **Host Bus Adapter** — The storage interface adapter on the host IO bus can implement RAID on the devices that are connected to it.

- ✓ **Storage Network Switches/Routers/Gateways** — These devices are a collection point for the storage resources and can easily implement RAID.

- ✓ **Storage Subsystems** — The controllers in the storage subsystems invariably provide RAID functionalities.

Note that these are the same places where storage virtualization can be implemented. That is not a coincidence when you consider RAID as a subset of the virtualization features.

Software implementation at the host system is a cost-effective solution, but the performance of such implementations is limited by the host's available processing, IO bus, and memory resources, and the implementation can stretch the limits of all these host resources. Software implementation is only suitable for small server configurations with few disk drives.

Host bus adapters were the first places where several RAID features were historically implemented. However, HBAs are also limited by the resources (processor, IO bus, storage channels) available on the adapter. In addition, such an implementation does not allow the sharing of RAID resources among multiple host computers.

Storage virtualization is one of the hot topics for storage gateway devices. Because these devices sit in the middle of the storage network, they are well positioned to implement several RAID functions. However, these devices might be physically far from the disk devices, and implementing low-level RAID functions at the network level might be difficult. You can still employ RAID functions such as mirroring and high-level striping on the network devices effectively.

Storage subsystem controllers are well positioned to implement many RAID functions. They are generally in close proximity to the disk devices and can easily implement low-level RAID algorithms. In addition, these controllers are built with special ASICs to accelerate RAID processing, such as hardware-accelerated XOR engines.

Speeding-Up Parity Calculations

Updating the parity information during a write operation is the performance-limiting factor in parity-based RAID levels (RAID4 and RAID5). As shown in Figure 16-2, a write operation requires the retrieval of the old data block and the old parity block. After the new parity is computed, the data and parity blocks can be updated. Overall, a single write operation requires two read operations and two write operations over the storage bus (or the network). This is known as the *read-update-write penalty*. For simplicity's sake, only the two disks that hold the data block and the parity block are shown in the figure. Normally, there are many more connected disks requiring similar operations.

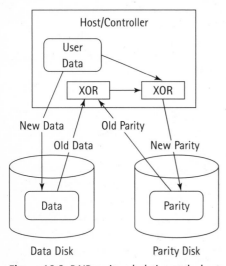

Figure 16-2: RAID parity calculation at the host or the RAID controller

Note also that in host-based (or controller-based) parity operations, the host is kept busy with all the reads, writes, and XOR calculations. Thus, when there are many (maybe hundreds) of disks to update, these operations may overwhelm any processing power the controller has.

To overcome the read-update-write penalty, some disk vendors have proposed disk-based XOR operations (Shim, 1996). The idea is to offload the XOR calculations to the storage devices and reduce the overhead in the controllers and storage bus. Disk-based XOR operations have been standardized in the SCSI-3 command set (INCITS, 1997).

Figure 16-3 illustrates the workings of the disk-based parity calculations. The data disk receives the new data, reads the old data, and calculates the parity information. This intermediate parity is returned to the host. The host then sends the intermediate parity to the parity disk, which calculates the new parity.

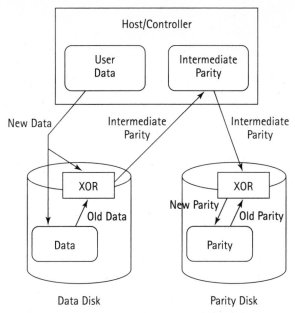

Figure 16-3: RAID parity calculation using disk-based XOR

Compared to the conventional parity calculations shown in Figure 16-2, the disk-based parity reduces the bus traffic by 25 percent and offloads the host from all XOR operations.

You can further reduce the bus traffic by letting the data disk send the intermediate parity information directly to the parity disk instead of the host, as shown in Figure 16-4. Normally, two disks cannot exchange data because both are SCSI targets. To enable direct parity exchange, the SCSI standard is extended to include *third-party XOR* operations (INCITS, 1997).

Compared to the host-based parity calculations, third-party XOR reduces the bus traffic by 50 percent and offloads all XOR overhead to the disks. Although third-party XOR looks like an excellent and easy alternative, it is plagued with technical problems that must be fixed. Third-party XOR can only work if all the drives support it. In addition, most drives today cannot handle multiple operations at the same time — they have single-threaded firmware. If two drives happen to send each other parity updates at the same time and wait on each other for the completion of the updates, a deadlock can occur (Shim, 1996). In addition, the interactions of the new read-modify-write commands with the standard SCSI commands might affect the caching and scheduling algorithms in the disk drives (Chang, 2002). Because of the deep command queues in the SCSI disks, cache segments may not be immediately available for disk-to-disk operations. Although some high-end storage arrays utilize disk-based XOR, because of the implementation difficulties, the usage of third-party XOR operations is not common.

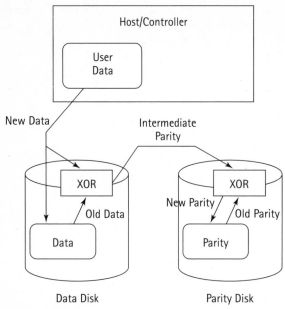

Figure 16-4: RAID parity calculation using third-party XOR

Intelligent Storage Devices

The "job description" of a disk drive is very simple. It writes data and then reads it. No matter how advanced disk drives are in terms of speed and reliability, their functionality stays the same. The latest disk drives incorporate processing elements with processing power equivalent to that of a low-end desktop computer. Disk drive manufacturers have difficulty differentiating their products by simply adhering to the simple write/read interfaces.

In order to utilize the processing power in the disk drives, academic researchers and disk drive manufacturers have been working on the concept of Object-Based Storage Devices (OSDs) (SNIA, 2000). The main idea is to move more functionality into the storage devices. Intelligent storage devices can be used to improve scalability and manageability. Academic projects with similar objectives include, but are not limited to, the following:

- ✓ Active Disks (Lim, 2001)
- ✓ Network-Attached Secure Disks (Gibson, 1997)
- ✓ Network-Attached Storage Devices
- ✓ iDISK

Generally, there are a large number of storage devices (for example, disks) per server in a computing system. These devices can form a large, distributed computing platform if a proper method of offloading work to them can be devised. Currently, one Storage Networking Industry

Association (SNIA) workgroup has developed an agenda to standardize the models and interfaces for Object-Based Storage Devices (OSDs). They have proposed a standard for augmenting the SCSI command set to include OSD-specific commands (INCITS, 2002).

Figure 16-5 shows an example of object-based storage. The left side of the figure depicts the standard (conventional) way to access block storage using file systems. On the right, you see an alternative architecture that uses OSD concepts to provide similar functionality.

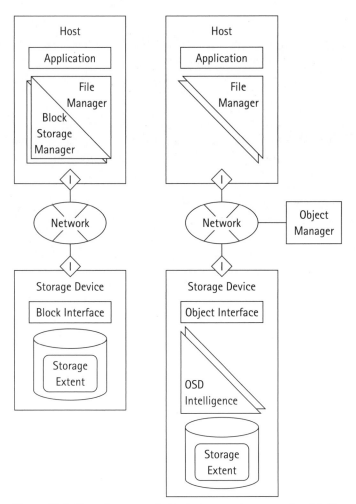

Figure 16-5: File system access to block storage using conventional (left) and Object-Based Storage Device architectures (right)

In the conventional file access method, the host is responsible for all the file system and block storage management tasks. Besides file system access control and directory management, host software also keeps track of free space management and block allocation on the storage devices. In the OSD model (Figure 16-5), part of the file system that deals with block and free space management is offloaded to the OSD. The host accesses the "objects" in the storage devices using a special object interface instead of the blocks in the conventional file system. Because OSDs have a higher level of functionality than simple storage devices, they are expected to be part of a LAN, and require special security and management considerations. An object manager on the network can be used to coordinate the discovery, allocation, and management of OSDs.

In addition, OSDs can execute user code to accelerate certain applications. Studies of this subject center on offloading database operations and multimedia editing functionality to storage devices.

OSDs can differentiate service levels for each access stream by implementing Quality of Service (QoS) interfaces. They can prioritize requests according to their QoS levels, and provide service-level guarantees. Data management functionality, such as mirroring, backup, snapshot, and defragmentation, can also be implemented as part the OSDs. By implementing distributed locking functionality in OSDs, distributed data sharing can be simplified.

OSDs are expected to take special optimization actions depending on the attributes of the stored data (like QoS levels previously mentioned). In this regard, OSD has very similar goals to the Microsoft VSS and VDS initiatives discussed in Chapter 14. Two main differences exist between OSD and VSS/VDS. First, OSD is targeted to all block storage devices — individual disk drives and large subsystems alike. VSS/VDS is mainly expected to be supported by subsystems with complex controllers. The second difference makes the first point more clear — the OSD interface is part of the SCSI command set and can be communicated in-band. VSS/VDS do not specify how the providers will communicate with the storage devices. This is expected to occur over secondary channels (most likely IP) using proprietary application program interfaces (APIs). In summary, OSD and VSS/VDS can co-exist and complement each other in the same storage network environment.

To date, there have been several research prototypes and interface standard proposals for OSDs. However, these are still works-in-progress — they are not commercially available products that can be classified as OSDs.

Summary

This chapter discussed storage subsystem configuration and tuning, and included the following topics:

Storage Subsystem Architectures

✓ Storage subsystems virtualize the capacity, speed, and failure characteristics of several smaller storage devices (disk drives) and present them as high-performance, highly available, larger storage units (logical units, LUs).

✓ The dominant subsystem architecture today has dual, redundant components that ensure high-availability and eliminate single points of failure.

✓ Number and speed characteristics of front-end networks and interfaces, storage controllers, cache, back-end networks and interfaces, and back-end storage devices all contribute to the overall subsystem performance, and any one of these components can become a performance bottleneck.

Data Layout Optimizations

✓ RAID systems provide performance and capacity improvements by striping the data over several disks, while protecting the data using mirror and parity redundancy.

✓ Different RAID implementations can be classified into RAID levels according to their striping and redundancy features. Different RAID levels exhibit different performance and availability characteristics, which also depends on the workload type.

✓ Some RAID implementations can tune RAID levels automatically by migrating data between RAID levels according to the access pattern history.

✓ Stripe unit size is one of the most important factors in striping performance. For synchronized arrays, stripe units must be large for highly concurrent, high transaction rate workloads. Small stripe units are appropriate for low concurrency, low-rate workloads. For unsynchronized arrays, stripe unit must be greater than a single request size.

✓ RAID functionality can be implemented at several layers of the storage network, and each layer exhibits different performance and ease of implementation characteristics.

Speeding-Up Parity Calculations

✓ Read-update-write penalty is a performance-limiting factor for parity-based RAID levels (RAID4 and RAID5).

✓ New extensions to the SCSI protocol enable the offloading of the parity operations to the disk drives using disk-based XOR. In this way, old parity information does not need to travel to the host.

✓ Third-party XOR commands further improve disk-based XOR performance by exchanging the intermediate parity information directly between the disk drives, without involving the host.

Intelligent Storage Devices

✓ Although storage devices have become more sophisticated over the years, the storage device interface still remains a simple block interface. Storage devices basically read and write data blocks.

✓ Object-based storage interfaces are being promoted to enhance storage device functionalities. Object-based storage devices can utilize device resources to perform enhanced storage functions such as free space management and block allocation.

✓ OSDs can be used to execute certain low-level application functions at the disk drive level.

References and Additional Resources

Chang, Tai-Sheng and David H C Du. 2002. *Efficient RAID Disk Scheduling on Smart Disks*. Tenth NASA Goddard Conference on Mass Storage Systems and Technologies, Adelphi, Maryland, USA, April 15–18.

Discusses the interaction of third-party XOR operations and standard disk scheduling and caching algorithms.

Chen, Peter M. and David A. Patterson. 1990. *Maximizing Performance in a Striped Disk Array*. Proc. 17th Annual Int'l Symp. on Computer Architecture, ACM SIGARCH, Computer Architecture News, pp. 322–331.

Discusses the importance of stripe unit size in striping performance and introduces heuristic formulas for optimal stripe unit sizes .

Ganger, G. R., B. L. Worthington, R. Y. Hou, and Y. N. Patt. 1993. *Disk Subsystem Load Balancing: Disk Striping vs. Conventional Data Placement*. Proc. of 26th Hawaii Int. Conf. on System Sciences, Vol. 1, pp. 40–49.

Discusses how disk striping eliminates many hot spots automatically, compared to the hand placement of data.

Gibson, Garth A., David F. Nagle, Khalil Amiri, Fay W. Chang, Eugene M. Feinberg, Howard Gobioff, Chen Lee, Berend Ozceri, Erik Riedel, David Rochberg, and Jim Zelenka. 1997. *File Server Scaling with Network-Attached Secure Disks*. SIGMETRIC '97, ACM, Seattle, WA, USA, pages 272–284..

INCITS T10 Committee. June 6, 1997. *SCSI-3 Block Commands (SBC)*, Project: 996D, Rev: 8a.

Section 5.1.15 describes the XOR and third-party XOR commands. Annex A contains examples of disk-based XOR usage. Available at www.t10.org.

INCITS T10 Committee. March 29, 2002. *SCSI Object Based Storage Device Commands (OSD)*, Project: 1355-D, Rev: 05.

Available at www.snia.org.

Kim, Michelle Y. November 1986. *Synchronized Disk Interleaving*, IEEE Transactions on Computers, C-35(11), pp. 978–988.

Performance study of rotationally synchronized disk striping.

Lim, H., V. Kapoor, C. Wighe, and D. Du. April 2001. *Active Disk File System: A Distributed, Scalable File System.*, Proceedings of the 18th IEEE Symposium on Mass Storage Systems and Technologies, San Diego, pp. 101–115.

Patterson, D. A., G. Gibson, and R. H. Katz. June 1988. *A Case for Redundant Arrays of Inexpensive Disks (RAID)*. Proceedings of ACM SIGMOD 88, pp. 109–116.

Introduces the original RAID level classifications.

Scheuermann, P., G. Weikum, and P. Zabback. 1994. *Disk Cooling in Parallel Disk Systems*. IEEE Data Engineering Bulletin, 17(3), pp. 29–40.

Discusses a technique that balances the load on storage devices by dynamically reallocating file system fragments. Striping is done on an individual file basis.

Shim, Sangyup, Yuewei Wang, Jenwei Hsieh, Tai-Sheng Chang, and David H.C. Du. 1996. *Efficient Implementation of RAID-5 Using Disk Based Read Modify Writes*. Technical Report, Department of Computer Science, University of Minnesota, 1996.

Discusses disk-based XOR implementation details and the solutions to possible deadlock problems.

Simitci, Huseyin and Daniel A. Reed. 1999. *Adaptive Disk Striping for Parallel Input/Output*. Proceedings of the Seventh NASA Goddard Conference on Mass Storage Systems, San Diego, CA, pp. 88–102.

Includes analytic queuing models of disk striping, which are used to drive optimization algorithms for striping parameter optimizations.

Storage Networking Industry Association (SNIA). January 17, 2000. *Usage Models for Object Based Storage Devices.*

Includes usage models for object-based storage devices in OLTP, file server, decision support system in Web server environments. Available at www.snia.org.

Wilkes, John, Richard Golding, Carl Staelin, and Tim Sullivan. 2001. *The HP AutoRAID Hierarchical Storage System*, in "High Performance Mass Storage and Parallel I/O Technologies and Applications," edited by Hai Jin, Toni Cortes, and Rajkumar Buyya. IEEE Computer Society Press and Wiley, New York, NY, USA, pp. 90–106.

Describes a method of migrating data between two RAID levels depending on the access patterns.

Chapter 17

Storage Network Tuning

In This Chapter

Storage networking technologies ensure that as long as a path exists between two devices, those devices can communicate. However, being able to communicate does not mean communicating efficiently. The number and size of network switches, the type and number of network links, and the placement of devices on the network end-points all affect the performance and availability characteristics of the network. This chapter discusses storage network design issues, including the following topics:

- ✓ Storage network topologies (mesh and core-edge designs)

- ✓ Improving performance by using faster links and link aggregation

- ✓ Logically partitioning the network using zoning and LUN masking

- ✓ Utilizing storage networks at storage subsystems' back-end

Storage Network Topologies

A storage network is constructed by connecting several switches together and attaching end-devices (network nodes) to available ports. The links between the switches are called *Inter-Switch Links (ISLs)*, and they enable the expansion of the networks into various topologies. Every ISL crossed during a network transmission is counted as a *hop*, and the number of hops is a measure of network distance.

Storage networks (whether using Fibre Channel or Internet Protocol) can be designed and implemented in various patterns (topologies). Some topologies are more efficient in terms of performance and availability than others. Ensuring that a storage network performs adequately is a mixture of choosing the right high-performance technologies and the proper network architectures. The remainder of this chapter discusses the performance aspects of storage network designs.

The spectrum of topologies with which a network can be designed is almost infinite. This chapter concentrates on mesh and core-edge topologies, using them as examples to study the factors affecting network performance. You could generalize and apply this discussion to other practical storage networks (for example, rings, strings, and so on).

For a more thorough discussion of storage network design topics, consult the references provided at the end of the chapter (for example, Brocade, Judd 2001, and Farley 2001).

Mesh Networks

The simplest network topology with high-availability features is called *full-mesh*. In a full-mesh topology, all the switches in the network have at least one link to all the other switches. The downside is the high number of ISLs that increase exponentially with the number of switches. For example, a full-mesh with eight 8-port switches will require seven ports used as ISLs on each switch, leaving only one port per switch for device connections. Moreover, adding another switch to this network without breaking the full-mesh topology will not be possible.

One possible solution to scaling is the use of so-called *partial-meshes*, where some ISLs are omitted between certain switches. Figure 17-1, for example, illustrates a two-tier topology, where all the switches are connected to all the other switches on the other tier. However, the switches on one tier are not directly connected amongst themselves. This two-tier topology might be useful if all the host computers can be connected to one of the tiers and all the storage devices to the other tier, providing complete connection from hosts to storage devices.

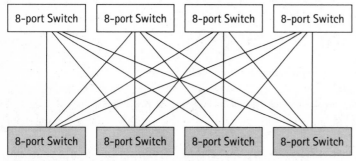

Figure 17-1: A partial-mesh topology arranged as a two-tier network

The drawbacks of the two-tier topology in Figure 17-1 are two-fold. First, there is only a single ISL between two switches on opposite tiers. This single ISL will limit the performance. If more than one ISL is used between each switch pair, there will be no ports left for devices. Second, even though it is possible to add another switch on one side by taking up a port from each switch on the other side, scalability is still limited by the number of ports on the switches.

Scalability and availability problems in full-mesh, two-tier, and similar network topologies have led to the proliferation of the core-edge designs, which are discussed next.

Core-Edge Designs

By introducing a third layer (tier) between the two tiers shown in Figure 17-1, you can scale the outer two tiers independently. The middle tier works like an interface between the outer tiers. Such network designs are known as *core-edge designs*.

Figure 17-2 depicts a core-edge design. The two 16-port switches in the middle constitute the *core* of the network, while eight 8-port switches constitute the *edges* of the network. Each edge switch is connected to each core switch and has dual paths to all the other switches.

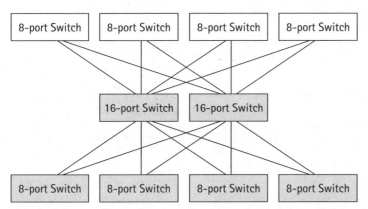

Figure 17-2: Core-edge topology example, with two core switches and eight edge switches

When you compare the two-tier topology in Figure 17-1 to the core-edge topology in Figure 17-2, you can see that core-edge designs are advantageous in several respects:

✓ In a core-edge design, there are at least two paths between edge switches. No single point-of-failure exists in the network itself.

✓ In a two-tier design, most of the edge switch ports are used for ISLs; however, in a core-edge design, two ISLs are adequate for basic connectivity. In the preceding examples, there are 32 (8×4) open edge ports in the two-tier design, and 48 (8×6) open edge ports in the core-edge design.

✓ The core-edge design can be scaled up to twice its size by adding eight more edge switches without requiring any changes to the core switches. Scaling to more devices can be achieved by upgrading the core switches or by adding two more core switches. These changes do not require any changes in the existing edge switches.

✓ System updates and additions can be performed without disrupting the ongoing traffic in a core-edge network. The traffic can be routed through any one of the two (or more) existing paths.

In core-edge networks, there are always two hops between two edge devices, compared to a single hop in a full-mesh topology. Two hops will add some latency to the communication.

Redundancy in a core-edge design is provided by multiple paths. However, keep in mind that those redundant paths are still part of a single fabric. If a problem occurs with the fabric (software bug or administrator error), the entire fabric is useless. To guard against such high-risk problems, a second, independent, redundant fabric, identical to the first, can be installed. So, even if the first fabric becomes unusable, the second fabric can take over the traffic. A second identical fabric doubles the cost of the network.

> Some Fibre Channel (FC) switch vendors provide a feature called *Virtual SANs (VSANs)*. VSANs are one or more logical SAN fabrics contained on the same, single physical fabric. Each VSAN has its own instances of fabric services, and provides isolation from fabric-wide faults and reconfigurations occurring in other VSANs.

The core-edge design is very flexible and can be modified according to cost and performance requirements. For example, as shown in Figure 17-3, the number of ISLs can be doubled if higher performance is required. Alternatively, additional ISLs can be added on the paths that are expected to be overloaded. The FC fabric routing algorithm, fabric shortest path first (FSPS), distributes the load among the available ISLs.

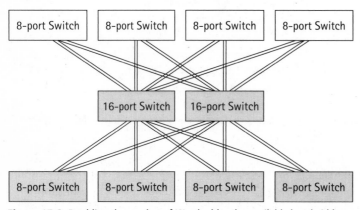

Figure 17-3: Doubling the number of ISLs doubles the available bandwidth

Although the basic core-edge design assumes that the hosts and storage devices are attached to the edges of the network, these devices can be located anywhere in the network if that will optimize the data traffic. For example, if a few storage devices are being used by many hosts, attaching the storage devices to the available core switch ports might be advantageous.

Figure 17-4 redraws Figure 17-2 such that the core switches are at the top. Otherwise, the networks in the two figures are identical.

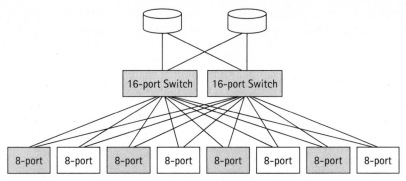

Figure 17-4: Attaching storage devices to the network core

In the figure, two storage devices are attached to two core switches. Note that the servers on the edge can access the storage devices with only a single hop. Alternatively, if a few high-performance servers are accessing many storage devices, the servers can be placed at the core switches and the storage devices on the edge switches. Still, a single hop occurs between servers and the storage devices.

Connecting switches using ISLs is easy. However, this does not mean you should connect all switches together just because you can. Connecting everything together creates a single-point-of-failure — the fabric itself.

Performance Requirements

The following terms are used to describe certain performance requirements in a storage network:

- ✓ **Fan-In** — Ratio of storage ports to host ports; an indication of storage load at a single host port.

- ✓ **Fan-Out** — Ratio of host ports to storage ports; an indication of host traffic load at a single storage port.

- ✓ **Open Edge Device Ports** — The total number of ports on the edge switches that are not consumed by ISLs and are available for end-device usage.

✓ **Core-to-Edge ISL Count** — Indicates the number of ISLs connecting any core switch to any edge switch. Higher ISL counts are required to achieve high-performance and load-balancing.

✓ **ISL Over-Subscription Ratio** — Over-subscription ratio is defined for a core-edge topology as the total number of open edge ports divided by the total number of ISLs. In other words, it indicates the number of edge connections per ISL, and is a function of the edge switch size, core switch size, and the core-to-edge ISL count. High over-subscription ratios point to a potentially overloaded design. The optimum ratio depends on the utilization of the edge ports. If edge-devices have high-performance requirements, this ratio could be one-to-one.

✓ **Maximum Number of ISLs per Switch** — Most fabric implementations have a limit of eight ISLs per switch.

✓ **Maximum Hops Between Devices** — Most fabrics limit the number of hops between any two devices to seven.

The optimum numbers for fan-in and fan-out depend on the characteristics of the host IO demand, the storage network, and the storage device performance. A rule of thumb is to keep fan-out one-to-one for a host that requires high-performance from a storage device. A higher ratio (for example, six-to-one) can be assumed for hosts that use the storage devices lightly.

While fan-in and fan-out indicate the ratio of edge device ports, ISL over-subscription is an indicator of the load at the core of the network. (See the sidebar for a comparison of the over-subscription ratios for two core-edge topologies.)

The placement of devices on the network relative to each other is another determinant in network performance. The optimal solution is putting every storage device on the same switch together with the hosts that will be using it. This localizes the data traffic to individual switches, without using any ISLs. However, this is not always possible because there may be many more hosts or storage devices than a switch can accommodate. Generally, the placement of devices should seek to minimize the number of network hops required between communicating devices.

ISL Over-Subscription Ratios

Compare the over-subscription ratios of the topologies in Figures 17-2 and 17-3.

In the core-edge topology shown in Figure 17-2, there are six open edge ports for every two ISLs. In total, there are 48 open edge ports and 16 ISLs, which results in the following ratio:

```
Over-subscription ratio = 48:16 = 3:1
```

In Figure 17-3, where the number of ISLs is doubled, there are 32 open edge ports and 32 ISLs in total. This results in the following ratio:

```
Over-subscription ratio = 32:32 = 1:1
```

Clearly, the second network will be able to serve hosts and storage devices with very high performance requirements.

The importance of traffic localization in storage networks cannot be overemphasized. A fabric enables you to attach a device anywhere on the network and still provides connectivity. However, this does not mean you should be indifferent to data sources and destinations. As much as possible, traffic should be localized to as few switches as possible (ideally, source and destination pairs should be on a single switch).

Some software tools help you plan and design storage networks. For example, Netreon's SANexec Designer is a commercial tool that can be used to plan, discover, and lay out SANs. The University of Minnesota FC Group has put out a research tool (SANTK, SAN Design Toolkit) that has a graphical interface for SAN topology designs (Strand, 2001). In addition, SANTK has a plug-in that can design a core-edge network automatically, based on connectivity and performance requirement inputs (Strand, 2002).

Improving the Network with Faster Links

When some storage network links experience continuous traffic overloading, two solutions can be used. You can either implement faster link speeds (if available), or you can increase the number of parallel links on that path.

The switches generally support the fastest available link speed, while the storage devices lag behind a couple of generations because of legacy components. This discrepancy can be used to optimize paths in a network. While the edge links are slower, you can utilize faster links at the network's core. In switched network terms, such networks are referred to as *fat-tree*, because they have faster and faster (fatter) links as you get closer to the network root.

Figure 17-5 shows a practical example of using faster links at the core. Because most FC switches support 2 Gb/s links, the ISLs between core switches are set at that speed, while edge connections are set at 1 Gb/s. The performance advantage of such a configuration will diminish as more and more edge devices start supporting the faster links. As 4 Gb/s and 10 Gb/s FC links become available, they can be utilized as the ISL connections.

Similar to FC, Ethernet networks have several bandwidth generations that enable core-to-edge bandwidth optimizations. For example, while the edges of the network can utilize 100 Mb/s, the next two levels of switches can utilize 1 Gb/s and 10 Gb/s Ethernet connections.

As previously mentioned, the other bandwidth solution is the addition of redundant links. However, adding more links in and of itself does not solve traffic congestion problems. The traffic must be distributed over the available links uniformly to achieve maximum performance. You can perform load balancing by statically assigning certain flows to certain ports using zoning (zoning is discussed in the next section) or proprietary switch management software. However, this static assignment requires the examination, modeling, and management of performance requirements, which is not always possible.

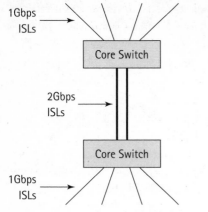

Figure 17-5: Using faster (2 Gb/s) links as ISLs

An easier solution for load balancing between multiple ISLs is provided by *link aggregation* (also called *ISL trunking*). ISL trunking combines multiple links and makes them appear as if they were a single, high bandwidth link. Trunking is available for Ethernet, IP, and FC switches.

Figure 17-6 illustrates the distinction between multiple, individual links and trunked links.

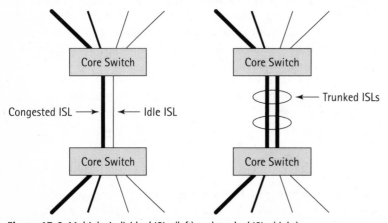

Figure 17-6: Multiple, individual ISLs (left) and trunked ISLs (right)

On the left side of the figure, you see four flows passing through two ISLs. The widths of the lines represent the amount of traffic on the link. The first ISL carries most of the traffic, while the second ISL is lightly loaded or is idle. This restricts the overall bandwidth close to a single link bandwidth. The right side of the figure shows the same situation but assumes that the two ISLs are trunked together. The load of the four flows is equally distributed among the ISLs, and the overall traffic bandwidth is almost doubled compared to individual links.

One obstacle for link trunking is preserving the frame order. Most storage devices do not have the capability to reorder frames that arrive out of order. This is not normally a problem because the FC switches ensure that the frames are delivered in order over a link. FC routing protocol

(FSPF) guarantees a single path between a source and destination pair. However, when link trunking is used, frames belonging to a single data flow might be distributed over two or more links. It is then the job of the switches on the two sides of the trunked links to guarantee that the frames leave the second switch in the order they arrive at the first switch.

Partitioning the Network with Zoning

An FC or IP fabric enables all the nodes in the network (switching elements, computing elements, storage elements, and so on) to see each other and communicate freely. As useful as this may sound, it creates a management nightmare. The entire fabric may constitute a single point of failure. Any event occurring at some remote corner of the network could affect the availability, performance, and security of the entire fabric. To solve this management problem, IP networks use Virtual LANs (VLANs) (Webb, 2001), and FC fabrics use *zoning* (Brocade, 2002).

VLANs and zoning create logical network partitions such that the elements in a VLAN or a zone can detect and communicate with the elements inside their own groups while unaware of the elements outside their groups. FC zones can be extended into IP networks using VLANs in the context of Internet Small Computer System Interface (iSCSI) and Internet Fibre Channel Protocol (iFCP). The performance and availability considerations for VLANs and zones have many parallels; the rest of this section focuses on FC zones only.

Figure 17-7 illustrates a simple FC fabric grouped into two zones. In this example, switch ports belong to one of the two zones, and devices attached to these ports can only communicate with the devices in the same zone. Overlapping zones, where some devices belong to two or more zones, are also possible. When zoning is enabled in a fabric, devices that do not belong to a zone are invisible and cannot be used.

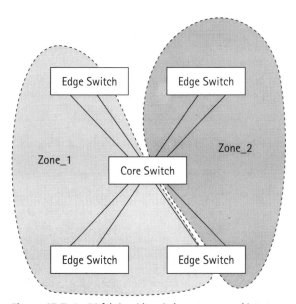

Figure 17-7: An FC fabric with switch ports grouped into two zones

Zoning can be applied to the switch ports or device names using FC World-Wide Names (WWNs). Two types of zones exist:

✓ **Hard Zones** — Hard zones are defined using the switch port numbers. The physical location of each port is specified in the zone configuration and the switches force this type of zoning in hardware. That is, the switch firmware allows frame exchanges only between ports belonging to the same zone. When a zone configuration is changed on one of the switches, the information is pushed out to the other neighboring switches, eventually reaching all the switches in the fabric.

✓ **Soft Zones** — Soft zones are defined using the port or device WWNs. When a device logs into a fabric, it queries the fabric name server for a list of available devices. If the zone is specified using WWNs, the name server returns a list of the devices only in that WWN's zone. Because the device is aware of only the devices in its zone, it does not have fabric addresses of the devices with which it is not supposed to communicate. However, this restriction is only advisory (Brocade, 2002), and a non-cooperating device may construct fabric addresses and try to communicate with those addresses. Therefore, soft zones are effective only if all the devices are voluntarily cooperating. Some implementations of soft zoning enforce zones in switches by checking addresses of frames in software. Such implementations add latency and overhead in the switches. In addition, software comparison of zone information is not as secure as hardware port zoning, as it is open to network spoofing and denial-of-service attacks.

Enforcing hard zones in hardware is a nice way of enforcing security between devices. On the other hand, because the ports are defined with their absolute position, any changes in the cable connections will require updating and distributing the zoning information.

Soft zones use WWNs and are independent of the physical port locations. Therefore, they allow the movement of devices between switch ports and different switches without any zoning modifications.

When a new device is inserted into the fabric or an existing device is removed from it, the fabric goes through a self-adjustment phase to accommodate the change. The fabric server generates State Change Notifications (SCNs) and sends them to all the connected devices to make them aware of the change. In a fabric with several (maybe hundreds of) devices, these SCN broadcasts (sometimes called *broadcast storms*) can be very disruptive to normal storage traffic.

In practice, SCN broadcasts are sometimes observed to cause the loss of connection between servers and storage devices due to connection time-outs. You should confine the scope of these SCNs.

Zoning is an effective way of restricting the effect of SCNs. When switches that support SCN isolation are used, SCNs are broadcast only in the affected zones. Consequently, devices in other zones do not receive any SCN broadcasts. This zoning advantage is surprisingly effective in improving the performance of large fabric installations.

Besides fabric zoning, some switched Fibre Channel Arbitrated Loop (FC-AL) implementations enable zoning in the arbitrated loops, as well. For example, Brocade QuickLoop zoning and Vixel Inspeed loop zoning enable the partition of the FC loops into logical loops that comprise zones. Similar to SCNs, loops generate Loop Initialization Primitives (LIPs) as a reaction to loop topology changes. And, similar to fabric zones, FC-AL zones allow the confinement of these LIPs to the affected zones.

Although zoning improves fabric manageability, having too many zones causes other management problems. When a configuration change occurs, you must think about the effects on all of the zones and update zone information on all switches. As with most things in storage networks, this is a trade-off.

Hard and soft zoning is enforced by networking equipment. You can implement a similar grouping function in the end-systems (hosts or storage devices) by voluntarily accepting or refusing connections to specific end-devices. This type of logical partitioning is termed *LUN masking*, because it controls access to particular storage volumes (LUNs). LUN masking can be implemented in host bus adapter device drivers by hiding certain LUNs from the host operating system and giving access to other LUNs. Storage subsystem controllers can perform a similar function by exposing/hiding some volumes to/from certain servers.

Design of Back-End Storage Networks

The current prominent storage subsystem architecture employs two array controllers connected to a couple of disk shelves using FC arbitrated-loop links. The arbitrated loop traverses the back-end disks and the shelves. When controllers with high-end processors and IO buses are used, the back-end disk connection can easily become the IO system bottleneck.

The disk shelves contain a backplane into which all the disks are inserted. The disks are part of an FC-AL connection routed in the backplane. A defective or missing disk can break the loop and render the entire shelf useless. To prevent this, the backplane contains *Port Bypass Circuit (PBC)* logic that routes the loop traffic around the defective ports. There is no controller logic in the shelves to present the disks as a RAID array, and individual disks are visible to the storage controller. Such disk shelves are called *Just a Bunch of Disks (JBODs)*.

Figure 17-8 depicts a typical JBOD with an FC-AL backplane. Although it is not shown in the figure for the sake of simplicity, most JBODs employ dual loops for high-availability.

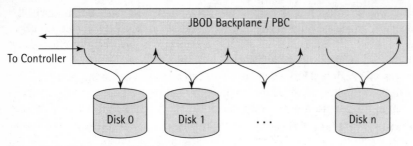

Figure 17-8: JBOD with an FC-AL backplane

Some availability and performance problems exist with a back-end JBOD such as the one shown in Figure 17-8. PBC can detect inoperable or missing disks and route around them. However, PBC is ineffective against misbehaving disks. If a disk starts sending frames on the loop without any regard to the loop protocol, the entire loop (together with the disks) might become unreachable. Even if there are dual loops, a single malfunctioning disk might take down both loops. The dual loops' failure modes are not independent.

On the performance side, the JBOD suffers from the usual performance drawbacks of arbitrated loops. The loop bandwidth is shared among all the nodes on the loop, and only one controller can talk to only one disk at a given time. In addition, the latency of the loop is a direct function of the number of elements on the loop. As the number of the disks in the JBOD or the number of JBODs in the loop increases, the latency increases considerably.

In spite of FC-AL's drawbacks, replacing them with FC fabrics at the back-end is not practical. Disk drives and JBOD boxes are not designed with enough processing power to support complex FC fabric services. A new breed of FC switches offers a solution for this problem. These embedded FC switches, pioneered by Vixel InSpeed, provide a switched loop environment, as illustrated in Figure 17-9.

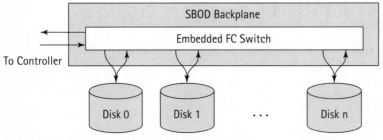

Figure 17-9: SBOD with an embedded switching backplane

These embedded switches provide FC-AL connections to individual disk drives and to the controllers. Neither the disks nor the controller firmware require any modifications. The switch makes sure that each link works like a loop with a single target device. The frames are actually passed through a crossbar fabric inside the switch. Such JBODs are called *Switched Bunch of Disks (SBOD)*.

Such an embedded switch topology has several advantages. Because the communication is performed in a switched environment, the latency is significantly reduced compared to that of the arbitrated loop. If a device wants to arbitrate for loop access, the embedded switch can immediately grant the arbitration to that device because it is the only device on the loop. In addition, in contrast to the loops, two controllers can have conversations with two separate disk drives at the same time.

In terms of availability, a switched backplane provides better fault isolation. A defective disk drive will not be able to take the entire SBOD down. The intelligence in the switch can detect a node with faulty behavior if it is not inline with the protocol, and stop transmitting frames in and out of that node. The switch's diagnostic tools (for example, fault statistics) can be used to track down misbehaving disk drives.

In current, prominent storage subsystems, the disk shelves (JBODS) are connected to the controllers using FC-AL. This is in addition to the FC-AL links inside the shelves. Such a storage subsystem is depicted in Figure 17-10.

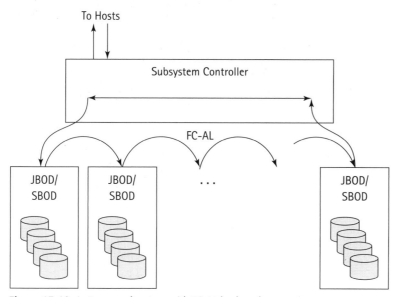

Figure 17-10: A storage subsystem with FC-AL back-end connections

This architecture experiences performance and availability problems similar to those of the FC-AL connections inside JBODs. It can be improved by using embedded switches between the controllers and the JBODs/SBODs, in addition to the switches in SBODs. Figure 17-11 illustrates a storage subsystem with a switched back-end connection to the disk shelves. With this architecture, the controllers can communicate with multiple disk shelves and multiple disks at the same time. Detecting and separating faulty disk shelves is facilitated.

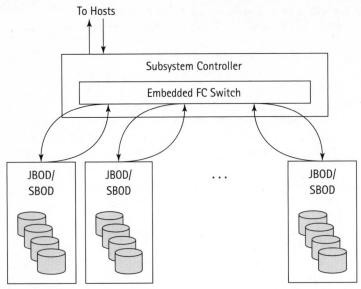

Figure 17-11: A storage subsystem with switched back-end connections

A switched back-end network can be used to carry cache mirror data between two controllers. This eliminates the need for a separate connection for cache mirroring and synchronization.

Summary

This chapter explained storage network design issues and covered the following topics:

Storage Network Topologies

✓ Utilizing Inter-Switch Links (ISLs) and network switches, you can construct an infinite number of network topologies. Some of these topologies are generally accepted, tested, and found to provide better performance and availability features than others.

✓ Full-mesh designs are appropriate for small networks. Core-edge designs have many scalability and availability characteristics that make them suitable for large-scale storage network installations.

✓ A core-edge topology's capacity can be studied in terms of the number and size of core and edge switches and the number of ISLs. The network paths passing through an ISL determine the over-subscription ratio of the design.

✓ Data traffic should be localized by keeping data sources and targets close to each other as much as possible.

Improving the Network with Faster Links

✓ Both FC and Ethernet/IP networks can be optimized by using faster link technologies at the network's core.

✓ Bandwidth at the core can be upgraded by adding more ISLs. ISL trunking balances the load between multiple links and makes them behave like a single, faster link.

✓ The switch hardware guarantees in-order delivery of frames inside a flow that is distributed among the links of a trunked ISL.

Partitioning the Network with Zoning

✓ To improve the performance, availability, and manageability of storage networks, fabrics should be partitioned into logical sets using zoning.

✓ If the fabric is not zoned, State Change Notification (SCN) broadcasts and the resulting reinitializations may cause availability and performance problems.

✓ Zoning can be augmented by proprietary grouping functions such as FC-AL zones and host/subsystem LUN masking.

Design of Back-End Storage Networks

✓ Today, the prominent storage subsystem back-end is a number of disk shelves (JBODs) connected using arbitrated loops. A loop that passes through hundreds of disk drives will have performance and reliability problems.

✓ Emerging embedded FC switches introduce switching to FC-ALs transparently to the disk drives and controllers. Switching backplane improves latency and bandwidth characteristics while providing failure containment.

✓ Embedded FC switches can also be utilized to connect back-end disk shelves to controllers to provide similar performance and reliability improvements.

References and Additional Resources

Brocade Communications Systems, Inc. 2002. *Brocade SAN Design Guide.* Document Number 53-0000231-05.

SAN design guidelines with an emphasis on Brocade equipment. Available at www. brocade.com.

Brocade Communications Systems, Inc. 2002. *Optimizing the Performance and Management of 2 Gbit/sec SAN Fabrics with ISL Trunking.* Brocade White Paper.

Available at www.brocade.com.

Brocade Communications Systems, Inc. 2002. *Brocade Zoning User's Guide.*

Available at www.brocade.com.

Judd, Josh, Chris Beauchamp, and Benjamin F. Kuo. January 2001. *Building SANs with Brocade Fabric Switches.* Syngress Media, Inc.

A detailed reference regarding SAN design principles, including transmission capacity and network topology decisions.

Farley, Marc. May 2001. *Building Storage Networks*, Second Edition. McGraw-Hill.

A comprehensive guide to everything related to storage networks.

Strand, Staffan. December 2001. *Storage Area Networks and SANTK.* Master of Science Thesis, University of Minnesota.

Describes the SANTK toolkit that helps in the design of SAN topologies. Available at www.borg.umn.edu/fc/papers/.

Strand, Staffan. May 2002. *Automatic Generation of Core/Edge Topology SANs Using SANTK.* University of Minnesota Fibre Channel Group.

Describes a plug-in for SANTK (SAN design toolkit). Includes algorithms for core-edge topology generation. Available at www.borg.umn.edu/fc/papers/.

Webb, Karen. May 2000. *Building Cisco Multilayer Switched Networks.* Cisco Press.

Provides details on IP network design, including Virtual LANs, and trunking.

Part VI

Case Studies

Chapter 18

Simulating Network Attached Storage Performance

In This Chapter

Simulation modeling can be used to study the performance of dynamic, complex systems. Developing simulation models requires a considerable amount of work and attention to detail. However, once you have a completed, accurate simulation model, it can be flexibly used to study the impact of several architectural alternatives, with rewarding results. This chapter presents the design of a simulation model for network attached storage (NAS) systems. This model has been used to evaluate and design NAS systems and was found to be reasonably accurate in predicting performance. The discussion in this chapter includes the following topics:

- ✓ Introduction of the main NAS concepts and components

- ✓ Simulation model development steps for networked storage, and the concept of top-down model development process

- ✓ Examples and tips on the details of the simulation module development

- ✓ Performance analysis examples that show the utility of a simulation model

Network Attached Storage IO Path

A NAS server is a specialized, optimized network file server. There is almost no difference in visualizing the IO path of a NAS server or a generic network file server. The differences are mostly in terms of cost and management, which do not show up in the IO access path.

Figure 18-1 depicts the main components involved in the access path between a NAS server and a client. Note that this figure can be generalized to large installations by parameterizing the number of clients and servers in the network. In other words, in an actual implementation, multiple clients will be accessing multiple servers.

The figure shows that a network file system consists of two main components. The part residing in the client is a file system redirector that intercepts all file IO in the client and decides where to route them. If the target file system is on a local disk, the IO is sent to a local attached block device. If the target file system is on a network-attached device (as is the case in the figure), the IO is routed to a file server through a network interface.

The NAS server is a "data mover" between the back-end storage devices and the front-end clients. It accepts network file system IO commands through a front-end network interface and performs them using the back-end block storage devices. The front-end network is almost exclusively an Ethernet-based IP network, even though other choices are theoretically possible (for example, IP over Fibre Channel, IP over InfiniBand, and so on). The back-end storage network is Fibre Channel (loop or fabric) in high-performance implementations and parallel Small Computer System Interface (SCSI) buses in medium performance servers. Low-end NAS servers use local Advanced Technology Attachment (ATA) disk drives for cost-effective storage.

Two common network file access protocols are Common Internet File System (CIFS) and Network File System (NFS). CIFS is the standard file access protocol in Microsoft Windows-based networks, while NFS is prominent in UNIX-based computer networks (Preston, 2002). Even though numerous differences exist between these two protocols, the basic access operations are similar. And, for the purposes of this chapter (that is, performance analysis), they will be treated the same. Whether the file access protocol is CIFS or NFS, the IO path in Figure 18-1 is valid. In addition, many NAS servers can serve both protocols at the same time. Most of the time, a NAS server will emulate one protocol on top of the other (Farley, 2001).

In a network file system, both clients and servers can contain data caches. Some portion of the file read requests can be satisfied from these caches. Write operations must access stable storage before the operation is considered complete. Write data can be buffered in battery-backed non-volatile RAM (NVRAM) that is used as a server cache.

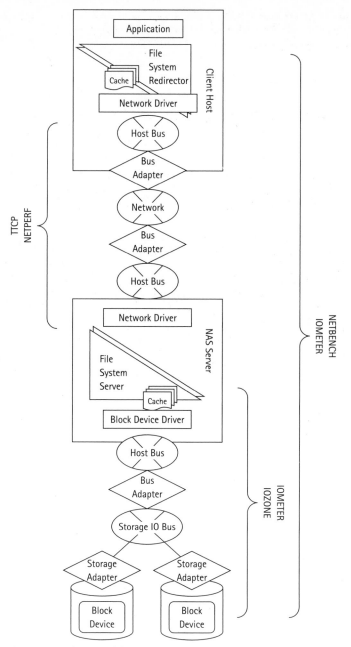

Figure 18-1: The IO path between a NAS server and its clients

Modeling Network Attached Storage

A system simulation model can be developed using the following steps:

1. Understand the system and the relationships and interactions between its components.

2. Determine the main system components and main modeling parameters.

3. Construct models for each component in an iterative fashion, increasing the modeling detail in each iteration.

4. Tune and verify modeling parameters through real-world measurement tests.

5. Use the simulation model to study the effects of interesting parameter combinations (what-if studies).

Figure 18-1 should help you understand the way NAS will be modeled. The figure shows the main components that directly affect the NAS's performance. In addition, it shows the scope of several benchmark programs. If a physical implementation is available, these benchmarks can be used to study the performance of several IO path segments, independently. The benchmark results can be used to estimate, tune, and validate several modeling parameters.

For example, network benchmarks such as TTCP and NETPERF can be used to estimate the performance of networking protocols. These benchmarks can generate Transmission Control Protocol (TCP) or User Datagram Protocol (UDP) traffic using various packet sizes. The result of such a benchmarking study would be realistic latency and bandwidth values for network modeling parameters. Similar benchmarking studies can be performed for block storage, file system, and network file system performance.

The next several sections discuss the modeling of the NAS IO path components.

Simulation Modules

There are endless ways to develop an analytic or simulation model for NAS. However, for the purposes of this chapter, an example simulation model implemented using HyPerformix Workbench will be presented. Discussing every detail of a complex NAS model in this chapter isn't possible, so the remainder of the chapter provides pointers, tips, and "best-practices" for a simulation modeling study.

The best approach to most simulation studies is a top-down design, starting with a few top-level modules and gradually introducing complexity into each one (Law, 1999). A top-level view of an example NAS model is shown in Figure 18-2. The figure contains the 15 modules that comprise the NAS simulation model, and the dependencies (dotted arcs) between the modules.

Two main modules are the `clients` and the `nas_servers` modules. The brackets in front of each indicate that they are dimensioned — in other words, an array of them is permitting the simulation of several clients and servers at the same time. The clients contain the `client_workload` module, which generates user-specified NAS workloads. Both servers and clients contain `networkSubsystem`, `cpu`, and `file_system` modules. In addition, the servers may contain an `iSCSI_server` module for future expansion of the model. NAS servers are expected to include iSCSI capabilities for simultaneous service of file-level and block-level data.

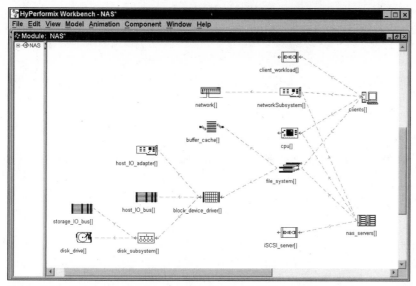

Figure 18-2: Modules and module dependencies in the NAS simulation model

NetworkSubsystem includes a network module that can simulate various kinds of networks by setting latency and bandwidth parameters. The file_system module uses block_device_driver and buffer_cache modules. The block_device_driver module simulates the access to the block storage devices through host_IO_bus, host_IO_adapter, and disk_subsystem modules. Finally, a disk subsystem contains storage_IO_bus and disk_drive simulation modules.

As is the case in the rest of the book, the main objective in this chapter and in the presented simulation model is to study performance. Therefore, only the main components and policies that affect performance directly are included in the model and in the discussion. Any detail that does not have an impact on performance is left out. This does not mean that all models should be performance models. Numerous other modeling objectives exist, such as cost, reliability, availability, and verification analysis.

Some of these modules are implemented in great detail for the study of various parameter and policy effects. Others are implemented as simple modules (mostly single queuing service centers) with latency and bandwidth parameters. The next couple of sections provide more implementation details on some of the modules.

Modeling the NAS Server

The NAS server is modeled using modules corresponding to both hardware and software components. Software components such as file systems and device drivers tax the cpu module for the duration of the software overhead. Hardware components add latency to each IO operation for the duration of the time spent in each component.

Figure 18-3 illustrates the `nas_servers` module's layout. At the highest level, a NAS server is modeled by a number of threads going around a circle, picking up client requests from the `networkSubsystem`, performing client commands in the `file_system` module, replying to the client using the `networkSubsystem`, and waiting for another client request to arrive. The number of server threads corresponds to the number of server daemons seen in real NAS servers and dictates the number of simultaneous operations.

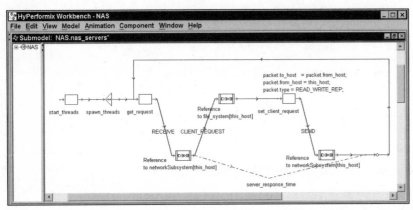

Figure 18-3: The simulation model for the `nas_servers` module

The `file_system` module determines whether the request should be satisfied from the buffer cache, or if it should be sent to the back-end storage. If the request requires device access, it is routed to the `block_device_driver` module shown in Figure 18-4. The device driver uses the `cpu` module for the duration of the software overhead and sends the request down to the `host_IO_bus`, `host_IO_adapter`, and the `disk_subsystem` modules.

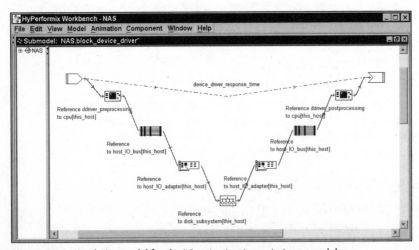

Figure 18-4: Simulation model for the `block_device_driver` module

Some of the modules in Figure 18-4 have similar complex models accessing other modules. On the other hand, some modules contain simple queuing models with service time computations based on latency and bandwidth characteristics. See the example in Figure 18-5, which illustrates the model for a `host_IO_bus`.

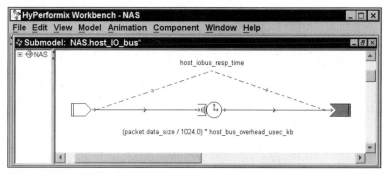

Figure 18-5: Simulation model for the `host_IO_bus` module

The service time in the `host_IO_bus` is computed using the packet data size and the bus's bandwidth (indicated here using the `host_bus_overhead_usec_kb` parameter).

Modeling Client Workloads

Clients include a `client_workload` module that is used to generate various network file access patterns. The simulation model for the workload module is shown in Figure 18-6.

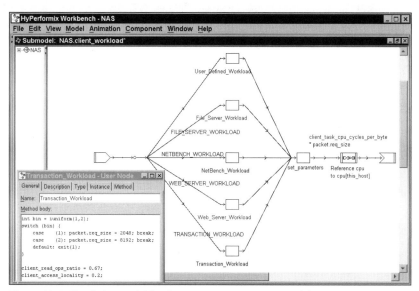

Figure 18-6: Simulation model for the `client_workload` module

As seen in the figure, the module contains four predefined workloads and one user-defined workload. File server, Web server, and transaction workloads are patterned after the generic workload definitions discussed in Chapter 9. NetBench workload models the access patterns of NetBench clients using the workload distributions shown in Chapter 12 (Figures 12-7 and 12-8).

The simulation model also allows the user to specify a specific workload in terms of the following:

✓ Average request size

✓ Ratio of write operations

✓ Spatial locality in the access pattern

✓ Client and server cache hit ratios

✓ Inter-request arrival times

Figure 18-6 also shows a possible definition of the transaction workload. In this example, the request size is either 2KB or 8KB with a 50 percent possibility. The read operations' ratio is 67 percent and the spatial locality is 0.2, which means that only a 20 percent chance exists that the successive requests are sequential.

Performance Analysis Using the Model

The NAS performance model described in the previous sections is tuned and validated against test results obtained on real computer networks in the lab. For this purpose, several benchmarks are used to measure different aspects of the NAS IO path, as shown in Figure 18-1. Each benchmark is used to tune different sets of simulation parameters. The model is capable of approximating the performance of several configurations within reasonable accuracy.

Once the model is found to be accurate, it can be used to study the effects of simulated parameters and policies on system performance. The following subsections present the results of such simulation studies. In most of the figures, the performance is presented in terms of the total bandwidth obtained by all clients, as a function of the number of clients. The number of clients generating workloads indicates the scalability of the NAS server's performance.

Unless otherwise noted, the simulation parameter values shown in Table 18-1 are used in the simulation tests.

TABLE 18-1 Default Simulation Parameter Values for the NAS Model

Parameter	Value	Parameter	Value
Number of NAS servers	1	Client queue depth	8
Disks per server	16	Server queue depth	512
Number of storage buses	2	Client cache hit ratio	0.2
Storage bus bandwidth	80MBs	Server cache hit ratio	0.2

Parameter	Value	Parameter	Value
Host bus bandwidth	266MBs	NVRAM size	0MB
Network bandwidth	400Mbs	Disk seek time	6ms
Access locality	20 percent	Disk rotational latency	4ms
Average request size	8KB	Write operation ratio	50 percent

Effects of Cache Hit Rates

Both clients and servers have file system caches that can be used to serve read operations quickly. Cache hits in these caches directly impact NAS performance. Figure 18-7 shows the total performance for various numbers of clients and three different server cache hit ratios. Higher cache hit ratios provide moderate increases in system bandwidth. Cache hits on the server eliminate back-end access, providing some speedup. However, note that achieving a cache hit rate of 60 percent requires a considerable amount of cache on the NAS server.

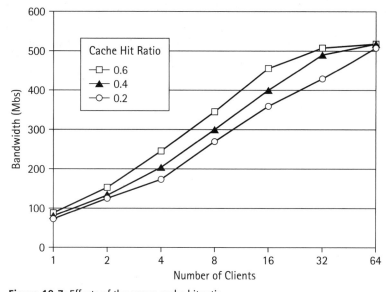

Figure 18-7: Effects of the server cache hit ratio

Figure 18-8 shows the effect of client-side cache hit ratios on system performance. Compared to the server-side caches, client caches cause considerable performance increase. There are two reasons for this. First, client cache is closer to the workload source (that is, the client). A server cache hit still requires traversing the network, while a client cache hit does not. Second, while there is a single server cache, each client has its own cache. Therefore, adding more clients adds more caches, resulting in better scalability. However, client caches have their own problems, such as data sharing, locking, and cache synchronization, which will not be discussed here.

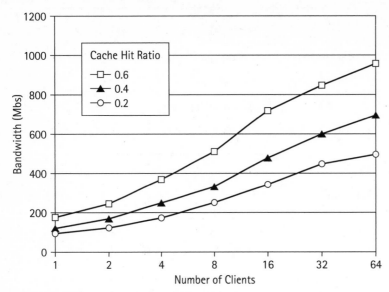

Figure 18-8: Effects of the client cache hit ratio

Server and Network Speed

Several different server CPU and network speeds are simulated to study their effects on performance. Figure 18-9 plots the system performance for server CPU speeds of 1GHz, 2GHz, and 3GHz. It shows that for the simulated setup, CPU performance corresponding to 2 and 3GHz is adequate, while a CPU performance corresponding to 1GHz limits the system performance for the number of clients beyond 16. In the model, CPUs are simulated using relative computing power. That is, a 2GHz CPU is assumed to be twice as fast as a 1GHz CPU.

Figure 18-10 shows that for the simulated setup, 1Gbs network link is adequate for the server, and faster network links do not improve performance. However, it clearly shows that a 100Mbs network will severely limit system performance.

Server NVRAM Size

Some NAS servers (and some array subsystems) include battery-backed NVRAM to buffer write operations before they are destaged (flushed) to disk drives. NVRAM's performance impact is dependent on the rate of arrivals to the buffer, rate of destaging from the buffer, and buffer size. If the arrival rate is equal to or greater than the rate of destaging, the buffer eventually fills up and the performance benefits of write buffering diminish.

Figure 18-11 plots the system performance for three NVRAM sizes — 0MB, 64MB, and 128MB. This simulation is executed for a short period (5 seconds). In this period, 64MB NVRAM fills up quickly with 8 or more clients, and it might even slow down the system. If all write operations wait for free space in NVRAM, the overhead of buffering exceeds the benefits and slowdown occurs. In that case, it is better not to buffer at all, as evidenced by the 0MB NVRAM plot in the figure. Another simulation, which bypasses the buffer if free space in NVRAM is not immediately available, shows that this slowdown can be avoided.

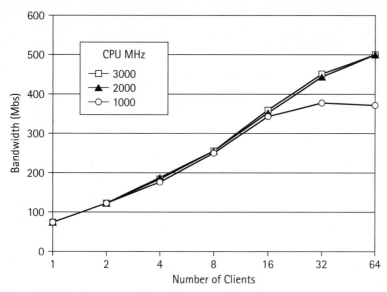

Figure 18-9: Performance scaling with server CPU speed

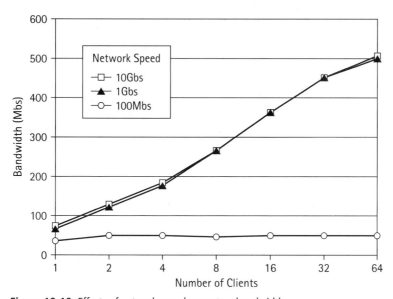

Figure 18-10: Effects of network speed on system bandwidth

Figure 18-12 shows the same set of experiments for a longer period of time (30 seconds). Because the client idle time between requests is assumed to be zero, the benefit of NVRAM is less pronounced over the long period compared to that seen in Figure 18-11. In addition, in these simulations, NVRAM is bypassed if it is full, and the slowdown effect is not experienced.

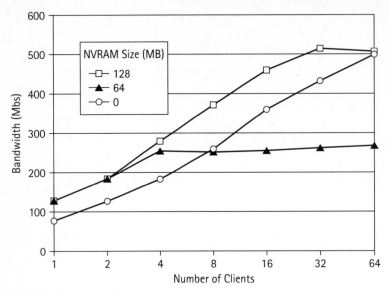

Figure 18-11: Impact of NVRAM cache size (5-second duration)

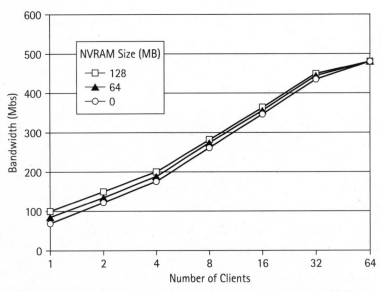

Figure 18-12: Impact of NVRAM cache size (30-second duration, bypass if full)

> **note**
>
> The real performance benefit of write buffering is experienced if enough idle gaps in the incoming stream enable the freeing up of enough space in the buffer for the successive write operations.

Summary

This chapter explored the performance of complex systems by utilizing simulation models, and included the following points:

Network Attached Storage IO Path

✓ NAS server access resembles network file server access in many respects, and they share a common IO path architecture.

✓ A NAS client contains a file system redirector layer that routes NAS requests through the network interface. The NAS server includes a file system layer that relays the requests from the network interface to the back-end storage devices.

✓ CIFS is the dominant network file protocol in Windows environments, and NFS is dominant in UNIX environments. In terms of the IO path, though, they share many commonalities.

✓ Both NAS clients and NAS servers contain file caches that influence system performance.

Modeling Network Attached Storage

✓ A simulation modeling study starts by understanding the system and identifying the main players (components) that affect the objective under study (performance, in this case).

✓ The chapter introduced a simulation model for NAS systems, which was developed using a top-down approach. The details of model modules are introduced gradually.

✓ The model contains modules corresponding to hardware and software components.

✓ Modules that contain interesting behavior and policies are implemented in detail, referencing many other submodules. Simpler modules are implemented using a single queuing center with predefined latencies.

Performance Analysis Using the Model

✓ The NAS model is tuned and verified against performance benchmark results. Several benchmark types are used to study various portions of the NAS IO path.

✓ The completed model is used to predict the effects of various configurations and policies on system performance.

✓ Example studies include the impact of cache hit rates, server and network speeds, and server NVRAM size on system performance and scalability.

References and Additional Resources

Berenbrink, P., A. Brinkmann, and C. Scheideler. February 2001. *Simlab — A Simulation Environment for Storage Area Networks*, in Proceedings of the 9th Euromicro Workshop on Parallel and Distributed Processing, Mantova, Italy, pp. 227–234.

Describes a simulation tool for SANs. Many concepts are applicable to NAS networks as well.

Farley, Marc. May 2001. *Building Storage Networks*, Second Edition. McGraw-Hill.

Includes comparisons of CIFS and NFS, and details on emulation of one protocol over another. Shows IO paths for SAN and NAS networks.

Law, Averill M. and W. David Kelton. December 1999. *Simulation Modeling and Analysis*, 3rd Edition. McGraw-Hill College Division.

Provides the fundamental theories behind simulation and statistical analysis.

Preston, W. Curtis. February 2002. *Using SANs and NAS*. O'Reilly & Associates.

Includes details on the usage of CIFS and NFS in NAS environments.

Chapter 19

Modeling Remote Storage Replication Performance

In This Chapter

This chapter presents an analytic queuing network model for storage data access over long distances as a case study of analytic modeling techniques. The performance of this kind of application depends on the latency of the link due to the distance between the sites. The model uses the most prominent characteristics of remote data access applications and simplifies the performance analysis. This study shows that the overall throughput is mainly determined by the link's latency and bandwidth, number of round trips required for each I/O operation, and number of simultaneously active I/O operations. Through laboratory and field experiments, the model is shown to be capable of approximating the performance of remote I/O operations within a very small error range. The discussion includes the following subjects:

✓ The usage models for remote data replication, and the technologies and protocols involved

✓ An analytic queuing model for remote data access that can be used to predict throughput, bandwidth, and response time

✓ Experimental test results that show the applicability of the analytic model

✓ Performance analysis studies that use the model to predict the impact of several system characteristics on the system's performance

Remote Storage Replication

Storage networks have emerged as a solution to the capacity and management problems caused by exponential growth in data repositories. This growth is produced by the proliferation of the Internet and the ever-increasing value of stored information. As the number of storage network deployments increases, so does the need for interconnecting geographically dispersed networks. Disaster recovery, data migration, and central management requirements drive remote storage connectivity activities. A plethora of standards, companies, and products are emerging to enable storage connectivity over metro/wide area network (MAN/WAN) distances.

The conversion from storage protocols (SCSI, FC) to network protocols (IP, ATM, SONET, and so on) can be performed at several points in the network. Figure 19-1 illustrates a typical remote SAN connection layout. In this case, two Fibre Channel storage area networks (FC SANs) are connected over Internet Protocol (IP) networks using FC-to-IP gateways. An alternative is to do **335** the conversion in a host adapter card—for example, an iSCSI (Internet SCSI) host bus adapter.

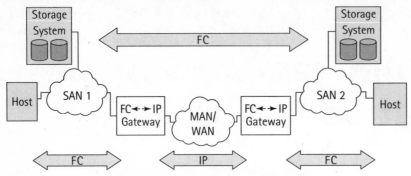

Figure 19-1: Remote data replication using FC SAN-to-IP gateways

Traditionally, the only choice for connecting FC networks has been the extension of FC signals over dark fiber (a telecommunications term to denote unused, physical fiber cables). With the latest developments in FC network equipment, FC extension can achieve distances up to 200km. However, the cost of leasing a dark fiber line or connecting to a Synchronous Optical Network (SONET) ring is still expensive. This led to the storage over IP developments. Some of these proposals were discussed previously in Chapter 8.

Both Fibre Channel over TCP/IP (FCIP) and Internet Fibre Channel Protocol (iFCP) are Internet Draft–level IETF proposals that try to leverage the existing dominance and availability of IP networks to transport FC traffic and connect islands of FC SANs together. FCIP is a tunneling protocol that connects existing FC SANs. iFCP's objectives are very similar to those of iSCSI (IPSWG, 2002) in regards to enabling a storage network natively based on IP networks.

Refer to the Simitci (2001) reference listed at the end of this chapter for a comparison of FC and iSCSI SANs for local storage networks.

Regardless of the encapsulation protocol used, a system that transports storage traffic over MAN/WAN IP networks can be depicted as shown in Figure 19-1. Storage traffic originating in local storage networks is routed to the IP network using gateway devices.

Introducing a long network connection in the middle dramatically changes the performance characteristics of storage networks. Over MAN/WAN distances, response time and throughput become a function of the latency between the two sites.

Latency in the network has several components, the most important of which is propagation delay. The speed of electromagnetic radiation in copper and light in fiber is finite. Roughly, a one-millisecond delay occurs for every 100 miles. The switches and routers in the network path also introduce processing delay. Queuing because of network congestion is another component of the latency.

Figure 19-2 shows the latency statistics for WorldCom's network backbone (WorldCom, 2002; WorldCom is one of the largest long-haul network providers). The latency data is collected from routers around the world in five-minute intervals. The figure shows the monthly average roundtrip latency that occurred in 2001. The average latency is around 50ms in North America, around 25ms in Europe, and 10ms in Japan. Trans-Atlantic roundtrip latency is between 80 and 90ms. Because these are only the core network latencies, one should expect that the routers and switches at the outer edges of the network will introduce additional delays.

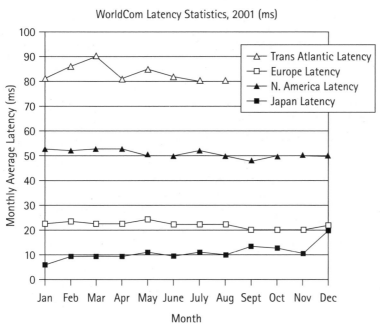

Figure 19-2: Monthly average latency statistics for WorldCom's core network

Storage traffic transported over IP networks will most probably occur over a line with a guaranteed service level in terms of latency and bandwidth. This can be achieved by dedicating a portion of a WAN link for storage traffic, using the Quality of Service (QoS) techniques described in Chapter 10. For the same 2001 time period, WorldCom reported (WorldCom, 2002) that packet delivery percentages of 99.9 percent and above were common. So, one can expect to get reliable connection and very few dropped packets.

Some of the most popular MAN/WAN link speeds are shown in Table 19-1, in increasing order of raw data speed. If TCP/IP/Ethernet protocols are used, they introduce additional space overhead and reduce the usable data bandwidth. The table's third column shows the usable payload bandwidth for these network services.

TABLE 19-1 Popular Link Speeds and Corresponding Payload Bandwidths

MAN/WAN Service	Link Bandwidth (Mb/s)	Payload Bandwidth (MB/s)
T1	1.5	0.2
T3	45	4.9
OC-3	155	17
OC-12	622	67
GbE	1,000	108
OC-48	2,488	270
OC-192	9,953	1,078
10GbE	10,000	1,078

This chapter presents an analytic queuing network model that models the performance characteristics of remote data access. A remote data replication application is used as the case study. This should cover most of the remote data access patterns. In terms of performance characteristics, remote data copy and asynchronous data mirroring are very similar.

As discussed in many places in this book, considerable research has been conducted to model and quantify the performance of storage systems and networks. However, no current research specifically focuses on queuing network models of storage performance over long distances, which is the subject of this chapter.

Queuing networks (see Chapter 3, or Jain [1991] in the reference section at the end of this chapter) have been used as an effective tool to model performance in several technical and social contexts for several decades now. Studies have been conducted that model storage systems at the end-points (Shriver, 1998; Uysal, 2001; Simitci, 1999). Blignaut (1999) provides an overview of the current practices for remote mirroring. He discusses the effects of various system characteristics, including synchronous and asynchronous copies. A series of papers written by H.P. Artis, of Performance Associates, Inc., (Artis, 1997; Artis, 1997b; Artis, 1998), discuss the performance characteristics of synchronous remote copy over Enterprise Systems Connectivity (ESCON) links. Artis drives formulas for access delays. Because these studies are focused on synchronous copy operations, queuing delays are not modeled. The model presented in this chapter accounts for queuing delays and is more suitable for modeling a broader set of remote access architectures.

The remainder of the chapter is organized as follows:

1. Modeling parameters that determine the performance of remote data access are discussed and an analytic queuing network model is developed.

2. Laboratory and real-world experimental data are compared with model outputs for verification.

3. The model is used to examine various aspects of remote storage access.

4. The chapter ends with a discussion on how the model can be adapted to different scenarios.

An Analytic Model for Remote Data Access

This section describes a simple analytic queuing network model that captures the performance characteristics of remote data access operations. Assume that the data will be transported between the two remote sites, as previously shown in Figure 19-1. For an FC write operation, the associated network traffic will look like that shown in Figure 19-3.

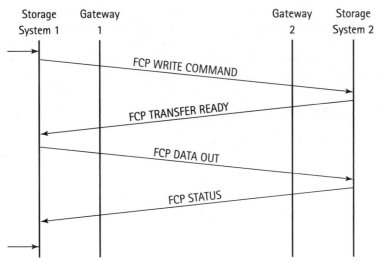

Figure 19-3: FCP command traffic across the WAN

The types and timings of individual messages may differ depending on the actual encapsulation protocol. The model parameters account for these differences. The FCP (FC SCSI Protocol) traffic in Figure 19-3 is accurate for FCIP and iFCP. For the sake of the discussion, the two sites will be referred to as the *source site* and the *target site*, even though these roles are interchangeable.

The steps portrayed in Figure 19-3 can be described as follows:

1. The transaction starts by spending some service time (S_1) in the source system.

2. FCP messages (in this case, two) are exchanged to prepare for the data transfer. Each of these messages incurs delays (D) at a number of gateways and routers (C; in this case, two). Each message is also subject to one-way latency (L) in the MAN/WAN connection.

3. The data is then transferred from the source to the target system. The service time (S_2) in the WAN connection depends on the link bandwidth (W).

4. The target site must spend some service time (S_3) on this data, after which it sends a final status message to the source system.

The total number of messages exchanged per transaction is denoted by M. There are N number of active transactions (queue depth) at a given point in time. When an I/O transaction is completed, another one is generated and inserted into the system. The average size of each I/O operation is denoted by B (buffer size).

Table 19-2 summarizes all the parameters used in the model. Besides the model input parameters previously discussed, the table also shows the model output parameters. The transaction throughput (X) is the number of I/O operations completed in a second. When multiplied by the buffer size (B), it gives the system's bandwidth in terms of bytes per second. The computed response time is represented by R. Another modeling parameter is the "think time" (Z), which is the sum of all nonservice time latencies. It will be discussed later in the next section.

TABLE 19-2 Parameters of the Remote Storage Access Model

Parameter	Description
S	Service time, seconds
D	Average switch delay, seconds
C	Number of switches/gateways
L	One-way, link latency, seconds
W	Link bandwidth, bytes per second
M	Number of one-way messages
N	Number of jobs, active transactions
B	I/O operation buffer size, bytes
X	Throughput, I/Os per second
R	Response time, seconds
Z	Think time, seconds

The latencies in the local SANs are ignored because they are generally negligible compared to the WAN latencies. If local latencies are not negligible, methods to overcome this assumption will be shown later in the chapter.

The next section presents the queuing network model that captures the behavior discussed for remote data access and generates throughput and response time approximations.

Closed Queuing Network Model

Given the assumptions in the previous section (especially the fact that there are always N number of active transactions), choosing a closed queuing network model for modeling remote data access is logical. A closed queuing network always has a finite (constant) number of jobs (transactions) in the system. The jobs circulate around the network, reentering the system after they finish each cycle. This is useful for modeling systems' throughput performance. This relation between throughput and the number of active jobs is in contrast to open queuing networks, where the system's throughput is determined by the input rate and the number of jobs in the system is variable (see Chapter 3 for a detailed discussion).

Figure 19-4 depicts the closed queuing network that will be used to model remote data access. Three service stations correspond to the source system, the WAN network, and the target system. Service stations can service one job at a time and queue the other arriving jobs. All the other latencies in the system can be combined in a delay center. In a closed queuing network model, this delay node can be modeled with the "think time" (Z). This is a station where the jobs wait for a specified time before reentering the system.

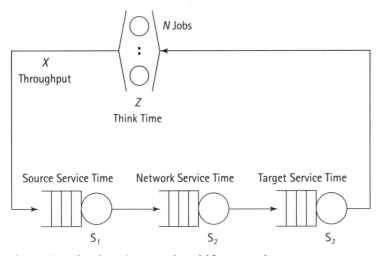

Figure 19-4: Closed queuing network model for remote data access

For a closed queuing network model, it can be shown that the order of service stations a job visits is not important for the purpose of performance computations. This observation allows reordering of the stations in the model, which is why it is possible to combine all the delay sources into the "think time."

The think time, Z, can be computed as the sum of WAN latencies and gateway delays incurred by all messages of a transaction, as shown in Equation 19-1.

Equation 19–1

```
Z = M (L + CD)
```

The computation of the service times in end systems (S_1 and S_3) are beyond the scope of this chapter. Much research has been conducted that models the performance of storage systems (see the references for Shriver [1998] and Simitci [1999] at the end of this chapter), as well as Chapters 6 through 9). In this chapter, these service times are assumed to be known through either modeling or experimentation.

The service time S_2 in the MAN/WAN link can be computed from the transaction size and the link bandwidth as shown in Equation 19-2.

Equation 19–2

```
S₂ = B ÷ W
```

At the steady state, all the service stations' throughputs are the same and equal the throughput of the system. No closed-form solutions exist for throughput in a closed queuing network. Generally, an iterative solution such as Mean Value Analysis (MVA) is used to compute the model outputs.

In Chapter 3, a sample script code (Listing 3-1) was presented for MVA computations. The MVA algorithm begins with the premise that in a system with zero active jobs, all the queue lengths are zero. Then it iterates over the number of jobs, computing the queue length in each iteration using the queue length found in the previous iteration (see Chapter 3 or Jain [1991] for further details).

In the model, the response time observed by each I/O transaction can be computed as R(N) + Z. This distinction is based on the fact that R(N) is only the response time for the service stations and from the end systems' perspective, the delay Z should be included in the response time.

Computing Bounds on System Throughput

In a closed queuing network, a limited number of active jobs put a bound on the possible queue length at each service station. This limits the maximum response time on each station. As a result, the lower bound for the expected throughput of N jobs can be computed as in Equation 19-3.

Equation 19–3

```
X(N) ≥ N / (Z + N ΣᵢSᵢ)
```

Chapter 3 showed that in a closed queuing network with N jobs, the throughput is bound by N / Z. In addition, the throughput is also bound by the throughput of the slowest performing service station. In summary, an upper bound for the system throughput can be computed as in Equation 19-4.

Equation 19–4

```
X(N) ≤ min(N/Z, minᵢ 1/Sᵢ)
```

One obvious result of the upper bound given in Equation 19-4 is that the number of active jobs (N, or queue depth) must be increased to overcome the throughput limitations due to the system's latencies (Z).

Experimental Verification of the Model

This section verifies the queuing network model for remote data access through experiments. It describes the experimental setup used in the tests and presents experimental results obtained in the laboratory environment. Later, real-world performance data collected in a MAN environment is presented. By comparing the model outputs with the experimental performance data, the model is shown to approximate the performance of these environments to a close degree.

Experimental Laboratory Setup

A MAN/WAN simulator is used to emulate a long distance network link. The simulator is a modified network switch with Gigabit Ethernet ports and can be configured to insert latencies into the communication between the ports. By using varying magnitudes of latencies, you can simulate several network distances. The accuracy of the WAN simulator is verified by using network ping commands and by checking the resulting delays. The observed latencies are very close to the intended numbers. The WAN simulator also allows throttling of the network speed at specified values. Therefore, you can also simulate several link bandwidths.

The setup shown in Figure 19-5 is used to simulate a remote data replication system over WAN links. The source and target storage systems are RAID arrays, with 16 disk drives, configured as RAID 10 (striped, mirrored) volumes. An experimental software application is used on the subsystems to replicate (copy) a local volume to another volume in the second subsystem. Originally, this replication is performed over FC links. By using FC-to-IP gateways at both ends, the replication can be performed over an IP/Ethernet network. In the experiments, 2GB volumes are copied between the two systems and the operation durations are recorded. You can compute the average throughput using these timings.

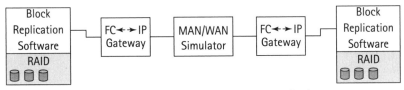

Figure 19-5: Experimental data replication setup using a WAN simulator

Experimental Results with the WAN Simulator

The experimental data replication software on the subsystems generates eight active copy transactions (N = 8), and then keeps a queue depth of eight by generating new transactions to replace the completed ones. Each copy transaction transmits 128KB of data ($B = 128KB$). Several measurements on the RAID arrays showed that the service times for 128KB read/write operations can be approximated as 3.8ms ($S_1 = S_3 = 3.8$ms).

Figure 19-6 shows the remote copy throughput values for various network round-trip latencies at GbE speed. The experiments are repeated several times to make sure the results are accurate. A comparison of the experimental throughput values with the computed MVA values shows that the difference is within 2 percent. The figure also shows the lower and upper bounds computed using Equations 19-3 and 19-4. The boundary lines align nicely with the experimental data.

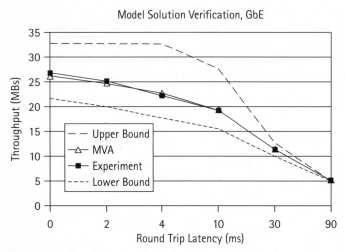

Figure 19-6: Experimental and model solution throughputs for remote copy over a GbE link

Similar experiments are repeated using T3 (45 Mbps) speeds. The throughput results in Figure 19-7 show that the MVA solution is within 6 percent of the experimental throughput, and the boundary solutions give a tight encapsulation of the experimental results.

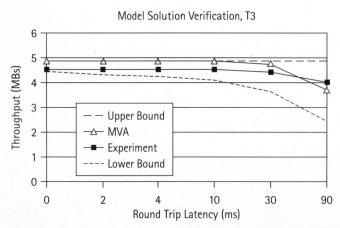

Figure 19-7: Experimental and model solution throughputs for remote copy over a T3 link

The following section presents similar comparisons for a real-world application of this remote data replication system.

Experiments Across Geographically Distant Sites

This section compares the remote copy throughput obtained between two geographically distant sites with the analytic model's throughput approximation. The two sites are approximately 50 miles apart, so 0.5ms is used for one-way propagation delay in the model ($L = 0.5$ms). In addition, the service times at the storage subsystems are computed as 3.3ms, faster than the 3.8ms seen in the previous section, probably caused by a faster RAID configuration. The link between the two sites is GbE and can be portioned at any speed desired below that. The rest of the setup uses the same experimental systems and FC-to-IP gateways as the laboratory experiments in the previous section.

Table 19-3 shows the throughput in terms of megabytes per second at three different link speeds. Experimental throughput numbers are the average of six operations that copied 4GB and 10GB volumes.

TABLE 19-3 Experimental and Model Throughput Performance for Three Link Speeds

Link Bandwidth (Mb/s)	Payload Bandwidth (MB/s)	Actual Copy Throughput (MB/s)	Analytical Lower Bound (MB/s)	MVA Model Solution (MB/s)	Analytical Upper Bound (MB/s)
150	17	16.0	13.0	16.3	17.0
300	34	25.4	21.1	24.3	34.0
1000	108	28.1	22.5	27.8	37.8

Similar to the experimental results previously shown, the results in Table 19-3 demonstrate the proximity of the calculated MVA solution to the real values. You can conclude that the described closed queuing network and its iterative solution accurately represent the performance of remote data access operations.

System Analysis for Remote Access

This section uses the remote data access model to anticipate the effects of several parameter changes on overall remote data access performance.

Link Speed Variations

One obvious way to increase the throughput of remote data access is to increase the link bandwidth. However, as Figure 19-8 shows, after a certain link speed the improvements on the throughput start to diminish because of the bottlenecks introduced by the other service times and latencies in the system. Ways to quantify these bottlenecks (upper bounds) were previously discussed.

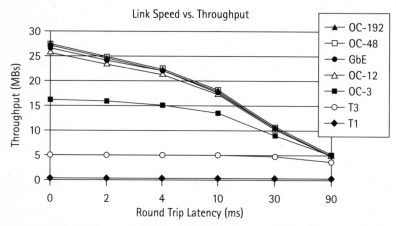

Figure 19-8: Remote copy throughput estimates for various link speeds (queue depth eight)

Queue Depth and Buffer Size Variations

Another alternative for improving the throughput is to keep more data in the long pipeline at all times. This can be achieved by either increasing the number of active operations (N, queue depth) or by increasing the size of the data carried in each operation (B, buffer size).

Figure 19-9 shows the effects of increasing the queue depth. Increasing this number might increase the throughput even at low network latencies. However, the figure demonstrates that to utilize the full bandwidth of a network with long latencies, very deep queue lengths are necessary.

Figure 19-10 shows the effects of the buffer size on throughput. For this figure, the service time at the end subsystems is assumed to increase linearly with the data size. Like Figure 19-9, this figure also demonstrates that the longer latencies require deeper buffer sizes to keep the throughput at a level when latencies increase.

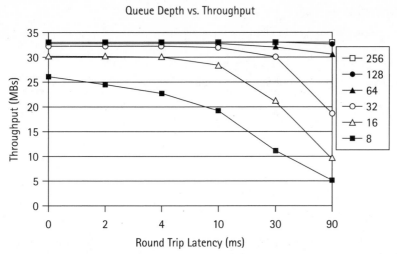

Figure 19-9: Effects of the number of active transactions on the throughput (buffer size 128KB)

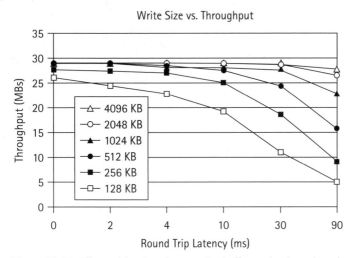

Figure 19-10: Effects of the size of transaction buffer on the throughput (queue depth eight)

Protocol Variations

The more messages sent per transaction, the slower the transaction will be. Figure 19-11 plots the throughput for three different numbers of messages. The implementation used in the experiments discussed earlier in the chapter requires four messages for each copy operation. The figure shows that you can double the throughput for longer latencies if a protocol can be devised to reduce the number of messages to two. Similarly, a protocol that might require eight messages will cut the throughput to half at longer latencies. In these calculations, as in the model, it is assumed that only one of these messages contains copy data; the others are short protocol messages.

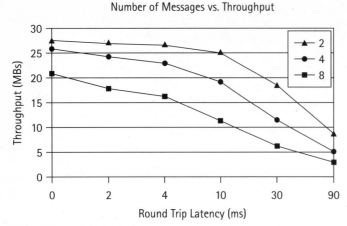

Figure 19-11: Effects of the number of messages per transaction on the throughput (queue depth eight, buffer size 128 KB)

Modeling Variations

The modeling framework described in this chapter can be varied to adapt to several system implementations. Queuing networks are powerful enough to include many different combinations.

For example, you can add two more service stations to the closed queuing network shown in Figure 19-4 to account for the link bandwidth in the local storage network — the connection between the subsystems and the gateways. The original model assumed that this connection does not limit performance. In addition, the latencies in the local networks are not included in the model and are observed as part of the delays at the gateway. If desired, this can be added explicitly to the think time model. Additions of new service stations and delay nodes will not change the nature of the MVA iterations, except the additions for response time and queue length computations to account for the additional nodes.

You can also account for the protocol used to exchange data between the two remote systems by varying the number of messages and the service times. It has been assumed that each transaction passes through each service station once. If a different storage protocol requires each transaction to pass through certain service stations multiple times, the queuing networks can easily account for this. In this case, the service demand at each station must be computed accordingly.

Although high-level (that is, FCP) storage protocol messages are used in the model, the underlying WAN connection will probably carry these messages in some other connection protocol (such as TCP). If the underlying protocol requires more crossings of the WAN connection than the modeled protocol, the model may be missing some latency components. For example, TCP must send acknowledgement messages for every packet. Thanks to some piggybacking optimizations, this creates a problem for the model only if the TCP window size is less than the data size in each I/O transaction. In this case, the source will need to wait for an acknowledgement before it can complete a data transfer. The model assumes that the TCP window size is large enough. If it is not, the model must be formulated to account for the extra messages required.

Another important assumption was reliable network connections. Data links used for storage data transfer will probably have very high delivery ratios and guaranteed latencies. Again, if this is not the case, the model parameters should be adapted.

A congested network can be modeled by increasing the latency, reducing the bandwidth, or by adding some retransmit ratio to the number of messages required.

Because the experiments were based on remote copy operations, the focus was on throughput computations. In addition to throughput, the MVA algorithm is equally capable of computing the response time of individual I/O operations, as shown previously in Chapter 3. Such response time computations may be useful for modeling real-time data mirroring applications, where the response time and the amount of asynchronous data must be balanced.

In addition, the experiments and the model focused on the performance of a single remote access flow. An inherent assumption was that single ports on the storage systems are used, which are connected to single ports on the gateway switches. An obvious extension is the modeling of multiple remote flows at the same time. Utilizing multiple ports on the end systems and the gateways will increase the utilization of the existing system capacity.

Summary

This chapter presented an analytic queuing network model for storage data access over long distances, and covered the following topics:

Remote Storage Replication

✓ Disaster recovery, data migration, and central management requirements lead to the connection of several storage network islands remotely. In such setups, remote data replication is the primary remote access operation.

✓ The most important characteristic of remote data access systems is the latency due to the propagation delay in the long network link.

✓ An analytic queuing network model was used to understand the behavior of remote storage data access over MAN/WAN distances.

An Analytic Model for Remote Data Access

✓ An analytic, closed queuing network model was developed using the most prominent factors determining the performance in such systems.

✓ The model incorporates such details as the number of messages required for each I/O operation, the size of each I/O operation, the number of active I/O operations at a given time, and the service time required at each remote end system.

✓ The model was used to demonstrate a framework to quantify the performance of remote data access. Model solutions include an iterative solution for system throughput and response time, and closed-form formulas for lower and upper bounds on throughput.

Experimental Verification of the Model

✓ Through laboratory and real-world experiments, the model is validated for providing accurate performance information for various network configurations.

✓ In laboratory experiments, a WAN simulator was used, which can introduce latencies and throttle network bandwidth to simulate various WAN characteristics.

✓ Field experiments were conducted between two sites that are 50 miles apart, and data copy experiments were repeated for various network speeds.

✓ In all cases, the replication throughput was predicted within 6 percent accuracy.

System Analysis for Remote Access

✓ The model was used to study various parameter tunings and their effects on system performance.

✓ The relationship between the link speed, queue depth, buffer size, number of protocol messages, and network latency were discussed.

✓ Modifications to the model were discussed to model different scenarios.

✓ The modeling framework described in this chapter can be used to research other variations, tunings, protocols, and similar new ideas for remote storage data access applications.

References and Additional Resources

Artis, H. P. December 1997. *Understanding the Performance Characteristics of Synchronous Remote Copy*. In proceedings of CMG '97. Orlando, Florida.

Artis, H.P. December, 1997b. *The Impact of Pipelining Protocols on Synchronous Remote Copy Performance*. In Proceedings of CMG '97, Orlando, Florida.

Artis, H.P. December, 1998. *DIBs, Data Buffers, and Distance: Understanding the Performance Characteristics of ESCON Links*. In proceedings of CMG '98, Anaheim, California.

Blignaut, R. September 1999. *Remote Copy — A Critical Examination of Current Practices*. In Proceedings of CMGA '99, Gold Coast, Australia.

A survey of remote copy techniques with extensive references to commercial applications.

IP Storage Working Group. September 5, 2002. *iSCSI*. Version 16.

Internet SCSI (iSCSI) is an IETF project that targets the mapping of the SCSI protocol over TCP/IP. This Internet-Draft status document can be found at http://www.ietf.org.

Jain, Raj. April 1991. *The Art of Computer Systems Performance Analysis*. John Wiley & Sons.

The classic computer performance analysis reference. Author's notes and errata can be found at www.cis.ohio-state.edu/~jain/books/perfbook.htm.

Shriver, Elizabeth A. M., Arif Merchant, and John Wilkes. June 1998. *An Analytic Behavior Model for Disk Drives with Readahead Caches and Request Reordering*. SIGMETRICS.

Presents detailed analytic models of disk drives with caches and command reordering.

Simitci, Huseyin and Daniel A. Reed. 1999. *Adaptive Disk Striping for Parallel Input/Output*. Proceedings of the Seventh NASA Goddard Conference on Mass Storage Systems, San Diego, CA, pp. 88–102.

Includes analytic queuing models of disk striping, which are used to drive optimization algorithms for striping parameter optimizations.

Simitci, H., C. Malakapalli, and V. Gunturu. August 2001. *Evaluation of SCSI over TCP/IP and SCSI over Fibre Channel Connections*. In Proceedings of HOT INTERCONNECTS 9, A Symposium on High Performance Interconnects, Stanford University, California.

Uysal, M., G. A. Alvarez, and A. Merchant. August 2001. *A Modular, Analytical Throughput Model for Modern Disk Arrays*. In Proceedings of the Ninth International Symposium on Modeling, Analysis and Simulation of Computer and Telecommunications Systems (MASCOTS 2001). Cincinnati, Ohio, USA, pp. 183–192.

WorldCom. January 2002. *Latency Statistics*, available at http://www1.worldcom.com/global/about/network/latency.

WorldCom publishes statistics on the performance of the worldwide network on the Web site shown above.

Chapter 20

Web and E-Commerce Data Center Performance Analysis

In This Chapter

Performance analysis is a systems-level study. You must look at the entire system to assess and improve performance. System performance is limited by its slowest component. This chapter demonstrates that even the most complex systems can be studied by using a simple, methodological approach. A multi-tier data center example shows that performance data, which is readily available from most performance tools, can be interpreted using operational analysis to find and improve performance bottlenecks. The topics discussed in this chapter include the following:

✓ The architecture of a multi-tier Web and e-commerce data center

✓ Operational analysis formulas and methods review

✓ Example performance data for a data center

✓ Identifying performance bottlenecks using operational analysis methods

✓ Using bottleneck analysis in performance improvement and capacity planning

Data Center Architecture

Storage networks do not exist in a void. They are part of larger computing systems. A computing system's effective performance from a customer or service provider perspective is determined by the slowest component in the system. This chapter introduces systems-level performance analysis using a data center example.

Most large-scale Web hosting and e-commerce service operations are located in data centers that comprise several layers of servers (Buch, 2001; Menasce, 2002). Figure 20-1 shows a multi-tier data center where the service is divided and shared by multiple tiers of servers.

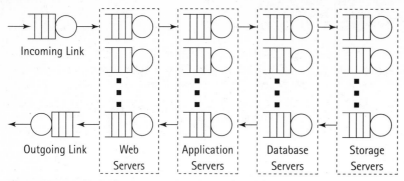

Figure 20-1: Multi-tier data center architecture and model

This particular example has four tiers:

  ✓ **Web Servers** — The incoming requests are received by front-end Web servers. Static pages or cached objects that can be serviced without further processing can be directly returned by the front-end Web servers. If the request requires further processing, it is forwarded to the application servers.

  ✓ **Application Servers** — Application servers contain the data center's business logic. Applications in this tier decide what to do with a request and take actions according to pre-programmed business logic objects. Example application objects include Active Server Pages (ASP) and Java Server Pages (JSP). These script-based objects create dynamic Web pages based on the parameters in the request. In addition, if the operations require access to persistent information, application servers access database servers.

  ✓ **Database Servers** — The servers in this tier execute database management services and reply to database queries. They access stable storage through storage servers.

  ✓ **Storage Servers** — Storage in a data center is accessed through storage subsystem controllers, network-attached storage (NAS) appliances, storage area network (SAN) devices, and other similar storage network components.

The data center is connected to the Internet through Internet Service Provider (ISP) links. Each tier consists of one or more servers. In a given data center, some of the tiers might be omitted or merged into other tiers. The simplest case is a single Web server computer that contains all the applications, databases, and storage devices.

The high-level model shown in Figure 20-1 can easily be turned into a queuing network model that can be implemented as either a closed or open network model for analytic or simulation solutions. As discussed earlier in the book (see Chapter 3), if the number of simultaneous requests in the system is (almost) constant, it can be modeled with a closed network model.

The rest of this chapter analyzes the preceding data center model using the fundamental performance analysis techniques introduced previously in the book. Even these most basic methods provide insights into the performance bottlenecks in the system and are useful in capacity planning and improvement studies.

Operational Analysis

The data center model will be analyzed using the two analytic laws that have the widest applicability among the other performance laws. You can apply these formulas to any system by simply observing the arrivals and departures to the system. In this regard, they are termed *operational analysis* (Denning, 1977), and their usefulness has been demonstrated in many performance studies over several decades (Gunther, 2000; Jain, 1991; Buch, 2001).

The first rule is Little's Law (Little, 1961), introduced in Chapter 3, and repeated in Equation 20-1 for reference.

Equation 20-1

$$N = X \times R$$

Little's Law states that the average number of requests (jobs, transactions, customers), N, in a service center is equal to the product of the center's average throughput, X, and the center's average response time, R.

The second law this chapter utilizes is the *Service Demand Law* (Equation 20-2), which states that the average service demand, D_i, of a request on service center i is equal to the division of the utilization, U_i, of the service center i by the system throughput, X. (See Chapter 3 for further details.)

Equation 20-2

$$D_i = U_i \div X$$

Both of these laws can be applied to arbitrary domains in the model, as long as the throughput, response time, and utilization are defined accordingly. Consider the example given in Figure 20-2 for the multi-tier data center model.

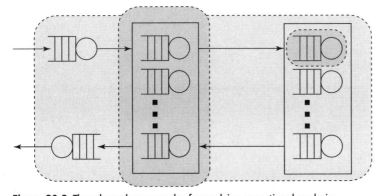

Figure 20-2: Three boundary examples for applying operational analysis

In this model, you can use Little's Law and the Service Demand Law at several layers, as shown by the three boundaries in Figure 20-2. First, they can be applied to the entire system by considering the overall throughput and response times. They can be applied to a particular tier or an individual server in a particular tier. As long as the throughput, response time, and utilization are defined according to the boundary you have defined, the laws are applicable.

> Utilizing the operational laws on real-world systems is easy because the parameters on which they depend (throughput, response time, utilization) are easily obtained by most available performance tools.

A Systems Performance Analysis Example

Several tools are available for measuring a Web server center's performance. For example, Microsoft provides the Web server stress tool called Microsoft Application Center Test (formerly Web Application Stress or WAS Tool), which emulates client browsers on several client computers and generates requests to a given Web source. Then, it collects performance data, including the throughput and response times. As shown in Chapter 12, you can collect server-specific response time and utilization data (CPU, disk, network, and so on) during these benchmark executions.

For simplicity and flexibility, this section uses the performance results obtained from a simulation model based on Figure 20-1. The simulation model includes five layers, from the network down to the storage servers. In addition, the number of servers is configurable in each tier. The model is a closed network that circulates a given number of user requests. Even though simulation results are used in this chapter, the techniques and analysis discussed should be equally applicable to real-world systems, because the techniques do not depend on the data itself.

Table 20-1 shows the performance data from a simulation test. The simulation configuration contained the following:

- ✓ A single ISP connection
- ✓ Four Web servers
- ✓ Two application servers
- ✓ Two database servers
- ✓ Two storage servers

The first column shows the number of simultaneous user requests circulating in the closed system. The second and third columns show the measured average throughput and response time values. Throughput is defined in terms of *transactions per second (tps)*. In this case, a transaction is defined as a completed Web request and could be different from a transaction in an e-commerce system, which might require multiple Web interactions. The fourth column contains the theoretical number of requests, which are computed using Little's Law. This column is the product of the throughput and the response time columns. Note that the theoretical numbers are identical or very close to the simulation numbers shown in the first column.

TABLE 20-1 Simulation Test Results for the Data Center

Number of Simultaneous Requests	System Throughput (tps)	Average Response Time (sec)	Computed Number of Requests
1	20.66	0.048	1.00
2	39.67	0.050	2.00
4	74.03	0.054	4.00
8	118.61	0.068	8.01
16	160.24	0.100	15.99
32	180.16	0.177	31.97
64	188.36	0.338	63.66

Little's Law ($N = X \times R$) can be used to perform sanity checks on measured data. Most benchmark tools keep a constant number of active requests on the system under study. Little's Law can be used to verify the consistency of the throughput and response time results obtained by the benchmark.

Next, Little's Law will be applied to a single server in the system. Table 20-2 shows the simulated queue length, throughput, and response time data for a single Web server, which was part of the system test given in Table 20-1. Because the system has four Web servers, the throughput of a single Web server (third column) is one-fourth of the system throughput. Again, the last column shows that the queue length computed using Little's Law is very close to the observed queue length.

TABLE 20-2 Simulated and Calculated Results for a Web Server

Observed Web Server Queue Length	System Throughput (tps)	Web Server Throughput (tps)	Web Server Response Time (sec)	Calculated Web Server Queue Length
0.05	20.66	5.17	0.010	0.05
0.09	39.67	9.92	0.011	0.10
0.22	74.03	18.51	0.012	0.21
0.46	118.61	29.65	0.016	0.46
0.84	160.24	40.06	0.022	0.89
1.60	180.16	45.04	0.037	1.67
3.79	188.36	47.09	0.078	3.69

Performance tools built into most operating systems enable you to collect utilization data for various system components. Although many other performance metrics (such as throughput, response time, number of visits, and so on) are difficult to obtain and interpret, utilization data is easily accessible. With utilization, you can predict the service demand of a single request on a given service center.

Table 20-3 contains utilization measurements obtained using the multi-tier data center simulation model for five different server tiers.

TABLE 20-3 Utilization Levels in the Simulation Tests

Number of Requests	Throughput (tps)	Network Utilization	Web Server Utilization	Application Server Utilization	Database Server Utilization	Storage Server Utilization
1	20.66	0.04	0.10	0.09	0.05	0.10
2	39.67	0.08	0.18	0.18	0.10	0.20
4	74.03	0.16	0.37	0.33	0.17	0.38
8	118.61	0.25	0.59	0.54	0.29	0.62
16	160.24	0.34	0.75	0.71	0.39	0.82
32	180.16	0.38	0.86	0.81	0.44	0.94
64	188.36	0.40	0.96	0.85	0.46	1.00

Using the service demand formula given in Equation 20-2 ($D_i = U_i \div X$), you can compute the demand on each server. When you divide the utilizations given in Table 20-3 by the throughput, you get the demand values shown in Table 20-4. Demand values are given in seconds, and they represent the amount of workload a request puts on a particular server.

TABLE 20-4 Computed Service Demands for Each Tier

Number of HTTP Requests	Throughput (tps)	Network Demand	Web Server Demand	Application Server Demand	Database Server Demand	Storage Server Demand
1	20.66	0.0021	0.0051	0.0043	0.0024	0.0048
2	39.67	0.0021	0.0045	0.0046	0.0025	0.0051
4	74.03	0.0021	0.0050	0.0045	0.0023	0.0051
8	118.61	0.0021	0.0050	0.0045	0.0025	0.0053
16	160.24	0.0021	0.0047	0.0045	0.0024	0.0051
32	180.16	0.0021	0.0048	0.0045	0.0024	0.0052
64	188.36	0.0021	0.0051	0.0045	0.0024	0.0053

Note that service demand is different than service time. In the preceding example, the demand on a Web server is computed as 5 ms (0.0050 sec) on average. There are four Web servers in the test configuration. A given request visits only a single Web server. Therefore, the probability that a request will visit a server is 0.25. Even though the request requires 20 ms service time on the receiving Web server, you can theoretically say that it requires 5 ms (0.25×20) service demand from all servers. This relationship is captured in Equation 20-3, which states that the demand on server i is equal to the visit count (V_i) to that server times the service time (S_i).

Equation 20–3

$$D_i = V_i \times S_i$$

In the preceding example, the visit count to a single Web server is 0.25, and the demand is 5 ms. Therefore, the service time should be 20 ms. However, for operational analysis, service time is not used directly. As the next section shows, knowing the service demand is good enough for many capacity-planning decisions.

Where Is the Bottleneck?

In the previous section, throughput, utilization, and service demand data were presented for the data center example. Although you can see that the storage servers, Web servers, and application servers have the highest utilization levels, quantifying the bottleneck on throughput just by looking at utilization values is difficult.

The Service Demand Law in Equation 20-2 ($D_i = U_i \div X$) provides a relationship between throughput, utilization, and service demand. If you assume 100 percent utilization and substitute $U_i = 1$ into the equation, you can compute the maximum possible throughput that can be supported by that server. Then, the maximum possible system throughput is the minimum of these throughput limits, as shown in Equation 20-4.

Equation 20-4

$$X_{max} = \min_i (1/D_i)$$

Table 20-5 contains the service demand and maximum throughput information for each tier. Now, it is clear from the table that the storage servers limit the throughput to 192 tps, while Web servers limit it to 200 tps. In addition, the limit of application servers (222 tps) is very close to the other two limits and will be the next bottleneck if storage and Web servers are upgraded. The table also shows the number of servers assumed in each tier.

TABLE 20-5 Throughput Limits for Each Tier

	Network	Web Server	Application Server	Database Server	Storage Server
Number of Servers	1	4	2	2	2
Demand (sec)	0.0021	0.0050	0.0045	0.0024	0.0052
Max Throughput (tps)	476.19	200.00	222.22	416.67	192.31

Removing the Performance Bottleneck

Removing all bottlenecks is impossible. One or more components in the system will always limit its performance. The best-case scenario occurs when the bottlenecks are alleviated to a level that enables at least the "desired" performance and the bottlenecks are spread across many components, such that you achieve a "balanced" system.

> **note**
>
> A system always contains a performance bottleneck. A corollary to this observation is the fact that a "balanced" system is one where almost all components are simultaneously (that is, equally) constrained.

In the multi-tier data center example given earlier in this chapter, there are two ways to improve performance. Both aim to reduce the service demand on a given tier.

First, it might be possible to add more servers to a tier to distribute the load to more service centers. This reduces the service demand on all the servers at that tier. For example, Table 20-5 shows that two storage servers have a service demand of 5.2 ms. If the number of storage servers is increased to four, the service demand decreases to 2.6 ms, effectively doubling the storage throughput limit from 192 tps to 384 tps.

Using twice as many storage servers decreases their utilization to half. You can see the difference in utilization levels by comparing Figures 20-3 and 20-4. Figure 20-3 shows the component utilizations in the original configuration with two storage servers.

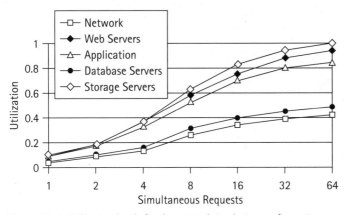

Figure 20-3: Utilization levels for the original simulation configuration

Figure 20-4 shows utilization after the number of storage servers is increased to four. You can see that the Web and application servers are now the performance bottlenecks.

Figure 20-5 shows the corresponding contributions to the overall response time as a percentage. Although there is less than 10 percent difference in utilization between Web and application servers, as shown in Figure 20-4, the majority of the response time is incurred at the Web servers. At utilization levels above 80 percent, a small increase in utilization causes major increases in response time. High utilization causes long queues at the service centers and increases the response time exponentially.

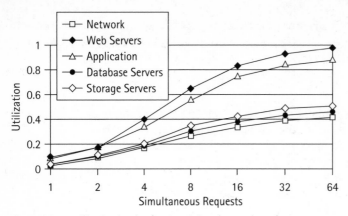

Figure 20-4: Utilization levels after increasing the number of storage servers

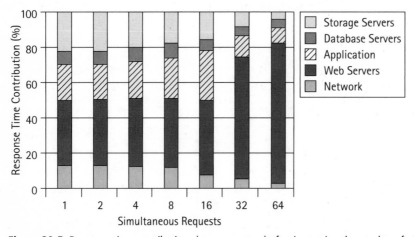

Figure 20-5: Response time contributions (as percentages) after increasing the number of storage servers

The second way of increasing the throughput limit is by decreasing the service time at a service center. This can be achieved by using faster components or optimized software or procedures on that service center. Assume you have a faster, optimized Web server software that decreases the service demand from 5 ms to 3 ms, while the number of Web servers stays at four. The Web server throughput limit is increased by 5/3.

Figure 20-4 showed that when a Web server's limit is lifted, the application servers become the next bottleneck. Assume that you can substitute three application servers instead of two. The resulting utilization levels are shown in Figure 20-6. Clearly, you can see that the storage servers are not the main bottleneck, while Web and application servers are equally performance bottlenecks.

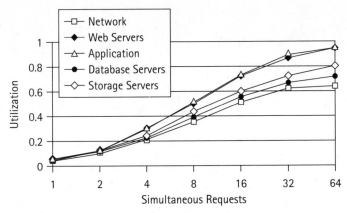

Figure 20-6: Utilization levels after all the upgrades

Theoretically, this exercise of upgrading several components can be continued indefinitely, each time removing one bottleneck and introducing another. You should end the cycle if you achieve a desired performance goal or you are in danger of exceeding the budget for adding more components.

Table 20-6 shows the final throughput limits after all the upgrades are complete, where the number of application and storage servers is increased and the service demand on the Web servers is decreased. It shows that the current throughput limit is 333 tps, a limit shared by the Web and application servers.

TABLE 20-6 Throughput Limits After Upgrades

	Network	Web Server	Application Server	Database Server	Storage Server
Number of Servers	1	4	3	2	4
Demand (sec)	0.0021	0.0030	0.0030	0.0024	0.0026
Max Throughput	476.19	333.33	333.33	416.67	384.62

Finally, Figure 20-7 illustrates the resulting simulated throughputs after each upgrade step. It shows that after upgrading the storage servers alone, the throughput does not change much because the Web and application servers are still the bottleneck. After upgrading Web and application servers, the throughput goes up to 320 tps for 64 simultaneous requests.

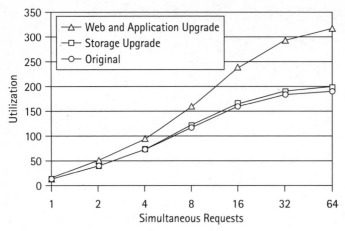

Figure 20-7: Comparison of throughputs in the original configuration and after each upgrade step

Summary

This chapter shows you how to study systems using a methodological approach and included the following points:

Data Center Architecture

✓ Storage networks and storage devices are parts of larger computing systems. A system's performance is limited by its slowest component.

✓ Large data centers used for Web serving and e-commerce consist of several tiers of servers, which can be divided into Web, application, database, and storage tiers.

✓ Each tier uses the bottom layers' services to service the higher layers. Storage devices and networks comprise the bottom layer and are abstracted in a storage servers tier for the purposes of this chapter.

Operational Analysis

✓ Operational analysis is a field of performance analysis that uses observational performance data to study a system's performance behavior and bottlenecks.

✓ Little's Law establishes a relationship between the number of active jobs in a system and the system throughput and response time.

✓ The Service Demand Law quantifies the additional load caused by each job on a given service center.

A Systems Performance Analysis Example

✓ Most benchmarks and operating system performance tools provide performance data on throughput, response time, and utilization levels.

✓ Little's Law can be used to perform a sanity check on the performance data obtained from performance tools.

✓ The Service Demand Law can be used to calculate the service demand values from measured utilization values.

Where Is the Bottleneck?

✓ A component provides maximum throughput when it is 100 percent utilized.

✓ A component's maximum throughput is equal to the inverse of the service demand on that component.

✓ The bottleneck in the system is the component(s) with the smallest throughput limit.

Removing the Performance Bottleneck

✓ A bottleneck that limits performance exists in every system. The purpose of bottleneck analysis is to reduce the bottleneck limits until desired performance is achieved.

✓ Improving the bottleneck performance is accomplished by reducing the service demand on a component.

✓ Service demand can be reduced by using more of the same component to distribute the load or by reducing the service time on each component.

References and Additional Resources

Buch, Deep K. and Vladimir M. Pentkovski. December 2001. *Experience of Characterization of Typical Multi-Tier e-Business System Using Operational Analysis*. CMG 2001 International Conference, Anaheim, California.

Shows that the predictions of operational analysis methods closely fit the performance data obtained from real, multi-tier e-business systems.

Denning, P. J. and J. P. Buzen. September 1977. *The Operational Analysis of Queueing Network Models*. Computing Surveys, Vol. 9-3, pp. 223–252.

The seminal paper that introduced operational analysis.

Gunther, Neil J.. October 2000. *The Practical Performance Analyst*. iUniverse.com.

A lively introduction to performance analysis with lots of practical insights and examples.

Jain, Raj. April 1991. *The Art of Computer Systems Performance Analysis*. John Wiley & Sons.

The classic computer performance analysis reference. Author's notes and errata can be found at `www.cis.ohio-state.edu/~jain/books/perfbook.htm`.

Little, J.D.C. 1961. *A Proof of the Queueing Formula $L = \lambda W$*. Operations Research, Vol. 9, pp. 383–387.

The first proof of Little's Law, which is named after its author.

Menasce, D. A. and V. A. F. Almeida. 2002. *Capacity Planning for Web Services: Metrics, Models, and Methods*. Prentice Hall, Upper Saddle River, NJ.

Provides performance analysis and capacity planning methods for e-business services.

Appendix

Glossary of Terms and Acronyms

A

access density A measure of performance per unit storage capacity. Generally computed as throughput (in IOPS) divided by the capacity (in Gigabytes).

access hot spot A disk, a volume, or an address range that is more heavily used compared to the other locations of the data.

actuator [disk drive] The step motor that moves all the arms together to seek to a particular track.

admission policy A policy in a system with QoS guarantees to determine whether enough resources are available to serve (admit) a request. Otherwise, the request is rejected.

AFR Annualized Failure Rate

aggregation The virtualization method of collecting various extents into a large storage pool. Or, the networking method of combining multiple links together to make a single, bigger link (trunking).

ALU Allocation Unit Size. File systems allocate disk storage to files using ALU.

analytical modeling The modeling technique that uses mathematical expressions to represent the relationships between modeled system components.

angular velocity [disk drive] Rotational speed of the spindle. It is measured in Revolutions Per Minute (RPM).

ANSI American National Standards Institute

API Application Programming Interface

arbitration The process of obtaining the connection ownership in a shared bus or loop connection, before a device can communicate on the shared medium.

arrival theorem [queuing theory] States that a job arriving at a queue in a closed queuing network with n jobs, will see a queue length in front of it as if the system had n-1 jobs.

ASIC Application Specific Integrated Circuit

ASPI Advanced SCSI Peripheral Interface. Provides a common interface for accessing SCSI devices under Windows operating systems.

ASU [SPC-1] Application Storage Unit

asynchronous I/O I/O operations that do not wait for the completion of the operation on the underlying storage devices before returning to the caller. Asynchronous I/O interfaces require special callback or check functions to denote the completion of the operation.

ATA Advanced Technology Attachment

ATAPI Advanced Technology Attachment Packet Interface. Enables Integrated Drive Electronics (IDE) devices to look like SCSI devices and accessed through ASPI.

ATM Asynchronous Transfer Mode

availability The degree to which a system stays up (running) within acceptable limits of performance and without any unrecoverable failures.

average [statistics] The sum of all the numbers in a sample divided by the number of elements (observations). Also called the mean, or the expected value.

B

backend storage The next layer of storage in a storage hierarchy behind any virtualization interface. For example, backend disks behind a disk array controller.

bandwidth Total amount of data transferred through a medium or system per unit of time. In data networks, it is a synonym for data transmission rate.

benchmark A set of well-defined, representative, repeatable workloads that can be executed on many systems to compare their performance.

BGP Border Gateway Protocol

block I/O interface I/O interface using absolute block addresses without any regard to the data format on the storage volume. Note that, higher levels that use these interfaces might be using their own data format, even though it is unknown (indistinct) at block level.

bottleneck The resource in the system that restricts the performance. In queuing theory, the queuing center with the least throughput.

BSU [SPC-1] Business Scaling Unit. The workload generator in SPC-1. One BSU represents a group of users, collectively generating a prescribed I/O demand. Each BSU demands 50 IO operations per second.

buffer credit [FC] The number allowable frames in-flight, in credit-based flow control.

buffer-to-buffer flow control (FC) Credit-based flow control between two directly connected FC ports.

bursty arrivals An arrival process, where the jobs arrive in bursts in short periods, followed by relatively idle periods. Self-similar distributions cause bursty arrivals. Most I/O traffic is bursty.

C

cache hit The state when the data resides in the accessed cache level; as opposed to a cache miss.

cache hit ratio The ratio of the number of accesses that are cache hits to the number of all accesses in a particular cache level.

cache miss The state when the data cannot be found in the accessed cache level; as opposed to a cache hit.

cache miss ratio The ratio of the number of accesses that are cache misses to the number of all accesses in a particular cache level.

capacity management The process of ensuring the current capacity is adequate and used in the most effective way.

capacity planning The process of determining which workloads will saturate a given system and designing the system so that the required service level agreements are met.

CD Compact Disc

CDF [statistics] Cumulative Distribution Function

checksum A computed value that depends on the contents of a data block, and transmitted or stored with the data block to check data integrity.

CIFS Common Internet File System. A network file system protocol based on Microsoft's SMB (Server Message Block), and is the native resource sharing protocol for MS Windows platforms.

CIM Common Information Model. CIM is an object-oriented information description language and methodology that enables the definition of component properties, methods, and relationships in an organized, standardized manner.

CIMOM Common Information Model Object Manager

closed queuing network [queuing theory] Queuing network in which there is always a finite (constant) number of jobs. The jobs circulate through the network, and reenter the system after they finish each cycle.

cold start Starting a process or a benchmark on a system after all caches and buffers are empty, so that the execution starts at a known, repeatable state.

confidence interval [statistics] The width of the expected range of the population mean around the sample mean.

confidence level [statistics] The probability that the population mean lies within a given confidence interval.

continuous-state model [simulation] A simulation model, where the state variables can take on continuous values. Generally, used in physical sciences, where the systems are continuous, as in a chemical process. Also called a continuous-event model.

control variable [DOE] Input variable that is expected to effect the output responses. Also called factor.

copy-on-write A snapshot method, where the original data is copied to the snapshot volume only after portions of the original data is overwritten.

core-edge design A network topology, where a middle tier (core) provides the connection between the outer tiers (edges). Provides independent scaling of outer tiers.

CoS Class of Service. The types of service. For example, FC class of service defines the message delivery guarantees. Might be similar to or different from QoS depending on the context.

CRC Cyclic Redundancy Check

credit-based flow control [FC] Flow control mechanism in FC, where the transmitter needs some credit (permission) amount from the receiver before the transmission can take place.

CRM Customer Relationship Management. Manages all aspects of relationships between businesses and customers. Collects and stores information from marketing, sales, and customer support into databases.

CTQ Command Tag Queuing. The ability to queue multiple commands simultaneously at a SCSI target device. SCSI and FC host bus adapters have parameters to dictate the length of the SCSI command queues.

customer [queuing theory] A transaction or job that requires service in a service center.

customer arrival rate [queuing theory] Total number of arrivals divided by the observation period.

cut-through switching Network switching method in which the switch looks at the destination address at the beginning of a packet, and starts forwarding the packet to the outgoing interface without storing it internally, potentially reducing latency.

cylinder [disk drive] Imaginary cylinder that consists of the corresponding tracks over all surfaces.

D

DAFS Direct Access File System. A network file system protocol based on RDMA networks like InfiniBand. Intends to improve network file system performance by eliminating operating system and network stack overheads.

DAS Direct Attached Storage. Storage devices that are connected explicitly to a single host. Is used to denote that there is no device sharing between hosts.

data warehouse A remote, centralized, large database that contains images of all enterprise databases. Used by planners and researchers to detect trends and categories.

data-mart A subset of a data warehouse specialized to specific functions or departments.

data-mover A computer, device, or software entity whose main job is to move data between two targets without much processing.

DBMS DataBase Management System. Suite of software programs that manage the storage of large, persistent business data. DBMS insures the security and integrity of the stored data while allowing dynamic updates and queries.

DDR Double Data Rate

defragmentation The process of checking the file layouts for gaps and moving and combining together the fragments.

delay The wait time induced by contention within a system component.

Design of Experiments (DOE) A branch of statistical mathematics, which aims to construct combinations of experiment inputs that provide statistically most significant results. The idea is to avoid insignificant experiments if their results could be predicted with the other significant experiments.

DHCP Dynamic Host Configuration Protocol

Differentiated Services (DiffServ) A standard for specifying service levels for IP datagrams. Uses a DiffServ Code Point value, which is assigned when the packet is entering a DiffServ network at an admission router. Each Code Point value is associated with a Per Hop Behavior (PHB).

direct IO An access mode supported by advanced file systems, and bypasses the buffer cache and copies application data directly to the physical storage interface.

Direct Memory Access (DMA) The method of using specialized hardware devices to move I/O data from HBAs to main memory, instead of using the main CPU to do the moves.

discrete-state model [simulation] A simulation model, where the state variables take only discrete values. Computer systems are generally modeled as discrete-state models, because the states are generally discrete. Also called discrete-event model.

disk array A collection of hard-disk drives that provides various performance and reliability features, accessed through an array controller.

DMA Direct Memory Access

DMI Desktop Management Interface

DMTF Distributed Management Task Force. Formerly Desktop Management Task Force

DOE Design of Experiments

DRAM Dynamic Random Access Memory

DSS Decision Support System

duplex link A communication link that allows traffic on both directions.

DVD Digital Versatile/Video Disc

dynamic model [simulation] A simulation model, where the time is a variable in the model.

E

E_Port [FC] Extension Port. Multiple switches connect together using E_ports, enabling extension of the fabric network.

e-business Electronic business. Performing business over the Internet.

ECC Error Correcting Code

EDO RAM Extended Data Out Random Access Memory

effect [statistics] The degree of a term's contribution to the outcome of the regression model. A term with a high coefficient multiplier in the regression formula will have a high effect on the output variable.

EIDE Enhanced Integrated Device Electronics

EISA Extended Industry-Standard Architecture

end-to-end flow control [FC] Credit-based flow control between two FC end-nodes, which may or may not be directly connected.

ESCON Enterprise Systems CONnectivity. An optical connection for mainframes.

event [simulation] Anything that causes a change in the state variables.

exchange [FC] A single cycle of communication between the initiator and the target, between the OPEN and CLOSE requests.

expected value [statistics] See average.

exponential distribution [statistics] A continuous probability distribution with the memoryless property.

extent A continuous storage chunk, with variable length, on a single disk. Extents are generally part of a larger logical volume.

F

F_Port [FC] Fabric Port. FC ports on FC switches. Connects to N_Ports and provides fabric connectivity to the end-devices.

fabric [FC] A network of FC devices using one or more interconnected switches. Loop devices can also participate in the fabric through special ports.

factor [DOE] See control variable.

fan-in Ratio of storage ports to host ports in a storage network. An indication of storage load at a single host port.

fan-out Ratio of host ports to storage ports in storage network. An indication of host traffic load at a single storage port.

fat-tree network A network topology, where the links are faster and wider (thus fatter) as the data moves from the edges to the center (root) of the network.

FC Fibre Channel

FC-AL FC Arbitrated Loop

FC-BB Fibre Channel Backbone protocol

FCFS [queuing theory] First Come First Serve. Service policy type. Also called FIFO.

FCIP Fibre Channel Over TCP/IP

FCP SCSI Fibre Channel Protocol. The mapping of the SCSI command set onto the FC physical layer. Enables storage access on a FC network (loop or fabric).

FCP-2 Fibre Channel Protocol 2. SCSI transport protocol over FC.

FIFO [queuing theory] First In First Out. Service policy type. Also called FCFS.

file system redirector Part of the network file system residing on the client, which intercepts all file IO in the client and decides where to route them. If the target file system is on a local disk, the IO is sent to a local attached block device. If it is on a network attached file system, the IO is routed to a file server through a network interface.

fit [DOE] The degree to which a regression model is able to explain experimental results.

FL_Port [FC] Fabric Loop Port. Ports on FC switches that provide fabric connectivity to NL_Ports on an FC loop.

fractional factorial design [DOE] An experimental design, where only a portion of the possible configurations are tested. Fractional factorial designs use only 1/2nd, 1/4th, 1/8th, etc. of the number of experiments generated by a full factorial design.

fragmentation Occurs after the file system is used for a long period with various file deletions and insertions. After these operations, the file system on the storage devices becomes fragmented with many small, disconnected regions. It becomes harder to find continuous space to put newer files.

frame [FC] Sections of a sequence, which are the unit of data exchange in FC.

frame buffer [Networking] Memory buffers at the ends of communication links for temporary storage of data frames.

FSPF [FC] Fabric Shortest Path First. Routing protocol between FC switches.

full factorial design [DOE] The basic experimental design in which every possibility (all combinations of factor values) are tested.

full-mesh Network topology, where all switches in the network have at least one direct link to all other switches.

G
Gb/s, Gbs Gigabits per second

GB/s, GBs Gigabytes per second

GbE, GE Gigabit Ethernet

general response time law [queuing theory] States that the total response time for a customer is the sum of all response times induced on all service centers in the queuing network.

H
hard zone [FC] A zoning method, defined using the switch port numbers. Physical location of each port is specified in the zone configuration and the switches force this type of zoning in hardware.

HBA Host Bus Adapter

HCA Host Channel Adapter

HDTV High Definition TV

heavy-tailed distribution A sewed probability distribution function with a large number of data points at small sizes, and a small number of data points at large sizes, hence heavy-tailed. Most workload data relating to network and file traffic have heavy-tailed distributions.

helical scan recording [tape drive] A tape recording method, where the tracks are laid in diagonal stripes, with a 6 degree angle, in a helical fashion.

hop [FC] An ISL crossed during a fabric transmission. The number hops is a measure of fabric distance.

host bus The data bus on a processor board, where all the external IO traffic converges.

Host Bus Adapter (HBA) Controller cards that reside on the host IO bus and connect external IO paths and peripheral devices (like storage devices) to the host computers.

Host Channel Adapter (HCA) InfiniBand host adapter that connects the host to InfiniBand target devices through the InfiniBand fabric.

host system Computer systems that are end users of the storage devices. Often connected to the storage network through host-bus adapters (HBAs).

HTTP HyperText Transfer Protocol

I

I/O path A virtual path that is envisioned to pass through all the devices that an input/output operation passes.

IB InfiniBand

IDE Integrated Device Electronics

iFCP Internet Fibre Channel Storage Networking

IID [statistics] Independent and Identically Distributed

infinite server [queuing theory] Service centers with no queuing. They appear to have infinite resources to accommodate all incoming traffic. Each customer incurs some amount of delay at the server. Because of this, they are sometimes called delay centers.

IO, I/O Input/Output

IOPS, IOps I/O Operations Per Second

IP Internet Protocol

IPX Internetwork Packet eXchange. A network layer protocol used by Novell NetWare based file servers.

ISA Industry-Standard Architecture

iSCSI Internet SCSI. SCSI transport protocol over IP. With this mapping, it is possible to exchange SCSI commands and data over any network that supports TCP/IP protocols.

IS-IS Intermediate System-to-Intermediate System

ISL [FC] Inter-Switch Link. The link between two E_Ports, that connect two switches.

ISL over-subscription ratio In core-edge topology, the total number of open edge ports divided by the total number of ISLs. In other words, it is an indication of the number of edge connections per ISL.

ISL trunking A link aggregation method that combines multiple links together and makes them appear like a single, high bandwidth link.

iSNS Internet Storage Name Service

IT Information Technology

J

JBOD Just a Bunch of Disks. Disk shelves without any RAID functionality, where individual disks are visible to the storage controllers.

jumbo frame [GbE] Oversized Ethernet frames, bigger than the IEEE 802.3 standard size. Jumbo frames defined by the Alteon Networks can be up to 9000 bytes long.

K

K (Kilo) Prefix denoting a thousand (1×10^3), and in some contexts 1024 (1×2^{10}).

KB/s, KBs, KBps Kilobytes Per Second

Kb/s, Kbs, kbs, kbps Kilobits Per Second

L

LAN Local Area Network

LAN-free backup A network backup setup, where backups are performed on a storage network separate from the application LAN.

latency The amount of time between the initiation of an action and the actual start of the action.

LBA Logical Block Address. In case of SCSI disks, one block corresponds to one sector, which is 512 bytes.

LBN Logical Block Number. Also called LBA.

LCFS [queuing theory] Last Come First Serve. Service policy type. Also called LIFO.

LDCM LANDesk Client Manager. Intel's DMI implementation, which supports SNMP and most enterprise management applications.

level [DOE] One of several possible values for a particular factor.

LIFO [queuing theory] Last In First Out. Service policy type. Also called LCFS.

line size The size of the data unit that is accessed at a particular cache level. The data is always kept and accessed in this size.

LIP Loop Initialization Primitive. Loops generate LIPs as a reaction to loop topology changes.

load time [tape drive] Time for the drive mechanism to wrap the tape around the head and get ready for tape movement.

Logical Unit (LU) In SCSI architectural model, a storage unit within a single device. LUs in a single device are distinguished using the LUNs (Logical Unit Numbers).

logical volume Virtualization of storage resources as logical disk drives, mostly performed as part of the operating system.

longitudinal recording [tape drive] A tape recording method, where the tracks run in parallel, along the length of the tape. Also called linear recording.

LU Logical Unit

LUN masking Hiding some LUNs from certain hosts. LUN masking can be implemented in host bus adapter device drivers by hiding some LUNs from the host operating system and giving access to other LUNs. Similarly, storage subsystem controllers can perform a similar function by exposing/hiding some volumes to/from certain hosts.

LVM Logical Volume Manager. Implements host-based virtualization functions (for example, software RAID).

M

MAC Media Access Control

MAN Metro Area Network

MB/s, MBs Megabytes Per Second

Mb/s, Mbs, mbs Megabits Per Second

mean [statistics] See average.

median [statistics] The value in the middle of the sample. Median might correspond to one of the sample values if it is unique or could be the average of two middle sample values.

memory hierarchy Layers of memory devices, where the layers below have higher capacity, but slower performance than the layers above.

memoryless distribution [statistics] A probability distribution in which previous values of the random variable do not have any effect on the successive values.

meta-data Data that describes data. In file systems, meta-data describes the layout of files on volumes using superblocks, inodes, and vnodes.

MIB Management Information Base. In SNMP, data structures and sets of parameters, used to query, or set management information.

MIF Management Information Format. Text files containing DMI information. Hardware and software vendors develop their own MIFs specific to their components.

min, m Minute

mirror set Two disk drives that are partners in disk mirroring. They may be a subset of a larger number of disk drives constituting a mirrored data volume.

MO Magneto-Optical disc

mode [statistics] The value that occurs the most number of times in a sample.

model An abstract description of the system under study. Models, often times, concentrate on the most important aspects of the system and leave out other details.

model validation The process of making sure that the conceptualized model is a valid representation of the real (modeled) system.

model verification The process of checking a model for implementation errors.

mount time [tape drive] Time required to grab and insert a particular tape cartridge into the tape drive. Applicable mostly to tape libraries with robotic tape mounting arms.

MPLS MultiProtocol Label Switching. A protocol agnostic QoS specification, where packets arriving at an edge router are stamped with labels that show their designated path inside the MPLS network.

ms Millisecond

MSS Maximum Segment Size

MTBF Mean Time Between Failures. The amount of time a component is expected to work without a serious failure.

MTTR Mean Time to Recovery. The average repair time to fix or replace a failed component and start using the system again.

MTU Maximum Transmission Unit

MVA [queuing theory] Mean Value Analysis. An iterative process for computing closed queuing network performance metrics.

N
N_Port [FC] Node Port. FC ports on end-nodes. For example, the HBAs on servers and storage subsystems have N_Ports.

NAS Network Attached Storage. Specialized file servers that serve file system data over a network (generally an IP network).

NAS head A NAS device that uses SAN attached storage as the backend storage instead of integrated storage devices.

NAS server/filer A Network Attached Storage device with integrated storage devices (disks).

NAT Network Address Translation

NDMP Network Data Management Protocol. A network-based backup protocol, proposed by Network Appliance, aiming to remedy the drawbacks of traditional backup configurations, with an architecture that offloads the backup responsibility to several devices.

network file system A client/server file system, where clients access file systems residing on the servers through network protocols. A single computer might contain both clients and servers at the same time.

NFS Network File System

NIC Network Interface Card

NL_Port [FC] Node Loop Port. End devices connect to an FC-AL chain using NL_Ports.

non-blocking switch A switch architecture in which a communication path inside the switch is not affected (blocked) by other communication occurring between other ports.

ns Nanosecond

NTP Network Time Protocol. Used for synchronizing the clocks of distributed systems on a network.

O

OLAP Online Analytical Processing. A class of business software used to extract relationships, trends, patterns, and exceptions in data.

OLTP Online Transaction Processing. Execution of business transactions in real-time. OLTP uses database systems for the consistency, availability, and security of transactions.

open queuing network [queuing theory] A queuing network in which customers arrive from an infinite, external source. Open queuing networks have no limitations on the number of customers that arrive in unit time, nor on the number of customers that exist in the system.

operational analysis [queuing theory] Performance analysis method that depicts a black-box look of a system, where transactions arrive on one side and they depart on the other side. Provides simple relationships between response time, throughput, and queue length.

OSD Object-based Storage Device. A storage device with advanced functionality and intelligence that can be used to improve scalability and manageability.

OSI Reference Model Open Systems Interconnect Reference Model. A framework of layers and protocols for standardization of communication between heterogeneous computers.

OSPF [FC] Open Shortest-Path First Interior Gateway Protocol. Link state routing protocol in Internet Protocol, where neighboring routers exchange their routing tables and similar network status information.

P

parity The result of XOR operations applied over all data in a data stripe.

parity block The block that contains the parity; as opposed to a data block.

parity disk The disk drive that contains the parity data; as opposed to a data disk.

PBC Port Bypass Circuit. Electronic circuits in FC-AL backplanes containing logic that routes the loop traffic around defective ports.

PCI Peripheral Component Interconnect

PCI-Express Formerly third-generation IO (3GIO), a high-speed, serial, packetized, chip-to-chip IO interconnect. The standard is governed by the PCI-SIG.

PDF [statistics] Probability Density Function. PDF is the first derivative of CDF.

PHB Per Hop Behavior. Used in DiffServ to construct several QoS scenarios.

PIO Programmed Input Output. As opposed DMA, PIO uses the host CPU to transfer data between the main memory and IO devices.

Poisson distribution [statistics] A discrete probability distribution with memoryless property. Widely used to model the number of events in unit time if the events are caused by independent factors.

population [statistics] The set of all possible values for a given random variable.

positioning time [tape drive] Time to seek to the start of the data on the tape.

priority queuing [queuing theory] A service policy type, where the customers are served according to their priorities, and higher priority jobs preempt the lower priority jobs.

processor affinity Assignment of specific processes or threads to small subsets of available processors to utilize processor caches more effectively.

PS [queuing theory] Processor Sharing. A service policy type, where each of the Q customers in the queue receives 1/Q of the server's capacity.

Q

QoS Quality of Service. The degree to which the expected outcome, according to some Service Level Agreement (SLA), is realized.

queue length [queuing theory] Average number of customers in the service center, waiting or receiving service.

queuing center [queuing theory] Model of a resource with arrival, queuing priority, and service time characteristics. Also called service center or service station.

queuing networks A modeling method that represents the systems as a network of service centers and their associated queues. Has been used to study computer system performance for several decades with great success.

queuing theory The study of the behavior of each individual queue in a queuing network.

queuing time [queuing theory] Average time spent by a customer waiting in the queue of a queuing center before it starts to receive service.

R

RAID Redundant Array of Inexpensive/Independent Disks

RAID levels Categorization of RAID implementations, which are basically different redundancy methods.

RAID0 RAID with striping, no redundancy.

RAID1 RAID with mirroring, full redundancy.

RAID10 RAID0 + RAID1, mirrored stripes, full redundancy.

RAID2 RAID with ECC protection, not used in practice.

RAID3 RAID with byte-interleaved parity, single designated parity disk.

RAID4 RAID with block-interleaved parity, single designated parity disk.

RAID5 RAID with block-interleaved parity, rotated parity blocks.

RAID5DP RAID5 with Double Parity blocks per stripe.

RAM Random Access Memory

random access Workload characteristic of a data stream in which there is no detectable correlation in the addresses of successive requests.

random variable [statistics] A term that can take on a value according to a given probability distribution.

RAS Reliability, Availability, Serviceability

rate-based flow control Flow control mechanism in TCP, Ethernet, and ATM, where the transmitter tries to estimate the sustainable rate using a feedback algorithm and transmits accordingly.

raw IO Access of IO devices directly by the applications without the involvement of any file systems. Since raw IO bypasses the file system cache, it generally has less latency. However, raw IO partitions cause some management problems.

RDRAM RAMBUS Dynamic Random Access Memory

read-update-write penalty The extra latency caused by the fact that a single write operation in a parity based RAID will require two read operations and two write operations over the storage bus (or the network).

redundancy The method of redundantly storing the data while distributing it onto the underlying storage extents, for reliability and performance improvements.

regression model [DOE] : In calculus, we say a variable y is a function of another variable x. If x and y are random variables (statistics), then we say random variable y is regressed upon random variable x. Alternatively, you can say there is a regression model of y using x.

reliability The degree to which a given computing component produces consistent results repeatedly without any incapacitating failures.

residual [DOE] The difference between the experimental measurement and the regression model output.

response [DOE] An output variable that is a function of the factors.

response time The time it takes to finish a given operation. The operation could be defined as any of the storage operations, read, write, open, close, search, or any mix of these. The response time is measured from the initiation of the operation (request) to the completion of the operation (reply). It is an end-to-end measurement and includes wait times (delays and latencies) and service times (actual work time).

rewind time [tape drive] Time to rewind the tape back to the beginning so that the next time it can start from a known position.

RIP Routing Information Protocol

rotational latency [disk drive] The time required for the target sector to rotate under the disk head before it can be read or written.

rotational speed [disk drive] The number of rotations completed in one minute. Denoted by Revolutions Per Minute (RPM).

RR [queuing theory] Round Robin. A service policy type, where the service is shared among the queued customers in a round robin fashion using fixed time periods.

RTT RoundTrip Time

S
SACK [TCP] Selective Acknowledgement. A mechanism that enables TCP to notify the sender of all the received segments, even if they are after a lost segment. This will increase the bandwidth in congested networks with frame losses or drops.

SAM Storage Area Management

sample [statistics] A random subset drawn from the population of a random variable.

sample variance [statistics] The sum of all square distances from the mean, divided by (n-1).

SAN Storage Area Network. Specialized networks for storage data that can connect multiple hosts to multiple storage devices.

SAS Serial-Attached SCSI. Enables point-to-point connections for SCSI similar to other serial interfaces, and scales up to 128 devices.

SATA Serial Advanced Technology Attachment

SBC-2 SCSI Block Commands 2. Standardizes the access to block-oriented SCSI devices like hard-disk drives.

SBOD Switched Bunch of Disks. A disk shelf containing a switched backplane.

scalability The ability of a system to grow without adversely affecting its service performance.

SCN [FC] State Change Notification. Notification messages generated by fabric servers and sent to all connected devices to make them aware of the changes in the fabric topology.

SCSI Small Computer System Interface

SDRAM Synchronous Dynamic Random Access Memory

sec, s Seconds

sector [disk drive] The minimum amount of data that can be read from or written to a disk drive. Typically 512 bytes.

seek profile [disk drive] A table or graph showing seek times against seek distances.

seek time [disk drive] An important contributor to the access time, required for positioning the head over the target track.

self-similar An object that repeats the same pattern at many scales. Fractals that repeat a pattern at several levels are a good visual example of self-similarity. For a workload definition, for example, the distribution of traffic on an annual scale might look similar to the daily traffic pattern, with similar ups and downs.

SEM [statistics] Standard Error of the Mean

sensitivity analysis [simulation] The process of checking the magnitude of model output changes with respect to model input changes.

sequence [FC] Subparts of a FC exchange, which correspond to the phases of a single IO operation.

sequential access Workload characteristic of a data stream in which all successive requests in order of occurrence have successive addresses.

server-free backup A backup configuration, where the backup data-flow occurs outside of the application server, backup server, and the LAN. Data is moved using data-movers on specialized devices or by storage devices.

service demand [queuing theory] Total service time that a single customer requires from a service center over all visits, before exiting the system.

service policy [queuing theory] Determines who gets the service next among the customers waiting at the queue of the service center.

service time [queuing theory] Average time it takes to receive service at a queuing center.

Shared Storage Model Storage Networking Industry Association's (SNIA) model for networked storage.

simplex link A one-way communication link.

simulation Representations of real world entities in computer program form. The represented entities could be anything from social institutions to mechanical components.

single point of failure A component in a system, failure of which can cause the system to fail. There can be multiple single points of failure in a system.

SLA Service Level Agreement

SLP Service Location Protocol. A standard protocol for discovering nodes and services on a network.

SMB Server Message Block. A file and printer sharing protocol for MS Windows based systems.

SMP Symmetric Multi-Processing

SNIA Storage Networking Industry Association

SNM Storage Network Management

SNMP Simple Network Management Protocol. Standard protocol for managing nodes on an IP network.

soft zone [FC] A zoning method, defined using the port or device WWNs.

SONET Synchronous Optical NETwork

spatial locality Workload characteristic of a data stream in which successive references have close addresses. These types of workloads are very suitable for cached devices with read-ahead buffers.

spatial reuse [FC] The use of the FC-AL loop, where one half of the loop transmits from the initiator to the target and the other half of the loop transmits from the target back to the initiator, effectively doubling the useable bandwidth.

SPC Storage Performance Council. A group comprised of companies predominantly in the data storage and server business, formed to develop industry-standard benchmarks for storage networks.

SPC-1 Storage Performance Council Benchmark-1. Represents a workload that is both throughput and response time sensitive. It is developed by studying the workload of transaction processing systems that require small size, mostly random, read and write operations (for example, database systems, OLTP systems, mail servers).

SPEC Standard Performance Evaluation Corporation. An industry consortium, which develops and publishes benchmarks for the evaluation of computing systems. SPEC has a broad range of benchmarks from CPU benchmarks to Web server benchmarks.

SPI-2 SCSI Parallel Interface 2. SCSI transport protocol over parallel SCSI.

split-mirror A snapshot method that first creates a mirror of the data volume and then splits the mirror to obtain a full copy of the data.

SPX Sequenced Packet Exchange. Transport layer protocol based on IPX for Novell NetWare based file servers.

SRM Storage Resource Management

SRP-2 SCSI RDMA Protocol. SCSI transport protocol over RDMA networks like InfiniBand.

SSC-2 SCSI Streams Commands 2. Standardizes the access to stream-oriented SCSI devices like tape drives.

SSD Solid State Disk. Used to cache storage data using nonvolatile RAM (NVRAM) devices. Most of the SSDs are implemented as battery-backed DRAM memory.

standard deviation [statistics] The square root of the sample variance.

standard error of the mean [statistics] (SEM) Shortly standard error is obtained by dividing the standard deviation by the square root of the number of the experiments in the sample. SEM is an approximate measure of the variation in the mean value if you were to repeat the set of experiments several times.

state variables [simulation] Parameters that define the state of the system at a given moment. By saving and loading back the state variables, you can restart a simulation without loss of information.

static model [simulation] A simulation model, where the time is not a variable in the model.

steady state [simulation] The state of a simulation model execution after its outputs settle down around a mean value.

storage hierarchy Layers of storage devices, where the layers below have higher capacity, but slower performance than the layers above.

storage network The overall system that encompasses all the storage related components, processes, and architectures.

storage provisioning The process of assigning storage resources to the users and applications, as they need it, statically or dynamically.

storage router Specialized routers that connect two different storage interconnect types. Might or might not have virtualization capabilities.

store-and-forward switching A network switching method, where the incoming packets are first stored in the switch's internal buffers, and then forwarded to the interface where the destination can be reached. See also cut-through switching.

streaming Processing data at the same time it is being communicated, possibly eliminating the latency and requirement of storing all data.

strided access A special sequential access pattern with regular gaps between successive references.

stripe depth See stripe unit.

stripe unit The amount of data written on a disk before the successive data is written to the next disk, while striping data. Also called stripe depth.

stripe width The total number of disks used for striping the data.

subsystem controller Processing board(s) that has the logic and processing elements to move data from the storage elements to the front-end connections. The controller is responsible for virtualization, RAID, access control, and availability tasks.

sustained bandwidth The data rate after accounting for all the overheads that might be needed for the transmission operations. Useable bandwidth.

synchronous I/O I/O operations that wait for the completion of the operation on the underlying storage devices before completing itself and returning to the caller.

synthetic workload A workload model used to capture the essence of the real workloads for use in performance studies. What constitutes "the essence" of a real workload is highly dependent on the system under study.

system bus The data and instruction bus on a processor board, which connects the CPUs, memory controllers, and IO bridges.

T

Tb/s, Tbs Terabits Per Second

TB/s, TBs Terabytes Per Second

TCA Host Channel Adapter. InfiniBand target adapter that connects the target devices to the InfiniBand fabric.

TCA [DiffServ] Traffic Conditioning Agreement. Negotiated between a customer and network provider to specify what kind of network traffic is allowed to enter to the network. Part of an SLA.

TCO Total Cost of Ownership. The total cost expectation for a product over its lifetime, including purchase, maintenance, management expenditures, and so on.

TCP Transmission Control Protocol

TCP slow-start algorithm A method used by TCP to gauge link bandwidth by starting with a small window size and gradually incrementing it until the link is congested.

TCP window size An adaptive parameter employed by TCP to determine the amount of in-transit data that can exist on the links. Used as a flow-control mechanism.

temporal locality Workload characteristic of a data stream in which the references that occur together in some time period are likely to occur together again in future time periods.

think time [queuing theory] The fixed amount of time a transaction waits before reentering the system in a closed queuing network.

third-party copy A data copy operation in which the initiator of the operation is not involved in the actual data move.

throughput The amount of work performed by a component or system over unit time. It is generally expressed in operations per second or transactions per second.

TOE TCP/IP Offload Engine

TOS Type of Service. A field in the IP datagram header.

TPC Transaction Processing Performance Council. A group of companies that produce benchmarks for transaction processing and database applications. Most of the TPC benchmarks are system level, end-to-end benchmarks that exercise almost all parts of the computing system, including the clients, the network, the servers, and the storage subsystems.

TPC-C Transaction Processing Performance Council Benchmark-C. TPC benchmark, which simulates an OLTP (Online Transaction Processing) environment with multiple terminal sessions in a warehouse-based distribution operation.

TPC-W Transaction Processing Performance Council Benchmark-W. Simulates a transactional web environment similar to e-commerce sites. It provides performance and price/performance metrics.

TPM, tpm Transactions Per Minute

tpmC Transactions per Minute for TPC-C. The TPC-C throughput metric.

TPS, tps Transactions Per Second

trace-based workload Workload generation based on the replay of workload parameters that are captured during an earlier execution of a real system.

track disk drive] Imaginary, circular, concentric track on a disk surface produced by successive data bits.

transient state [simulation] The period of a simulation model execution while the model outputs may fluctuate randomly, before the model reaches a steady state,

trashing Excessive page file activity due to the lack of adequate memory.

traverse recording [tape drive] A tape recording method, where the tracks are perpendicular to the length of the tape.

TSC [SPC-1] Tested Storage Configuration

U
UFS Unix File System

ULP [FC] Upper Layer Protocol. High-level protocol that is mapped onto the FC transport. Corresponds to OSI application layer (L7).

uniform distribution [statistics] A probability distribution, where the random variable has known minimum and maximum boundaries and can take on values in this range with equal probability.

utilization [queuing theory] The fraction of time a resource or service center is busy.

V
VDS Virtual Disk Service. Storage management interface introduced by Windows .NET, which provides a unified management interface to multiple-vendor storage subsystems.

VIA Virtual Interface Architecture. Uses RDMA methods to transfer messages directly between application layer buffers without buffering in the operating system device drivers. Supported by Ethernet and Fibre Channel standards. In addition, InfiniBand uses VIA as its native transport protocol.

virtualization The process of collecting several underlying storage extents and presenting them to the upper layers as a different set of Logical Units, possibly after applying aggregation, partitioning, and redundancy transformations.

visit count [queuing theory] The number of visits (passes) each transaction makes to a particular service center before it leaves the system.

VLAN [IP] Logical partition of the network such that the elements in a VLAN can detect and communicate with the elements inside their own groups, while they are unaware of the elements outside of their groups. Used for better security and management.

VSAN Virtual SAN. One or more logical SAN fabrics contained on the same, single physical fabric. Each VSAN has its own instances of fabric services.

VSS Volume Shadow Copy Service. Introduced in the Windows XP and Windows .NET operating systems and designed to make backup operations easier by always providing consistent file system copies without a need for backup windows.

VxFS Journaling file system developed and marketed by Veritas.

W

WAN Wide Area Network

WBEM Web-Based Enterprise Management. An initiative for standardizing the access to management information over the Web. The standard is currently governed by DMTF. WBEM defines the interfaces and access methods for the software agents and management applications that comprise the enterprise management framework.

workload The amount, type, and other characteristics of the work that is completed in a specific time period.

WWN [FC] World Wide Name. A 64-bit name, assigned by the device manufacturers to each FC device. This name is unique and assigned out of a pool provided to the manufacturer by IEEE.

X

XCOPY Extended Copy operation. A third-party copy technique supported by SCSI-3.

XFS Extended File System. Journaling file system developed by SGI.

XML Extensible Markup Language

XmlCIM Extensible Markup Language Common Information Model. Defines a standard way of encoding CIM models in Extensible Markup Language (XML) and transporting them over Hypertext Transfer Protocol (HTTP).

XOR Exclusive OR. The binary exclusive OR operation.

Z

zoned bit encoding [disk drive] The method of putting more sectors to outer tracks of a disk surface than the inner tracks, which are shorter in length. Enables better utilization of the disk surface in terms of data capacity. Also called zoned bit recording.

zoning [FC] Logical partitioning of a FC fabric such that the elements in a zone can detect and communicate with the elements inside their own groups, while they are unaware of the elements outside of their groups. Used for better security and management.

SYMBOLS

μs, us Microseconds

σ [statistics] See standard deviation.

σ^2 [statistics] See sample variance.

Index

Symbols and Numerics

σ (standard deviation). *See* standard deviation

σ^2 (sample variance). *See* sample variance

μs (microsecond), 15

2^k factorial designs, 85

A

access density, 20, 99, 107–109, 367

access hot spot, 367

access latency, hard-disk drive, 107–108

access probability, 101

access time, average, 101–103

Active Disk File System: A Distributed, Scalable File System, 301

actuator, hard-disk drive, 104, 367

adapters, HBAs, 7

Adaptive Disk Striping for Parallel Input/Output, 126, 301, 351

Addetia, S. (*Structure and Performance of the Direct Access File System*), 268

admission policy, 187, 367

Advanced SCSI Peripheral Interface (ASPI), 140, 367

Advanced Technology Attachment (ATA), 137–138

Advanced Technology Attachment Packet Interface (ATAPI), 140, 368

Advances in Network Simulation, 82

affinity. *See* processor affinity

AFR. *See* Annualized Failure Rate

aggregation, 5, 367

aliasing (DOE). *See* confounding (DOE)

Allocation Unit (ALU), 259, 367

Almeida, V. A. F. (*Capacity Planning for Web Services: Metrics, Models, and Methods*), 211, 366

Alvarez, Guillermo A.

   Minerva: An Automated Resource Provisioning Tool for Large-Scale Storage Systems, 211, 252

   A Modular, Analytical Throughput Model for Modern Disk Arrays, 351

Amiri, Khalil (*File Server Scaling with Network-Attached Secure Disks*), 300

An Analysis of Three Gigabit Networking Protocols for Storage Area Networks, 169

An Analytic Behavior Model for Disk Drives with Readahead Caches and Request Reordering, 126, 351

An Analytic Model of Hierarchical Mass Storage Systems with Network-Attached Storage Devices, 126

An Analytic Performance Model of Disk Arrays, 125

An Analytical Model for Designing Memory Hierarchies, 125

analytical modeling

   bottleneck analysis, 64

   for data centers, 355–356

   definition of, 47–48, 367

   for Fibre Channel storage networks, 165–166

   for hard-disk drives, 110–113

   performance bounds, 63–64

   performance laws for, 48–53

   queuing networks, 53–63

   for remote storage replication, 339–345

   used in performance evaluation, 26

Anderson, D. (*Managing Energy and Server Resources in Hosting Centers*), 211

Anderson, Eric (*Ergastulum: An Approach to Solving the Workload and Device Configuration Problem*), 211, 252

angular velocity, 367

Annualized Failure Rate (AFR), 114–115

Appia: Automatic Storage Area Network Fabric Design, 212

Appia tool, 209

Application Center Test (Microsoft), 356

Application layer (L7), OSI network model, 150

application layer, storage networking model, 4

Application Specific Integrated Circuit (ASIC), 289

Application Storage Unit (ASU), 219

application-level benchmarks, 229–230

applications. *See also* backups; software

   activity levels of, 258

   as benchmarks, 230

   optimizing, 269–272

arbitrated loops, 143–146, 162–163

arbitration, 367

An Architecture for Differentiated Services, 198

Arena package, 74

arrival policy, 53

arrival process, 54

arrival rate (queuing theory). *See* customer arrival rate

arrival rate, workload parameter, 179

arrival theorem, 60, 367

Arsham, Hossein (*Excel for Introductory Statistical Analysis*), 46

H

continued